Causes and Consequences of Nuclear Proliferation

This book offers valuable insights into the causes and consequences of nuclear proliferation.

Through the development of new datasets and the application of cutting edge research methods, contributors to this volume significantly advance the frontiers of research on nuclear weapons. Essays in this volume address why states acquire nuclear weapons, why they engage in nuclear cooperation, and also explore the relationship between nuclear weapons possession and a variety of security and diplomatic consequences. In addition to accelerating the development of an empirical research agenda, the chapters combine to form a coherent storyline that shows nuclear technology and capabilities have been underappreciated as a cause of proliferation in recent scholarly literature. For scholars and practitioners alike, there is a strategic logic to nuclear assistance that is essential to understand. Moreover, several of the essays show that the consequences of nuclear proliferation are more complex than is conventionally understood. Nuclear weapons can have both stabilizing and destabilizing effects. Nuclear weapons may simultaneously cause their owners to become more influential, more successful in the wars they choose to fight, and to have less intense conflicts, when these conflicts occur.

This book will be of much interest to students of arms control and nuclear proliferation, war and conflict studies, security studies, and IR.

Robert Rauchhaus is Assistant Professor of Political Science at the University of California, Santa Barbara.

Matthew Kroenig is Assistant Professor of Government at Georgetown University, Washington, DC.

Erik Gartzke is Associate Professor of Political Science at the University of California, San Diego. He has authored numerous journal articles.

Routledge Global Security Studies
Series editors: Aaron Karp, Regina Karp and Terry Terif

Causes and Consequences of Nuclear Proliferation

Edited by Robert Rauchhaus,
Matthew Kroenig, and Erik Gartzke

Routledge
Taylor & Francis Group

LONDON AND NEW YORK

First published 2011
by Routledge
4 Park Square, Milton Park, Abingdon, Oxon OX14 4RN
605 Third Avenue, New York, NY 10017

Routledge is an imprint of the Taylor & Francis Group, an informa business

First issued in paperback 2013

British Library Cataloguing in Publication Data
A catalogue record for this book is available from the British Library

Library of Congress Cataloging-in-Publication Data
A catalog record has been requested for this book

ISBN: 978-0-415-59833-0 (hbk)
ISBN: 978-0-415-72397-8 (pbk)

Typeset in Baskerville
by Wearset Ltd, Boldon, Tyne and Wear

Contents

Contributors

Victor Asal is an Associate Professor of Political Science at Rockefeller College at the University at Albany, SUNY. He is also a Research Associate for the National Center for the Study of Terrorism and Responses to Terrorism (START). Dr Asal's research has focused on terrorist behavior, including the US as a target of terrorists, structural and social antecedents to terror, non-state actor mobilization online, and international crisis behavior.

Kyle Beardsley is an Assistant Professor of Political Science at Emory University. He received his Ph.D. from the University of California, San Diego in 2006 and his undergraduate degree from the University of Maryland in 2001. His published research includes work on international mediation, nuclear proliferation, rebel groups, and quantitative methodology, in addition to ongoing research projects on the United Nations.

Brett V. Benson is an Assistant Professor of Political Science at Vanderbilt University. He received his Ph.D. in Political Science from Duke University in 2006. His research focuses on international relations theory, third-party commitments, and nuclear development and disarmament.

Robert Brown is an Assistant Professor of Political Science at Temple University in Philadelphia, PA. He is also Director of the Public Policy and Nuclear Threats Program at the University of California Institute on Global Conflict and Cooperation. His research examines international cooperation in international organizations. He is currently writing a book analyzing delegation by the international community to the International Atomic Energy Agency.

Jennifer L. Erickson is an Assistant Professor of Political Science at Boston College. She received her Ph.D. in Government from Cornell University in 2009, and was a Post-Doctoral Research Fellow at Dartmouth College in 2009–10. Her current research focuses on conventional arms transfers, sanctions and arms embargoes, international reputation, and domestic politics and compliance with international commitments.

Matthew Fuhrmann is an Assistant Professor of Political Science at the University of South Carolina and a Nuclear Security Fellow at the Council on Foreign Relations. He has previously held fellowships at Harvard University's Belfer Center for Science and International Affairs and the Center for International Trade and Security at the University of Georgia. His research on international security and nuclear proliferation has been published in *International Security, Journal of Conflict Resolution, Journal of Peace Research,* and *Foreign Policy Analysis,* among other journals.

Erik Gartzke is Associate Professor of Political Science at the University of California, San Diego. His primary area of study involves the impact of information and institutions on war and peace. Dr Gartzke's work has appeared in leading journals including *American Political Science Review, American Journal of Political Science, International Organization, International Studies Quarterly,* and *World Politics.*

Martin Hellman is Professor Emeritus of Electrical Engineering at Stanford University and a member of the National Academy of Engineering. His primary interest is how fallible human beings might survive while possessing the god-like power granted by technology. Within that area, he focuses on potential failure mechanisms for nuclear deterrence and methods for creating societal awareness of the need for change.

Michael C. Horowitz is an Assistant Professor of Political Science at the University of Pennsylvania. He primarily studies international conflict issues. His first book, *The Diffusion of Military Power: Causes and Consequences for International Politics,* was published in 2010 by Princeton University Press.

Dong-Joon Jo is an Associate Professor of Political Science and International Relations at Seoul National University. He received his Ph.D. from Pennsylvania State University and has previously taught at the Department of International Relations, University of Seoul. His research interests include nuclear proliferation, voting behavior and internal politics within international organizations, and diffusion of international norms.

Matthew Kroenig is an Assistant Professor of Government at Georgetown University and a Research Affiliate with the Project on Managing the Atom at Harvard University. He is the author of *Exporting the Bomb: Technology Transfer and the Spread of Nuclear Weapons.*

Alexander H. Montgomery is an Assistant Professor of Political Science at Reed College. He has published articles in *International Security, International Organization,* and the *Journal of Conflict Resolution,* among others, on dismantling proliferation networks and on the effects of social networks of international organizations on interstate conflict. His research interests include political organizations, social networks, weapons of mass disruption and destruction, social studies of technology, and interstate social relations.

Paul Nelson is Professor Emeritus of Computer Science, Nuclear Engineering and Mathematics, at Texas A&M University, where he also serves as Associate Director for International Programs in the Nuclear Security Science and Policy Institute. He is a Fellow of the American Nuclear Society, and a member of the Special Committee on Nuclear Nonproliferation of that society.

Robert Rauchhaus is an Assistant Professor of Political Science at the University of California, at Santa Barbara. His research and consulting focuses on how individuals and organizations formulate and implement strategy under conditions of uncertainty and risk. His recent research interests include conflict management, nuclear deterrence, and the *Pax Americana.*

Scott D. Sagan is the Caroline S.G. Monro Professor of Political Science at Stanford University and co-director of Stanford's Center for International Security and Cooperation (CISAC). His books include *The Limits of Safety* (1993) and (with Kenneth N. Waltz) *The Spread of Nuclear Weapons: A Debate Renewed* (2003).

Christopher Way received his Ph.D. from Stanford University and is Associate Professor of Government at Cornell University. His early research focused on the politics of economic policy, and he published papers on central bank independence, the politics of financial market deregulation, and the political economy of fixed exchange rates. In recent years his work has shifted in focus towards WMD proliferation and the non-proliferation regime.

Quan Wen is a Professor of Economics at Vanderbilt University. He received his Ph.D. in Economics from the University of Western Ontario in 1991. His research focuses on economic theory, repeated games, and bargaining theory.

James Wirtz is the Dean of the School of International Graduate Studies (SIGS) at the Naval Post Graduate School, and Director of the Global Center for Security Cooperation (GCSC), Defense Security Cooperation Agency. His most recent publications are *Complex Deterrence: Strategy in the Global Age* (University of Chicago Press: 2009) and *Strategy in the Contemporary World* (Oxford University Press: 2010).

Acknowledgments

A number of individuals and organizations contributed to this project's success. As editors, we were especially fortunate to work with such a talented and professional group of scholars. We also benefitted from early feedback at an annual meeting of the American Political Science Association where panelists and audience members helped a number of our contributors to sharpen their arguments.

We owe special thanks to Bruce Russett and members of the editorial staff at the *Journal of Conflict Resolution*. We would also like to thank the *JCR* and its publisher, Sage Press, for permission to reproduce and build on essays from the April 2009 special issue, including the introduction (Chapter 1), conclusion (Chapter 14), and half of the substantive chapters (4–5, 8–11). Another debt of gratitude is owed to Andrew Humphrys and the staff at Routledge for seeing the value of this project and encouraging us to expand its scope and include six new essays. We are also thankful to the Engineering Honor Society for permitting Martin Hellman to build on an essay published in the Spring 2008 issue of *Tau Beta Pi*.

We are grateful for generous financial support from the Department of Political Science at the University of California at San Diego, the Government Department at Georgetown University, the University of California's Institute on Global Conflict and Cooperation (IGCC), and the Project on Managing the Atom and the International Security Program, both at Harvard University's Belfer Center for Science and International Affairs. We also thank Susan Shirk and the Public Policy and Nuclear Threats (PPNT) program at IGCC – many of the scholars involved in this project received training and funding from this superb program. The University of California at Santa Barbara also provided financial support that allowed us to secure research assistance. We thank Alisa Rod for being an excellent RA.

1 Introduction

The causes and consequences of nuclear proliferation

*Matthew Kroenig, Erik Gartzke, and
Robert Rauchhaus*[1]

Nuclear weapons have occupied a central role in international politics ever since their introduction onto the world stage in 1945. The use of nuclear weapons by the United States on Hiroshima and Nagasaki is widely believed to have compelled the Japanese surrender and brought World War II to a close.[2] The vast nuclear arsenals of the United States and the Soviet Union were fundamental to the bi-polar, strategic relationship that structured international politics for over 50 years during the Cold War. And while many analysts hoped that the collapse of the Soviet Union would lead to a reduction in the influence of nuclear weapons in international affairs, it was not to be.

The threat of nuclear proliferation resurfaced as India, Pakistan, and more recently North Korea, have conducted nuclear tests. Iraq, Libya, South Africa, and other regional powers have pursued nuclear capabilities in the past, and evidence suggests that Iran is doing so at present. The September 11 attacks on the New York World Trade Center and on the Pentagon in Washington also raised concerns about the prospects for nuclear terrorism.

There is little doubt that if terrorists could acquire nuclear weapons, they would attempt to carry out mass-casualty attacks. The ease with which states or terrorists could potentially acquire sensitive nuclear materials and know-how was exemplified by the black-market nuclear proliferation ring operated by Pakistani scientist A.Q. Khan. Indeed, according to the Obama administration's 2010 National Security Strategy, nuclear proliferation poses one of the greatest threats to US national security.[3]

The real-world importance of nuclear weapons has led to the production of a voluminous scholarly literature on the causes and consequences of nuclear proliferation (e.g., Schelling 1966; Betts 1987; Powell 1990; Sagan and Waltz 1995; Sagan 1996/1997; Singh and Way 2004; Hymans 2006; Solingen 2007). Scholars have thoroughly examined *why* states want nuclear weapons (e.g., Sagan 1996/1997) and the broad effects of nuclear proliferation on the stability of the international system (e.g., Sagan and Waltz 1995). Missing from this debate is an analysis of *how* states acquire nuclear weapons and a systematic empirical examination of how nuclear weapons affect the security and the diplomacy of proliferators.

The chapters in this book address these twin deficits by focusing on the causes and consequences of nuclear proliferation. We aim to accelerate the development of an empirical research agenda by employing robust research methods. Quantitative studies have been underrepresented in the expansive nuclear proliferation literature, which was historically dominated by comparative, historical, and qualitative analyses of the spread of nuclear weapons and nuclear deterrence. This edited volume brings together a new generation of nuclear scholarship, advancing novel theoretical positions through models and arguments, and performing quantitative tests on both the causes and consequences of proliferation. We also include two qualitative essays, one that helps identify an underdeveloped research frontier, and another that provides a critical review of all the studies contained in this volume.

This book makes theoretical, empirical, and methodological contributions to the field by centering on two observations. First, whether states want nuclear weapons is irrelevant if they are unable to acquire them. Our basic argument, grounded in the tradition of realist and security-based approaches to nuclear proliferation and nuclear deterrence, is that nuclear weapons on average and across a broad variety of indicators enhance the security and diplomatic influence of their possessors. Because states stand to gain by possessing nuclear weapons, the supply-side factors that enable nuclear development are among the most important determinants of nuclear proliferation. Second, nuclear weapons potentially have a wide variety of effects on their possessors. Nuclear weapons alter the timing, intensity, duration, and outcome of conflicts and may also affect a state's diplomatic influence.

Our theoretical claims also mark a significant departure from the contemporary scholarly literature on the causes of nuclear proliferation. First, recent studies suggest that psychological, economic, and domestic considerations are the principal determinants of nuclear proliferation (e.g., Hymans 2006; Solingen 2007). We do not dispute that these considerations can be important, but emphasize that the strategic benefits of nuclear weapons should not be overlooked. Second, scholars have argued that what is most surprising about nuclear proliferation is how few states have acquired atomic bombs (e.g., Hymans 2006; Solingen 2007). These analysts point to countries like Japan and Germany that have the technical capability to produce nuclear weapons but have refrained from doing so. This leads these scholars to conclude that a state's demand for nuclear weapons, and not the capability to produce nuclear weapons, is the key to explaining nuclear proliferation. We agree that there are countries that can produce nuclear weapons, but have not, just as there are countries like Egypt, Libya, and Iraq that have wanted nuclear weapons, but were unable to produce them. Therefore, the causal significance of either demand-side or supply-side factors cannot be dismissed by offering counterexamples. We advocate for a more careful scholarly analysis of the supply-side of nuclear proliferation. We emphasize that the ability to produce nuclear weapons is a necessary condition for nuclear proliferation to occur.

Common objectives and baselines

Our main goal is to offer a systematic account of the process of nuclear proliferation and its consequences. We explore – theoretically and empirically – our basic assumptions that nuclear weapons, on average and across a broad variety of indicators, have beneficial effects for their possessors and that, partly for this reason, supply-side factors are among the most important causes of nuclear proliferation.

For all of the chapters in this edited volume, a key variable will be the same: nuclear weapons possession. Six chapters in this edited volume treat nuclear weapons possession as a dependent variable and seek to explain the factors that lead states to acquire nuclear weapons. Six other chapters treat nuclear weapons possession as the key independent variable. These chapters seek to understand how the possession of nuclear weapons influences state behavior. Due to the centrality of proliferation to the studies, it is necessary to define and measure nuclear proliferation carefully. The chapters in this edited volume focus on the process of horizontal nuclear proliferation. By horizontal, we mean the spread of nuclear weapons to new states as opposed to the multiplication of nuclear warheads within existing nuclear-armed states.

To create consistency across studies, all of the chapters in this volume use a common set of nuclear proliferation dates (listed in Table 1.1). States are defined as having acquired nuclear weapons when they first

Table 1.1 Nuclear weapons proliferation, 1945–present

Country	Date
United States	1945
Soviet Union/Russia	1949
United Kingdom	1952
France	1960
China	1964
Israel	1967[4]
India	1988[5]
South Africa	1982–1990[6]
Pakistan	1990[7]
Belarus	Never[8]
Kazakhstan	Never[9]
North Korea	Never[10]
Uzbekistan	Never[11]

assemble a nuclear weapon that could be delivered against an enemy target. The first five nuclear weapon states, the United States, the Soviet Union, Great Britain, France, and China, immediately tested their nuclear weapons. Measuring when these states crossed the nuclear threshold is as simple as recording the date of the first nuclear test. The subsequent nuclear powers, however, have either never conducted a nuclear test, or have waited a significant period of time before weaponizing a potential nuclear capability. For example, North Korea is believed to have possessed enough separated plutonium to build one or two nuclear bombs by 1994, yet it is not known when North Korea assembled its first nuclear device. North Korea conducted nuclear tests in October 2006 and May 2009, but some experts considered these tests to be failures and question whether North Korea actually has a functioning nuclear weapons arsenal to this day. North Korea could plausibly be coded as acquiring nuclear weapons in 1994, 2006, 2009, or never. Similarly, India conducted a "peaceful nuclear explosion" in 1974, but it is not believed to have fashioned a deliverable nuclear warhead until 1988. Should India be coded as a nuclear power beginning in 1974 or in 1988? To code the remaining nuclear powers, we scoured historical, archival, and policy materials to determine when the country first assembled a deliverable nuclear device. Because there may be disputes about the precise date at which some countries acquired nuclear weapons, and because critics may question how the choice of dates influences the results, the authors employ a variety of robustness checks to test the sensitivity of their findings to the coding decisions.

The text addresses nine nuclear proliferation-related dependent variables:

- nuclear proliferation
- nuclear cooperation
- nuclear disarmament
- probability of conflict
- frequency of conflict
- timing of conflict
- intensity of conflict
- outcome of conflict
- diplomatic influence

We examine why states acquire nuclear weapons, under what conditions they give them up, why they engage in nuclear cooperation, and explore the relationship between nuclear status and a variety of security and diplomatic outcomes. This list does not cover the full range of possible nuclear proliferation issues that could be subjected to scholarly scrutiny, but a focus on these seven critical variables does offer several advantages. First, these outcomes are substantively important. Second, they can be measured, allowing us to quantitatively analyze nuclear proliferation across cases and over time. Third, this list covers a broader range of outcomes than are considered in the existing literature. Indeed, some of these relationships are conceptualized and subjected to empirical scrutiny for the first time in this book.

The authors in this volume generally situate their research in the tradition of realist and security-based approaches to nuclear proliferation and nuclear deterrence. The authors build on earlier work to develop theoretical propositions that are then evaluated in the chapters of this volume. Our view is that a strategic, security-based approach can explain much about the causes and consequences of nuclear proliferation, though certainly it does not explain everything.

As Sonali Singh and Christopher Way (2004) have argued, statistical analysis is particularly appropriate for the study of nuclear proliferation for three reasons. First, statistical studies can examine the entire universe of cases, avoiding the problems associated with selecting cases on the dependent variable. Second, most of the claims made by theorists of nuclear proliferation are probabilistic, making statistical analysis the most appropriate research tool for their examination. Large sample studies can help to avoid the deterministic conclusions implied by some case-based research. Third, the causes and consequences of nuclear proliferation are multi-causal. Statistical analysis can help the researcher to test and control for complex relationships and interactions that interfere with simple inference.

To this list, we add a fourth reason. The monadic and dyadic units of analysis that form the backbone of datasets in international relations mesh well with our research focus on the causes and consequences of nuclear proliferation on the part of individual states.

These studies are not the first to employ quantitative analysis to examine nuclear proliferation issues. Quantitative research on nuclear proliferation traces its roots to earlier work by Kegley (1980) and Meyer (1984). Unfortunately, the methodological tools available to these pioneering efforts were insufficient to test more complex theories of interest. In recent years, scholars (Geller 1990; Singh and Way 2004; Jo and Gartzke 2007; Asal and Beardsley 2007; Fuhrmann 2008a) have begun to quantitatively analyze the causes and consequences of nuclear proliferation. Still, this research has not yet generated the critical mass of scholarship that has proven necessary for productive research in other fields.

We are advocating for a broad empirical research approach that sharpens and tests theories of nuclear proliferation by conducting systematic tests using large statistical samples. We view this endeavor as complementary to other research approaches. Statistics are a tool that, in combination with other research methods, can help scholars to resolve important puzzles concerning nuclear proliferation and to identify critical sources of variation.

This book offers a systematic account of the process of nuclear proliferation and its consequences. The 13 chapters that follow are organized into three parts. Part I contains six chapters that focus on the causes of nuclear proliferation. Part II contains six chapters on the consequences of the spread of nuclear weapons. Part III consists of an analytical review essay that offers a critique of the substantive chapters.

The causes of nuclear proliferation

The six chapters in Part I offer explanations for why states acquire nuclear weapons. These authors expand on, and refine, recent quantitative work on nuclear proliferation by Singh and Way (2004) and Jo and Gartzke (2007), focusing in particular on the supply-side of nuclear proliferation. In Chapter 2, Robert Brown discusses the disagreement among policymakers about the importance of international institutions and international organizations (IOs) for achieving cooperation on international non-proliferation goals. IR scholars share a parallel concern about why non-proliferation institutions exist and whether (or for whom) they serve functional interests. As with other issue areas, the persistence of these arguments reflects the fact that rigorous empirical studies of international cooperation have lagged behind the development of diverse theoretical claims. Brown argues that we can learn from the broader study of IOs, which have applied principal–agent (PA) theories of delegation. Using new quantitative measures of delegation, Brown's chapter tests competing realist, institutionalist, and constructivist explanations for why we observe an increase in the delegation to an important non-proliferation IO, the International Atomic Energy Agency (IAEA). His analysis indicates that power, purpose, and beliefs are all important for a complete explanation of why the IAEA intervenes in international nuclear non-proliferation efforts.

In Chapter 3, Jennifer Erickson and Christopher Way focus on the Nuclear Non-Proliferation Treaty. The authors begin with a puzzle: if the NPT entails high costs for non-nuclear countries, why have so many countries joined and done so relatively quickly? The authors argue that NPT leaders may have helped to reduce the costs of signing the NPT by providing alternative means of protecting members' security – namely, enhanced access to conventional arms. The authors explore the idea through a statistical analysis of conventional weapons transfers from the United States and the Soviet Union/Russia from 1970 to 2001, as well as from the United Kingdom, France, and (West) Germany. Their results reveal that informal inducements provided a "signing bonus" to states that join the NPT.

Matthew Kroenig's analysis in Chapter 4 examines the relationship between the international transfer of nuclear materials and technology and the proliferation of nuclear weapons. He notes that policy analysts have frequently claimed a link between nuclear assistance and nuclear proliferation, but that academic studies of nuclear proliferation have not treated international assistance as a potential cause of the spread of nuclear weapons. Kroenig argues that international nuclear transfers can help states to overcome the common technical and strategic obstacles that they encounter as they attempt to develop nuclear weapons. Applying nonparametric matching techniques and event-history models to a new dataset on international nuclear transfers, he finds that states that receive nuclear assistance are more likely to acquire nuclear weapons than are similar states that do not receive such help. More broadly, Kroenig finds overwhelming support for a supply-side approach to nuclear proliferation. Controlling for demand-side factors, he finds that states that have the ability to produce nuclear weapons, either through domestic capacity or international assistance, are at a greater risk of acquiring the bomb.

The demonstration of a link between nuclear assistance and nuclear proliferation begs for an explanation of the sources of nuclear assistance. This question has been largely unexplored in the vast literature on nuclear proliferation. Scholars have strained to explain why states want nuclear weapons, but very few (e.g., Kroenig 2010; Fuhrmann 2008b) have examined what is arguably the more puzzling question: why do states provide nuclear assistance? In Chapter 5, Matthew Fuhrmann uses new data on civilian nuclear cooperation agreements to examine this question. Contrary to the claims of many pundits and policy analysts, he finds only mixed support for the idea that economic considerations drive nuclear cooperation. Instead, his study finds that states offer civilian nuclear assistance for mainly strategic reasons. These include assisting allies, helping the enemies of one's enemies, and efforts by democracies to strengthen other democracies.

In Chapter 6, Brett Benson and Quan Wen develop a game-theoretic model that examines bargaining over nuclear weapons. The model examines the interdependent decision-making that occurs between states attempting to acquire nuclear weapons and those engaged in counter-proliferation efforts. The authors identify conditions that determine when, and under what conditions, different counter-proliferation strategies are most appropriate. Their analysis suggests that when verification is possible, pure disarming strategies (e.g., bribery and use of force) always exist. The authors also show that ambiguous development can be an effective policy for extracting concessions from concerned counter-proliferators.

The analysis of the causes of nuclear proliferation concludes with an analytic essay which points to a relatively unexplored research frontier. In Chapter 7, James Wirtz suggests that, although there are both necessary and sufficient conditions behind national decisions to acquire, sustain, or discard a nuclear arsenal, scholars often ignore nuclear politics. His analysis shows that analysts frequently fail to recognize that nuclear deterrence represents an ongoing national commitment that is constantly being adapted, modified, and revised. For sustaining national nuclear capabilities over decades there must be a favorable climate of nuclear politics. As the only qualitative analysis in this volume, Wirtz's chapter captures important nuances that can be lost in quantitative analyses.

The consequences of nuclear proliferation

The six chapters contained in Part II focus on the consequences of nuclear proliferation. The chapters provide considerable support for the argument that nuclear weapons enhance the security and diplomatic power of their possessors. While nuclear weapons do not always reduce the frequency of conflict, they appear to affect the timing, duration, severity, and outcomes of conflicts. The evidence suggests that nuclear weapon states engage in conflicts that are shorter and less intense, and they tend to emerge victorious from them. Furthermore, nuclear powers enjoy enhanced international bargaining power.

In Chapter 8, Gartzke and Jo's study examines the effects of nuclear weapons possession on the probability of conflict and international bargaining. They find that nuclear weapons states are neither more nor less likely to be involved in international disputes. However, their study suggests that even if nuclear weapons do not directly affect the likelihood of conflict, nuclear weapons status can still increase the influence of nuclear capable states. To test the hypothesis that nuclear weapon states enjoy greater international influence, Gartzke and Jo examine whether nuclear possession affects patterns of diplomatic missions. Important states send and attract diplomatic missions to and from other nations. The authors build on previous research on diplomatic missions and carefully control for other relevant factors including population and economic size. They find that states with nuclear weapons tend to host (and send) greater numbers of diplomatic missions. The primary effect of nuclear proliferation on international politics is not a reduction or increase in the probability of conflict, but to produce greater diplomatic leverage for their possessors.

The subject of experience with nuclear weapons is addressed in Chapter 9 by Michael Horowitz. Does the length of time states have nuclear weapons influence their behavior and the behavior of opponents in militarized disputes? If a state's capabilities and resolve, and the way in which a state's capabilities and resolve are perceived by adversaries, influence the probability of conflict, then the probability of conflict may change over time as nuclear learning occurs. Using multiple statistical models, Horowitz finds that when states acquire nuclear weapons they are more likely to reciprocate international disputes and are also more likely to have their disputes reciprocated. Over time, however, the effect of nuclear weapons reverses. Inexperienced nuclear states are more dispute-prone, while experienced nuclear states are less so. Consistent with the theme of this book, nuclear weapons improve the strategic position of their possessor. The longer a state possesses nuclear weapons, the less likely it is to become involved in disputes. This finding also has important implications. Any static understanding of nuclear proliferation is likely to be incomplete because it ignores how nuclear possession interacts with time to influence international conflict behavior.

In Chapter 10, Robert Rauchhaus offers a direct examination of the relationship between nuclear weapons and conventional conflict. His study builds on Democratic Peace Theory research designs and employs generalized estimating equations (GEE) to measure the intensity of conflict involving nuclear powers. His study examines a wide range of conflicts, including militarized disputes, disputes that include the use of force, and conflicts with fatalities, and full-scale wars. His study suggests that the presence of nuclear weapons tends to shift the intensity of disputes toward the lower end of the conflict scale. Symmetric nuclear dyads are less likely to become involved in a full-scale war, though nuclear status increases other types of dispute behavior. Rauchhaus' findings support the existence of the stability–instability paradox – nuclear weapons induce lower levels of violence, but deter full-scale war. Consistent with the themes of this book, nuclear powers can expect to enjoy an improved strategic environment in the form of lower incidences of large-scale violence.

Kyle Beardsley and Victor Asal (Chapter 11) examine the outcome of conflicts involving nuclear-armed states. To test the effects of nuclear status on crisis outcomes, they draw on data from the International Crisis Behavior dataset. They find that when nuclear weapon states face a non-nuclear weapon state (an asymmetric dyad), nuclear weapon states are more likely to win concessions and more likely to experience shorter crises. The findings do not hold for symmetrical nuclear dyads, however. Nuclear weapon states facing a nuclear-armed opponent are no more (or less) likely to experience enhanced bargaining leverage or shorter crises. Beardsley and Asal carefully test the robustness of these findings with a selection model that enables them to rule out the possibility that the results were driven by selection into crises. Again, nuclear weapon states possess a strategic advantage when facing nonnuclear weapon states: they enjoy shorter crises and emerge victorious from these crises.

Taken together with the findings of Gartzke and Jo, the chapter by Beardsley and Asal suggests that the possession of nuclear weapons enhances a state's diplomatic influence. This is an important corrective to much of the previous scholarly literature that has tended to assert that nuclear weapons provide little diplomatic benefit to their possessors.

Additionally, there is further significance to these findings. Nearly all of the theoretical work on nuclear deterrence has assumed nuclear symmetry. In fact, the field lacks a coherent theory of the behavior of asymmetric nuclear dyads. Combined with the findings of Rauchhaus, Beardsley and Asal's chapter suggests the beginning of a theory of interstate conflict within asymmetric nuclear dyads. Nations with nuclear weapons may be able to fight nonnuclear opponents without the fear that the opponent will invade the homeland or challenge the fundamental interests of the nuclear state. Unsurprisingly, the outcomes of these conflicts tend to favor the nuclear-armed state. This empirical finding could become the basis for further theoretical and empirical work on the subject of asymmetric nuclear dyads.

Chapter 12 and 13 present studies that use risk analysis to assess the consequences of nuclear weapons proliferation. While risk analysis has made important contributions in many disciplines, it has not been widely applied in security relations. Martin Hellman helps address this deficit by taking aim at the nuclear optimist's argument that approximately 50 years of success is evidence that all is well and that no changes should be made in our nuclear posture. His study shows that risk analysis extracts more information from the available data by viewing each year as more than just a simple success or failure, and taking near misses into account. The preliminary risk analysis presented in his chapter suggests that there is approximately a 10 percent chance that civilization will be destroyed during the expected lifetime of a child born today. Further, depending on assumptions and key parameters, the true failure rate could be an order of magnitude larger, as high as 50–50 chance.

Paul Nelson (Chapter 13) comes to a different conclusion by applying risk analysis to nuclear disarmament. Using a two-event dynamic model, his study shows that over a variety of risk functions, nuclear disarmament may entail many hidden dangers. Proponents of nuclear disarmament, while well intentioned, make arguments that the author finds dubious. Nelson examines the intellectual underpinnings of nuclear disarmament, paying special attention to the hidden assumptions of *conventional nondeterrence* and *benign disarmament.* His analysis shows that the advantages of disarmament may only hold under specific conditions that may be more limited than is conventionally appreciated. His study suggests that nuclear disarmament could make the world less safe.

Looking forward

The chapters in this book offer valuable insights about the causes and consequences of nuclear proliferation. Access to nuclear technology and capabilities has been underappreciated as a cause of proliferation in the recent scholarly literature. There is a strategic logic to nuclear assistance, one worth understanding for those who seek to limit the spread of nuclear weapons. Nuclear weapons are neither potent causes of war, nor irrelevant to world politics. They cause their owners to become more influential, more successful in the wars they choose to fight, and to have less intense conflicts, when these conflicts occur. Still, this is a beginning more than an end. Good empirical research often raises as many questions as it answers. We hope that the effort here prompts readers to wonder, and to explore further a topic of global import.

We defer any effort to critique the chapters to Chapter 14. We invited Alex Montgomery and Scott Sagan to comment on individual chapters and the project as a whole. As experts on the politics of nuclear proliferation with perspectives as practitioners of qualitative research methods, Montgomery and Sagan are both supportive of this project and critical of it. Their chapter suggests that they believe the approaches advanced in this volume can contribute to our knowledge and understanding of the causes and consequences of nuclear proliferation, but they also argue that the quantitative research methods suffer from inherent drawbacks that prevent the examination of some important theoretical relationships. We believe Montgomery and Sagan's critique provides the reader with an important vantage point from which to assess possible limitations of our approach. They also offer a series of suggestions for further research. We very much welcome these suggestions as we are eager to encourage additional research on this important subject.

Notes

1 For helpful comments on earlier drafts of this introduction, we would like to thank Bruce Russett, and the contributors to this book.
2 For a recent effort to undermine the consensus position, see T. Hasegawa (2005) *Racing the Enemy: Stalin, Truman and the Surrender of Japan*, Cambridge: Belknap Press.
3 M. McConnell (2007) "Annual Threat Assessment of the Director of National Intelligence for the Senate Armed Services Committee," Unclassified Statement for the Record, February 27.
4 According to Cohen (1998: 273–276), Israel began separating plutonium in 1966 and assembled two makeshift nuclear weapons on the eve of the 1967 war.
5 According to Perkovich (1999: 293–297), India first readied two dozen nuclear weapons for quick assembly and delivery by aircraft between 1988 and 1990.
6 According to Albright (1994: 43), South Africa constructed its first nuclear device in 1979, but the first deliverable device was not ready until 1982. The 1982 device was deliverable in the sense that it could have been "kicked out of the back of a plane." South Africa began dismantling its nuclear program in 1990.
7 According to Jones *et al.* (1998: 132, 140n.), Pakistan had enough enriched uranium to produce nuclear weapons in 1987, but it was not until 1990 that it manufactured the metal components for a nuclear device.
8 The nuclear weapons in Belarus, Ukraine, and Kazakhstan were generally believed to have been under de facto Russian/CIS control and that in order to acquire the nuclear weapons, the newly independent states would have had to seize them from Russian forces. See, for instance, Miller (1993).
9 See the note on Belarus.
10 North Korea tested its first nuclear device in October 2006. Many experts believe, however, that this test was a failure and evidence of the fact that North Korea still lacks a deliverable nuclear weapon.
11 See the note on Belarus.

Bibliography

Albright, David (1994) "South Africa and the affordable bomb," *Bulletin of the Atomic Scientists* 4: 43.

Asal, Victor and Kyle Beardsley (2007) "Proliferation and international crisis behavior," *Journal of Peace Research* 2: 139–155.

Betts, Richard K. (1987) *Nuclear Blackmail and Nuclear Balance*, Washington, DC: Brookings Institution.

Blair, Bruce G. (1993) *The Logic of Accidental Nuclear War*, Washington, DC: Brookings University Press.

Cohen, Avner (1998) *Israel and the Bomb*, New York: Columbia University Press.

Fuhrmann, Matthew (2008a) "Exporting mass destruction? The determinants of dual-use trade," *Journal of Peace Research* 5: 633–652.

Fuhrmann, Matthew (2008b) "The nuclear marketplace and grand strategy," Ph.D. dissertation, University of Georgia.

Geller, Daniel S. (1990) "Nuclear weapons, deterrence, and crisis escalation," *Journal of Conflict Resolution* 34: 291–310.

Hymans, Jacques E.C. (2006) *The Psychology of Nuclear Proliferation*, Cambridge: Cambridge University Press.

Jo, Dong-Joon and Erik Gartzke (2007) "Determinants of nuclear weapons proliferation: a quantitative model," *Journal of Conflict Resolution* 1: 167–194.

Jones, Rodney W. and Mark G. McDonough with Toby F. Dalton and Gregory D. Koblentz (1998) *Tracking Nuclear Proliferation: A Guide in Maps and Charts*, Washington, DC: Carnegie Endowment for International Peace.

Kegley, Charles W. (1980) "International and domestic correlates of nuclear proliferation: a comparative analysis," *Korea and World Affairs* 4: 5–37.

Kroenig, Matthew (2010) *Exporting the Bomb: Technology Transfer and the Spread of Nuclear Weapons*, Ithaca: Cornell University Press.

Meyer, Stephen M. (1984) *The Dynamics of Nuclear Proliferation*, Chicago, IL: University of Chicago Press.

Miller, Steven E. (1993) "The case against a Ukrainian nuclear deterrent," *Foreign Affairs* 3: 67–80.

Perkovich, George (1999) *India's Nuclear Bomb: The Impact on Global Proliferation*, Berkeley, CA: University of California Press.

Powell, Robert (1990) *Nuclear Deterrence Theory: The Search for Credibility*, Cambridge, New York: Cambridge University Press.

Sagan, Scott D. (1993) *The Limits of Safety: Organizations, Accidents, and Nuclear Weapons*, Princeton, NJ: Princeton University Press.

Sagan, Scott D. (1996/1997) "Why do states build nuclear weapons? Three models in search of a bomb," *International Security* 3: 54–86.

Sagan, Scott D. and Kenneth Waltz (1995) *The Spread of Nuclear Weapons: A Debate*, New York: W.W. Norton & Company.

Schelling, Thomas C. (1966) *Arms and Influence*, New Haven, CT: Yale University Press.

Singh, Sonali and Christopher R. Way (2004) "The correlates of nuclear proliferation: a quantitative test," *Journal of Conflict Resolution* 6: 859–885.

Snyder, Glenn (1965) "The balance of power and the balance of terror," in Paul Seabury (ed.) *Balance of Power*, San Francisco, CA: Chandler.

Solingen, Etel (2007) *Nuclear Logics: Contrasting Paths in East Asia and the Middle East*, Princeton, NJ: Princeton University Press.

2 International nonproliferation

Why delegate to the International Atomic Energy Agency?

Robert Brown

Introduction

During the past two decades, the International Atomic Energy Agency (IAEA) pushed the international community into a confrontation with North Korea to enforce the Nuclear Nonproliferation Treaty (NPT), interfered with enforcement of the NPT against Iran, and contradicted the claims of one of its most powerful members with respect to Iraq (Mathews 2004; Williams 2004; du Preez and Sobrado 2004). Whether the IAEA becomes involved in international nonproliferation efforts with North Korea, Iran, and Iraq appears to have a significant effect upon the outcome of those efforts. Why do IAEA member states choose to give it more money or expand its authority over the nuclear nonproliferation regime? Why ask it to play a role in international negotiations, monitor more states, or monitor states more intrusively? And when do they withdraw its authorities or resources? Explaining international cooperation through the IAEA is significant as one case of international security cooperation but also important to the broader debate over why states cooperate through international organizations.

IR scholars disagree about why IOs intervene in the interaction among the interests and capabilities of states that produces outcomes. Realists argue international institutions are the tools of powerful states, used to coerce compliance with their short-term interests (Krasner 1983; Mearsheimer 1994), Institutionalists look for the functional utility of IOs to facilitate cooperation (Keohane 1984), and Constructivists focus on international institutions as creating or spreading particular norms of appropriate behavior (Barnett and Finnemore 2004; Finnemore and Sikkink 1998). This debate persists because empirical studies of international cooperation continue to lag behind theory development (Hafner-Burton *et al.* 2008). Also, while international institutions and IOs are increasingly included as factors in many analyses of nuclear motivations, the role they play is underspecified (Jo and Gartzke 2007; Sagan 1997).

This chapter analyzes why states cooperate to control proliferation threats by delegating as an international community to an IO. This chapter applies a new measure of the level of IO empowerment – the international delegation of resources and authority (Brown 2010) – to the IAEA to explain why international delegation for nuclear nonproliferation has increased over the course of the nuclear age. The results indicate that power, purpose, and beliefs are all important to a complete explanation of why the IAEA is asked to intervene in international nuclear nonproliferation efforts.

Why delegate to the IAEA?

IAEA history

The United States had a monopoly on nuclear weapons in 1945 and there was no prospect yet for commercial nuclear energy. Many US nuclear scientists joined the advocates of complete and general disarmament, world peace, and a world government in calling for nuclear technologies to be put under international controls. This became the core goal of the disarmament, and later nonproliferation, movement: if some states could credibly deny themselves a class of weapons, others would no longer find the pursuit of these weapons to be necessary.

When the United States presented the Baruch Plan to the world in 1946, the United Nations (UN) General Assembly endorsed this first call for the internationalization of all things nuclear. Still, US allies in Europe were quietly skeptical despite their public support: many feared the US would abandon them to advance its own interests and some wanted to keep the nuclear option open for themselves. Meanwhile, the USSR rejected internationalization outright if it was expected to abandon its nuclear program even before the United States disarmed. Despite the apparently heartfelt collective desire for nuclear disarmament, the widening chasm of the Cold War was replicated on nuclear issues as states important to successful cooperation instead feared the costs if others cheated.

President Dwight D. Eisenhower's 1953 "Atoms for Peace" speech before the UN was another US attempt at an international solution to the threat of nuclear weapons. When bilateral talks with the Soviets again floundered, however, the United States shifted to negotiating with the major Western nuclear technology and uranium supplier states and together they endorsed a draft text based on "Atoms For Peace" (Bechhoefler 1973; IAEA 1997; McKnight 1971).[1] The draft's formula for national representation and proposal to require safeguards only for states accepting assistance (and not as a condition of membership) anticipated the need to later include Communist and Non-Aligned Movement states in the negotiations (Bechhoefler 1973). The West was able to bring into the bargaining process the developing nuclear powers that could otherwise prevent the new institution from being effective, but did so after achieving some consensus about its structure and purpose.

The compromise document presented to 81 countries at the Conference on the Statute of the International Atomic Energy Agency in 1956 was accepted with little amendment, and the Statute entered into force as an international treaty on July 29, 1957, creating the IAEA (US Senate 1957: 20). The main goal of the IAEA was to help divert scarce nuclear materials from military uses to peaceful ones by offering assistance with costly peaceful nuclear energy programs while attempting to prevent lowest-common-denominator controls on nuclear trade (IAEA 1998). In exchange, the recipients would accept IAEA verification, or "safeguards," of the non-diversion of nuclear materials. Safeguards could take many forms but used on-site inspections to measure the flows of nuclear materials: differences between the measured and the expected quantities would be evidence of a diversion. The USSR had argued a nuclear weapons no-use treaty was more important, but it was content to accept a plan that imposed constraints on Western governments' nuclear programs while reinforcing a strong UN Security Council role (Timerbaev and Welsh 1994).

The negotiators believed safeguards would be extended over more national nuclear programs as states contracted with the IAEA for assistance. However, the IAEA never received from the major nuclear suppliers the resources necessary to become such a provider. The extension of safeguards happened instead when the major nuclear suppliers began demanding them of recipient states as a condition for trade in nuclear materials and technologies. The IAEA's responsibilities further increased in the 1960s with the transfer of bilateral safeguards from the United States and with new Soviet support for safeguards after the Cuban missile crisis (Goldschmidt 1977: 75). The major extension of IAEA safeguards, however, occurred in the 1970s because of international expansion of the nuclear industry and because the 1968 Nuclear Nonproliferation Treaty and various nuclear weapons-free zones called for treaty implementation to be monitored through IAEA safeguards (Goldschmidt 1977).[2]

Still, there has been continuous debate over how intrusive safeguards must be to verify that states are not proliferating. The safeguards process was not defined by states in the IAEA Statute nor later in the NPT, but was relegated to the IAEA itself to later determine. The recent push for states to accede to the Additional Protocol has generated a new fracture line over the safeguards process. Some states resist additional intrusiveness while others argue that the safeguards used so far were shown by Iraq in 1991 and Iran today to be insufficient to prove compliance with the NPT (Official, IAEA 2005).

In short, the belief in the 1950s was that the nuclear industry was not commercially viable; nuclear materials and technologies were so expensive that no state could consider them unless the real goal was nuclear weapons. The authority delegated to the IAEA to fulfill its primary mission – implementing safeguards only when providing assistance and then withholding that assistance from noncompliant states – became its weakness. As a result of requests to safeguard nuclear programs to monitor the implementation of various treaties, however, over time the IAEA's approach to safeguards became more in tune with controlling than promoting proliferation. The IAEA's escape from institutional infancy required developing legitimacy from its expertise in safeguards, but why does the international community increasingly rely on the IAEA to implement the nonproliferation regime by intervening in the incentives to proliferate?

International relations theory and the IAEA

The IAEA's creation required convergence on a bargain among nuclear suppliers that was acceptable to developing state interests, but which would also not tip the balance in the US–Soviet Cold War. After its creation, the IAEA's delegated authorities and resources rose, and also occasionally fell, over subsequent decades. Explaining why seems to defy easy answers and IR scholars have long had a problematic time explaining when states will cooperate through international institutions and then how these international institutions affect state behavior (Martin and Simmons 1999; Simmons 1998).

Realists assume international institutions are epiphenomenal to anarchy and the distribution of power: compliance with the provisions of security institutions like alliances and arms control agreements occurs out of short-term self-interest (Mearsheimer 1994). Some accept that international institutions may play a role in perpetuating a hegemon's interests or at least slowing any changes in the international distribution of benefits as the distribution of power changes (Keohane 1984; Krasner 1983). In short, however, Realists argue international cooperation is impeded by anarchy and that international institutions are created only when a hegemon creates and enforces them (Wallander *et al.* 1999). Hegemonic Stability Theory, however, does not explain why the hegemon sometimes chooses to cooperate through an IO and is unclear whether international institutions are created during its ascent or decline (Gilpin 1981; Keohane 1984; Keohane and Nye 1989).

Rational Institutionalists accept most of the core assumptions of Realists but recognize the functional utility of international institutions in assisting cooperation. Institutions, they argue, reduce transaction costs to bargaining, monitoring, and enforcing cooperation, including reducing information asymmetries, providing negotiating fora, and resolving distributional effects (Haggard and Simmons 1987; Keohane 1984; Keohane and Martin 1999; Martin and Simmons 1999; Morrow 1994). IOs can further reduce the transaction costs of cooperating by empowering an agent to increase specialization, manage policy externalities, facilitate bargaining, resolve disputes, create policy bias, and enhance the credibility of commitments (Hawkins *et al.* 2006b). Therefore, while Realists may view the NPT and IAEA as products of American hegemony, Institutionalists focus on the demand for cooperation as states seek mechanisms to facilitate mutually advantageous outcomes.

Finally, Constructivists argue states embrace international institutions out of a "desire to conform to shared ideas and norms of behavior" (Moravcsik 2000: 224). An individual international institution, such as the IAEA, is an array of interrelated norms that embody appropriate behavior for actors with a given identity (Finnemore and Sikkink 1998: 251). In this case, the norm of nonproliferation is an extension of the "nuclear taboo," a norm "against the use of nuclear weapons ... which, although not (yet) a fully robust prohibition, has stigmatized nuclear weapons as unacceptable weapons" (Tannenwald 2007: 2). Similar to the problem facing Realists, though, Constructivists have trouble explaining why cooperation on nuclear nonproliferation takes the forms it does: even if institutionalization helps norm transmission and internalization, why create and expand the IAEA rather than some non-IO alternative? Embracing the norm by institutionalizing it may occur because this is the most appropriate vehicle for cooperation among the international community (March and Olsen 1998), but this requires proving a recursive interaction between two distinct norms: the norm of nonproliferation and the norm of international cooperation through IOs. Still, Constructivists would expect states internalizing the nonproliferation norm and the nuclear taboo to feel obligated to then engage in costly supportive action, such as expanding the IAEA.

Hypotheses, research design, and data

Hypotheses

The three basic approaches offer almost mutually exclusive explanations for the persistence and level of international support for the IAEA, each inspiring hypotheses for testing. One hypothesis, proposed by some Realists, argues international institutions only reflect the international distribution of power: they are created by powerful states to serve their short-term interests and should therefore wax and wane along with the power of their most powerful members (Mearsheimer 1994, 2001). Hegemonic Stability Theory argues the rise of international institutions should be negatively correlated with the hegemon's power: because they are costly to change, the hegemon employs them to prolong an existing distribution of benefits (Gilpin 1981; Keohane 1984). The first hypothesis is, therefore, that delegation to an IO should be correlated with the power of the strongest state(s), though the direction (positive or negative correlation) is debated and the criteria for "power" is under-specified.

Delegation to IOs may also occur because of the functional benefits anticipated by the states trying to cooperate. As Rational Institutionalists argue, the contribution of powerful states may be necessary to help overcome collective action problems (Olson and Zeckhauser 1966), but the IOs themselves grow in response to greater demand for their services (Hawkins *et al.* 2006b). If true, the second hypothesis is that delegation to the IAEA should be driven by greater demand for cooperation on nuclear issues because of a greater risk of nuclear weapon acquisition and use.

Finally, if delegation for nonproliferation is occurring because of increased international socialization in anti-nuclear norms, as Constructivists argue, then delegation should correlate with this recursive process. The third hypothesis, therefore, is that delegation to the IAEA is correlated with strengthening norms of nonproliferation. I now turn to operationalizing the competing, but abstract, concepts: delegation, power, nuclear threats, and the strength of nuclear nonproliferation norms.

Measuring the DV: delegation

The empirical study of international organizations (IOs) has been recently advanced using principal–agent (PA) theories of delegation (Bradley and Kelley 2008b; Brown 2009; Gould 2006; Hawkins *et al.* 2006a; Pollack 1997). PA theory generally incorporates strongly functionalist assumptions but also offers a useful direction for distinguishing among the relevant actors and identifying the structure of their interactions. Individuals form a collective principal if they agree to a single contract by which they conditionally transfer decision-making authority to an agent (Hawkins *et al.* 2006a). While international decision-making bodies may pool the sovereignty of the participating states, as with the United Nations General Assembly, this is not delegation by states to an agent (Lake and McCubbins 2006; Lake 2007).[3] The grant of authorities to the UN Secretariat and the UN Security Council in the UN Charter, and to the IAEA through the Statute of the IAEA, are delegation by a collective principal to an IO agent. Importantly, an individual state does not become a principal of the IAEA by signing a safeguards agreement, no more than obtaining a license to operate a nuclear reactor in the United States makes one a principal of the US Nuclear Regulatory Commission. Rather, a state joins the collective principal of the IAEA, its Conference of States Parties, only by ratifying the Statute and being a member in good standing.

States transfer to their IO agent the authority and capacity to make decisions or take actions (Bradley and Kelley 2008a: 1), but also constrain the IO's autonomy to limit its ability to act opportunistically with respect to their interests (Hawkins and Jacoby 2008: 4; Huber and Shipan 2002). Brown (2010) identifies the ten key components of the delegation of and constraints on authority and capacity as being the agent's level of assistance with intra-principal bargaining, monitoring, and judging and enforcing compliance, its fiscal autonomy, its autonomy from its principal to select its staff and make policy decisions, the size of its staff and budgetary resources, and the principal's legal obligation to abide by the delegation contract. Agents are scored on these components and higher scores indicate greater delegation, making dissimilar acts of delegation theoretically comparable. Brown's (2010) three measures of delegation to the IAEA, 1958–2003, are employed in this analysis: the full delegation score, the resource delegation score (staff and budget size), and the institutional delegation score (composed of all authority measures). Differences in the direction and magnitude of changes in the resource and institutional scores could be occurring for different reasons; disaggregation should therefore improve inference for evaluating the hypotheses.

Illustrated in Figure 2.1, these data show that the level of delegation to the IAEA (the vertical axis is the index score) has increased over time (the horizontal axis). While greater autonomy to determine its rights of access for verifying safeguards compliance has been responsible for much of the increase in the institutional delegation score, the IAEA's Secretariat has also parlayed its technical expertise and knowledge of its principals' interests to increase its role in proposing and negotiating changes in its role with respect to its principals. The IAEA's resources, measured as the number of staff and the budget, have generally also increased over time. However, even once the budget is adjusted for inflation by using constant 2003 US dollars and for international economic conditions by then taking its share of world GDP, the resource indicators reveal no growth in a surprising number of years and even some retractions of delegation. For example, the IAEA lost millions from its budget after international inspectors were ejected from Iraq in 1998. At present, the level of international delegation to the IAEA by its principals is nearly double that at its founding in 1957.

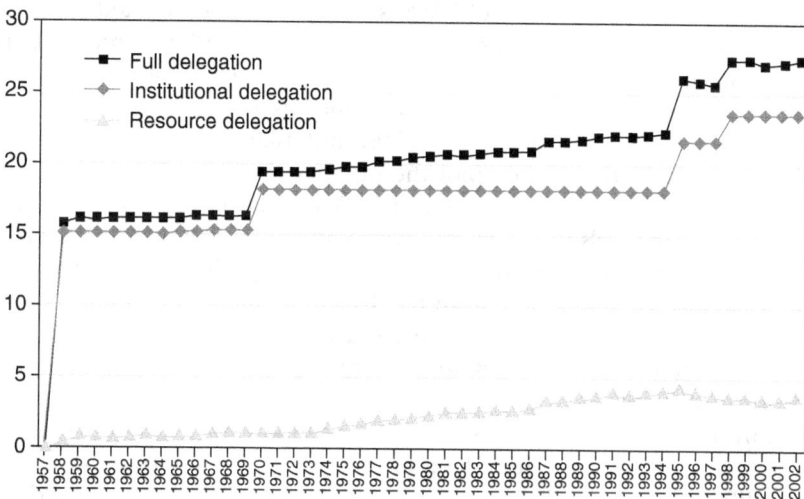

Figure 2.1 IAEA Delegation: full delegation score and institutional and resource components.

Causal variables

Three hypotheses are proposed for evaluation: Realist, Rational Institutionalist, and Constructivist. To test the Realist hypothesis, I use the Composite Index of National Capability (CINC) scores as an indicator of aggregate power (Singer 1987). If Mearsheimer is correct, delegation to the IAEA should reflect, and therefore they should be positively and significantly correlated with, the United States CINC scores (Mearsheimer 1994, 2001). If Krasner is correct, the opposite should be true: powerful states in decline will use IOs to reinforce the existing distribution of benefits against change in the underlying distribution of power (Krasner 1983). The US share of world power decreases 1945–75 and holds steady through the early 1990s before beginning to increase. I also introduce a dummy variable to control for potential structural effects caused by the end of the Cold War (ColdWar = 1 for 1947–1990, = 0 for 1991–2002).

If the Institutionalist hypothesis is correct, the creation of and delegation to the IAEA could be one response to greater threats from proliferation. This threat increases with more states trying to become nuclear weapons states (NWS), more NWS, and more NWS involvement in armed conflicts in which nuclear weapons could theoretically be used. The number of NWS and states with nuclear programs is compiled from the list generated by Jo and Gartzke (2007) and the number of NWS conflicts is a simple interaction term between the number of NWS and the count of the number conflicts in which those states are involved, as reported in the PRIO-UPPSALA Armed Conflict Dataset (Gleditsch *et al.* 2002: version 3–2005). The number of nuclear weapon program states is just four in 1946, increases to seven in 1966, and peaks at 14 in 1984 before declining to ten after 1991. The number of NWS is one in 1946 (the United States), five in 1964 (China, France, Soviet Union, United Kingdom, and United States), and peaks at ten in 1991, but is eight in 2002. Finally, the interaction term averages 3.7 in the 1950s and increases to average 4.6 in the 1960s, 4.9 in the 1970s, 7.6 in the 1980s, and 10.9 in the 1990s, before peaking at 17 in 2001. I also employ the number of "Minutes to Midnight" on the Bulletin of the Atomic Scientists' "Doomsday Clock," their representation of "the perils posed by nuclear weapons" (Scientists 2009). The "Clock" indicates periods of relatively low nuclear peril in the 1950s and mid-1980s with times-to-midnight in the 16–18 minute range, highly perilous years in the 8–11 minute range from the post-Cuban missile crisis 1960s until the early 1980s, and absolute peak danger in the 3–6 minute range from 1991–98.

Finally, if normative pressures are driving support for IAEA delegation, this socialization process should be apparent in state internalization of nonproliferation norms. Tannenwald argues the increasing normative delegitimization of nuclear weapons has been embedded in nuclear arms control agreements and implies this is reflected in the increasing number and scope of these agreements ratified by members of the international community (Tannenwald 1999). Following Simmons, one operationalization of the diffusion of norms is the proportion of states in the international system that have signed related treaties that, by themselves, do not offer material rewards (or the avoidance of costs) for accession (Simmons 2002; Smith 2007).[4] To proxy for the diffusion of nonproliferation norms, I measure the share of states that have ratified or otherwise acceded to the NPT.[5] The share of states ratifying the NPT is zero before its opening for ratification in 1967, is only 2.5 percent in 1968, but reaches 33.8 percent by entry into force in 1970, 50 percent by 1977, 60 percent by 1984, 70 percent by 1991, and 90 percent by 1996.[6]

Methods

Problems of autocorrelation in observations of the variables are endemic to IR time-series data. In this analysis, path dependence in the IAEA's level of delegation creates time-induced trending in the data. Brown (2010) attempts to correct for this by "detrending" the budget data, a common source of serial correlation, by using the IAEA's share of global GDP in constant 2003 US dollars, as discussed above. To correct for the remaining lack of independence in the observations revealed by correlogram and Lagrange multiplier (LM) tests, the hypotheses are therefore tested using Prais-Winsten Feasible Generalized Least Squares (FGLS).[7] The FLGS model conducts a Prais-Winsten transformation of time-series variables, estimating the amount of auto-correlation and re-weighting the standard errors to produce more efficient results. The time-series analyzed is 1966–2002 to include a small period of time prior to the opening for ratification of the NPT. The results are robust to alternative specifications of the time-series start year: starting a few years earlier or later, including after the NPT is open for ratification, yielded substantively identical results. The results are reported in Table 2.1, coded by the employed dependent variable: "F" for Brown's full IAEA delegation score, "I" for institutional score, and "R" for resource score.

Results

The results indicate that delegation to the IAEA changes over time for complicated reasons. The results of eight Prais-Winsten FGLS models are reported in Table 2.1 and summarized in Table 2.2. First, US power appears to have no significant effect upon IAEA delegation when taken in isolation from other potential factors (F1). It is only with the inclusion of the functionalist and normative variables that the power of the United States has a strong, positive, and significant effect upon delegation to the IAEA ($p < 0.001$ for all F and I models).

Table 2.1 IAEA Delegation (Prais-Winsten FGLS; F1 is 1958–2002, all others are 1966–2002)

Dependent variable:	Full delegation			Institutional delegation		Resource delegation	
Model:	F1	F2	F3	I1	I2	R1	R2
US CINC Score	-4.43 (17.25)	54.20*** (14.08)	57.17*** (10.56)	54.80** (15.11)	58.51*** (11.08)	4.60 (5.39)	2.35 (4.83)
Cold War (dummy variable)	-0.36 (0.82)	-1.13 (0.62)	-0.96 (0.62)	-0.76 (0.66)	-0.62 (0.65)	-0.23 (0.17)	-0.27 (0.18)
# of nuclear weapons states (NWS)		-0.57*** (0.14)	-0.66*** (0.14)	-0.99*** (0.15)	-1.10*** (0.15)	0.15* (0.07)	0.16* (0.07)
# of nuclear weapon program states		-0.11 (0.12)		-0.12 (0.13)		0.03 (0.04)	
Interaction: NWS (count × conflicts)			0.10 (0.06)		0.11 (0.06)		0.01 (0.01)
BAS "Minutes to Midnight"		0.08* (0.04)	0.04 (0.04)	0.04 (0.04)	0.00 (0.04)	0.01 (0.02)	0.01 (0.02)
Share of states ratifying NPT		15.90*** (1.21)	15.49*** (1.23)	14.30*** (1.30)	13.86*** (1.29)	1.50* (0.61)	1.41* (0.59)
Constant	22.49*** (4.77)	9.60* (3.88)	8.42** (3.02)	11.13* (4.15)	9.78** (3.16)	-0.21 (1.43)	0.28 (1.18)
Adj_R2	0.03	0.97	0.97	0.94	0.95	–	–
N	46	37	37	37	37	37	37

Notes
* $p < 0.05$, ** $p < 0.01$, *** $p < 0.001$. Standard errors in parentheses. Models are coded "F" for full delegation measure, "I" for institutional delegation scores only, and "R" for resource delegation only.

Table 2.2 Results summary: direction of significant coefficients

Independent variables:	Dependent variable: IAEA delegation		
	Full score (F)	*Institutional score (I)*	*Resource score (R)*
Realist variable:			
US CINC	+	+	0
Functionalist variables:			
NWS (#)	–	–	+
Minutes to Midnight	+	0	0
Constructivist variables:			
NPT accession share	+	+	+

Note
Variables excluded for insignificance include Cold War, Number of Nuclear Weapon Program States, and number of NWS conflicts.

The more nuanced models show a complete shift in the direction of the effect of the US share of world power: controlling for other factors, increases (decreases) are now positively correlated with increased (retracted) delegation to the IAEA. The basic Realist assumption that power is important to explaining international outcomes, including the decision to create and perpetuate international institutions, is supported but only when other factors are taken into account. The differences in size and significance of the coefficients indicates a stronger United States, causes increased institutional delegation but is largely unrelated to the IAEA's level of resources.[8]

The inclusion of the functionalist and normative variables does not just magnify the effect of US power as they themselves have significant effects delegation to the IAEA. First, the functionalist variables employed as partial analogies for the demand for IAEA services have a significant but mixed effect. The number of NWS is negatively correlated with institutional delegation (each additional NWS appears to cause institutional delegation to decrease by about 1 point, significant to $p < 0.001$ level) but is positively correlated with increased delegation of resources (significant to $p < 0.10$ level). While more states with nuclear weapons appears to cause a decrease in delegation, moving beyond the coefficients to the historical record provides a real context: the disarmament of South Africa and the nuclear-armed Soviet successor states in the 1990s, all of whom sought to join the NPT to assert the legitimacy of their regimes, occurs as the IAEA expands to verify disarmament efforts there and in Iraq. Then, the IAEA sees its resources contract as verification in Iraq ends in the same year as India and Pakistan, both outside the NPT, test nuclear weapons and declare themselves to be NWS. It is also interesting that the popular sense of the threat from nuclear weapons expressed by the Bulletin of the

Atomic Scientists' clock does translate into greater delegation. Change in the number of "Minutes to Midnight" is positively correlated with changes in delegation, but only for the aggregate or full score.[9] Among the functionalist variables, it is surprising that the number of NW program states is never significant, though these states were rarely under IAEA safeguards.

Second, the models that indicate nonproliferation norms exert a very strong and positive influence on delegation to nuclear IOs. As noted above, this result is robust to alternative starting points for the time-series analysis, including to starting in 1970 when the NPT enters into force and more than a third of states had already ratified. Specifically, there is strong support for the hypothesis that greater socialization of states in the system in the norms of nonproliferation leads to increasing support for the IAEA quite independently of any apparent functional advantages: as more states accede to the NPT, greater resources *and* authority are transferred to the IAEA. It is important to remember that states acceding to the NPT are not required to join the IAEA, only sign a safeguards agreement. Even then, many NPT states have no nuclear program to speak of, many European states rely on safeguards verification implemented by EURATOM on the IAEA's behalf, and, for other states acceding to the NPT, signing an IAEA safeguards agreement is not a forgone conclusion, as exemplified by the North Korean experience.[10] Instead, it appears the increasing universality of the NPT represents a real normative shift within the international community.

Conclusions

This chapter began by posing an empirical puzzle: why do states cooperate on international nonproliferation through an international organization (IO), such as the IAEA? Most Realists emphasize the importance of the distribution of power and argue the IAEA has persisted and expanded because the major powers sought to create and lock in an international nonproliferation regime that served its interests. Rational Institutionalists rarely dispute the importance of power but argue that international institutions must also serve some functional advantage in facilitating cooperation. To be worth the costs of its creation and maintenance, which is not only financial but also leads to the loss of some control of the nonproliferation agenda, the IAEA must actively facilitate cooperation on nonproliferation such that its members on average are better off than without it. Finally, Constructivists argue both Realists and Institutionalists overstate the importance of materialist forces and neglect developing international nuclear norms. International socialization in the norms of nuclear weapon illegitimacy, and nuclear nonproliferation occurs in parallel with the international community's twentieth-century embrace of international nonproliferation institutions.

These hypotheses are often represented as mutually exclusive explanations and that parsimony requires one to be "right." Using data on delegation to the IAEA, this chapter shows that the world is more complex. First, the expansion of the IAEA would not have occurred without strong US support, which was greater with a relatively greater American capacity to act (as measured by its CINC score). The quantitative results therefore coincide with Realist expectations. A stronger United States, though, did not cause a larger IO, only one with greater authority.

Second, there is some significant observable relationship between the demand for nonproliferation-related services and delegation to the IAEA. The proxies for demand – the number of NWS, of nuclear programs, and of "Minutes to Midnight" – are clearly incomplete and do not reflect all sources of demand. Other sources could include, for example, the bargaining problems that result from preference heterogeneity or the increasing monitoring workload as the nuclear industry expanded. Still, there is a real functionalist story in the data that connects the demand for cooperation to its supply with IOs.

The third finding will possibly be the most remarkable to materialists. The normative variable attempts to quantify the strength of nonproliferation norms and appears to capture a strong and positive correlation with delegation to the IAEA. Increased accession to the NPT largely affects the expanded delegation of institutional authority and has a smaller (but still significant) effect upon the IAEA's resources. Constructivists must still explain why a stronger nonproliferation norm requires an expanded IAEA (one with greater delegations of authority and resources) rather than the also observed alternatives: unilateral actions, other arms control agreements, and even new IOs (as in the IOs created to implement the disarmament of Iraq and the Comprehensive Test Ban Treaty).

Why do states cooperate on nonproliferation through the IAEA? Why create and maintain an international organization with substantial financial and agenda-setting costs? While the support of the United States is important to facilitating cooperation through the IAEA, this story is incomplete. Even within a materialist frame, a focus on power cannot explain the *form* of cooperation: the decision to use an IO. Instead, IR scholars must examine the complex incentive structure facing states. Before the international community will delegate authority over an issue of such importance to their national security as nuclear weapons, two things must occur. First, states must see a demand for nonproliferation-related services as a response to their nuclear insecurities. Rational Institutionalists provide one answer for why cooperation should occur through an IO: the greater efficiency of cooperation produced by reducing the transaction costs of negotiation but also of monitoring and enforcement. Second, though, they must also come to believe nonproliferation is the appropriate way to address their nuclear insecurities: a normative judgment. The increasing universality of the NPT, combined with the opprobrium cast upon states choosing unilateral solutions, suggests these strategies for resolving nuclear insecurities are made with attention to factors beyond a strict cost-benefit analysis.

What can we expect from institutionalized cooperation on nonproliferation in the future? Much depends on the capacity – not simply the will – of the United States to lead the international community. When the United States escapes its wars in Afghanistan and Iraq, and the economic recession, is probably less important than how well it does so relative to other powerful countries. As noted above, it appears important whether the advancement of the nonproliferation regime is challenged by a hegemonic contender: the USSR in the Cold War and China today. Much also depends on whether the anticipated nuclear renaissance is realized: new expansion of the commercial nuclear energy industry should lead to expanded international nuclear delegation. Finally, as the NPT has achieved near universality, continued strengthening of international nonproliferation norms should lead to pressure for new position-taking (Hathaway 2002). This should include pressure to bring into force existing treaties (the Comprehensive Test Ban Treaty) or new treaties (a fissile-material cut-off treaty, for example), or to threaten or implement enforcement of existing treaties. Any difficulty with negotiating new treaties may then increase the prospects for enforcement of the rules of the existing international regime as defined by the NPT and IAEA.

Notes

1 These states included Australia, Belgium, Canada, France, Portugal, South Africa, the UK, and the US. West Germany did not formally regain its sovereignty until May 1955 (Haftendorn 2005). US government documents indicate that the "fourth country problem" (after the UK, US, and USSR) focused on Canada, China, France, Israel, Japan, and Sweden (Burr 2005).

2 Nuclear weapon-free zones (NWFZs) are regional treaties abolishing nuclear weapons programs or possession in the territories controlled by their member states. They generally follow the same pattern as used in the NPT of delegating to the IAEA the authority to implement safeguards (Quester 1973; McKnight 1971; Jensen 1974; Wittner 1997; Pilat 2005; US Senate 1978).

3 Others argue delegation to an international legislature occurs when a group of actors agrees to accept decisions made according to less-than-consensus rules (Bradley and Kelley 2008b; Cooper et al. 2008; Vaubel 2006).

4 This represents only one Constructivist perspective (Hymans 2006; Rublee 2009). As one alternative, Kelley suggests we can learn about the strength of a norm by observing actors that cheat and the responses by other actors (Kelley 2008). However, the vast majority of enforcement events concern ancillary elements of the nonproliferation norm, such as reporting or acquiring enrichment or reprocessing technologies, and not the core norm against acquiring nuclear weapons.

5 Accession to the IAEA Statute is the oldest independent international nuclear arms control agreement but presents endogeneity problems. Accession to the

1963 Limited Test Ban Treaty (LTBT) was analyzed as an alternative normative independent variable but yielded no significant results.

6 Ratification appears further from universality than usually reported because the employed total number of states in the system includes microstates (Gleditsch and Ward 1999).

7 Maximum likelihood models, including ordered probit, are inappropriate because of the small number of observations but also because they discard the significant variation in the dependent variable. Models, not reported, yielded similar results but an expectation of unreliable and biased errors from the constrained sample and fewer controls. Though often used, lagged dependent variable (LDV) tests are inappropriate with many autoregressive processes (Keele and Kelly 2005: 203).

8 As the USSR was strongly supportive of nonproliferation but served as a counterweight to the United States during the Cold War, the role of USSR/Russian power (CINC score) was included in several analyses (not reported). The Soviet/Russian share of world power is steady from the early 1950s until the fall of the USSR in 1989, whereupon the Russian CINC score drops dramatically for several years before stabilizing by about 1993 at a reduced level. Soviet/Rusisan power consistently yields a negative and significant effect ($p < 0.10$ level), and this persists when truncating the analysis to 1966–89 to exclude the collapse of the USSR. Russian power 1991–2002, though, is insignificant as a correlate.

9 The inclusion of the USSR/Russian CINC score as a variable (see above) increases the significance level of the Minutes to Midnight variable in models with the full delegation score as the dependent variable but also reduces slightly the significance of the number of nuclear weapons states for models using IAEA resources as the dependent variable.

10 The NPT allows safeguards agreements to be concluded "either individually or together with other States" (Treaty on the Non-Proliferation of Nuclear Weapons 1970: Article III Para. 4), creating a loop-hole in which the European members of EURATOM could be safeguarded by that body as long as the IAEA could certify safeguards compliance was occurring (on EURATOM's special status, see: Bunn 1992; Fischer 1997; McKnight 1970; Young 1969).

References

Barnett, Michael and Martha Finnemore (2004) *Rules for the World: International Organizations in Global Politics*, Ithaca, NY: Cornell University Press.

Bechhoefler, Bernhard G. (1973) "Historical Evolution of International Safeguards," in M. Willrich (ed.) *International Safeguards and Nuclear Industry*, Baltimore, MD: Johns Hopkins University Press.

Bradley, Curtis A. and Judith G. Kelley (2008a) "The Concept of International Delegation," *Law and Contemporary Problems* 71: 1.

Bradley, Curtis A. and Judith G. Kelley (eds) (2008b) *Law and Contemporary Problems, Special Issue: The Law and Politics of International Delegation*. Vol. 71: 1.

Brown, Robert L. (2009) "Measuring Delegation," *Review of International Organizations (Online First)* 5:1.

Brown, Robert L. (2010) "Measuring Delegation," *Review of International Organizations* 5: 141–75.

Bunn, George (1992) *Arms Control By Committee: Managing Negotiations with the Russians*, Stanford, CA: Stanford University Press.

Burr, William (2005) "National Intelligence Estimates of the Nuclear Proliferation Problem: The First Ten Years, 1957–1967," Washington, DC: National Security Archive.

Cooper, Scott, Darren Hawkins, Wade Jacoby, and Daniel Nielson (2008) "Yielding Sovereignty to International Institutions: Bringing System Structure Back In," *International Studies Review* 3: 501–24.

du Preez, Jean and María Lorenzo Sobrado (2004) *IAEA Board Gives Iran Yet Another Chance* [website]. CNS (Center for Nonproliferation Studies) Research Story, September 27 [cited September 27, 2004]. Available at http://cns.miis.edu/pubs/week/040927.htm.

Finnemore, Martha and Kathryn Sikkink (1998) "International Norm Dynamics and Political Change," *International Organization* 52: 4.

Fischer, David A.V. (1997) *History of the International Atomic Energy Agency: The First Forty Years*, Vienna: International Atomic Energy Agency.

Gilpin, Robert (1981) *War & Change in World Politics*, Cambridge, MA: Princeton University Press.

Gleditsch, Kristian Skrede and Michael D. Ward (1999) "Interstate System Membership: A Revised List of the Independent States since 1816," *International Interactions* 25: 393–413.

Gleditsch, Nils Petter, Peter Wallensteen, Margareta Sollenberg Ericksson, and Harvard Strand (2002) "Armed Conflict 1946–2001: A New Dataset," *Journal of Peace Research* 5: 615–37.

Goldschmidt, Bertrand (1977) "A Historical Survey of Nonproliferation Policies," *International Security* 1: 69–87.

Gould, Erica R. (2006) *Money Talks: The International Monetary Fund, Conditionality, and Supplemental Financiers*, Stanford, CA: Stanford University Press.

Hafner-Burton, Emilie M., Jana von Stein, and Erik Gartzke (2008) "International Organizations Count," *Journal of Conflict Resolution* 2: 175–88.

Haftendorn, Helga (2005) "Germany's Accession to NATO: 50 years on," *NATO Review*, Summer.

Haggard, Stephan and Beth A. Simmons (1987) "Theories of International Regimes," *International Organization* 3: 491–517.

Hathaway, Oona (2002) "Do Human Rights Treaties Make A Difference?," *Yale Law Journal* 111: 1935–2042.

Hawkins, Darren and Wade Jacoby (2008) "Agent Permeability, Principal Delegation and the European Court of Human Rights," *Review of International Organizations* 1: 1–28.

Hawkins, Darren, David A. Lake, Daniel Nielson, and Michael J. Tierney (2006a) *Delegation and Agency in International Organizations*, Cambridge (UK): Cambridge University Press.

Hawkins, Darren, David A. Lake, Daniel Nielson, and Michael J. Tierney (2006b) "States, International Organizations, and Principal–Agent Theory," in D. Hawkins, D.A. Lake, D. Nielson, and M.J. Tierney (eds) *Delegation and Agency in International Organizations*, Cambridge: Cambridge University Press.

Huber, John D. and Charles R. Shipan (2002) *Deliberate Discretion? The Institutional Foundations of Bureaucratic Autonomy*, New York, NY: Cambridge University Press.

Hymans, Jacque E.C. (2006) "Theories of Nuclear Proliferation," *Nonproliferation Review* 13: 3.

IAEA (1997) "The IAEA Turns 40: Key Dates and Historical Developments," Vienna, Austria: The International Atomic Energy Agency.

IAEA (1998) "The Evolution of IAEA Safeguards," Vienna, Austria: The International Atomic Energy Agency.

Jensen, Lloyd (1974) *Return from the Nuclear Brink*, Lexington, MA: Lexington Books.

Jo, Dong-Joon and Erik Gartzke (2007) "Determinants of Nuclear Weapons Proliferation," *Journal of Conflict Resolution* 1: 167–94.

Keele, Luke and Nathan J. Kelly (2005) "Dynamic Models for Dynamic Theories: The Ins and Outs of Lagged Dependent Variables," *Political Access* 14: 186–205.

Kelley, Judith G. (2008) "Assessing the Complex Evolution of Norms: The Rise of International Election Monitoring," *International Organization* 2: 221–55.

Keohane, Robert O. (1984) *After Hegemony: Cooperation and Discord in the World Political Economy*, Princeton, NJ: Princeton University Press.

Keohane, Robert O. and Lisa L. Martin (1999) "Institutional Theory, Endogeneity, and Delegation," Paper read at Progress in International Relations Theory: A Collaborative Assessment and Application of Imre Lakatos's Methodology of Scientific Research Programs, January 15–16, at Scottsdale, AZ.

Keohane, Robert S. and Joseph S. Nye (1989) *Power and Interdependence*, 2nd edn, Glenview: Scott, Foresman and Company.

Krasner, Stephen D. (1983) "Structural Causes and Regime Consequences: Regimes as Intervening Variables," *International Organization* 36: 2.

Lake, David A. (2007) "Delegating Divisible Sovereignty: Sweeping a Conceptual Minefield," *Review of International Organizations* 2: 219–37.

Lake, David A. and Mathew D. McCubbins (2006) "The Logic of Delegation to International Organizations," in D. Hawkins, D.A. Lake, D. Nielson, and M.J. Tierney (eds) *Delegation and Agency in International Organizations*, Cambridge: Cambridge University Press.

McKnight, Allan (1970) "Nuclear Non-Proliferation: IAEA and EURATOM," New York, NY: Carnegie Endowment for International Peace.

McKnight, Allan (1971) *Atomic Safeguards: A Study in International Verification*, New York: United Nations.

March, James G. and Johan Olsen (1998) "The Institutional Dynamics of International Political Orders," *International Organization* 52: 4.

Martin, Lisa L. and Beth A. Simmons (1999) "Theories and Empirical Studies of International Institutions," in J. Katzenstein, R.O. Keohane, and S.D. Krasner (eds) *Exploration and Contestation in the Study of World Politics*, Cambridge, MA: MIT Press.

Mathews, Jessica Tuchman (2004) "UN Inspection in Iraq Was No Sham," *YaleGlobal*, March 24.

Mearsheimer, John J. (1994) "The False Promise of International Institutions," *International Security* 3: 5–49.

Mearsheimer, John J. (2001) *The Tragedy of Great Power Politics*, New York: Norton.

Moravcsik, Andrew (2000) "The Origins of Human Rights Regimes: Democractic Delegation in Postwar Europe," *International Organization* 2: 217–52.

Morrow, James D. (1994) "Modeling the Forms of International Cooperation: Distribution Versus Information," *International Organization* 3: 387–423.

Official, IAEA (2005) IAEA Interview 01, Vienna, Austria, July 20.

Olson, Mancur and Richard Zeckhauser (1966) "An Economic Theory of Alliances," *Review of Economic and Statistics* 48: 266–79.

Pilat, Joseph F. (2005) "Reassessing Security Assurances in a Unipolar World," *Washington Quarterly* 2: 159–70.

Pollack, Mark A. (1997) "Delegation, Agency, and Agenda Setting in the European Community," *International Organization* 1: 99–134.

Quester, George H. (1973) *The Politics of Nuclear Proliferation*, Baltimore, MD: Johns Hopkins University Press.

Rublee, Maria Post (2009) *Nonproliferation Norms: Why States Choose Nuclear Restraint*, Athens, GA: University of Georgia Press.

Sagan, Scott D. (1997) "Why Do States Build Nuclear Weapons?," *International Security* 21: 54–86.

Scientists, Bulletin of the Atomic (2009) *Doomsday Clock: Timeline* 2009 [cited June 1, 2009]. Available at www.thebulletin.org/content/doomsday-clock/timeline.

Simmons, Beth A. (1998) "Compliance with International Agreements," *Annual Review of Political Science* 1: 75–93.

Simmons, Beth A. (2002) "Why Commit? Expaining State Acceptance of International Human Rights Obligations," in D. Hawkins, D.A. Lake, D. Nielson, and M.J. Tierney (eds) *Conference on Delegation to International Organizations*, Bringham Young University.

Singer, J. David (1987) "Reconstructing the Correlates of War Dataset on Military Capabilities of States, 1816–1985," *International Interactions* 14: 115–32.

Smith, Heather M. (2007) "Ratification of Global Human Rights Treaties: Signaling for Aid during Regional Crises," Ph.D. in Political Science, UC San Diego, La Jolla, CA.

Tannenwald, Nina (1999) "Nuclear Taboo," *International Security* 53: 3.

Tannenwald, Nina (2007) *The Nuclear Taboo*, New York, NY: Cambridge University Press.

Timerbaev, Roland and Susan Welsh (1994) "The IAEA's Role in Nuclear Arms Control: Its Evolution and Future Prospects," *The Nonproliferation Review* 3: 18–31.

Treaty on the Non-Proliferation of Nuclear Weapons (1970) London, Moscow, and Washington, DC (Opened July 1, 1968, Entered into force March 5, 1970).

United States Senate (1957) Committee on Foreign Relations and Senate Members of the Joint Committee on Atomic Energy, 85th Congress 1st Session. *Statute of the International Atomic Energy Agency. Hearings before the Committee on Foreign Relations, United States Senate, and Senate Members of the Joint Committee on Atomic Energy, 95th Congress, 1st session, on Executive I Statute of the International Atomic Energy Agency (May 10, 14, 15 and 20, 1957)*.

United States Senate (1978) Committee on Foreign Relations 95th Congress 2nd Session. *Ex. 1, Additional Protocol I to the Treaty for the Prohibition of Nuclear Weapons in Latin America (Treaty of Tlatelolco). Hearing Before The Committee on Foreign Relations 95th Congress 2nd Session (August 15, 1978)*.

Vaubel, Roland (2006) "Principal–agent Problems in International Organizations," *Review of International Organizations* 1: 125–38.

Wallander, Celeste A., Helga Haftendorn, and Robert O. Keohane (1999) "Introduction," in H. Haftendorn, R.O. Keohane, and C.A. Wallander (eds) *Imperfect Unions: Security Institutions over Time and Space*, Oxford: Oxford University Press.

Williams, Ian (2004) "Blix Not Bombs," *The Nation* 278: 13.
Wittner, Lawrence S. (1997) *Resisting the Bomb: 1954–1970*, 3 vols, Vol. 2. Stanford, CA: Stanford University Press.
Young, Elizabeth (1969) "The Control of Proliferation: The 1968 Treaty in Hindsight and Forecast," *Adelphi Paper 56*, London.

3 Membership has its privileges

Conventional arms and influence within the Nuclear Non-Proliferation Treaty

Jennifer Erickson and Christopher Way

The Nuclear Non-proliferation Treaty (NPT) is unusual both for its breadth of membership and for its institutionalized inequality. In an international system of sovereign equal states, the NPT requires signatories to give up access to what is arguably the most powerful means available to guarantee their security, while nevertheless allowing a handful of countries the exclusive possession of those very means.[1] Yet it has also managed to become one of the most widely supported pieces of international treaty law, currently with 189 members. To be sure, signatories receive some benefits in exchange for giving up their right to the bomb, such as enhanced access to nuclear energy technology and know-how. For many, however, these benefits are marginal at best and fail to address effectively their security needs and goals. The NPT "bargain" seems to offer a poor deal for many of its signatories. Why, then, have so many countries signed the NPT, and (for the most part) signed it relatively quickly?

Although the formal provisions of the treaty offer scant security benefits, informal behavior by regime supporters may provide important inducements to increase the attractiveness of the NPT bargain. More specifically, we argue that the costs of the NPT "bargain" can be reduced if a substitute means of protecting members' sovereignty and territorial integrity is provided. For example, some nuclear weapons states have occasionally pledged never to use nuclear weapons against non-nuclear signatories of the treaty, presumably enhancing the security of NPT members. However, those pledges lack any credible commitment, rendering them of limited value. Instead, we examine the possibility of a more concrete extratreaty side-payment: major conventional arms transfers. In this chapter, we ask whether NPT membership grants signatories enhanced access to conventional arms, in essence providing them with a valuable security side-payment or "signing bonus" for joining. If states gain conventional arms in exchange for eschewing unconventional weapons, the NPT bargain may be a better deal after all.

By exploring the potential provision of conventional arms to reward NPT membership, we contribute to our understanding of both the growth and functioning of the non-proliferation regime and of international regimes more broadly. Indeed, while it is easy to speculate that side-payments and other forms of informal encouragement must be a common currency of regime promotion and upkeep, they remain understudied. In terms of the NPT, although it has been claimed that a tacit agreement assuring "a system of relative free trade in conventional weaponry" (Smith 1987: 258) underpinned the explicit bargain of the treaty, whether such an agreement has played out in practice has never been studied systematically. Moreover, our claim is somewhat different: rather than maintaining a system of *free* trade in arms, we suggest that NPT promoters can use *selective* and *conditional* access to conventional arms to support the treaty. To explore this possibility empirically, we conduct a statistical analysis of major conventional weapons exports from the United States and Soviet Union/Russia from 1970 to 2001, examining whether and how conventional arms transfers may be linked to NPT support among recipient states. We demonstrate that informal inducements have provided a "signing bonus" to states that join the NPT. Conditional, extra-treaty benefits to members can play an important role in recruiting new signatories and, in doing so, help to broaden regime membership. These findings, in turn, suggest lessons for bolstering the NPT, frequently described as a "regime in crisis," although we argue difficult trade-offs are inescapable.

History of the NPT and theoretical background

After a decade of nuclear crisis, an escalating superpower arms race, and the addition of China and France to the list of nuclear military powers, the Nuclear Non-proliferation Treaty opened for signature in July 1968 and went into effect in March 1970. Although Finland and Ireland introduced the treaty, the United States and Soviet Union quickly adopted it as one of their major foreign policy objectives (Nye 1988; Shaker 1980). The core of the treaty cements five countries (the United States, Soviet Union, United Kingdom, France, and China) as nuclear weapons states (NWS) and requires the remaining non-nuclear weapons states – those that had not tested nuclear devices before January 1, 1967 – to give up their right to develop and diffuse nuclear weapons technology. In exchange, the nuclear members pledged their assistance in providing peaceful, civilian applications of nuclear technology and committed themselves "to pursue negotiations in good faith" aimed at nuclear disarmament (although this pledge lacked concrete commitments). At a time when nuclear weapons were seen not as taboo but rather as a practical means for states to acquire international status and security, this built-in inequality would seem to make the NPT a difficult sell for many states.

Nevertheless, almost every country has signed the NPT. Participation is the rule, not the exception. By 1970, the NPT had already gathered 95 signatures and entered into force. Participation rates have increased steadily over time to include 189 member states in the present day. Only three states have staunchly refused to join (India, Israel, and Pakistan), and only one has exercised its option to withdraw in the event of "extra-ordinary events" as outlined in Article X (North Korea in 2003).[2] To be sure, the treaty promises access to civilian nuclear technology, offering the peaceful benefits of the atom in exchange for giving up the military bene-fits. Yet, in practice, this benefit has not materialized: NPT members have actually received *less* peaceful nuclear assistance than non-members (Fuhrmann, this volume). Even in the absence of peaceful benefits, giving up their right to the bomb is not a costly decision for some states. For those lacking significant security concerns or the resources to invest realis-tically in nuclear weapons development,[3] the benefits of signing the NPT may outweigh the costs, even without factoring in any extra side-payments. For many more states, however, the benefits of the NPT bargain are not so clear-cut. For those with the resources and/or faced with security threats to make nuclear weapons appear a plausible and effective addition to their military arsenals, trading away the right to nuclear military technology in exchange for nuclear civilian technology might require some added incen-tives to make even the long-run sacrifice pay off. And, as Goodliffe and Hawkins (2006) observe, states are less likely to sign on to treaties when the commitment costs of doing so are high, and those costs vary substan-tially from one state to another according to their situations. In particular, states facing challenging security environments pay a higher cost in com-mitting to the NPT than states in more benign regions.[4]

As a result, the conditions for creating international regimes[5] are often much more difficult to establish than the conditions for maintaining them (Keohane 1984). Scholars frequently point to the importance of hegem-onic leaders in spearheading regime formation by offering incentives to join or by increasing the costs of not joining. However, in the case of the NPT, a strict reading of hegemonic stability theory, emphasizing a single dominant leader, has been found wanting (Smith 1987). Alternatively, a handful of cooperating system-determining states (Keohane 1969),[6] like the US and USSR in the 1960s and 1970s, may be the best resource- and incentive-equipped states to promote regime membership and com-pliance. Events in the 1960s – particularly France and China's nuclear tests and their demonstration that early assumptions about the difficulty of mas-tering nuclear weapons technology were inaccurate – fostered a consensus among the system-determining states of the time in favor of stemming the spread of nuclear weapons (Paul 2003).

That consensus underpinned superpower cooperation in drafting the NPT. Considering the text that emerged, it is not hard to see why the superpowers were willing to make the investment in treaty promotion. By freezing the legitimate possession of nuclear weapons, the US and USSR could, to a large extent, ensure their continued dominance within their own spheres of influence and prevent the rise of serious challengers to that dominance elsewhere (Paul 1998). The treaty legalized their monopoly of nuclear weapons and protected their ability to intervene (conventionally) across the globe. To be sure, the negotiations of the treaty were frequently contentious (Shaker 1980). On the one hand, the treaty that emerged is a genuine bargain that reflects the desires of non-nuclear states for access to nuclear energy and commitments to reducing both horizontal and vertical proliferation. On the other hand, it legalized the inequality between nuclear and non-nuclear states and promised to slow the spread of weapons that might limit the ability of the superpowers to impose solutions on others.[7]

Given the relatively meager attractions of the NPT for many states, and the fact that states faced highly differential costs in joining, what inducements could the superpowers provide to encourage other states to sign on? Without any built-in assurances to compensate for non-nuclear states' security concerns, little in the way of rewards for joining in terms of access to civilian nuclear technology (Fuhrmann, this volume), and weak normative pressures to join, at least initially, lead states would likely need to offer extra-treaty side-payments to broaden international support. It is therefore useful to consider a wider range of policy inducements, beyond specific treaty provisions, to understand better the means leading states employ to facilitate international cooperation and regime creation. Informal inducements can be integral to attracting regime membership, and yet are not often explicitly addressed in systematic analyses of negotiated regime formation.[8] We define informal inducements as positive material incentives[9] not delineated in the treaty that regime supporters can use to encourage membership (or compliance). Although the NPT itself outlines a number of benefits to its members, the security costs it entails may still outweigh the short list of formal benefits it provides. Regime promoters may therefore reach beyond those formal boundaries to draw on a wide range of resources not explicitly mentioned in the treaty or even overtly related to nuclear non-proliferation (i.e., informal inducements).

Informal inducements must, of course, be distinguished not only from formal inducements, but also from coercive measures or negative sanctions. Rather than punishing non-supporters to impose costs for non-commitment, incentives or inducements entail rewards or "the granting of a political or economic benefit in exchange for a specified policy adjustment by the recipient nation" (Cortright 1997: 6; see also Baldwin 1971; Long 1996). Such foreign policy strategies can be used to "create and/or guide change in favorable directions" by increasing another state's interests in behaving in a desired way (George and Smoke 1974: 605, 608). Indeed, the use of positive benefits in foreign policy is predicated on the assumption that other states' preferences may, in some cases, be open to change, and that such change can affect the possibility for interstate cooperation (Long 1996: 8–11).

For the NPT, positive inducements aimed at reducing the security costs of joining the regime might be particularly effective. Upon joining the NPT, states are required to foreswear what is arguably the most powerful and effective means of assuring their existential security and a potential way for them to level the playing field with more powerful rivals. Any inducement linked to treaty membership that enhances non-nuclear weapons states' security should therefore reduce the costs entailed in joining (and complying with) the treaty. One possible inducement is assurance against nuclear attack by the nuclear weapons states.[10] The treaty itself lacks any guarantee by the nuclear weapons states not to threaten to use or use nuclear weapons against non-nuclear weapons states party to the treaty (Athanasopulos 2000). However, just 17 days after the draft treaty was adopted by the General Assembly, the Soviet Union, United States, and United Kingdom jointly sponsored a Security Council resolution designed to offer such assurances, as part of their drive to gain signatures for the NPT. Resolution 255 endorses the intention stated by those three powers to provide immediate support, in accord with the UN Charter, to any non-nuclear weapons state party to the NPT which is the victim of aggression using nuclear weapons (Lenefsky 1970).[11]

In addition, some nuclear weapons states have occasionally pledged unilaterally never to use nuclear weapons against non-nuclear signatories of the treaty, presumably enhancing the security of NPT members. Russia offered such a pledge in 1993 (thus modifying Leonid Brezhnev's blanket no first-use pledge issued in 1982), as has the United States at various times (initially in 1978 and reaffirmed by the Clinton administration in a 1997 Presidential Decision Directive).[12] Non-nuclear weapons states have occasionally sought such NPT-linked assurances in exchange for their continued support of the regime (Bunn and Timerbaev 1993), as did Nigeria at the 1990 NPT review conference, or have sought to provide greater credibility to existing pledges (for example, Egypt at the same venue). Concerns about the lack of legal effect and credibility of such pledges were later to be borne out. When circumstances change, such pledges can easily be withdrawn, as the unraveling of the US qualified no first-use pledge in 2002 illustrates.[13]

These negative security pledges failed to provide any credible commitment,[14] rendering them of limited value. We point instead to enhanced access to major conventional arms as a more tangible, and possibly more credible, extra-treaty side-payment. If regime leaders can provide conventional arms transfers in place of unconventional arms, they may be able to assuage some members' security concerns and sweeten the NPT deal substantially. As William Long points out, "As a policy matter, states often employ trade or technology transfer measures to strengthen an ally or decrease the dependency or vulnerability of a potential ally or friend to a common adversary" (1996: 5). Conventional weapons transfers from NPT proponents to promote regime membership are *positive* incentives, we hypothesize, in the sense that the superpowers will transfer them in larger and more frequent amounts to states once they have joined the NPT – in essence, a "signing bonus" or reward for joining. If conventional arms are in fact used as we suggest, they are also *informal* incentives, not among the membership inducements outlined in the NPT and serving instead as side-payments at the discretion of the arms-exporting state to support the regime.

Conventional arms as tools of foreign policy

Major conventional arms transfers would be a natural informal inducement for NPT promoters to offer potential new members, especially during the Cold War. First, the superpowers had long viewed arms transfers as a standard tool of foreign policy, useful for winning over non-aligned states and influencing states within their respective blocs (Neuman 1986; Pierre 1982; Stanley and Pearton 1972). Although smaller exporters were typically motivated by economic necessity to export arms, the United States and Soviet Union saw their economic utility as equal to or surpassed by their political utility. Access to arms in the form of both sales and aid could provide concrete assurances of a security relationship, buy and reward bilateral friendship, sway the course of proxy wars, enhance conventional deterrence, and win supporters to a superpower's foreign policy causes.[15] As a result, exporters were particularly reluctant to formalize any agreements on conventional arms and preferred instead to leave the terms of exchange up to individual exporters. Moreover, they placed a premium on arms trade secrecy, arguing that importers would look elsewhere for goods if sales were made public.

With decreased demand and increased supply for conventional arms in the post-Cold War era, experts suggest that the arms trade has become both increasingly commercialized and reduced in value as a political tool. Still, the United States in particular has continued to employ conventional arms transfers as a foreign policy tool, using arms as inducements for allies in the War on Terror and in support of other favored policy initiatives. Even with the collapse of the Soviet Union, Russia too remains a top producer and supplier of weapons and their component parts in the post-Cold War era.

Second, within the context of the NPT, arms transfers could provide a means to offset the security costs of signing. Enhanced access to conventional arms could provide a substitute to nuclear weapons, reducing the commitment costs of the treaty. By improving insecure recipients' military capabilities, increased arms transfers would not only directly assuage security concerns but also provide a symbol of a concrete military relationship with a nuclear-armed superpower. Furthermore, observers have speculated that conventional arms transfers may sometimes be used to stave off a state's nuclear ambitions – even if it creates a "dove's dilemma" in the process. From this point of view, the price of some increased regional instability that may come with building recipients' conventional arsenals may be worth it, if they can be dissuaded from building far more dangerous nuclear arsenals. The rationale is that an enhanced conventional arsenal (and closer relationship with a superpower) will reduce a state's perception of insecurity and, in turn, of its need for nuclear weapons (Gelb 1976/77; Nolan 1997; Pierre 1982).

Thus, although not formally related to the NPT, conventional arms have an implicit but recognized connection to nuclear proliferation and the NPT. As Roger Smith states, "The non-proliferation regime is ... 'nested' within an extensive set of other international arrangements" (1987: 274). The interconnected nature of these issues and arrangements, we argue, opens the door to the possibility of NPT proponents wielding new or increased conventional arms supplies – especially within their political blocs – as an inducement to support the regime. Even states that already receive conventional arms from a supplier could be persuaded by the offer of more or better arms and related technology, whether to enhance their security, prestige, or both. To uncover whether this relationship exists in practice, we turn to a large-N statistical analysis, which enables us to find whether such export patterns exist to a wide range of importers over a span of 30 years.

Research design and data

The statistical models examine the relationship between US and Soviet/Russian major conventional arms exports (the outcome of interest) and 180 potential recipient states' accession to the NPT (our variable of interest) from 1970 to 2001.[16] In particular, we focus on whether the two superpowers used conventional arms as an inducement to broaden NPT membership, particularly during the Cold War era. To provide context, we also examine export patterns from the third major NPT proponent, the United Kingdom, as well as those of the top five major conventional arms exporters as a whole: the United States, Soviet Union, France, the United Kingdom, and (West) Germany. The following sections describe our dependent, independent, and control variables, as well as expected relationships among them.

Dependent variable: major conventional weapons transfers

Major conventional weapons (MCW) are defined as large weapons with a military purpose, falling into one of nine categories: aircraft, armored vehicles, artillery, sensors, air defense systems, missiles, ships, engines, or "other" fulfilling specified qualifications (SIPRI 2007: 428–9). We use annual, dyadic MCW transfer data collected and standardized by the Stockholm International Peace Research Institute (SIPRI). SIPRI's database extends back to 1950 and presents the most up-to-date and comprehensive multi-country source available on MCW transfers.[17] Its export–import records are compiled from public sources, including government documents, news reports, reference works, and books and journals, and past years are continually updated as new information becomes declassified (430). As Brzoska and Pearson (1994) note, SIPRI "provides the most painstakingly researched database available" (20) and is an established source for researchers exploring cross-national arms transfer trends over time.[18] We begin the analysis in 1970, when the US and Soviet Union sign on to the NPT and work toward promoting membership among their respective blocs.[19]

To standardize data values across country, time, sophistication of equipment, and mode of payment, SIPRI codes its records as continuous "trend-indicator values" (TIVs) for each dyad-year. A TIV represents the quantity and technological quality of weapons transfers between an exporter and importer every year and is assigned from "an index that reflects [the weapon's] value as a military resource in relation to other weapons," factoring core weapons prices into its scale wherever possible (SIPRI 2007: 429).[20] Because arms transfers can come in the form of sales, gifts, or aid, can include new or used equipment, and can be financed through a number of means, such as gifts, discounts, cash, credit, and bartering, the TIV is much more representative of a transfer's value in both qualitative and quantitative terms than export sales figures. Importantly for our purposes, the standardized value also allows scholars to compare data across time and space (Brzoska 2004).

As Figure 3.1 shows, the United States and the USSR/Russia have long dominated major conventional arms transfers, together accounting for approximately 80 percent of transfers from the top five supplier states. The figure also demonstrates that arms transfers peaked in 1983, afterwards trending downwards with the exception of upturns in the mid 1990s and after 2001. In general, transfers have been notably lower in the post-Cold War years, as states' military budgets, armed forces, and security needs have shrunk to reflect the "peace dividend." The United States and Russia have remained the top exporters, but their arms transfers, too, have declined. Moreover, as some smaller states have acquired production capacity since the 1980s and former Eastern Bloc members began to sell off their used weapons stocks in the early 1990s, the market shares of the major exporters have declined a bit. Nevertheless, the United States, Russia, and Europe continue to dwarf their competition in arms exports. From 2002–2006, SIPRI (2007) estimates that the United States, Russia, and the big European suppliers (the United Kingdom, France, and Germany) still accounted for approximately 90 percent of the total global market in major conventional arms transfers.

Variable of interest and controls

NPT status

Our independent variable of interest is potential arms recipients' NPT status: is an importing country inside or outside of the treaty regime? To record NPT status, we create two dichotomous variables, one coding

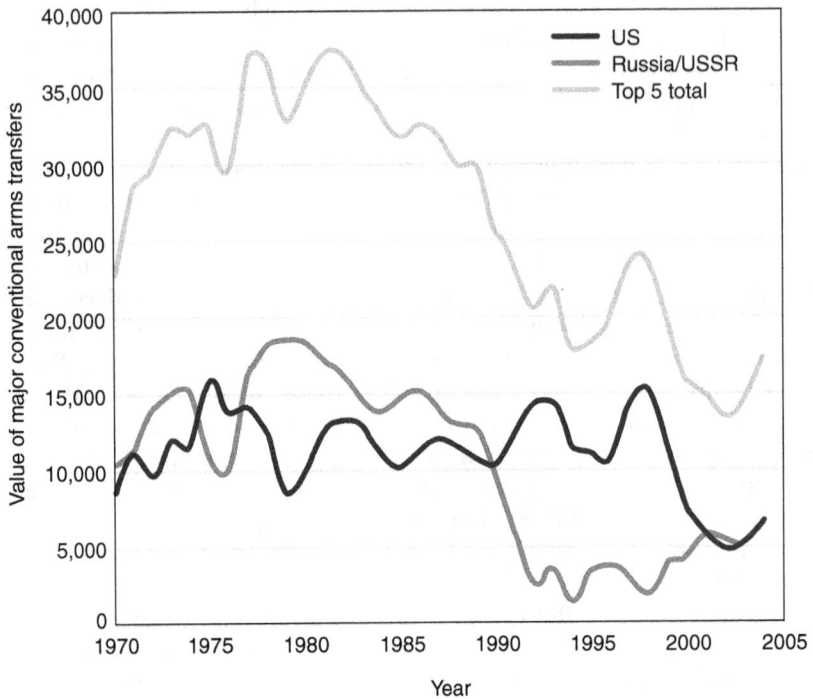

Figure 3.1 Trends in global arms transfers, 1970–2004.

treaty membership as starting with signature and the other with ratification. The variables are coded "1" for the year in which a state initially signed/ratified the NPT and every year thereafter. Countries that are not members or have withdrawn their membership are coded as "0." We employ both versions of NPT status in the analyses. In practice, this makes little difference since most countries ratify very shortly after signing the treaty, but in a handful of cases (for example, South Korea) the gap lasts several years.[21] We therefore report findings using both regressors. In general, NPT membership has increased gradually over time, with larger waves of states joining in the early 1970s after the treaty entered into force, and in the early 1990s, after the break-up of the Soviet Union.

Control variables

If NPT membership were assigned to states by a random process, this would be the end of the story. We could simply compare arms transfers in NPT membership country-years with those in non-membership country-years and draw valid inferences from the results. But, of course, countries select themselves into the NPT by a highly non-random process. As a result, the average NPT country-year differs systematically from the average non-NPT country-year on several important observable variables. In addition to the independent variable of interest, we therefore include control variables chosen because of their potential effect on *both* the amount of major conventional arms transfers *and* recipients' willingness to join the NPT. In doing so, this approach avoids the "garbage can" or "kitchen sink" models against which methodologists have recently warned. Such models rely not only on fragile and highly contingent specifications but also risk masking nuances in the relationship of interest.[22] In order to concentrate on the potential link between NPT status and the receipt of major conventional arms, we therefore limit our control variables to potentially confounding variables.

Specifically, NPT country-years differ, on average, from non-NPT country-years in their *security, economic,* and *political* circumstances. With regard to potential members' *security,* we use two variables to proxy for members' generally less threatening security environments: involvement in enduring rivalries and militarized interstate disputes (MIDs).[23] Unlike those facing severe security threats, countries outside of rivalries and with low rates of dispute involvement are both more likely to join the NPT and less likely to have a high demand for conventional weapons.

In terms of states' *economic* situations, annual GDP per capita provides an indicator of level of economic development. Since arms are a normal good (Murdoch and Sandler 1982), richer countries are likely to import more of them. They are also better positioned to take advantage of the nuclear energy technology offered by the NPT, providing them with greater reasons to join the regime.[24] We also expect that smaller (i.e., less populous) countries will purchase, on average, fewer arms, and have less inhibitions in joining the NPT, since their defense needs are less likely to be met by nuclear arms. Larger populations, in contrast, have been associated with a higher probability of conflict, possibly due to more severe internal pressures on environmental and social resources,[25] and may therefore have a higher demand for conventional and nuclear weapons alike.

Turning to recipients' *political* circumstances, countries more closely aligned with one of the superpowers may prove more likely both to follow their lead in joining the NPT and to have greater access to arms exports from their patron.[26] To account for this possibility, we include a variable for the similarity of their foreign policy positions with potential exporting nations, using a measure of similarity in UN voting records (*affinity*), scored from −1 to 1, for each exporter–importer dyad-year (Gartzke 2006).[27] Finally, to tap the obvious *time trends* in exports, we include (depending on the regressions) either dummies splitting the observations into three time periods (the period of export growth, 1971–1982; the period of gradual decline, 1983–1990; and the post-Cold War years 1991–2002) or dummies for each year.

Results and discussion

Our findings reveal, as expected, a strong relationship between NPT membership and major conventional weapons transfers from the two superpowers. We emphasize, however, that there is no simple direct correlation between NPT membership and the receipt of larger amounts of conventional arms. Let us explain this by way of introducing our data and analysis. Our unit of observation is the exporter–importer dyad-year. We thus have data pairing the United States and Russia/USSR with 180 potential arms importers for years spanning 1970 to 2001. As a starting point, Figure 3.2 compares the average level of imports received from either the United States or the USSR/Russia by NPT signatory dyad-years with those received by non-NPT signatory dyad-years. The figure shows that the average amount of arms received per year by states within the NPT is less than that received by those outside the NPT: On average, NPT signatories received just over $13 million of imports per year, whereas states outside the NPT received a little less than $18 million.[28]

However, potential confounding relationships between NPT membership and access to conventional arms, as described above, provide compelling reasons to take the direct relationship depicted in Figure 3.2 with more than a few grains of salt.[29] To better explore the relationship between arms transfers and NPT membership, we need to estimate arms transfers conditional on these potentially confounding variables. Countries' security, economic, and political circumstances are likely to affect both their access to conventional weapons *and* their willingness to join the NPT. Consequently, excluding variables to account for these

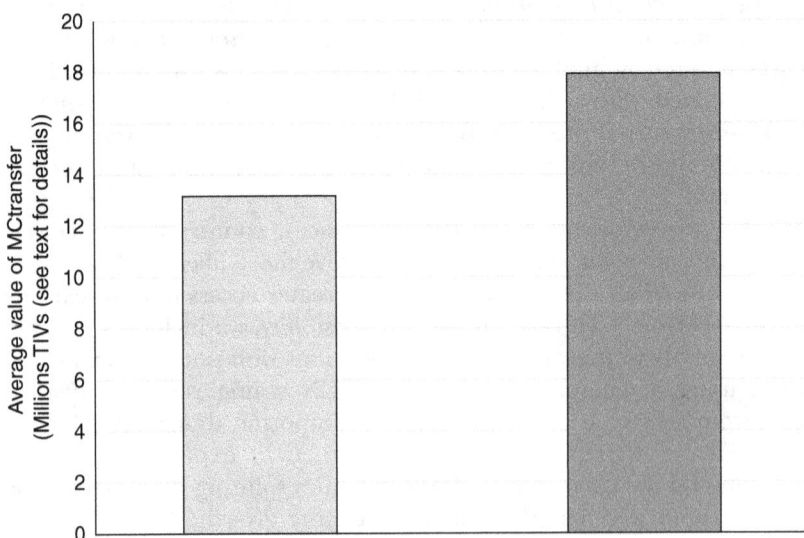

Figure 3.2 Conventional arms transfers and NPT membership.

circumstances risks obscuring the size and direction of the relationship between NPT membership and conventional arms transfers. To this end, we estimate pooled time-series models of arms transfers between the United States, Russia/USSR, and 180 other states from 1970 to 2001, limiting our models to include only potential confounding variables as controls. This enables us to explore the relationship of interest between NPT membership and conventional arms transfers (as opposed to understanding all the determinants of arms transfers).

As is well known, pooled models of this sort are vulnerable to violations of the assumptions underpinning OLS regression models. Specifically, errors are likely to be heteroskedastic by panel and autocorrelated over time within panel. Diagnostic tests indicate that we can reject both the assumptions of panel-homoskedasticity and non-correlated errors over time in our data.[30] Following the recommendations of Beck and Katz (1995, 1996), we use panel-corrected standard errors to control for possible bias in the standard errors and Prais-Winsten correction for first-order autocorrelation.[31] The dependent variable, major conventional weapons (*mctransfer*), is highly skewed; it is, however, log-normal and we thus use the natural log of *mctransfer* as our dependent variable.[32] The independent variable of interest is NPT status, for which we examine recipients' signatures and ratification of the NPT. For control variables, as described above, we included proxies for security environment, wealth, closeness of relations with the exporting nation, and population size.

Table 3.1 reports the results of models pooling the two main promoters of the NPT, the US and USSR, as exporters. The pattern of results accords with expectations. Participants in enduring rivalries, richer countries, and more populous countries all receive greater amounts of arms transfers. The coefficients on MID involvement and affinity of UN voting pattern with exporter are also positive, although not statistically significant by standard criteria.[33] The time dummies indicate that the level of exports began to decline gradually after 1982 and then more sharply after the end of the Cold War, and models including year fixed effects instead of period dummies produce very similar results. And most importantly, our primary regressor of interest, NPT status, is positive and significant at greater than the 1 percent level in all four specifications. After conditioning on an appropriate set of control variables, it appears that NPT membership is positively associated with greater arms shipments from the US and USSR/Russia.

In these models, our dependent variable is in logs whereas the explanatory variables are not (that is, these are semi-logarithmic equations), meaning the coefficients can be read as partial elasticities: the coefficient indicates roughly the approximate percentage change in arms transfers for a one unit change in the explanatory variable. For example, the model in column two indicates that signatories of the NPT receive roughly 21.1 percent (and precisely, 23.5 percent) more arms transfers than non-NPT

Table 3.1 Influence of NPT status on major conventional arms transfers

	Signing/Accession		Ratification/Accession	
NPT Status	0.211*** (0.053)	0.234*** (0.056)	0.175*** (0.051)	0.199*** (0.052)
Rivalry	0.72*** (0.11)	0.72*** (0.11)	0.73*** (0.11)	0.71*** (0.11)
Dispute Involvement	0.039 (0.043)	0.038 (0.043)	0.038 (0.043)	0.037 (0.043)
GDP per Capita	0.007*** (0.0009)	0.007*** (0.0009)	0.007*** (0.0009)	0.007*** (0.0009)
Affinity With Exporter	0.06 (0.048)	0.04 (0.051)	0.06 (0.049)	0.04 (0.051)
Population	0.0002** (0.00008)	0.0002** (0.00008)	0.0002** (0.00008)	0.0002** (0.00008)
1971–1982	0.061 (0.039)		0.058 (0.039)	
1983–1990	-0.114** (0.047)		-0.116** (0.047)	
1991–2002	-0.330* (0.058)		-0.331*** (0.058)	
Constant	0.37*** (0.06)	0.49*** (0.11)	0.41*** (0.06)	0.48*** (0.11)
Year Fixed Effects	No	Yes	No	Yes
Wald Chi-Square	162.8	195.9	158.8	192.1
Dyads	360	360	360	360
Observations	9,758	9,758	9,758	9,758

Notes
*Significant at 10%; **Significant at 5%; ***Significant at 1%.

signatories, and the model in column five implies that NPT ratifiers receive roughly 20 percent (and precisely, 22 percent) more weapons.[34] Clearly, this represents a substantial "signing bonus" for joining the NPT regime. Not surprisingly, enduring rivalry participation has the largest effect: countries in an enduring rivalry receive 105 percent more arms than those without. Richer countries also import more arms: each $1,000 increment increase in per capita GDP is associated with receiving 7 percent more arms. The "NPT bonus" is roughly equivalent to a quarter of the effect associated with participation in an enduring rivalry or with about a $3,500 increase in per capita national income.

The results in Table 3.1 indicate that access to major conventional arms from the two main promoters of the NPT is positively associated with treaty membership. However, by pooling the US and Russia/USSR as exporters in the same models, we have assumed similar export behavior by the two states. Obviously, this assumption may not be justified. Moreover, by including *all* exporter–importer dyads, we included some pairs for which it is virtually impossible to imagine arms transfers transpiring (and thus a non-zero value on the dependent variable). Specifically, during the Cold War era cross-bloc arms transfers simply did not happen. The possibility that the US would dangle access to major conventional arms as a carrot to induce Romania, for example, to sign the NPT is fanciful (to say the least), as is the possibility that the USSR would do the same with Canada. Our causal story makes sense for each superpower's relations within its own bloc and with states that are "in play" (that is, neither in one's bloc nor that of the other side), but not for cross-bloc relationships.

In response to these concerns, we estimated exporter-specific models excluding cross-bloc dyads and restricting analysis to the Cold War/NPT era of 1970 to 1990. We also estimated a model for the third, less engaged principal of the NPT negotiations: the United Kingdom. The results reported in Table 3.2 indicate that although the US and USSR differed in some aspects of their export behavior, both transferred greater quantities of arms to NPT members.[35] Notably, however, this pattern was more pronounced for the United States than for the USSR: countries in the NPT received over 59 percent more arms transfers (relative to those outside the NPT) from the US compared to just over 23 percent more from the USSR. Also of note is the coefficient for affinity with the exporter: it is large and highly significant for both superpowers when we restrict the years to 1970–1990. During the Cold War, close alignment with either the US or USSR was strongly associated with greater arms transfers.[36]

The results in Table 3.2 also reveal that the United Kingdom failed to follow the export pattern of the US and USSR – at least with regard to NPT status. Not surprisingly, the United Kingdom transferred more arms to countries facing security challenges, to richer countries, and to larger countries, but its pattern of exports have no discernible relationship to NPT status of the importer. Part of the explanation for this pattern, of

Table 3.2 Country-specific models of NPT promoters, Cold War era

	United States	Russia/USSR	United Kingdom
NPT Status	0.47*** (0.08)	0.21** (0.07)	-0.09 (0.088)
Rivalry	1.06*** (0.18)	0.63*** (0.21)	0.48*** (0.12)
Dispute Involvement	0.05 (0.08)	0.22** (0.09)	0.111* (0.061)
GDP per Capita	0.013*** (0.002)	0.0009 (0.001)	0.008*** (0.001)
Affinity with Exporter	0.76*** (0.13)	1.11*** (0.23)	0.27 (0.19)
Population	0.0008*** (0.0002)	0.0006** (0.0001)	0.0006*** (0.0001)
Constant	0.17* (0.09)	-0.63*** (0.17)	0.05 (0.13)
Year Fixed Effects	Yes	Yes	Yes
Wald Chi-Square	287.6	97.4	212.8
Dyads	151	142	152
Observations	2,890	2,635	2,891

Notes
NPT Status variable is signing. Cross-bloc dyads are excluded.
*Significant at 10%; **Significant at 5%; ***Significant at 1%.

course, is that the UK makes large transfers to its former colonies, including two prominent NPT holdouts that are also major arms importers (Pakistan and India). Yet even with these countries removed, the UK's exports fail to reveal an NPT–arms transfer linkage similar to that of the US and USSR.

The difference between the export patterns of the US and USSR, on the one hand, and that of the UK, on the other, raises an interesting possibility. Perhaps NPT members merely substitute imports from the US and USSR (arguably the most desirable sources of major conventional weaponry) for exports from other major conventional arms exporters? If so, they may not receive a net *increase* in arms transfers as a result of joining the NPT but may simply be substituting one source for another. To explore this possibility, we estimated models of *total* arms transfers received from major exporters. In doing so, the unit of observation shifts from the exporter–importer dyad-year to the importing country-year. This allows us to assess whether countries gain access to a greater overall quantity of sophisticated conventional arms by joining the NPT.

The results reported in Table 3.3 suggest that they do. Here, we estimate models for the total arms transfers from the top three (US, Russia/USSR, UK) and top five (plus France and West Germany/Germany) exporters of major conventional arms. The same variables are included as before, with the exception of the dyadic affinity variable, and all are significant at better than the 1 percent level. Greater arms imports are associated with participation in an enduring rivalry, greater MID involvement, higher GDP per capita, larger populations, and, of greatest interest, having ratified the NPT. Whether focusing on the top five or just the top three exporters, country-years of NPT membership are associated with receiving roughly 44 percent more aggregate arms transfers compared to country-years of

Table 3.3 Total arms imports by recipient

	Big 3 Exporters	*Big 5 Exporters*
NPT Status	0.363*** (0.125)	0.368*** (0.161)
Rivalry	1.79*** (0.21)	3.05*** (0.337)
Dispute Involvement	0.59*** (0.09)	0.546*** (0.143)
GPD per Capita	0.019*** (0.001)	0.028*** (0.002)
Population	0.003*** (0.0003)	0.004*** (0.0004)
Constant	−0.0004*** (0.0001)	−0.0005*** (0.0001)
Year Fixed Effects	Yes	Yes
Wald Chi-Square	1,383	1,579
Countries	177	177
Observations	4,902	4,902

Notes
NPT Status variable is signing. Cross-bloc dyads are excluded.
*Significant at 10%; **Significant at 5%; ***Significant at 1%.

non-NPT membership.[37] As the old American Express slogan puts it, "membership has its privileges," and, in the case of the NPT, one of those privileges is access to additional conventional arms.

We conclude this section with a few examples of upticks in conventional arms flows from the United States following NPT ratification. In the early 1970s, South Korea was dragging its feet about ratifying the NPT. During the same years, arms transfers from the US were meager, the highlight being several dozen F-5E Tiger II fighter-bombers, complemented by little more than an occasional patrol boat (all arms transfers are according to various editions of the SIPRI Yearbook). However, after South Korea finally ratified the NPT in 1975, the floodgates opened. In the next few years, the US transferred the more sophisticated F-4 E/D Phantom aircraft, the new A-10A attack plane, thousands of TOW anti-tank missiles, Honest John surface-to-surface missiles, the new Harpoon anti-ship missile, hundreds of AIM 9-L and AIM-7E air-to-air missiles to equip the new fighter aircraft, two destroyers and four LSTs – and this is just a partial list of the cavalcade of arms transferred. This step-change in arms flows is clearly reflected in SIPRI's "trend value indicator" measure of arms flows: between 1971 and 1972, as South Korea hesitated to ratify the NPT, this figure averaged 273 per year, whereas from 1976 to 1980 it jumped up to 719 per year.

Like South Korea, Indonesia hesitated for a while before joining the NPT in 1979. From the mid to late 1970s, the country received little in the way of arms transfers from the United States, and what it did receive was almost exclusively training or transportation equipment, such as T-2C Buckeye trainers, Beech Musketeers, and Beech King Air 100s. However, after joining the NPT in 1979, Indonesia begin to receive more sophisticated, combat equipment: A-4E Skyhawk attack aircraft, C-130H transports, M-101-A1 artillery pieces, and a variety of helicopters. As with Korea, the change is captured in TIV values: from 1975 to 1979, US transfers averaged 48 per year, whereas from 1980 to 1984 it averaged 135. Shifting to a later, post-Cold War period, Argentina's accession to the NPT in 1995 marked another step-change in US arms transfers. From 1990 to 1994, Argentina received an average of 21 TIV of arms transfers from the US per year. After joining the NPT, Argentina's arms imports from the US over the next five years more than sextupled to 136 per year.

Robustness and sensitivity analysis

Earlier, we noted that the control variables in our regressions are "good controls" in that all are plausible causes of both arms transfers and willingness to join the NPT, whereas NPT membership is unlikely to influence any of them in turn. If this is correct, the fact that none of the control variables are caused by our regressor of interest makes it more reasonable to attach a causal interpretation to the coefficient on NPT membership. If, however, NPT membership itself causes changes in the value of control variables, the coefficient would be misleading (in a causal sense). Although this is unlikely for most of our controls, NPT membership could perhaps affect enduring rivalries by, for example, facilitating a reduction of tensions among rivals and helping tame a security-dilemma driven arms race.

To investigate this possibility, we explored the relationship between joining the NPT and exiting enduring rivalries. Eleven countries in our data exited enduring rivalries between 1968 and 2001.[38] Eight of these 11 exited their enduring rivalries *before* ratifying the NPT. Among these eight, the average time gap between exiting rivalries and joining the NPT was six years. In contrast, among the three that joined first and *then* exited rivalries, an average of 17 years elapsed between the two events.[39] This reinforces our confidence that enduring rivalry status is a "good control." It may well influence NPT status in that states are more likely to join when their threats dissipate, but NPT membership does not seems to cause rivalry status.[40]

Having explored the possibility that our variable of interest is casually influencing other regressors, we now turn to influence analysis and the exploration of outliers. Our analysis, which includes all countries in the world for which we have relevant data, includes a very heterogeneous set of countries. It is thus important to determine if specific importing countries or exporter–importer dyads have a disproportionate influence on the estimated values of coefficients. To this end, we used both graphical and numerical analysis to look for countries that might be strongly influencing the coefficient estimates.

Visual inspection of plots of leverage against squared residuals (LVR2 plots) suggested a handful of importing countries that might combine relatively high leverage with relatively high residuals.[41] China yields the greatest number of suspect observations, and Iran and India also emerge as possibilities. DFITS provide a numerical means for detecting observations, combining high leverage with large residuals (Bollen and Jackman 1990). An examination of DFITS values reinforces the suspicions raised by the LVR2 plots. The only countries yielding eight or more observations above a size-adjusted cut-off were China, India, and Israel.

To explore the sensitivity of our results to the four countries flagged by graphical and numerical analyses (China, India, Iran, and Israel), we re-estimated the models leaving out each possible combination of the four importers in turn. Deleting these suspect countries, either singly or in all possible combinations, fails to alter substantially the estimated coefficient on our variable of interest. For the model reported in column 4 of Table 3.1, for example, the lower and upper bounds on estimated coefficients are 0.186 and 0.212, respectively, compared with the baseline of 0.199 for results featuring all countries. Using signings instead of ratifications produces parallel results, with lower and upper bounds of 0.218 and 0.251

straddling the all-importers estimate of 0.234.[42] With or without these potentially influential importing countries, our conclusion remains the same: NPT membership is associated with larger conventional arms imports.

Conclusions

In recent years, it has become commonplace for commentary on the NPT to begin by calling the treaty a regime in crisis (Ali 2007; Braun and Chyba 2004; Cirincione and Newland 2000; Goldschmidt 2006; Howlett *et al.* 2005; Langmore 2008; Ogilvie-White and Simpson 2003; Pilat 2007; Sauer 2006; Squassoni *et al.* 2006; Wesley 2005; Wilson *et al.* 2005). We agree. Without a doubt, recent years have seen new challenges emerge, exposing weaknesses in the non-proliferation regime and highlighting the desirability of revision. And although many of the challenges facing the non-proliferation regime suggest the necessity of revising the NPT, policies of key states in recent years make that task difficult. Indeed, the UN High Representative for Disarmament Affairs, Sergio Duarte, characterizes the 2005 NPT review discussions as hampered by "mistrust, mutual suspicions, intransigence, and perceptions of bad faith" (Duarte 2008: 5).

Yet rumors of the treaty's death appear to be greatly exaggerated. In the United States, the Obama administration's commitment to negotiating deep cuts in nuclear arsenals promises to answer non-nuclear states' desire for nuclear weapons states to take their Article VI commitments to stemming vertical proliferation seriously. Similarly, the changed dynamic at the third Preparatory Committee meeting raised hopes for the 2010 NPT review conference (Johnson 2009). In our view, revitalizing the NPT requires a careful understanding of the negotiation, promotion, and expansion of the original treaty framework. Partly, we believe this because the world has turned and left us in a situation resembling that in which the NPT was originally negotiated and promoted. In the late 1960s, recent proliferation incidents had sown fears of proliferation cascades and shown that technological advances had rendered the acquisition of nuclear weapons easier than had been anticipated (Athanasopulos 2000). At the same time, nuclear energy was heralded as a promising and attractive source of electricity, generating great interest in access to the technology.

Today, another round of realized and potential proliferation incidents sharpens fears of proliferation cascades, the specter of nuclear terrorism heightens concerns, and technological advances have made the acquisition of nuclear technology easier to conceal. Nuclear energy is back in style, with demand stoked by rapid industrialization in the BRICs and concerns over global carbon emissions, and supply fueled by safer, more efficient Generation III reactors and the promise of new technologies, such as the pebble bed reactor in the Generation IV initiative. The NPT was originally enabled by a combination of fear and desire: fear of nuclear weapons proliferation, and desire for nuclear energy. That combination is back in spades. This similarity, in our view, makes understanding the mechanisms behind the successful spread of the NPT instructive for assessing strategies for extending and deepening the treaty.

In this chapter we add one small piece to this picture by exploring how promoters can use informal inducements to foster the spread of a treaty. Even though the terms of the NPT bargain are, on the face of it, rather unappealing for many states, informal inducements and side-payments can reduce the costs of joining for many states. We investigated this possibility with statistical models of major conventional arms transfers from leading exporters over a 30-year time frame. Countries within the NPT received substantially greater arms transfers from the superpowers compared to those outside the regime. This "signing bonus" was far from trivial. Countries in the NPT received an estimated 45 percent larger amount of major conventional arms transfers than those outside the regime.[43] When it comes to access to conventional arms, NPT membership has its privileges. This is important because the inducement makes treaty membership more attractive and lowers the security costs of joining by providing enhanced access to conventional weaponry in exchange for renouncing unconventional weapons.

The lesson for current negotiations is straightforward. If informal inducements were an important part of the promotion and spread of the original NPT, they will probably be an important ingredient of any recipe for renewal. Concerns of key states need not be addressed in formal provisions if those concerns can be assuaged informally. Yet this particular inducement poses difficult trade-offs. After all, nuclear disarmament proponents seek a safer and more peaceful world. However, greater trade in major conventional weapons may undercut that goal. If our analysis of the role of access to conventional weapons in the spread of the NPT is correct, this suggests that an idea much discussed in the early NPT era may also have regained relevance: the dove's dilemma. This acknowledges a possible trade-off between efforts to stem nuclear weapons proliferation and efforts to slow conventional weapons transfers (Dunn 1981). In the 1960s and 1970s, conventional arms controls were rarely, if ever, a policy concern, leaving NPT leaders to wield them in support of favored policy initiatives at their own discretion. In contrast, today, conventional arms transfer controls have become an issue in their own right. Regional and international efforts to stem the flow of conventional weapons to unstable regions and governments engaged in conflict and human rights abuses abound. As a result, even as the US and Russia have been among the few states to resist such controls, the ability of NPT proponents to use conventional arms as informal inducements regardless of the recipient government in question may be reduced in the years to come.

To be sure, states will have to make difficult trade-offs and painful compromise to strengthen the non-proliferation regime. Our analyses suggest, however, that they were made the first time, and there is no reason to expect painful trade-offs can be – or must be – avoided this time. Even today, international normative constraints on nuclear weapons development and expectations for NPT membership are on uncertain ground. However, if regime leaders wish to offer the incentives to cooperate (whether formal or informal), many states may be inclined to pay attention. The costs of nuclear non-proliferation can be mediated, even if it may be at the expense of conventional proliferation. As economists are fond of reminding us, there are no free lunches, and part of the price for slowing the spread of nuclear weapons may be ensuring the flow of conventional ones.

Notes

1 Of course, the treaty did commit the five designated nuclear weapons states "to pursue negotiations in good faith" aimed at nuclear disarmament, but progress on this front has been non-existent (at least until recently). Moreover, the expectation that the treaty would not interfere with their own nuclear weapons acquisition was crucial to the superpower consensus, which was essential to the creation and promotion of the treaty. For an excellent discussion of the formation and persistence of the regime, see Paul (2003); for a broad overview of the regime, Way (2008), and for an insightful discussion of its somewhat anomalous status in view of regime theory, Smith (1987).

2 There is some debate about the legality of North Korea's withdrawal and the interpretation of the provisions of Article X. See, for example, Strohmaier and Phillips (2005).

3 One should be cautious in asserting that developing nuclear weapons is beyond a given state's means. Four states that have developed nuclear weapons have been among the world's poorest in terms of GDP per capita at the time they successfully invested in acquiring a nuclear weapons capability: China, North Korea, Pakistan, and India.

4 For studies arguing that security challenges are the major demand-side driver of interest in nuclear weapons, see Paul (2000); Thayer (1998). Recent quantitative studies also emphasize, like these earlier qualitative studies, security situation as a main determinant of nuclear proliferation (Jo and Gartzke 2007; Singh and Way 2004).

5 Stephen Krasner (1983) defines international regimes as "sets of implicit or explicit principles, norms, rules, and decision-making procedures around which actors' expectations converge in a given area of international relations" (2). This has become the commonly accepted definition of regimes in international relations.

6 System-determining states, in Keohane's terminology, are the most powerful in the system: those whose policies for the most part shape international politics (Keohane 1969).

7 Indeed, the treaty marked the first time in history that a disarmament resolution jointly sponsored by the two superpowers failed to gain the unanimous support of the UN General Assembly (Athanasopulos 2000), illustrating the lukewarm support it received from many states. The superpowers' joint draft was adopted on June 12, 1968 by a 95–4 vote with 21 abstentions.

8 The literature on regime formation is vast. For a selection, see Adler (1992); Goodliffe and Hawkins (2006); Haas (1990); Hasenclever *et al.* (1997);

Keohane (1983, 1984); Milner (1992); Moravcsik (2000); Oye (1986); and Young and Osherenko (1993).

9 Although David Cortright suggests that inducement has "a more holistic and inclusive connotation" than incentive, he acknowledges that, in practice, "it is not necessary to distinguish rigidly between them" (1997: 6). Examples of incentives (or positive sanctions) include import/export subsidies, most-favored-nation status, foreign aid, favorable taxation, military cooperation, security assurances, access to advanced technology, and debt relief, among many other potential economic, social, political, and military benefits (Baldwin 1985: 42; Cortright 1997: 6–7).

10 This possibility was in fact proposed for inclusion in the treaty by the Soviet Union. Known as the Kosygin Clause (after Soviet Premier Aleksei Kosygin), this text would have prohibited the use of nuclear weapons against non-nuclear signatories, provided they harbored no nuclear weapons on their territory. The clause was opposed by the NATO countries and did not become part of the NPT (Singh and McWhinney 1989). Some states, like Brazil, explicitly sought such assurances as part of the treaty.

11 However, this guarantee is highly problematic, since such action under the UN Charter would be vulnerable to a veto by the NWS, all of whom are permanent members of the Council.

12 Other NWS states have issued similar qualified negative assurances at times (Bunn and Timerbaev 1993), although not always explicitly linked to NPT membership. For a careful argument in favor of no first-use policies, see Sagan (2009).

13 The United Kingdom joined the United States in also withdrawing its own pledge in 2002.

14 For a good discussion of various ways that claims can engender credibility, see Dixit and Nalebuff (1991). The negative security assurances offered by the superpowers obviously left much to be desired on this score.

15 As a result, the superpowers were not eager to impose external constraints on their ability to transfer conventional weapons, preferring to retain their freedom to transfer arms as they saw fit in pursuit of political goals. The US under the Carter administration presents one notable exception to this trend. President Carter sought both to impose unilateral constraints on US arms export policy and to establish multilateral constraints with its European allies and the Soviet Union. However, he failed to achieve any meaningful implementation of US unilateral restraints and could not reach an agreement with the Soviet Union on multilateral constraints.

16 Recall that the United States and Soviet Union both deposited their ratifications in 1970 and, in doing so, brought the treaty into force. Among other top five arms exporters, the United Kingdom joined in 1968, West Germany signed in 1969 and ratified in 1975, and France did not join until 1992.

17 The US State Department also collects global arms trade data through its World Military Expenditures and Arms Transfers (WMEAT) project, formerly with the Arms Control and Disarmament Agency. However, WMEAT's dyadic data is only publicly available for US transfers, rarely updated or standardized across years, and combines small and major conventional arms transfers in a single figure. US data on Foreign Military Sales (FMS) is also limited to US transfers and does not consider gifts, aid, or direct commercial sales approved by the State Department. Since our research question requires us to consider exporters other than the US and all forms of major conventional arms transfers that can be used as inducements to encourage/reward NPT membership (not just sales), SIPRI data serves the project better than sources restricted to US sales.

18 Quantitative analyses on conventional arms transfers are few and typically limited to exports from the United States (Blanton 2000, 2005). However, SIPRI data is standard for researchers wishing to illustrate worldwide trends in conventional arms transfers over time. For post-Cold War examples of research using SIPRI data, see: Durch (2000); Golde and Tishler (2004); Harkavy (1994); Kinsella (1994); Sanchez-Andres (2004); Sanjian (1991, 1998); Wulf (1993).

19 There are a number of important differences between the pre- and post-1970 arms market. In the early post-World War II period, the arms market was more strongly shaped by colonial relations but began to open up to competition across blocs as empires collapsed and new groups came to power in the developing world (SIPRI 1971: 3). In addition, during the 1960s, some European exporters, like West Germany, were still rebuilding their postwar arms industries. Substantial arms transfers outside of the NATO and Warsaw pact countries to the developing world – apart from cleaning obsolete and vintage technologies out of suppliers' inventories to make room for new and better equipment – did not get underway until the late 1960s (Pierre 1982: 10, 12). The constellation of states that continues to dominate as the top five exporters today solidified in the 1970s, during which time the arms market more than doubled from the previous decade and grew in political importance.

20 See SIPRI (2007) for a complete description of its method for calculating TIVs (429–30).

21 A word on legal terminology is in order here. Accession is the act whereby a state agrees to join and be bound by a treaty that has already been negotiated and signed by other states and has entered into force. It has the same legal effect as ratification. Signature either establishes consent to be bound by the treaty (if no ratification by another body is required), or, if the signature is subject to ratification, creates a good faith obligation to refrain from acts contrary to the treaty. For states joining after the treaty entered into force at the end of 1970, the only method of joining was accession and any distinction between signing and ratifying evaporates. The distinction in our data thus only matters for states which signed between 1968 and 1970, but delayed ratification (an extreme example being Egypt, which signed in 1968 but ratified only in 1981). For more details, see the United Nations Treaty Reference Guide: http://treaties.un.org/Pages/Overview.aspx?path=overview/treatyRef/page1_en.xml (last accessed May 20, 2010).

22 See, for example, Achen (2002, 2005); Berk (2004); Ray (2003, 2005).

23 Enduring rivalry memberships is a dichotomous variable taking on a value of one if a country is involved in one or more enduring rivalries in a given year and zero otherwise. Enduring rivalry participation is coded (see Bennett 1997, 1998). Recent rate of MID involvement is calculated as the five-year moving average of the number of disputes per year in which a state is involved according to version 3.1 of the MID dataset (Ghosn and Palmer 2003).

24 The vast majority of the world's nuclear energy plants are in high GDP per capita regions: the United States, Japan, and Western Europe.

25 See, for example, Choucri (1984); Hauge and Ellingsen (1998); Hirshleifer (2001); Homer-Dixon (1994); Tir and Diehl (1998).

26 Regime type, and particularly democracy, is a possible additional political variable. However, it makes little sense to suppose the Soviet Union favored democracies as arms recipients, so we leave it out of the overall regressions. We did explore the effect of democracy in the exporter-specific models, and report those results in footnotes below.

27 Existence of a military alliance provides another possible indicator of political alignment. We prefer affinity because it taps broader similarities in foreign

policy positions, but we also substituted the alliance variable for affinity in all regressions. Military alliances are positively associated with arms transfers, especially during the Cold War years, but including it instead of affinity does not significantly alter the results for our variable of interest (NPT membership).

28 All dollar values are for 1990 US dollars.

29 We point out that these variables are "good controls," in the language of Angrist and Pischke (2009), since they almost surely influence NPT membership but are not themselves plausibly caused by the regressor of interest. For example, it is implausible to think of NPT membership as causing population growth or more rapid increases in GDP per capita. More plausibly, NPT membership *might* improve the security environment by reducing tensions, or improving relations with the US or Russia, but even here we find the existence of a strong causal effect to be unlikely. Nonetheless, we explore these possibilities later in the paper.

30 Following the advice of Wilson and Butler (2007), we do not implement the "cure" unless we have reason to think we have the "disease." A test for autocorrelation in panel models (Wooldridge 2009) rejects the null of zero correlation at better than the 1 percent level, and a likelihood ratio test for panel-level heteroskedasticity does the same for the null of panel-homoskedasticity.

31 Beck and Katz's recommendation of lagged dependent variables has been more controversial than their advocacy of panel-corrected errors; we choose to use the Prais-Winsten correction for autocorrelation instead of lags, but this choice does not influence our findings.

32 More precisely, we take the natural log of *mctransfer* +1 because many of the dyad-years feature zero arms transfers.

33 As we show below, the affinity variable is highly significant during the Cold War era.

34 The coefficients in the table can be read as a *rough approximation* of the partial elasticity, but as values increase in size the approximation becomes progressively less accurate. The precise proportional change in the outcome variable resulting from a non-infinitesimal change in the explanatory variable is calculated as $\exp(b\,X) - 1$ (the percentage change reported in the text multiplies this result by 100). Thornton and Innes (1989) provide a careful explanation of the proper interpretation of semi-logarithmic regressions.

35 To explore possible regime-type effects, we experimented with adding various indicators of democracy to the country-specific models. Interestingly, the United States favored democracies during the Cold War era whereas the Soviet Union shunned them, and the United Kingdom showed no discernible preference for democracies. Adding an indicator for democracy had minor effects on the NPT variable: for the US, reducing the coefficient a bit to 0.43; for the USSR, increasing it a bit to 0.23; and for the UK, leaving it unchanged at –0.9. These patterns hold with both continuous and dichotomous versions of the Polity index and with the dichotomous ACLP classification.

36 The high level of statistical significance here, as opposed to the near significance of the affinity variable in the models in Table 3.1, is due to the restriction to the Cold War era. Affinity becomes similarly significant in the models in Table 3.1 when those are restricted to years 1970–1990. The relationship between affinity and arms transfers disappears after the Cold War.

37 And this is despite the fact that NPT membership trends up over time whereas the value of arms transfers trends broadly down (after the early 1980s).

38 By exit, we mean switching from a state of being in at least one enduring rivalry to being in none. Thus, if a country were in more than one enduring rivalry and one ended, it would not be coded as exiting since it is still involved in another one. This accounts for the odd number of exiting countries.

39 Moreover, two of these countries were the United States and United Kingdom, key promoters of regime. It would be a stretch to link their joining of the NPT with the demise of the Cold War more than 20 years later. The third country in this group is Laos, which ratified the NPT in 1970 and exited an enduring rivalry in 1976.
40 A similar pattern obtains between MID involvement and NPT accession: frequency of dispute involvement tends to decline before joining the NPT, but not the other way around. Dispute involvement does not seem to be caused by NPT membership.
41 Leverage is defined as the diagonal of the hat matrix.
42 It is interesting to note that India exerts the largest downwards influence on the estimate, whereas China exerts the largest upwards estimate.
43 This is the figure derived from the model of exports from the "big five" presented in Table 3.3.

References

Achen, Christopher H. (2002) "Toward a New Political Methodology: Microfoundations and ART," *Annual Review of Political Science* 5: 423–50.

Achen, Christopher H. (2005) "Let's Put Garbage Can Regressions and Garbage Can Probits Where They Belong," *Conflict Management and Peace Science* 22: 327–39.

Adler, Emanuel (1992) "The Emergence of Cooperation: National Epistemic Communities and the International Evolution of the Idea of Nuclear Arms Control," *International Organization* 46: 101–45.

Ali, Adel M. (2007) "Treaty on the Non-Proliferation of Nuclear Weapons and Its Recent Issues: A Legal Perspective," *International Journal of Nuclear Law* 1: 305.

Angrist, Joshua David and Jèorn-Steffen Pischke (2009) *Mostly Harmless Econometrics: An Empiricist's Companion*, Princeton, NJ: Princeton University Press.

Athanasopulos, Haralambos (2000) *Nuclear Disarmament in International Law*, Jefferson, NC: McFarland & Co.

Baldwin, David A. (1971) "The Power of Positive Sanctions," *World Politics* 24: 19–38.

Baldwin, David A. (1985) *Economic Statecraft*, Princeton, NJ: Princeton University Press.

Beck, Nathaniel and Jonathan N. Katz (1995) "What to Do (and Not to Do) with Time-Series Cross-Section Data," *The American Political Science Review* 89: 634–47.

Beck, Nathaniel and Jonathan N. Katz (1996) "Nuisance vs. Substance: Specifying and Estimating Time-Series–Cross-Section Models," *Political Analysis* 6: 1–36.

Bennett, Scott D. (1997) "Testing Alternative Models of Alliance Duration, 1816–1984," *American Journal of Political Science* 41: 846–78.

Bennett, Scott D. (1998) "Integrating and Testing Models of Rivalry Termination," *American Journal of Political Science* 42: 1200–32.

Berk, Richard A. (2004) *Regression Analysis: A Constructive Critique, Advanced Quantitative Techniques in the Social Sciences*, Thousand Oaks, CA: Sage Publications.

Blanton, Shannon Lindsey (2000) "Promoting Human Rights and Democracy in the Developing World: U.S. Rhetoric versus U.S. Arms Exports," *American Journal of Political Science* 44: 123–31.

Blanton, Shannon Lindsey (2005) "Foreign Policy in Transition? Human Rights, Democracy, and U.S. Arms Exports," *International Studies Quarterly* 49: 647–67.

Bollen, Kenneth A. and Robert W. Jackman (1990) "Regression Diagnostics: An Expository Treatment of Outliers and Influential Cases," in J. Fox and J.S. Long (eds) *Modern Methods of Data Analysis*, Newbury Park: Sage.

Braun, Chaim and Christopher F. Chyba (2004) "Proliferation Rings: New Challenges to the Nuclear Nonproliferation Regime," *International Security* 29: 5.

Brzoska, Michael (2004) "The Economics of Arms Imports after the End of the Cold War," *Defence and Peace Economics* 15: 111–23.

Brzoska, Michael and Frederic S. Pearson (1994) *Arms and Warfare: Escalation, De-Escalation, and Negotiation*, Columbia: University of South Carolina Press.

Bunn, George and Roland M. Timerbaev (1993) "Security Assurances to Non-Nuclear-Weapon States," *The Nonproliferation Review* 1: 11–17.

Choucri, Nazli (1984) *Multidisciplinary Perspectives on Population and Conflict*, 1st edn, Syracuse, NY: Syracuse University Press.

Cirincione, Joseph and Kathleen Newland (2000) *Repairing the Regime: Preventing the Spread of Weapons of Mass Destruction*, New York: Routledge.

Cortright, David (1997) "Incentives and Cooperation in International Affairs," in D. Cortright (ed.) *The Price of Peace: Incentives and International Conflict Prevention*, Lanham, MD: Rowman & Littlefield Publishers.

Dixit, Avinash and Barry Nalebuff (1991) "Making Strategies Credible," in R. Zeckhauser (ed.) *Strategy and Choice*, Cambridge, MA: MIT Press.

Duarte, Sergio (2008) "Making the 2010 NPT Review Conference a Success," Speech at the Annual Meeting and Luncheon of the Arms Control Association, June 16, Washington, DC: Arms Control Association.

Dunn, Lewis A. (1981) "Some Reflections on the 'Dove's Dilemma'," *International Organization* 35: 181–92.

Durch, William J. (2000) *Constructing Regional Security: The Role of Arms Transfers, Arms Control, and Reassurance*, New York: Palgrave.

Fuhrmann, Matthew (This Book) "Taking a Walk on the Supply-Side: The Determinants of Civilian Nuclear Cooperation."

Gartzke, Erik (2006) "The Affinity of Nations Index, 1946–2002. Version 4.0." Available at http://dss.ucsd.edu/~egartzke/.

Gelb, Leslie H. (1976/77) "Arms Sales," *Foreign Policy* 25: 3–23.

George, Alexander L. and Richard Smoke (1974) *Deterrence in American Foreign Policy: Theory and Practice*, New York: Columbia University Press.

Ghosn, Faten and Glenn Palmer (2003) *Codebook for the Militarized Interstate Dispute Data, Version 3.0* 2003. Available at http://cow2.la.psu.edu.

Golde, Saar and Asher Tishler (2004) "Security Needs, Arms Exports, and the Structure of the Defense Industry: Determining the Security Level of Countries," *Journal of Conflict Resolution* 48: 672–98.

Goldschmidt, Pierre (2006) "The Urgent Need to Strengthen the Nuclear Non-Proliferation Regime," *Policy Outlook* (January), Washington, DC: Carnegie Endowment for International Peace.

Goodliffe, Jay and Darren G. Hawkins (2006) "Explaining Commitment: States and the Convention Against Torture," *Journal of Politics* 68: 358–71.

Haas, Peter M. (1990) *Saving the Mediterranean: The Politics of International Environmental Cooperation*, New York: Columbia University Press.

Harkavy, Robert E. (1994) "The Changing International System and the Arms Trade," *Annals of the American Academy of Political and Social Sciences* 535: 11–28.

Hasenclever, Andreas, Peter Mayer, and Volker Rittberger (1997) *Theories of International Regimes*, New York: Cambridge University Press.

Hauge, Wenche and Tanja Ellingsen (1998) "Beyond Environmental Scarcity: Causal Pathways to Conflict," *Journal of Peace Research* 35: 299–317.

Hirshleifer, Jack (2001) *The Dark Side of the Force: Economic Foundations of Conflict Theory*, New York: Cambridge University Press.

Homer-Dixon, Thomas (1994) "Environmental Scarcities and Violent Conflict: Evidence from Cases," *International Security* 19: 5–40.

Howlett, Darryl, John Simpson, Harald Müller, Bruno Tertrais, and Burkard Schmitt (2005) "Effective Non-Proliferation – The European Union and the 2005 NPT Review Conference," *EU-ISS Chailoot Paper 77*, Paris: Institute for Security Studies.

Jo, Dong-Joon and Erik Gartzke (2007) "Determinants of Nuclear Weapons Proliferation," *The Journal of Conflict Resolution* 51: 167–94.

Johnson, Rebecca (2009) "Enhanced Prospects for 2010: An Analysis of the Third PrepCom and the Outlook for the 2010 NPT Review Conference," *Arms Control Today* (June): 16–22.

Keohane, Robert O. (1969) "'Lilliputians' Dilemmas: Small States in International Politics," *International Organization* 23: 291–310.

Keohane, Robert O. (1983) "The Demand for International Regimes," in S.D. Krasner (ed.) *International Regimes*, Ithaca, NY: Cornell University Press.

Keohane, Robert O. (1984) *After Hegemony: Cooperation and Discord in the World Political Economy*, Princeton, NJ: Princeton University Press.

Kinsella, David (1994) "Conflict in Context: Arms Transfers and Third World Rivalries during the Cold War," *American Journal of Political Science* 38: 557–81.

Langmore, John (2008) "Pulling Back from the Nuclear Precipice," *Eureka Street* 18: 27.

Lenefsky, D. (1970) "The United Nations Security Council Resolution on Security Assurances for Non-nuclear Weapons States," *New York University Journal of International Law and Politics* 3: 59–70.

Long, William J. (1996) *Economic Incentives and Bilateral Cooperation*, Ann Arbor, MI: University of Michigan Press.

Milner, Helen (1992) "Review: International Theories of Cooperation among Nations: Strengths and Weaknesses," *World Politics* 44: 466–96.

Moravcsik, Andrew (2000) "The Origins of Human Rights Regimes: Democratic Delegation in Postwar Europe," *International Organization* 54: 217–52.

Murdoch, James C. and Todd Sandler (1982) "A Theoretical and Empirical Analysis of NATO," *Journal of Conflict Resolution* 26: 237–63.

Neuman, Stephanie G. (1986) *Military Assistance in Recent Wars: The Dominance of the Superpowers*, New York: Praeger.

Nolan, Janne E. (1997) "United States," in A.J. Pierre (ed.) *Cascade of Arms: Managing Conventional Weapons Proliferation*, Washington, DC: Brookings Institution Press.

Nye, Joseph S. (1988) "US–Soviet Cooperation in a Non-proliferation Regime," in A.L. George, P.J. Farley, and A. Dallin (eds) *US–Soviet Security Cooperation: Achievements, Failures, Lessons*, New York: Oxford University Press.

Ogilvie-White, Tanya and John Simpson (2003) "The NPT and its 2003 Prepcom Session: A Regime in Need of Intensive Care," *The Nonproliferation Review* 10: 40.

Oye, Kenneth A. (1986) *Cooperation under Anarchy*, Princeton, NJ: Princeton University Press.

Paul, T.V. (1998) "The NPT and Power Transitions in the International System," in R.G.C. Thomas (ed.) *The Nuclear Non-Proliferation Regime*, New York: St Martin's Press.

Paul, T.V. (2000) *Power Versus Prudence: Why Nations Forgo Nuclear Weapons*, Ithaca: McGill-Queen's University Press.

Paul, T.V. (2003) "Systemic Conditions and Security Cooperation: Explaining the Persistence of the Nuclear Non-proliferation Regime 1," *Cambridge Review of International Affairs* 16: 135–54.

Pierre, Andrew J. (1982) *The Global Politics of Arms Sales*, Princeton, NJ: Princeton University Press.

Pilat, Joseph F. (2007) "The End of the NPT Regime?," *International Affairs* 83: 469–82.

Ray, James Lee (2003) "Explaining Interstate Conflict and War: What Should Be Controlled For?," *Conflict Management and Peace Science* 20: 1–31.

Ray, James Lee (2005) "Constructing Multivariate Analyses (of Dangerous Dyads)," *Conflict Management and Peace Science* 22: 277–92.

Sagan, Scott D. (2009) "The Case for No First Use," *Survival* 51: 163–82.

Sanchez-Andres, Antonio (2004) "Arms Exports and Restructuring in the Russian Defence Industry," *Europe-Asia Studies* 56: 687–706.

Sanjian, Gregory S. (1991) "Great Power Arms Transfers: Modeling the Decision-Making Processes of Hegemonic, Industrial, and Restrictive Exporters," *International Studies Quarterly* 35: 173–83.

Sanjian, Gregory S. (1998) "Cold War Imperatives and Quarrelsome Clients: Modeling US and USSR Arms Transfers to India and Pakistan," *Journal of Conflict Resolution* 42: 97–127.

Sauer, Tom (2006) "The Nuclear Nonproliferation Regime in Crisis," *Peace Review* 18: 333–40.

Shaker, Mohammed I. (1980) *The Nuclear Non-Proliferation Treaty: Origin and Implementation 1959–1979*, London: Oceana Publications.

Singh, Nagendra and Edward McWhinney (1989) *Nuclear Weapons and Contemporary International Law*, 2nd revised edn, Boston, MA: Martinus Nijhoff Publishers.

Singh, Sonali and Christopher Way (2004) "Paths to Non-Proliferation: The Need for a Quantitative Test of Nuclear Weapons Proliferation Theory," *Journal of Conflict Resolution* 48: 859–85.

Smith, Roger (1987) "Explaining the Non-Proliferation Regime: Anomalies for Contemporary International Relations," *International Organization* 41: 253–81.

Squassoni, Sharon, Steve Bowman, and Steven A. Hildreth (2006) "Proliferation Control Regimes: Background and Status," *CRS Report for Congress*, Washington, DC: Congressional Research Service.

Stanley, John Paul and Maurice Pearton (1972) *The International Trade in Arms*, London: Chatto and Windus for the International Institute for Strategic Studies.

Stockholm International Peace Research Institute (SIPRI) (1971) *The Arms Trade with the Third World*, New York: Humanities Press.

Stockholm International Peace Research Institute (SIPRI) (2007) *SIPRI Yearbook 2007: Armaments, Disarmament and International Security*, New York: Oxford University Press.

Strohmaier, James and Joe Phillips (2005) "The World vs. Kim Jong-il: The Legal Case Against a Nuclear-Armed North Korea," *Pacific Focus* 20: 193–239.

Thayer, Bradley A. (1998) "The Causes of Nuclear Proliferation and the Utility of the Non-proliferation Regime, in R.G.C. Thomas (ed.) *The Nuclear Non-Proliferation Regime*, New York: St Martin's Press.

Thornton, Robert J. and Jon T. Innes (1989) "Interpreting Semilogarithmic Regression Coefficients in Labor Research," *Journal of Labor Research* 10: 443–7.

Tir, Jaroslav and Paul F. Diehl (1998) "Demographic Pressure and Interstate Conflict: Linking Population Growth and Density to Militarized Disputes and Wars, 1930–89," *Journal of Peace Research* 35: 319–39.

Way, Christopher (2008) "Proliferation, Nuclear," in W. Darity Jr (ed.) *Oaxaca, Ronald – Quotas, Trade*, Detroit, MI: Macmillan Reference USA.

Wesley, Michael (2005) "It's Time to Scrap the NPT," *Australian Journal of International Affairs* 59: 283–99.

Wilson, Nick, John Loretz, and Julia Johnstone (2005) "Lessons from the Unsuccessful 2005 Nuclear Non-Proliferation Treaty Review Conference," *Medicine Conflict and Survival* 21: 274.

Wilson, Sven E. and Daniel M. Butler (2007) "A Lot More to Do: The Sensitivity of Time-Series Cross-Section Analyses to Simple Alternative Specifications," *Political Analysis* 15: 101–23.

Wooldridge, Jeffrey M. (2009) *Introductory Econometrics: A Modern Approach*, 4th edn, Mason, OH: South-Western Cengage Learning.

Wulf, Herbert (1993) "Arms Industry Limited: The Turning-Point in the 1990s," in H. Wulf (ed.) *Arms Industry Limited*, New York: Oxford University Press.

Young, Oran R. and Gail Osherenko (1993) "Testing Theories of Regime Formation: Findings from a Large Collaborative Research Project," in V. Rittberger (ed.) *Regime Theory and International Relations*, New York: Oxford University Press.

4 Importing the bomb

Sensitive nuclear assistance and nuclear proliferation

Matthew Kroenig[1]

Why do nuclear weapons spread? Politicians, policymakers, and pundits often worry that nuclear-capable states will provide sensitive nuclear assistance to other states or terrorist networks, contributing to the international spread of nuclear weapons.[2] The idea that states that get help with their nuclear programs will be more likely to acquire nuclear weapons has intuitive appeal, but international nuclear transfers may have no meaningful effect on nuclear proliferation. Indeed, existing scholarly approaches to nuclear proliferation have examined why states want nuclear weapons (e.g., Sagan 1996/1997) and the relationship between domestic capacity and nuclear acquisition (e.g., Singh and Way 2004; Jo and Gartzke 2007), but have not examined the relationship between international nuclear transfers and the spread of nuclear weapons. This raises an interesting question about the sources of nuclear proliferation: does international nuclear assistance contribute to the spread of nuclear weapons?

To answer this question, I begin with a simple logic of the technical and strategic advantages that potential nuclear proliferators can gain by importing sensitive nuclear materials and technologies from more advanced nuclear states. I argue that states that receive sensitive nuclear assistance can better overcome the common obstacles that states encounter as they attempt to develop a nuclear weapons arsenal. They can: leapfrog technical design stages, acquire tacit knowledge from more advanced scientific communities, economize on the costs of nuclear development, and avoid international pressure to abandon a nuclear program.

Drawing on a new dataset on the international transfer of sensitive nuclear materials and technology, this chapter demonstrates that sensitive nuclear assistance is an important determinant of nuclear proliferation. States that receive sensitive nuclear assistance from abroad are more likely to acquire nuclear weapons. I also find that states above a certain level of industrial development are more likely to acquire nuclear weapons. Taken together, these findings provide strong support for the supply-side approach to understanding the causes of nuclear proliferation advocated in this issue

(Kray, Gartzke, Rauchhaus, this issue). States that have the ability to acquire nuclear weapons, either through international assistance or domestic capacity, are more likely to do so.

Explaining nuclear proliferation

There is a vast scholarly literature on the causes of nuclear proliferation. Dong-Joon Jo and Erik Gartzke (2007) have recently categorized this research into two camps: arguments that focus on a state's *willingness* to acquire nuclear weapons (or demand-side approaches); and those that privilege a state's *opportunity* to acquire nuclear weapons (supply-side approaches). The bulk of scholarly research on nuclear proliferation has focused on demand. This school has sought to identify the factors that drive states to pursue and abandon nuclear weapons programs. Scott Sagan (1996/1997) argues that there are three primary reasons why states seek nuclear weapons. Sagan maintains that states in competitive security environments desire nuclear weapons as a means to deter external aggression, that domestic political lobbies (primarily the domestic nuclear complex) can encourage states to pursue a national nuclear weapons program for parochial reasons, and that international norms of prestige or opprobrium associated with nuclear weapons can influence states' nuclear decisions. Sagan concludes that none of these causes is dominant, but that they are each in operation to varying degrees in different cases.

Other scholars have suggested additional factors that may influence a state's demand for nuclear weapons. Etel Solingen (1994, 1998, 2007) maintains that domestic political coalitions and their associated economic development strategies determine a state's demand for nuclear weapons. "Liberalizing coalitions" are internationalist, pursue export-oriented industrialization strategies, and will be reluctant to jeopardize international trade and investment on controversial foreign policies such as the pursuit of nuclear weapons. On the other hand, states controlled by "inward looking, nationalist, and radical-confessional coalitions" oppose liberalization, choose an autarchic path to economic development, and are more likely to pursue nuclear weapons because they face fewer international economic costs to doing so and because they are more beholden to nationalist appeals.

Individual psychological drivers have also been invoked to explain a state's willingness to acquire nuclear weapons. Jacques Hymans (2006) argues that leaders' conceptions of their countries' national identities is the key to explaining state demand for nuclear weapons. Other research has drawn on these and other factors to explain why states pursue and abandon nuclear weapons programs (e.g., Quester 1973; Paul 2000).

In contrast, the supply-side approach to nuclear proliferation recognizes that an analysis of a state's demand for nuclear weapons can only provide a partial explanation for nuclear proliferation (Singh and Way

2004; Jo and Gartzke 2007; Meyer 1984; Lavoy 1993, 1995). Whether or not a state wants nuclear weapons is irrelevant if it is unable to acquire them. States may badly desire nuclear weapons, but lack the technology, resources, and expertise required to build them. Moreover, opportunity can shape willingness. States that could conceivably produce a nuclear weapons arsenal will face a great temptation to go nuclear. According to this view, "once a country acquires the latent capacity to develop nuclear weapons, it is only a matter of time until it is expected to do so" (Singh and Way 2004: 862). The supply-side approach to proliferation claims that states with an advanced industrial capacity can more easily create and maintain a nuclear weapons program and are thus more likely to acquire nuclear weapons than are less developed states. This line of argumentation has roots in earlier scholarship (Meyer 1984; Lavoy 1993, 1995) and has been revived by recent quantitative analyses of nuclear proliferation (Singh and Way 2004; Jo and Gartzke 2007). The quantitative studies have found that measures of economic development and industrial capacity are associated with a greater risk of becoming a nuclear power. These authors do not consider, however, how the supply of international nuclear assistance may advance a country's ability to produce nuclear weapons, nor do they explicitly examine the relationship between international nuclear assistance and nuclear proliferation.

The literature on "proliferation rings" has argued that nuclear capabilities in "second-tier" supplier states like Pakistan, Iran, and North Korea, could increase the availability of nuclear materials and technology on the international marketplace, threatening the nuclear nonproliferation regime (Braun and Chyba 2004; Chestnut 2007). Alex Montgomery (2005) has countered that without the tacit knowledge that comes from deep experience with a nuclear weapons production program, states that receive nuclear assistance will still struggle to acquire nuclear weapons. Yet, these scholars do not examine systematically the effect of nuclear assistance on the spread of nuclear weapons.

Scholars have also examined the causes of international nuclear assistance. Drawing on the nuclear deterrence literature, Matthew Kroenig (2009, 2010) has argued that the spread of nuclear weapons is more threatening to relatively powerful states than it is to relatively weak states and, applying this insight to the problem of sensitive nuclear transfers, finds that states are more likely to provide sensitive nuclear assistance under three strategic conditions. First, the more powerful a state is relative to a potential nuclear recipient, the less likely it is to provide sensitive nuclear assistance. Second, states are more likely to provide sensitive nuclear assistance to states with which they share a common enemy. Third, states that are less vulnerable to superpower pressure are more likely to provide sensitive nuclear assistance. Matthew Fuhrmann has examined why states trade in dual-use WMD technologies (2008) and why states sign civilian nuclear cooperation agreements (this issue). Fuhrmann also finds that strategic, and not economic, or normative concerns drive states to export civilian nuclear technologies. Unlike this analysis, however, these studies explore the causes, but not the consequences, of international nuclear assistance.

Importing the bomb

A state's ability to produce nuclear weapons often hinges on the availability of external assistance from a more advanced nuclear state. There are a number of common hurdles that states face as they attempt to develop a nuclear weapons program, but sensitive nuclear assistance from a more advanced nuclear state can help a state to overcome these technical and strategic challenges.[3]

First, the designs for many sensitive nuclear technologies, such as uranium enrichment plants and implosion-type nuclear weapons are not available in the public realm. States pursuing these technologies, without external assistance, must fashion designs for these complicated and advanced technologies indigenously. Second, the construction and successful operation of nuclear facilities requires much trial and error. Previous scholarship has emphasized the importance of tacit knowledge in successful nuclear weapons programs (MacKenzie and Spinardi 1995; Montgomery 2005). For example, the operation of a gaseous-centrifuge, uranium enrichment plant requires the spinning of large metal cylinders at a rate of 300 meters per second, roughly the speed of sound. Inexperienced engineers often struggle to prevent the cylinders from spinning out of control and crashing on the ground. The kind of trial and error required for the indigenous development of advanced nuclear technology often ends in failure. For example, from 1981–1991, Iraq tried and failed in multiple attempts to produce highly enriched uranium using several different methods including: gaseous centrifuge, chemical enrichment, ion exchange, and laser isotope separation, before finally settling on electromagnetic isotope separation.[4] Third, the development of a nuclear weapons infrastructure from scratch is an expensive enterprise. A state must, at a minimum: procure the relevant raw materials and technologies at home or on the open market; develop an advanced industrial and nuclear infrastructure; train, and provide for, a specialized cadre of physicists, mathematicians, engineers, and metallurgists; and provide adequate finances to continue to develop and support the program throughout its lifetime. For example, it is estimated that Iraq spent many billions of dollars in its unsuccessful bid to develop nuclear weapons.[5]

Fourth, states striving for a nuclear weapons capability must overcome these significant technical challenges under intense international pressure. Other states, international organizations, and nongovernmental organizations opposed to nuclear proliferation apply a variety of economic, diplomatic, and military pressures to dissuade states from fulfilling their nuclear ambitions. In 1981, for example, Iraq's nuclear reactor at Osiraq, then the centerpiece of Iraq's nuclear program, was destroyed by Israel in a preventive military strike.

International nuclear assistance can ease each of the challenges faced by potential nuclear weapon states. First, nuclear suppliers can provide the aspiring nuclear weapon state with proven designs for nuclear technology. With a guaranteed design in hand, scientists and technicians can leapfrog technical design stages and focus their effort on replicating a model that has proven effective elsewhere. For example, without access to Chinese nuclear bomb designs, it is believed that Pakistan would have had great difficulty developing a design for the implosion-type nuclear weapon that now consti-tutes its nuclear arsenal (Corera 2006: 46). Second, nuclear assistance can reduce the amount of trial and error needed to successfully operate nuclear facilities. States supplying nuclear assistance can construct and even operate nuclear facilities for the recipient state. For example, when China provided Pakistan with uranium enrichment technology in the early 1980s, Chinese technicians remained in Pakistan until the uranium enrichment facility was fully operational (Jones *et al.* 1998: 50, 57n.). In this way, the nuclear recipi-ent benefits from the tacit knowledge acquired by the scientific community in the more advanced nuclear state. Third, importing sensitive nuclear tech-nology can help states to economize on the costs of nuclear development. Procuring sensitive nuclear assistance from abroad can be less expensive than the indigenous development of a complete nuclear infrastructure. In fact, previous research has demonstrated that states have often received sub-stantial amounts of sensitive nuclear materials and technology at little or no cost because nuclear suppliers had a strategic interest in helping them to acquire sensitive nuclear technology (Kroenig 2010). For example, from 1958–1960, the Soviet Union "loaned" China the key component parts for the Lanzhou uranium enrichment facility and the Jiuquan plutonium reprocessing plants, partly because Moscow feared a US attack on the Chinese mainland following the Second Taiwan Straits Crisis, and wanted to enhance China's defensive and deterrent capabilities (Goncharenko 1998; Lewis and Xue 1988). Fourth, and finally, sensitive nuclear assistance can help a state to avoid international scrutiny. The receipt of sensitive nuclear materials and technology from abroad can quickly remake a state without a nuclear weapons program into a state with a latent nuclear weapons capabil-ity, presenting the international community with a *fait accompli* and preempt-ing international efforts at dissuasion. For example, France provided Israel with nuclear assistance from 1958–1965, transforming Israel from a state with a rudimentary, civilian nuclear research program into a nuclear weapon state in less than a decade. The United States was strictly opposed to nuclear proliferation in Israel, but by the time US intelligence agencies recognized the extent of Israel's nuclear program, the United States had few remaining policy options to dissuade Israel from its nuclear course (Richelson 2006; Cohen 1998).

The above discussion suggests that the receipt of sensitive nuclear assistance increases the probability of nuclear proliferation. This logic leads us to the central hypothesis of this chapter:

Hypothesis 1: States that receive sensitive nuclear assistance will be more likely to acquire nuclear weapons.

There are clearly other, alternative explanations for why states acquire nuclear weapons. I therefore control for a wide set of opportunity and willingness determinants of nuclear proliferation. I discuss these variables in the sections that follow in which I describe the data and examine the evidence for the above hypotheses.

Empirical analysis

To examine the relationship between sensitive nuclear assistance and nuclear proliferation, I employ qualitative and quantitative research methods. Nuclear proliferation and sensitive nuclear assistance are both rare events. From 1945–2000, the time period under study, nine countries acquired nuclear weapons, and of these, three (Israel, China, and Pakistan) received sensitive nuclear assistance.[6] The relatively small number of positive cases allows me to examine the role of sensitive nuclear assistance in the positive cases and to compare these countries to other similar countries that did not receive sensitive nuclear assistance. The qualitative analysis is only the first step, however. To analyze the relationship between sensitive nuclear assistance and nuclear proliferation in the entire universe of cases and to control for potentially confounding factors, a large-N statistical analysis will form the core of the empirical investigation.

Case studies

A brief review of important cases of nuclear proliferation demonstrates that assistance from abroad can be an important factor in determining whether or not a state eventually acquires nuclear weapons. For example, in 1958, Israel's nuclear program consisted of nothing more than a national atomic energy commission and a small, research reactor at Nahal Soreq. From 1958–1965, however, France provided nuclear assistance to Israel, greatly enhancing Israel's ability to produce nuclear weapons. France constructed a large, plutonium-producing nuclear reactor and a plutonium reprocessing facility at Dimona, transferred a nuclear weapon design, trained Israeli scientists at nuclear facilities in France, and allowed Israeli observers at French nuclear weapon tests (Cohen 1998). By 1967, after seven full years of sustained French assistance, Israel was able to assemble its first nuclear weapon.

Other states with nuclear arsenals received substantial assistance from abroad. In fact, much of the history of nuclear proliferation can be read as a history of a chain of cases of sensitive nuclear assistance. From 1958–1960, the Soviet Union provided China with key component parts for uranium enrichment and plutonium reprocessing plants and trained Chinese technicians, contributing to China's ability to conduct its first nuclear weapon test in 1964 (Lewis and Xue 1988). Thereafter, China itself became a nuclear supplier. From 1981–1986, China transferred significant quantities of highly enriched uranium, uranium enrichment technologies, and a nuclear weapon design to Pakistan (Corera 2006). While Pakistan refrained from testing a nuclear device until 1998, it is believed that with China's assistance, Pakistan assembled its first nuclear weapon in 1990 (Jones *et al.* 1998: 132, 140n.). More recently, from 1987–2002, Pakistan, with the help of Pakistani nuclear scientist A.Q. Khan, distributed sensitive nuclear technology and materials to Iran, Libya, and North Korea.[7] Since the end of cooperation in 2002, Libya has agreed to give up its nuclear program, but North Korea tested its first nuclear device in 2006, and Iran is making steady progress on developing its nuclear capability. In fact, according to a 2007 US National Intelligence Estimate, Iran may soon be able to produce nuclear weapons, thanks in large part to uranium enrichment assistance from Pakistan.[8]

On the other hand, states with a persistent demand for nuclear weapons, but that were unable to acquire substantial international assistance, failed to sustain national nuclear weapons programs. Egypt, over the course of many decades, has been rebuffed in numerous attempts to secure an international nuclear supplier and, to this day, lacks a nuclear weapons arsenal. Beginning in the 1960s Egypt sought sensitive nuclear assistance, first from the Soviet Union, and then from China, but was denied by both states.[9] There is also evidence to suggest that Egyptian officials may have met with representatives from the A.Q. Khan network, but Egypt never received sensitive nuclear assistance from Pakistan.[10] Unlike Israel and other current nuclear weapon states that received substantial imports of sensitive nuclear materials and technology, Egypt presently maintains a rudimentary civilian nuclear program. Other states that have shown a historical interest in nuclear weapons, but that have not yet acquired the bomb include states that have received little sensitive nuclear assistance from abroad, including Iraq and Taiwan, and states that have received no sensitive nuclear assistance whatsoever, such as Argentina, Saudi Arabia, Syria, and South Korea.

Nuclear proliferation data

To test the effect of sensitive nuclear assistance on the spread of nuclear weapons, I construct an original sensitive nuclear assistance dataset. The dataset contains yearly information for all states in the international system from 1945–2000. The unit of analysis is the country-year. I also draw on data from Singh and Way (2004) and Jo and Gartzke (2007) to construct other nuclear proliferation variables.

Dependent variable

The dichotomous dependent variable is *Nuclear proliferation*. This variable measures whether a state acquires nuclear weapons in a given year.[11] To construct this variable I draw on the nuclear proliferation dates from Gartzke and Kroenig (this issue). A state is coded as acquiring nuclear weapons when it first explodes a nuclear device or, if it does not immediately conduct a nuclear test, when it first assembles a deliverable nuclear weapon.

Independent variable

I construct independent variables to test the hypotheses about the effects of nuclear assistance explicated above. *Sensitive nuclear assistance* is a dichotomous variable measuring whether a state has ever received the key materials and technologies necessary for the construction of a nuclear weapons arsenal from a capable nuclear-supplier state.[12] Sensitive nuclear assistance takes three forms. States receive sensitive nuclear assistance when they: receive assistance in the design and construction of nuclear weapons; receive significant quantities of weapons-grade fissile material; or receive assistance in the construction of uranium enrichment or plutonium reprocessing facilities that could be used to produce weapons-grade fissile material.[13]

Sensitive nuclear assistance excludes other types of nuclear cooperation less relevant to the development of a nuclear weapons program. I exclude the receipt of the platforms that could potentially be used to deliver nuclear weapons, such as bombers and ballistic missiles. The receipt of nonsensitive nuclear assistance, such as scientific exchanges, assistance in the surveying and mining of natural uranium, fuel-cycle services, and the construction of research and power reactors, does not qualify as sensitive nuclear assistance.

To code the sensitive nuclear assistance variable, I began with an online nuclear weapons database maintained by the Nuclear Threat Initiative. I also drew on prominent reviews on the proliferation of nuclear weapons and on historical studies of countries' nuclear weapons programs. To be included in the dataset, a case of sensitive nuclear transfer had to be verified by at least two sources.[14] A list of the cases of sensitive nuclear assistance can be found in Table 4.1.[15]

Control variables

I also include a number of variables to control for other factors thought to influence the likelihood of nuclear proliferation. All control variables are drawn from Singh and Way (2004), unless otherwise specified.[16] To assess

Table 4.1 Cases of sensitive nuclear assistance

Recipient	Year of first assistance	Supplier(s)	Type of assistance
China	1958	Soviet Union	Plutonium reprocessing, uranium enrichment
Israel	1959	France	Plutonium reprocessing, nuclear weapon design
Japan	1971	France	Plutonium reprocessing
Pakistan	1974	France, China	Plutonium reprocessing, uranium enrichment, nuclear weapon design
Taiwan	1975	France	Plutonium reprocessing
Iraq	1976	Italy	Plutonium reprocessing
Brazil	1979	Germany	Plutonium reprocessing, uranium enrichment
Egypt	1980	France	Plutonium reprocessing
Iran	1984–95	China, Pakistan	Plutonium reprocessing, uranium enrichment, nuclear weapon design (?)
Algeria	1986	China	Plutonium reprocessing
Libya	1997	Pakistan	Plutonium reprocessing, uranium enrichment, nuclear weapon design
North Korea	1997	Pakistan	Plutonium reprocessing, uranium enrichment, nuclear weapon design (?)

a country's domestic capacity to produce nuclear weapons, I include a measure of economic development. *GDP* is measured as a country's GDP per capita in constant 1996 dollars. To test for a nonmonotonic relationship between level of economic development and nuclear acquisition, I include a squared term, *GDP squared.*[17] *Industrial capacity* is a dichotomous variable that measures whether a country produces steel domestically and has an electricity generating capacity greater than 5,000 MW. States above a certain threshold of industrial development may be better able to support a nuclear weapons program.

Scholars (e.g., Sagan 1996/1997) have argued that states may pursue nuclear weapons in order to improve their security. If this is the case, we may expect that states in threatening security environments may be more likely to acquire nuclear weapons. To test the effect of a state's security environment on its risk of acquiring nuclear weapons, I include a *Rivalry* variable that measures whether a state is involved in at least one enduring rivalry (Diehl 1998; Bennett 1998). *Alliance* is a dichotomous variable that assesses whether a state is in a defense pact with a nuclear-armed state. States under an ally's nuclear umbrella may have fewer incentives to develop nuclear weapons.

A number of variables gauge the institutional and economic determinants of nuclear acquisition. Scholars have argued that democratic states, due to their position in the "core" of the international system, may feel more secure and may be less likely to pursue nuclear weapons (e.g., Chafetz 1993). On the other hand, democratic states may be more beholden to nationalist appeals and to domestic political lobbies that favor nuclear proliferation (Sagan 1995/1996). I include *Regime type*, which measures a country's domestic political regime type, drawing on data from the Polity IV index (Jaggers and Gurr 1995). Scholars have also argued that states that are open to the international economy, or that are pursuing a strategy of economic liberalization, are less likely to seek nuclear weapons because they are reluctant to risk international trade and investment on controversial foreign policies (Solingen 1994, 1998, 2007; Paul 2000). *Openness* assesses a state's openness to the international economy and is calculated as a country's trade ratio (exports plus imports, divided by GDP). *Liberalization* measures changes in a country's trade ratio over spans of three, five, and ten years.

Data analysis

My central hypothesis concerns the importance of international nuclear assistance for understanding nuclear proliferation. I employ Cox proportional hazard models to test claims about the correlates of nuclear acquisition (Box-Steffensmeier and Jones 1997). Robust standard errors are adjusted for clustering by country.[18]

Several types of statistical analyses prove useful in exploring the evidence for or against each of the hypotheses described earlier. To begin the investigation, I examine the simple bivariate relationship between *Sensitive nuclear assistance* and *Nuclear proliferation* (Table 4.2, model 1). To control for potentially confounding factors, I then evaluate the effect of *Sensitive nuclear assistance* after including the control variables (Table 4.2, model 2).[19] I then estimate a trimmed model that includes only the variables that were statistically significant in the previous model (Table 4.2, model 3). To assess the relationship between *Sensitive nuclear assistance* and *Nuclear proliferation* among the states that actively pursued nuclear weapons, I use a censored hazard model of the risk of nuclear acquisition contingent on a state possessing a nuclear weapons production program (Table 4.2, model 4) as measured by Jo and Gartzke (2007).[20]

I first evaluate the hypothesis that sensitive nuclear assistance is positively related to nuclear acquisition. Hypothesis 1 states that states that receive sensitive nuclear assistance will be more likely to acquire nuclear weapons than are similar states that do not receive sensitive nuclear assistance. Turning to the hazard models, we see that the relationship between *Sensitive nuclear assistance* and *Nuclear proliferation* is positive and statistically significant in each and every model. There is strong empirical support for the causal significance of sensitive nuclear assistance for understanding nuclear proliferation.

Next, I examine the control variables to assess the relative support for the supply-side, as opposed to the demand-side, approach to nuclear proliferation. International assistance and domestic capacity are the primary means by which a state acquires the capability to produce nuclear weapons. I have already found a relationship between sensitive nuclear assistance and nuclear proliferation. *GDP* and *GDP squared* are statistically significant and have positive signs on the coefficients in two of the three models in which they are included, providing some support for the existence of a nonmonotonic relationship between economic development and nuclear proliferation. Furthermore, we see that *Industrial capacity* is positive and statistically significant in every model, demonstrating that states above a certain level of industrial development are more likely to acquire nuclear weapons. Taken together, the results provide strong support for the supply-side approach to understanding nuclear proliferation. States that can more easily produce nuclear weapons, due to international assistance or domestic capacity, are more likely to do so.

Turning to the demand variables, we find that *Rivalry* is positive and statistically significant in two of the three models in which it is included. Consistent with security-based approaches to nuclear proliferation, and the findings of previous quantitative studies (Singh and Way 2004; Jo and Gartzke 2007), states in a threatening security environment are more likely to acquire nuclear weapons. Next, we find that the protection provided by a nuclear umbrella appears to mitigate a state's demand for nuclear weapons. *Alliance* is negative and statistically significant in two of the three

Table 4.2 Hazard models of nuclear proliferation

Independent variable	Model			
	1	*2*	*3*	*4*
Sensitive nuclear assistance	3.323**** (0.951)	2.093**** (0.641)	2.024*** (0.786)	1.478** (0.694)
GDP		0.649*** (0.240)	0.625*** (0.227)	0.609 (0.378)
GDP squared		-5.13e-05**** (1.54e-05)	-5.69e-05*** (2.03e-05)	-4.60e-05 (3.02e-05)
Industrial capacity		3.430**** (0.387)	3.606**** (0.497)	3.276**** (0.756)
Rivalry		2.382* (1.367)	2.371* (1.252)	1.517 (1.651)
Alliance		-1.800* (1.061)	-1.705* (0.945)	-0.8253 (0.835)
Regime type		0.114** (0.050)	0.112** (0.055)	0.112** (0.050)
Openness		-0.022 (0.018)		-0.027 (0.026)
Liberalization		0.028 (0.026)		0.059** (0.028)
Log likelihood	-32.669	-18.784	-19.260	-15.413
Number of countries	156	156	156	18
Total observations	5,901	5,901	5,901	387

Notes
Statistically significant parameter estimators are denoted by * (p 0.10), ** (p 0.05), *** (p 0.01), **** (p 0.001). Coefficients are estimates for Cox proportional hazard models; robust standard errors, adjusted for clustering by country, are in parentheses. GDP=gross domestic product.

models in which it is included. States that are in a defense pact with a nuclear-armed state are less likely to acquire nuclear weapons. The sign on the coefficient of *Regime type* is positive and statistically significant in each model. This finding provides support for the idea that democratic states may be more prone to nuclear proliferation because they may be subject to pressure from domestic constituencies that favor nuclear development. The alternate hypothesis that democratic states will be less likely to acquire nuclear weapons because they form the secure core of the international system, does not find support. There is no discernible relationship between economic openness and nuclear proliferation. *Openness* is not statistically significant in any of the models in which it is included. States that are open to the international economy are neither more nor less likely to acquire nuclear weapons. Neither is there support for the idea that liberalizing states will seek to avoid controversial foreign policies such as nuclear weapons proliferation. *Liberalization* is statistically significant in model 4 only, but the sign on the coefficient is positive. This suggests, contrary to theoretical expectation, that liberalizing states may be more, not less, likely to acquire nuclear weapons. Taken together, I find modest support for demand-side approaches to the study of nuclear proliferation. Security environment and domestic politics appear to play some role in shaping the likelihood that a state will acquire nuclear weapons, but a state's relationship to the international economy does not.

Table 4.3 interprets the substantive effect of the variables that were statistically significant in all of the above models on *Nuclear proliferation*, using the results from the uncensored hazard model reported in Table 4.2, model 2 and the censored hazard model reported in Table 4.2, model 4. The entries represent the percent change in the baseline hazard ratios of nuclear acquisition for a given change in the independent variable. Focusing my comments on the results from model 2, the table reveals that providing a state with sensitive nuclear assistance increases the risk that it will acquire nuclear weapons by more than 700 percent. *Sensitive nuclear assistance* has not just a statistically significant effect, but also a substantively

Table 4.3 Substantive effects of the explanatory variables on the likelihood of nuclear proliferation

Variable	Percent change in the hazard ratios	
	Uncensored	*Censored*
Sensitive nuclear assistance	+711	+338
Industrial capacity	+2,986	+2,546
Regime type	+12	+12

Note
Hazard ratios on whether a state acquires a nuclear weapon are based on the hazard models reported in Table 4.2, models 2 and 4.

significant effect on nuclear proliferation. Turning now to the substantive effect of the control variables, Table 4.3 shows that *Industrial capacity* has a substantive effect on *Nuclear proliferation*. States above a certain threshold of industrial capacity have a hazard ratio of nuclear proliferation that is over 29 times greater than the hazard ratio for similar states below the industrial capacity threshold. In contrast, *Regime type* has a smaller substantive impact. Increasing a state's level of democracy by one point on the 20-point scale, increases the risk that it will acquire nuclear weapons by 12 percent.

The hazard analysis is only the first step, however. To address problems related to nonrandom assignment of the treatment, I use nonparametric, matching techniques as recommended by Ho *et al.* (2007). It is possible that the findings presented above are biased because states that receive sensitive nuclear assistance are quite different from those that do not. Sensitive nuclear assistance is not randomly assigned. If countries that received sensitive nuclear assistance and those that did not are very different, the above findings could be largely the result of extrapolations from the available data.

To correct for this problem, Ho *et al.* (2007) recommend preprocessing data using matching techniques in which treated cases are matched with similar untreated cases. Observations within the control group (in this study, states that did not receive sensitive nuclear assistance) are matched as closely as possible with the treated cases (states that did receive sensitive nuclear assistance) to form a matched sub-sample of data. This allows the researcher to make inferences about the causal effect of sensitive nuclear assistance based on a comparison of the most similar cases. Matching reduces the role of functional form and specification assumptions of the parametric model, resulting in more reliable causal inferences. When comparing cases in which other causal variables are as similar as possible, any remaining differences between the cases can be attributed to the treatment. In order to adjust for any remaining imbalances, Ho *et al.* (2007) recommend using the same parametric model one would have applied to the entire dataset on the matched sub-sample of data.

To begin the analysis, I first identify the confounding factors on which to match observations. Confounding factors are those variables that: may influence the dependent variable conditional on treatment, may be correlated with the treatment variable, and are causally prior to treatment. According to Ho *et al.* (2007: 216), "All variables in X_i that would have been included in a parametric model without preprocessing should be included in the matching procedure." I include, therefore, as confounding factors, the control variables detailed above: *GDP*, *GDP squared*, *Rivalry*, *Alliance*, *Regime type*, *Openness*, and *Liberalization*.

Next, to preprocess the data, one-to-one nearest neighbor matching with replacement was employed, using GenMatch (Sekhon forthcoming; Sekhon and Diamond 2008; Sekhon and Mebane 1998). Table 4.4 presents the

Table 4.4 Balance statistics

Variable		Mean treated	Mean Control	t-test p-value	K-S test p-value	Var. ratio (Tr/Co)	Mean std. eQQ diff
GDP	Before Matching	7057.7	5452.5	0.000	2.479e-11	1.077	0.114
	After Matching	6943.9	6608.6	0.574	0.144	1.0629	0.046
GDP squared	Before Matching	86540299	63991650	0.031	2.565e-11	0.97574	0.105
	After Matching	84853891	78135099	0.625	0.144	1.154	0.045
Industrial capacity	Before Matching	0.746	0.229	2.22e-16		1.079	0.259
	After Matching	0.751	0.726	0.571		0.940	0.012
Rivalry	Before Matching	0.761	0.269	2.22e-16		0.929	0.246
	After Matching	0.766	0.741	0.564		0.934	0.012
Alliance	Before Matching	0.462	0.466	0.915		1.004	0.002
	After Matching	0.453	0.532	0.111		0.995	0.040
Regime type	Before Matching	-0.523	-0.274	0.647	0.124	0.968	0.035
	After Matching	-0.692	-0.557	0.860	0.114	0.936	0.049
Openness	Before Matching	39.030	52.432	1.589e-10	5.0538e-07	0.370	0.096
	After Matching	38.304	38.621	0.902	0.273	1.239	0.028
Liberalization	Before Matching	-0.195	2.587	0.008	0.195	0.697	0.033
	After Matching	-0.185	0.0439	0.869	0.330	1.037	0.029

before and after balance statistics. The Table presents five standard indicators of balance: the difference in means; the *p*-values from a *t*-test on the
difference of means; where possible, the *p*-values from a K-S test of similar
distributions; the ratio of the variances of the treated and control samples,
and the mean standardized differences from the QQ plot (Imai *et al.* 2006;
Sekhon 2008).[21]

The balance statistics indicate that excellent balance was achieved. The
p-values on all *t*-tests are above 0.56, with the exception of the *t*-test on
Alliance, which is still well balanced at 0.11. QQ statistics improve in all cases
except *Alliance* and *Regime type*, which were both well balanced before matching ($p = 0.915$ and 0.647 on the *t*-tests, respectively), and continued to be
well balanced after matching ($p = 0.11$ and 0.860 on the *t*-tests, respectively).

Next, I analyze the preprocessed data, using a Cox proportional hazard
model. Table 4.5 presents the effect of sensitive nuclear assistance on
nuclear acquisition as estimated by the Cox regression in the matched
sample. I only present the coefficients for the treatment variable in Table
4.5. The coefficients for the confounding factors are substantively mean-
ingless because I matched on those variables. The results of the Cox estimation on the matched sub-sample provide further support for hypothesis
1. The sign on the coefficient is positive and statistically significant, demonstrating that states that receive sensitive nuclear assistance are more
likely to acquire nuclear weapons. Furthermore, the analysis on the
matched data suggests that *Sensitive nuclear assistance* may have an even
larger substantive effect than indicated by the analysis performed on the
unmatched sample. On the unmatched sample, we saw that *Sensitive
nuclear assistance* increased the risk of *Nuclear proliferation* by over 700
percent. In the matched sample, however, *Sensitive nuclear assistance*
increases the risk of *Nuclear proliferation* by over 1,200 percent (not shown).
If anything, it appears that not correcting for the nonrandom assignment
of sensitive nuclear assistance underestimates the effect of sensitive
nuclear assistance on nuclear proliferation.

Robustness checks

I explore the robustness of my findings by examining the extent to which
my results depend on the coding of the dependent variable, model specifi-

Table 4.5 Hazard model of nuclear proliferation, post-matching

Matched observations	280
Number of countries	48
Coefficient	2.552
Standard error	1.029
p-value	0.013

cation, and the nuclear proliferation behavior of a few key states. It is difficult to define precisely when some states acquired nuclear weapons. For states that conduct a nuclear test, the date of nuclear acquisition is quite clear. For nuclear weapon states that did not conduct nuclear tests, however, the date of the first assembly of nuclear weapons requires an examination of the countries' historical records of nuclear development and some guesswork. Robustness checks performed using alternate codings of *Nuclear proliferation* reveal that the results are not sensitive to different measurements of the dependent variable. Next, to ensure that my results were not being driven by the inclusion of specific control variables, I reran dozens of models, omitting right-hand side variables one at a time. Again, the core results were not affected. Finally, to assess whether the findings are being driven by the proliferation behavior of particular states, I dropped the observations containing certain key countries and repeated the analysis. Sequentially removing the observations containing China, Israel, and Pakistan, and reestimating the models did not affect the findings.[22]

Conclusion

This chapter sought to explain why states acquire nuclear weapons. I found that in order to explain patterns of nuclear proliferation, one must look to international transfers of sensitive nuclear materials and technology. States that receive sensitive nuclear assistance from more advanced nuclear states are more likely to acquire nuclear weapons than are similar states that do not receive sensitive nuclear assistance. The receipt of sensitive nuclear assistance helps potential nuclear proliferators overcome the common obstacles that states encounter as they attempt to develop a nuclear arsenal. By importing the bomb states can: leapfrog technical design stages, benefit from tacit knowledge in more advanced scientific communities, economize on the cost of nuclear weapons development, and avoid international scrutiny.

In broader terms, this chapter provided strong support for the supply-side approach to nuclear proliferation advocated in this issue (Gartzke and Kroenig this issue). States that have the ability to produce nuclear weapons, either through international assistance or domestic capacity are much more likely to do so. In contrast, this chapter found only modest support for key demand-side variables. This may be because nuclear weapons provide states with a variety of security and diplomatic benefits (Gartzke and Kroenig, Gartzke and Jo, Horowitz, Beardsley and Asal, this issue), muting demand-side differences across states. In short, variation in nuclear proliferation outcomes is best explained, not by analyzing which states want nuclear weapons, but by understanding which states are able to get them.

The argument of this chapter began with the simple insight that the ability to construct nuclear weapons spreads from state to state. As such, this argument about the relationship between nuclear assistance and nuclear acquisition treats nuclear proliferation as a transnational phenomenon. Scholarly approaches to nuclear proliferation have focused largely on the characteristics of individual states and have failed to theorize fully the international dimensions of nuclear proliferation. Academic nonproliferation studies have been criticized for a "tendency to isolate individual states and to examine their unique motives for going nuclear, prevent(ing) us from giving due importance to the varieties of international collaboration that were common and indispensable to all early developers of nuclear programs" (Abraham 2006: 55). Indeed, it is somewhat peculiar that studies about the "proliferation," "diffusion," and "spread" of nuclear weapons have not explicitly recognized that nuclear weapons technologies and materials literally spread from state to state. A complete understanding of nuclear proliferation, therefore, requires further research on the causes and consequences of nuclear assistance.

Notes

1 For helpful comments on earlier versions of this chapter, the author would like to thank the authors in this special issue, Bruce Russett, and two anonymous reviewers. Replication data and an online appendix are available at http://jcr.sagepub.com/supplemental.
2 See, for example, President Bush's Statement on North Korea Nuclear Test. October 9, 2006. Available at www.whitehouse.gov/news/releases/2006/10/20061009.html.
3 I define international nuclear assistance as the international transfer of nuclear materials and technologies to a nonnuclear weapon state.
4 Nuclear Threat Initiative website. Iraq Country Overview. Available at www.nti.org/e_research/profiles/Iraq/Nuclear/index.html.
5 Ibid.
6 North Korea received sensitive nuclear assistance in the 1990s and tested its first nuclear device in 2006. Because North Korea acquired nuclear weapons after the end of the time period under investigation, it is not included in the analysis as a positive case of nuclear proliferation.
7 Pakistani assistance to Iran, Libya, and North Korea from 1987–2002 was state-sponsored according to any reasonable definition of the term. Recent evidence reveals that senior government officials, including heads of state and Army chiefs of staff, actively supported the policy of nuclear transfer (Corera 2006).
8 Office of the Director of National Intelligence (2007) *Iran: Nuclear Intentions and Capabilities*, November. Available at www.dni.gov/press_releases/20071203_release.pdf.
9 Nuclear Threat Initiative website. Egypt Country Overview. Available at www.nti.org/e_research/profiles/Egypt/index.html.
10 See e.g., "The A.Q. Khan Network: Case Closed?," Hearing before the Subcommittee on International Terrorism and Nonproliferation of the Committee on International Relations, House of Representatives, May 25, 2006.
11 I do not include variables measuring state decisions to explore, pursue, or possess nuclear weapons because my theoretical interest is limited to the effect of nuclear assistance on nuclear acquisition. Nevertheless, robustness tests performed using these alternate measures of nuclear proliferation produce similar results.

12 The line between nonsensitive and sensitive nuclear assistance is often fuzzy in practice, yet there is a fairly widespread scientific consensus that sensitive fuel-cycle facilities, such as uranium enrichment facilities, represent a direct nuclear proliferation threat, while other less sensitive, civilian technologies are relatively resistant to proliferation. By drawing the line between nonsensitive and sensitive nuclear assistance at sensitive fuel-cycle facilities, my definition follows this preexisting consensus.

13 Nuclear weapons experts have long recognized that a necessary, and the most difficult, step to building a nuclear arsenal is the acquisition of the weapons-grade fissile material that forms the core of the nuclear device. International Atomic Energy regulations assume that 8 kg of plutonium and 25 kgs of weapons-grade highly enriched uranium are sufficient for the construction of a basic nuclear device. Assistance on fuel-cycle facilities includes the construction of complete facilities or the transfer of key component parts for the construction of such facilities, such as centrifuges for uranium enrichment plants or hot cells for plutonium reprocessing plants. Assistance on uranium enrichment includes assistance on any of the various types of uranium enrichment processes including jet-nozzle, gaseous diffusion, gas-centrifuge, and laser isotope enrichment. For a primer on nuclear weapons and their construction see Jones *et al.* (1998): 317–322.

14 The secretive nature of sensitive nuclear transfers raises the potential for a missing data problem. It is difficult, however, for countries to maintain a secret nuclear program, and sensitive nuclear transfers that countries attempt to conduct in secret generally become known within a few years. Given the time frame of this study, which ends in 2000, I assess that missing data does not pose a significant problem to this analysis.

15 See Kroenig 2010 for a description of the cases of sensitive nuclear assistance, a list and description of selected cases that do not qualify as sensitive nuclear assistance according to the above definition, an explanation of key coding decisions, and the sources used in coding the variable.

16 To date, Singh and Way (2004) is the only study that uses quantitative methods to assess the correlates of nuclear acquisition. Jo and Gartzke's study on nuclear proliferation (2007) examines the determinants of nuclear possession, not nuclear acquisition.

17 Including a variable and its squared term in the model is a common method for testing for a nonmonotonic relationship (Ramsey and Schafer 2002: 244–245).

18 Using Logit or Probit estimators, or hazard models with a Weibull distribution to characterize the baseline hazard function, produces virtually identical results.

19 I conceive of the demand-side and supply-side variables as additive in their effects. In other words, a state that has a strong desire for nuclear weapons will be more likely to acquire nuclear weapons, holding all other factors constant, because the benefits to doing so may be higher. Similarly, a state that has the ability to produce nuclear weapons will be more likely to proliferate, *ceteris paribas*, because the costs to doing so may be lower.

20 As a robustness check, I replicated the findings of Singh and Way (2004) and Jo and Gartzke (2007) and then added the sensitive nuclear assistance variable to their models. In each and every model, sensitive nuclear assistance was positive and statistically significant.

21 QQ plots are available in the online appendix.

22 When I deleted any two of these three states and reestimated the models, *Sensitive nuclear assistance* was no longer statistically significant. This result is not terribly surprising given that dropping two of these three states leaves only a single positive case where a country received sensitive nuclear assistance and then went on to acquire nuclear weapons.

Bibliography

Abraham, Ittly (2006) "The ambivalence of nuclear histories," *Osiris* 21: 49–65.

Bennett, Scott D. (1998) "Integrating and testing models of rivalry termination," *American Journal of Political Science* 42:1200–1232.

Box-Steffensmeier, Janet M. and Bradford S. Jones (1997) "Time is of the essence: event history models in political science," *American Journal of Political Science* 41: 1414–1461.

Braun, Chaim and Christopher Chyba (2004) "Proliferation rings: new challenges to the nuclear nonproliferation regime," *International Security* 29: 5–49.

Chafetz, Glenn (1993) "The end of the Cold War and the future of nuclear proliferation: an alternative to the neorealist perspective," in Zachary S. Davis and Benjamin Frankel (eds) *The Proliferation Puzzle: Why Nuclear Weapons Spread (and What Results)*, Portland, OR: Frank Cass.

Chestnut, Sheena (2007) "Illicit activity and proliferation: North Korean smuggling networks," *International Security* 32: 80–111.

Cohen, Avner (1998) *Israel and the Bomb*, New York: Colombia University Press.

Corera, Gordon (2006) *Shopping for Bombs: Nuclear Proliferation, Global Insecurity, and the Rise and Fall of the A.Q. Khan Network*, Oxford: Oxford University Press.

Diehl, Paul F. (1998) *The Dynamics of Enduring Rivalries*, Urbana, IL: University of Illinois Press.

Fuhrmann, Matthew (2008) "Exporting mass destruction? The determinants of dual-use Trade," *Journal of Peace Research* 45: 633–652.

Gartzke, Erik (2006) *Codebook for the Affinity of Nations Index, 1946–2002, version 3.0.* Available at www.columbia.edu/~eg589.

Gartzke, Erik and Dong-Joon Jo (2009) "Bargaining, nuclear proliferation, and interstate disputes," *Journal of Conflict Resolution* 53.

Gartzke, Erik and Matthew Kroenig (2009) "A strategic approach to nuclear proliferation," *Journal of Conflict Resolution* 53.

Ghosn, F. and G. Palmer (2003) *Codebook for the Militarized Interstate Dispute Data, version 3.0.* Available at http://cow2.la.psu.edu.

Goncharenko, Sergei (1998) "Sino-Soviet military cooperation," in Odd Arne Westad (ed.) *Brothers in Arms: The Rise and Fall of the Sino-Soviet Alliance, 1945–1963*, Washington, DC: Woodrow Wilson Center Press.

Ho, Daniel, Kosuke Imai, Gary King, and Elizabeth Stuart (2007) "Matching as nonparametric preprocessing for reducing model dependence in parametric causal inference," *Political Analysis* 15: 199–236.

Horowitz, Michael (2009) "The spread of nuclear weapons and international conflict: does experience matter?," *Journal of Conflict Resolution* 53.

Hymans, Jacques E.C. (2006) *The Psychology of Nuclear Proliferation: Identity, Emotions, and Foreign Policy*, Cambridge: Cambridge University Press.

Imai, Kosuke, Gary King, and Elizabeth A. Stuart (2006) "The balance test fallacy in matching methods for causal inference." Available at http://gking.harvard.edu/projects/cause.shtml.

Jaggers, Keith and Ted R. Gurr (1995) "Tracking democracy's third wave with the Polity III Data," *Journal of Peace Research* 32: 469–482.

Jo, Dong-Joon and Erik Gartzke (2007) "Determinants of nuclear weapons proliferation: a quantitative model," *Journal of Conflict Resolution* 51: 167–194.

Jones, Rodney W. and Mark G. McDonough with Toby F. Dalton and Gregory D. Koblentz (1998) *Tracking Nuclear Proliferation: A Guide in Maps and Charts*, Washington, DC: Carnegie Endowment for International Peace.

Kroenig, Matthew (2009) "Exporting the bomb: why states provide sensitive nuclear assistance," *American Political Science Review* 103: 113–133.

Kroenig, Matthew (2010) *Exporting the Bomb: Technology Transfer and the Spread of Nuclear Weapons*, Ithaca, NY: Cornell University Press.

Lavoy, Peter R. (1993) "Nuclear myths and the causes of nuclear proliferation," in Z.S. Davis and B. Frankel (eds) *The Proliferation Puzzle: Why Nuclear Weapons Spread (and What Results)*, Portland, OR: Frank Cass & Company.

Lavoy, Peter R. (1995) "The strategic consequences of nuclear proliferation," *Security Studies* 4: 695–753.

Lewis, John W. and Xue Litai (1988) *China Builds the Bomb*, Stanford, CA: Stanford University Press.

MacKenzie, Donald and Graham Spinardi (1995) "Tacit knowledge, weapons design, and the uninvention of nuclear weapons," *American Journal of Sociology* 100: 44–99.

Meyer, Stephen M. (1984) *The Dynamics of Nuclear Proliferation*, Chicago, IL: University of Chicago Press.

Montgomery, Alexander H. (2005) "Ringing in proliferation: how to dismantle an atomic bomb network," *International Security* 30: 153–187.

Paul, T.V. (2000) *Power Versus Prudence: Why Nations Forgo Nuclear Weapons*, Montreal: McGill-Queen's University Press.

Quester, George (1973) *The Politics of Nuclear Proliferation*, Baltimore, MD: Johns Hopkins University Press.

Ramsey, Fred L. and Danniel W. Schafer (2002) *The Statistical Sleuth: A Course in Methods of Data Analysis*, Belmont, CA: Duxbury Press.

Rauchhaus, Robert (2009) "Evaluating the nuclear peace hypothesis: a quantitative approach," *Journal of Conflict Resolution* 53.

Richelson, Jeffrey T. (2006) *Spying on the Bomb: American Nuclear Intelligence from Nazi Germany to Iran and North Korea*, New York: W.W. Norton & Company.

Sagan, Scott D. (1996/1997) "Why do states build nuclear weapons? Three models in search of a bomb," *International Security* 21: 54–86.

Sekhon, Jasjeet S. (Forthcoming) "Multivariate and propensity score matching software with automated balance optimization: the matching package for R," *Journal of Statistical Software*.

Sekhon, Jasjeet S. and Alexis Diamond (2008) "Genetic matching for estimating causal effects: a general multivariate matching method for achieving balance in observational studies," Working paper.

Sekhon, Jasjeet S. and Walter Mebane (1998) "Genetic optimization using derivatives," *Political Analysis* 7: 187–210.

Singh, Sonali and Christopher R. Way (2004) "The correlates of nuclear proliferation: a quantitative test," *Journal of Conflict Resolution* 48: 859–885.

Solingen, Etel (1994) "The political economy of nuclear restraint," *International Security* 19: 126–169.

Solingen, Etel (1998) *Regional Orders at Century's Dawn: Global and Domestic Influences on Grand Strategy*, Princeton, NJ: Princeton University Press.

Solingen, Etel (2007) *Nuclear Logics: Contrasting Paths in East Asia and the Middle East*, Princeton, NJ: Princeton University Press.

5 Taking a walk on the supply side

The determinants of civilian nuclear cooperation

Matthew Fuhrmann[1]

In a historic address before the United Nations General Assembly in December 1953, US President Dwight D. Eisenhower encouraged the nuclear suppliers to "serve the peaceful pursuits of mankind" by providing "abundant electrical energy in the power-starved areas of the world" (Eisenhower 1953). Since Eisenhower's speech, civilian nuclear cooperation – the transfer of nuclear technology, materials, or knowledge from one country to another for peaceful purposes – has been a prominent feature of international politics.[2] Indeed, countries have regularly signed bilateral nuclear cooperation agreements (NCAs) pledging to assist in the development of peaceful nuclear programs. Every country with a civil nuclear program has received assistance via NCAs. Iran received assistance from the United States, Germany, and Russia in developing its peaceful nuclear program. France, Brazil, and Italy assisted Iraq in reactor development, nuclear fuel, and plutonium reprocessing during the 1970s. And India received nuclear-related technology and knowledge from Canada and the United States prior to conducting a nuclear test in 1974. More recently, the 2005 US–India nuclear deal has spotlighted international attention on civilian nuclear cooperation. This agreement is controversial because India's status outside the nuclear Nonproliferation Treaty (NPT) undermines a long-established norm that requires a legal commitment forswearing nuclear weapons as a precondition for the supply of nuclear technology (e.g., Perkovich 2005).

This chapter examines why countries assist one another in developing civil nuclear programs.[3] Although very little scholarly research has examined this matter, it is both substantively important and theoretically interesting. In this book, Matthew Kroenig finds that countries receiving "sensitive" nuclear assistance are more likely to acquire nuclear weapons. I agree with Kroenig that sensitive assistance contributes to proliferation, but I argue that the relationship between peaceful nuclear aid and the spread of nuclear weapons is broader. Other types of nuclear aid – including assistance in constructing research and power reactors, fuel fabrication facilities, uranium conversion facilities, and training in nuclear engineering – offer countries experience in matters that have both peaceful and military applications (e.g., Bunn 2001). Importing dual-use technology, therefore, reduces the expected costs of a nuclear weapons program and enhances states' ability to successfully build the bomb. Based on this logic, countries receiving atomic assistance via nuclear cooperation agreements are more likely to desire the bomb and successfully manufacture it – even controlling for the sensitive transfers as defined by Kroenig and military assistance explicitly intended to facilitate proliferation (Fuhrmann 2009, 2010). This evidence suggests that analyzing all civilian nuclear cooperation can provide a fuller understanding of how nuclear weapons spread.

Civilian nuclear assistance brings to light an interesting puzzle. If countries generally oppose the spread of nuclear weapons and peaceful nuclear assistance can lead to proliferation, why do supplier states engage in civil nuclear cooperation? My argument is that countries offer civilian assistance because it is useful in meeting strategic objectives and the dual-use nature of nuclear technology and knowledge allows suppliers to convince themselves – rightly or wrongly – that their aid will not facilitate proliferation. I argue in this chapter that countries provide nuclear assistance for three strategic reasons: (1) to strengthen their allies and alliances; (2) to strengthen their relationship with enemies of enemies; and (3) to strengthen existing democracies and bilateral relationships with these countries (if the supplier is also a democracy). Under these conditions, the strategic value of civilian nuclear cooperation is enough to counter the chance that it *could* contribute to the spread of nuclear weapons. I find that these strategic motivations described above are more salient in explaining civilian nuclear commerce than variables rooted in nonproliferation, such as whether the importing state is exploring nuclear weapons or has signed the NPT. Consistent with the overarching themes of this book, this argument focuses on the supply side of nuclear proliferation and the strategic logic that motivates state behavior on nuclear issues. I test these hypotheses using statistical analysis and a new, comprehensive dataset on civilian nuclear assistance between 1950 and 2000 that I created based on the coding of NCAs. The empirical analyses lend robust support to my hypotheses.

This chapter makes several contributions to theory and policy. It offers the first comprehensive analysis of all peaceful nuclear cooperation that has occurred in the atomic age. My argument and findings bring to light a tragic irony of the nuclear marketplace. It is the stated policy of all nuclear suppliers to promote nonproliferation. Yet, nuclear assistance can be a valuable tool in achieving strategic objectives and the dual-use dilemma creates uncertainty about the end use of assistance. These circumstances collectively lead countries to offer nuclear aid. In the end, suppliers end up raising the risks of nuclear proliferation even though they are committed to nonproliferation and many find the spread of nuclear weapons the most pressing threat to their national security. In exposing this dilemma, I add to our scholarly understanding of when states transfer technology and knowledge that could be used to build nuclear weapons (e.g., Fuhrmann 2008, 2009, 2010; Kroenig 2009) and contribute to our understanding of how nuclear weapons spread (e.g., Montgomery 2005). This is especially important in light of recent evidence suggesting that nuclear weapons have security implications beyond those that have been well known to scholars and practitioners for decades (Waltz and Sagan 1995; Gartzke and Jo, this volume; Horowitz, this volume; Rauchhaus, this volume; Beardsley and Asal, this volume; Fuhrmann and Kreps 2010).

My finding that supplier states' strategic interests are more important than limiting the spread of nuclear weapons is troubling from a nonproliferation standpoint. While an NPT commitment reduces the probability a state will pursue nuclear weapons (Jo and Gartzke 2007), it does not make it any more likely to receive nuclear technology even though all treaty members are entitled to assistance for "peaceful purposes."[4] States with high energy needs may be more likely to sign the NPT (Way and Sasikumar 2007; see also Erickson and Way, this volume) but my results indicate that the promise of nuclear energy assistance often goes unfulfilled. Ultimately, this casts some doubt on the effectiveness of the NPT, which is a point that I discuss further in the conclusion.

This chapter proceeds by reviewing the existing literature relevant to my research question. Next, it develops the argument and hypotheses on peaceful nuclear assistance, describes the empirical approach to testing these hypotheses, and discusses the results. It concludes by summarizing the findings and highlighting the contributions of this study.

Existing studies

The recent literature on nuclear proliferation examines the factors that motivate countries to pursue nuclear weapons (e.g., Sagan 1996/97; Singh and Way 2004; Hymans 2006; Solingen 2007; Jo and Gartzke 2007). As the editors highlight in the introduction of this book, scholars have devoted much less attention to *how* countries proliferate (Rauchhaus, Kroenig and Gartzke, this volume). In particular, very little research has been conducted on civilian nuclear cooperation, which is an important but overlooked factor affecting how nuclear weapons spread. A few studies analyze the nuclear exports of a single country to a small group of countries (Lowrance 1976; Boardman and Keeley 1983; Potter 1990; Paul 2003; Corera 2006; Bratt 2006). These studies make important contributions to the literature but they are largely policy-oriented and their intention is not to offer generalizable explanations for civilian nuclear assistance.

Kroenig's work is, to my knowledge, the only other research seeking to explain cross-national variation in nuclear assistance over time. His chapter in this book underscores that countries receiving sensitive aid – including bomb designs, enrichment/reprocessing facilities, and significant quantities of weapon-grade uranium or plutonium – are more likely to acquire nuclear weapons. This highlights the importance of explaining sensitive nuclear assistance, which Kroenig does in a recent study (Kroenig 2009). He argues that relatively weak states offer sensitive aid to countries that they cannot project power against to constrain the capabilities of more powerful countries by promoting the spread of nuclear weapons. This research offers a number of important contributions to the literature on nuclear proliferation. But the argument explains a very small sub-set of peaceful nuclear assistance. The transfers identified by Kroenig constitute less than 1 percent of the NCAs that were signed from 1950 to 2000. Moreover, many of the exports he studied were provided explicitly to promote the spread of nuclear weapons. In other words, they did not have a civilian purpose. I argue that scholarly understanding of proliferation can be enhanced by developing a theory that explains all civilian nuclear cooperation, since even seemingly "innocuous" nuclear aid raises the risk that nuclear weapons will spread (Fuhrmann 2009).

Theoretical framework

As I highlighted in the introduction, it is puzzling that countries provide nuclear assistance because they generally are supportive of non-proliferation, and civilian nuclear cooperation raises the risks that nuclear weapons will spread. In this section I present my argument for peaceful nuclear assistance. Before discussing my argument in detail I briefly explain how the dual-use dilemma and the strategic value of nuclear aid set the stage for states to assist other countries' civil nuclear programs.

The dual-use dilemma

To understand why countries provide civilian nuclear assistance we must first revisit the dual-use dilemma. All nuclear technology and materials are dual-use in nature (see, e.g., Fuhrmann 2008). They can be used either to produce energy or to enhance a country's ability to build nuclear weapons. Studies show that because of this, countries receiving nuclear assistance are more likely to pursue and acquire nuclear weapons (Fuhrmann 2009). But there is a probabilistic – not deterministic – relationship between peaceful aid and proliferation. Fuhrmann (2009) finds that 13 percent of the countries that receive nuclear assistance via nuclear cooperation agreements later began weapons programs while only 4 percent of states began programs without receiving any aid. Thus, nuclear assistance significantly increases the likelihood that the recipient country will want nuclear weapons but it does not guarantee this outcome. Importantly, this distinguishes nuclear assistance from arms transfers and other types of military cooperation. When a country transfers conventional munitions, there is little doubt what their end use will be. In exporting F-16s to Pakistan, for example, the United States is certain that it is augmenting the capabilities of the Pakistani military. It cannot convince itself or domestic audiences that the fighter aircraft might be used for peaceful purposes.

On the other hand, uncertainty plagues the nuclear marketplace. At the end of the day, recipients can reassure suppliers that assistance they provide will not be used for military purposes. Suppliers can also convince themselves that their assistance will not facilitate proliferation – even if there are reasons to believe that this might be the case. This is even true for the most sensitive transfers relating to the nuclear fuel cycle. For instance, in the 1970s West Germany pledged to supply Brazil with the complete fuel cycle, including assistance in building a uranium enrichment facility. Although West Germany was well aware that this technology could be used to produce fissile material for a bomb and it did not want Brazil to acquire nuclear weapons, Bonn pledged to provide nuclear technology in part because it convinced itself that enrichment assistance would not contribute to proliferation (e.g., Lowrance 1976).

This issue is compounded because countries may calculate that one transfer is unlikely to singlehandedly carry a country over the nuclear tipping point. Nuclear weapons production is extremely complex and it usually requires assistance from several foreign suppliers in more than one aspect of the fuel cycle. India, for instance, signed 19 NCAs from eight different suppliers prior to conducting its first nuclear test in 1974. No single transfer was alone sufficient to enable New Delhi to produce the bomb. Even the Canadian-supplied heavy water reactor, which was the most useful foreign-supplied technology in producing the bomb, required heavy water from the United States in order to function. The bottom line is that suppliers realize that assistance they provide will help recipients make progress towards bomb production but that they will likely need additional help to go nuclear. This allows states to convince themselves that assistance will not harm their security interests by spreading nuclear weapons.

Nuclear assistance and statecraft

There is a second consideration that helps us more fully understand why countries would accept even modest proliferation risks associated with nuclear commerce. I argue that some risks are accepted because atomic assistance is a potentially effective instrument of statecraft. There are two reasons why this is the case. First, nuclear assistance bolsters the capabilities of the recipient country. Energy plays a critical role in facilitating economic growth and it is an important element of national power (e.g., Singer *et al.* 1972). Since nuclear power reactors improve a state's energy production capacity, they directly affect a country's material capacity. Receiving nuclear assistance also indirectly enhances a state's capabilities since enhanced energy production capacity frees up resources that can be used to bolster its military capabilities (e.g., Gowa 1994).

Second, civilian nuclear assistance can strengthen relations between the supplier and recipient countries. Hans Morgenthau (1962) argues that foreign aid fosters closer political relationships by signaling favorable intentions and evoking a sense of gratitude that makes recipients more likely to cooperate with the supplier country in a wide variety of domains. Assistance is especially valuable in strengthening bilateral relations if the asset being exchanged is valuable to the recipient and if it depends on the supplier country to obtain that asset (Walt 1987: 43). Civilian nuclear cooperation meets these criteria. Countries value nuclear energy because it stimulates economic growth, symbolizes technological modernity and scientific competence, fosters energy independence, and provides a foundation that a weapons program could draw on in the future (e.g., Poneman 1982; Bratt 2006).[5] At the same time, countries are generally dependent on foreign suppliers in order to experience the benefits of nuclear energy. Most countries simply do not have the indigenous capabilities required to construct reactors, fuel-cycle facilities, or other infrastructure relevant for a civil nuclear program. Others that probably could build facilities indigenously given sufficient time and political commitment recognize that they can build a civil nuclear program much more quickly if they receive foreign aid. Even the United States, the largest nuclear supplier, has received help from European countries in building uranium enrichment facilities.

For these reasons, civilian nuclear assistance can effectively strengthen bilateral relations. Supplier countries are well aware of this. For example, Jules Leger, the Canadian Undersecretary of State for External Affairs, said this about nuclear assistance to India in the 1950s: "politically, it would do more to strengthen our relations with India than anything I could think of" (Donaghy 2007). Similarly, the United States believes that the 2005 nuclear deal with India is not only the most important initiative aimed at improving Indo-American relations, it is necessary for a strategic partnership to develop (e.g., Burns 2005).

Strategic incentives and nuclear assistance

The logic advanced above helps explain why countries would ever provide assistance that could lead to the spread of the most destructive weapon known to man. There is no guarantee that assistance will lead to proliferation and the value of atomic assistance as an instrument of statecraft can outweigh proliferation risks under certain conditions. In an anarchic international system where the prospect of nuclear war looms large, countries are unlikely to accept even modest proliferation risks unless they receive strategic benefits. My argument is that countries provide nuclear assistance for three strategic reasons: to strengthen their allies and alliances; to develop closer relationships with enemies of enemies; and – if the supplier is a democracy – to strengthen democracies and relationships with democracies. What follows is a more detailed discussion of these arguments.

Strengthening allies and alliances

States enter alliances in order to enhance their security. Alliances may be formed in order to establish a balance of power and constrain threatening states (e.g., Waltz 1979; Walt 1987). They may also represent attempts to bandwagon with more powerful states in security-enhancing ways (e.g., Schweller 1994). Since they are useful instruments for balancing and bandwagoning, countries perceive that alliances deter third party aggression and promote peace (e.g., Gelpi 1999). Major powers sometimes seek alliances for other purposes such as managing weaker countries or obtaining autonomy benefits including the right to establish military bases or acquire over-flight rights (Sprecher and Krause 2006).

The anticipated benefits stemming from alliances are vital to states' strategic interests. But the payoffs that countries expect when they form alliances do not always materialize. The absence of costly enforcement mechanisms, incentives to free ride, and changes in the strategic environment over time provide countries with incentives to abandon their alliance commitments (Skålnes 2000: 16–17). Data on the dependability of allies in war underscore that allies are often unreliable. Alan Sabrosky (1980) finds that allies fought together in only 27 percent of the cases and actually opposed one another 12 percent of the time in wars between 1816 and 1965. In a more recent analysis, Brett Ashley Leeds, Andrew Long, and Sarah McLaughlin Mitchell (2000) find that alliances are relatively reliable but allies still do not aid one another in war roughly 25 percent of the time. A military alliance also does not guarantee cooperation in areas short of war. A country cannot assume that its allies will support its positions at the United Nations Security Council, ratify treaties that serve its strategic interests, share sensitive intelligence, restrict potentially lucrative trade with a third party, or work together to combat issues such as terrorism and weapons proliferation. The United States, for instance, has occasionally had trouble convincing France, Germany, and its other European allies to institute harsh economic sanctions against Iran in response to Tehran's alleged pursuit of nuclear weapons. All of this suggests that a military alliance alone does not guarantee that an ally will provide assistance in achieving strategic objectives.

Countries, therefore, have incentives to make sure that bilateral relationships with their allies remain strong even after a formal alliance is forged. By keeping intra-alliance relations strong, countries help to ensure that they actually experience the benefits that led them to create the alliance in the first place. Imagine an alliance where State A agrees to assist State B if it is attacked by State C. State B can increase the likelihood that State A will actually come to its aid if it works to continually strengthen bilateral relations with it. Likewise, State A will be more likely to cooperate with State B in a variety of other strategic domains if the partnership between the two countries is strong. And State A's cooperation will be more meaningful if its capabilities are enhanced. For example, the stronger State A is, the more likely it will effectively deter third party aggression.

Countries routinely use atomic assistance to strengthen alliance ties. Nuclear assistance is not the only tool countries can use to achieve this objective but it can be a particularly effective one since countries value civil nuclear programs but usually depend on assistance to develop them, as I argued above. American civil nuclear cooperation with Japan beginning in the late 1950s is a textbook example of using atomic assistance to strengthen an alliance (see United States 1960). The United States depended on its alliance with Japan to balance against the Communist bloc, defend the Western Pacific from Soviet aggression, house American military bases essential to any operation conducted in the Far East. At the same time, Washington recognized that it could not take its partnership with Tokyo for granted. In 1958, the United States signed its first nuclear cooperation agreement with Japan to strengthen the alliance that the two countries had forged six years previously. By fostering Japanese economic growth via civil nuclear cooperation, the United States believed that it would strengthen Japan in ways that would reinforce the American–Japanese alliance and help ensure that Washington could depend on Tokyo to help attain strategic objectives (Lester 1982).

Hypothesis 1: Suppliers are more likely to export nuclear technology to their military allies than non-allies.

The value of atomic assistance in strengthening intra-alliance relations is partially contingent on restricting aid to adversaries. Lars Skålnes (2000) argues that attempts to bolster relations with allies by adopting discriminatory foreign economic policies can be undermined by granting enemies similar benefits because it sends mixed signals to both allies and adversaries. Building on this logic, I argue that countries refrain from assisting enemies' nuclear programs to make nuclear assistance to allies more meaningful. Since suppliers restrict nuclear technology to some destinations, recipient countries view atomic assistance as a credible signal of intent to forge a strategic partnership.

Additionally, states want to avoid contributing to the capabilities of an adversary. They prefer that those they are fighting, or likely to fight in the future, are relatively weak because this increases their chances of victory. Countries also want to weaken their adversaries to increase their relative bargaining power and political influence. These considerations generally compel states to restrict foreign economic cooperation – including atomic assistance – with their enemies (e.g., Hufbauer *et al.* 1990). The classic example of this is the American-led restriction of nuclear assistance and other sensitive dual-use technologies to the Soviet Union and its allies during the Cold War (e.g., Mastanduno 1992).

> *Hypothesis 2*: Suppliers export less nuclear technology to states with which they are engaged in militarized conflict.

Strengthening enemies of enemies and relations with enemies of enemies

States have incentives to constrain the power of those they find threatening and often do so by cooperating with threatening states' enemies (e.g., Waltz 1979). As I discussed above, State A and State B are likely to form an alliance if both actors are threatened by State C (Walt 1987). But countries that share enemies do not always formally ally. Today, for instance, the United States and India have a common enemy – China – but they do not share a defense pact or other formal alliance. Yet both countries are cooperating in a wide variety of areas, partially because they each fear China's rising influence in Asia. This type of strategic cooperation in the absence of a formal alliance is often referred to as "soft balancing" (Pape 2005; Paul *et al.* 2004). I argue that civilian nuclear cooperation is one type of soft balancing countries can employ to counter the capabilities of potentially threatening states.

Nuclear assistance is useful in achieving this strategic objective for two reasons. First, it allows a supplier state to develop a closer relationship with the importing state, improving its ability to balance the threatening state's power. For example, India's civilian nuclear assistance to Vietnam beginning in the late 1990s was intended to forge an Indo-Vietnamese partnership to counter the rising influence of China in the region (Singh 2007). Likewise, US officials pushed a civil nuclear deal with India because they believed that it could foster a bilateral partnership and provide "a strategically important counterweight to China" (Kessler 2007: 57).

Second, civilian nuclear cooperation with a threatening state's enemy also constrains its power by making it more difficult for the threatening state to exert influence or aggression against its enemy (e.g., the recipient). For instance, the United States sought to provide nuclear aid to Iran in the 1970s, to strengthen it economically and politically, which made it more difficult for the Soviet Union – a common enemy in this case – to influence or attack Tehran. Nuclear assistance to enemies of enemies has another added benefit for suppliers. Since nuclear technology is dual-use in nature, the threatening state may worry that nuclear trade for peaceful purposes could enhance the recipient state's ability to build nuclear weapons.[6] This is almost never the explicit intent of assistance, but third parties may not be aware of this. Consequently, atomic aid under such circumstances can divert the threatening state's attention towards the recipient state's nuclear energy program and away from other power-maximizing objectives.

One of the most well-known cases of using nuclear assistance as a means of soft balancing is China's aid to Pakistan in the 1990s. T.V. Paul (2003) argues that China's nuclear exports to Pakistan can be explained by a desire to "limit India's power capabilities to South Asia and thereby constrain New Delhi's aspirations to become a major power in Asia." Since Chinese nuclear assistance strengthens its bilateral relationship with Pakistan, it makes it more difficult for India to assert regional dominance. It also constrains India because it reduces its political influence vis-à-vis Pakistan. Moreover, from Beijing's perspective, if India is worried about a nuclear arms race with Pakistan it would be less concerned with its rivalry with China. In this sense, atomic assistance could be an effective diversion that takes Indian attention away from strategic objectives that China finds threatening.

Hypothesis 3: Suppliers are likely to export nuclear technology to enemies of enemies.

In international politics, states are most threatened by the strongest countries in the international system (e.g., Waltz 1979). Consequently, nuclear suppliers are especially likely to provide assistance to those states that are enemies of superpowers. Such behavior allows the supplier to counter the dominant state's influence by forging a partnership with its enemy. It further constrains the powerful state's capabilities by making it more difficult for it to exert pressure or aggression against its enemy. For example, in the post-Cold War era Russia, China, and other nuclear suppliers have continually offered nuclear commodities to states that are enemies of the United States such as Iran and Syria. Russian nuclear cooperation with Iran is perhaps the most well-known case in recent years aimed at countering American influence (Pape 2005). Although Russian pledges to provide assistance related to the fuel cycle in the mid-1990s never fully materialized, they represented an attempt to counter US influence by strengthening a partnership with Iran. Moscow also hoped that if Washington was concerned about Iran possibly acquiring nuclear weapons, it would focus less on policies it finds threatening such as the deployment of a missile defense system in Eastern Europe or the eastward expansion of the North Atlantic Treaty Organization (NATO).

Hypothesis 4: Suppliers are likely to export nuclear technology to states that are enemies of the most powerful states in the international system.

Strengthening democracies and relations with democracies

Scholars of international relations have long recognized that a country's regime type can affect international security. This fact is most evident in the democratic peace theory, which suggests that two democratic states are unlikely to fight each other because democracies share values and a respect for the rule of law and democratic leaders face institutional constraints that make conflict particularly costly (e.g., Doyle 1983). The logic of this theory not only implies that democracies are less likely to engage in conflict, but also that they are more likely to cooperate with one another. Indeed, democracies cooperate more than other pairs of states because they share similar interests and expect that accommodating behavior will be reciprocated (Leeds and Davis 1999).

Democratic states, therefore, have incentives to prop up other democracies because this puts them in a better position to achieve strategic objectives. A relatively weak democracy like the Philippines, for example, can better assist the United States in countering terrorism or weapons proliferation if its capabilities are enhanced. This is in large part why the influential Princeton Project on National Security urges the United States to "sustain the military predominance of liberal democracies and encourage the development of ... like-minded democracies" (Ikenberry and Slaughter 2006: 8). While shared values provide the foundation for strong relations between democracies they do not always guarantee a close relationship, just as an alliance does not ensure that an ally will always be willing to cooperate. Despite being the largest and second largest democracies in the world, for instance, India and the United States have only recently developed a close bilateral relationship. Sometimes, additional measures are necessary to develop strong relations – even between two democracies.

Strengthening a democracy can also limit the influence of non-democracies. There are two reasons why this is the case. First, strengthening a democratic state makes it more difficult for a non-democracy to assert itself as a regional hegemon. If India becomes stronger, for instance, it will be more difficult for China to emerge as the clear leader in Asia. Second, strengthening a democracy makes it more difficult for an autocratic country to exert influence against it, possibly weakening the democracy's commitment to the rule of law. During the Cold War, the United States worried that the Soviet Union would pressure weak democracies in the developing world and attempt to convert them into communist states. Washington recognized that it could stymie this strategy by strengthening these countries, making them less susceptible to Soviet aggression or influence. Limiting the influence of non-democratic states in these two respects serves a democratic state's strategic interests by constraining countries with which it could experience future conflict. Since it is more likely to fight a non-democratic state, a democracy prefers these countries to be relatively weak.

The 2005 US–India deal is a recent high-profile case that underscores the relationship between civilian nuclear cooperation and democracy. Virtually every senior US decision-maker involved in the deal – including President George W. Bush, Secretary of State Condoleezza Rice, and Undersecretary of State Nicholas Burns – has publicly justified atomic assistance to India on the grounds that it will transform relations with a democratic country in ways that enhance American security. As Undersecretary Burns said in 2005, "a strong, democratic India is an important partner for the United States ... By cooperating with India now, we accelerate the arrival of the benefits that India's rise brings to the region and the world."

Hypothesis 5: Democratic nuclear suppliers are more likely to offer peaceful nuclear assistance to democracies than non-democracies.

Methodology and data

I adopt a time-series cross-sectional data structure for the period 1950 to 2000. The unit of analysis is the directed dyad year. Included in the dataset are all nuclear suppliers and all potential recipient dyads in the international system. Nuclear suppliers include the "traditional exporters" and the "emerging suppliers" as defined by Potter (1990).[7] All suppliers are included in the dataset beginning in the first year subsequent to 1950 that they acquire a nuclear engineering or uranium production capability. To determine when this occurred, I consult data on nuclear production capabilities compiled by Jo and Gartzke (2007). Table 5.1 provides a list of the major nuclear suppliers including the first year subsequent to 1950 that they acquired this capability.[8] All states in the system are potential recipients of nuclear-related commodities.

Table 5.1 List of nuclear suppliers

Country	Year of first capable supply	Country	Year of first capable supply
Argentina	1950	North Korea	1950
Belgium	1950	Pakistan	1963
Brazil	1950	Russia	1950
Canada	1950	South Africa	1950
China	1950	South Korea	1961
France	1950	Spain	1950
Germany	1959	Sweden	1950
India	1950	Switzerland	1957
Israel	1950	United Kingdom	1950
Italy	1961	United States	1950
Japan	1959	Yugoslavia	1959
Netherlands	1950		

Dependent variable and measurement

Civilian nuclear cooperation is the state-authorized transfer of nuclear facilities, technology, materials, or know-how from one country to another for peaceful purposes. This definition captures all transfers enabling the recipient country to develop, successfully operate, and expand a civil nuclear program. Operationally, there are five general categories of civilian nuclear cooperation: (1) reactors; (2) nuclear materials; (3) fuel-cycle facilities; (4) nuclear safety; and (5) intangible transfers (e.g., knowledge).

Prior to this chapter, comprehensive data on civilian nuclear cooperation did not exist. Kroenig (2009) produces a unique dataset on "sensitive" nuclear assistance. But the transfers Kroenig identifies as sensitive (e.g., bomb designs, reprocessing/enrichment facilities, and significant quantities of bomb-grade fuel) make up only a tiny fraction of all civilian nuclear cooperation and some of these transfers were provided explicitly to facilitate weapons proliferation, as I indicated above.

To analyze all peaceful nuclear assistance I produce a new dataset. To identify the universe of cases of civilian nuclear cooperation, I consulted a list compiled by James Keeley (2003) of all bilateral NCAs signed between 1945 and 2003. NCAs are agreements signed by supplying and importing countries authorizing nuclear transactions. In his list, Keeley includes all agreements dealing with the five operational domains listed above.[9] But he also includes agreements that do not meet my definition of peaceful nuclear assistance such as those dealing exclusively with safeguards or nonproliferation assurances. Therefore, I collected additional information on each NCA to be sure that I only include agreements in my sample that constitute civilian nuclear cooperation.

Having identified and coded the agreements that constitute civilian nuclear cooperation, the next step is to determine the identity of the supplier and recipient countries for each NCA.[10] Making a determination on this issue is important since I am interested in studying exporting states' motivations for engaging in civilian assistance and the effects that receiving aid has on importers' proliferation choices. But it is not always easy to identify suppliers and recipients (Keeley 1985). Sometimes the treaty text makes it clear that only one state is the supplier. More often, however, an NCA is written in such a way to imply reciprocity of supply but in reality only one state is doing the supplying. In some instances, agreements written in this manner genuinely involve reciprocal nuclear assistance. In other cases the deal implies reciprocal supply when common sense dictates that this is not the case. When the treaty text does not specify the supplier[s], I conduct additional research to identify the exporting and importing countries.[11] When further research does allow me to determine this, I assume that countries having the capacity to supply nuclear technology at the time the agreement was signed are exporters under the terms of the NCA.[12]

Based on these criteria, I construct a dichotomous dependent variable and code it annually. This variable measures whether a supplier and recipient state signed a NCA that involves the supply of nuclear items in a given year.[13] There are 2,470 "1s" in the sample, indicating that an average of 48 nuclear cooperation agreements were signed each year between 1950 and 2000.[14] Figure 5.1 plots the number of NCAs that have been signed over time. As the figure illustrates, there have been some fluctuations in nuclear assistance over time but there has been a general upward increase in the number of NCAs signed since 1950. This is in large part because more nuclear suppliers have emerged and more countries have become interested in nuclear energy.

Independent variables and measurement

A number of independent variables are employed to operationalize the hypotheses described above. Shared enemies, superpower enemies, military alliances, and joint democracy all increase the likelihood of nuclear cooperation while militarized conflict reduces it. Data on shared enemies and superpower enemies were self-coded from the New Rivalry Dataset compiled by Klein, Goertz, and Diehl (2006).[15] I create a dichotomous variable and code it 1 if two states are part of a rivalry with the same state in year *t*-1 and 0 otherwise. I create a second dichotomous variable and code it 1 if the importing state is a rival of either the Soviet Union between 1950 and 1991 or the United States between 1950 and 2000 in year *t*-1 and 0 otherwise. To determine whether states are military allies, I consulted version 3.0 of the Correlates of War (COW) Formal Alliance Data (Gibler and Sarkees 2004).

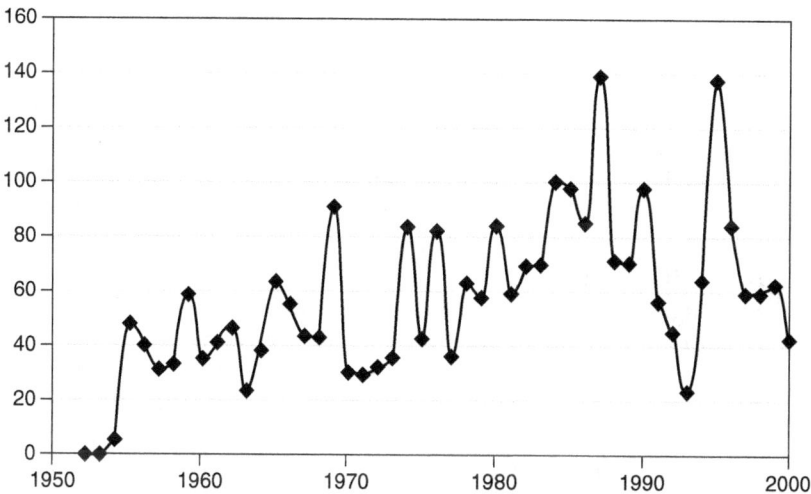

Figure 5.1 Number of Nuclear Cooperation Agreements, 1950–2000.

I include a dummy variable that equals 1 if the supplier and recipient share a formal defense pact in year *t*-1 and 0 otherwise. Democracy data were obtained from the Polity IV dataset (Beardsley and Gleditsch 2003).[16] I include a dummy variable and code it 1 if the recipient and supplier states both have a score of at least 7 on the Polity scale in year *t*-1 and 0 otherwise. Data on militarized conflict are taken from version 3.0 of the COW Militarized Interstate Dispute (MID) dataset (Ghosn *et al.* 2004).[17] I include a dummy variable and code it 1 if the supplier and recipient states were involved in a MID in year *t*-1 and 0 otherwise.

Control variables and measurement

There are other variables that could affect civilian nuclear cooperation. In the interest of tight model building, I control for possible confounding variables that flow from the principal competing explanations and exclude intervening variables (e.g., Achen 2005). In an online appendix, I show that my core findings remain unaltered when additional controls are added to the model.

Economics, particularly a desire to maximize profits, could drive the nuclear marketplace. If this were the case, we would expect that suppliers would behave in ways that maximized economic – not necessarily strategic – efficiency. A number of economic variables could influence the supply and demand for civilian nuclear commodities. It remains widely accepted that a state's capacity to supply exports as well as a state's demand for imports is directly related to its GDP (Anderson 1979). I include variables measuring the GDP of the exporting state and the GDP of the importing state in year *t*-1.[18] The distance between countries controls for the transportation and transaction costs associated with trade. These costs are expected to rise as the distance between two countries increases. I include a variable measuring the "great circle" distance between the capitals of states.[19]

Factors related to nuclear nonproliferation might also affect civilian nuclear cooperation. States that are at least exploring nuclear weapons might be less likely to be on the receiving end of a nuclear cooperation agreement since supplier states generally do not want their exports to contribute to proliferation. I create a dichotomous variable and code it 1 if the recipient state is at least "exploring" nuclear weapons in year *t*-1 based on Singh and Way's (2004) proliferation data. Nonproliferation pledges on the part of the importing state might enhance suppliers' confidence that exported commodities will not be used for unauthorized purposes. I include two dummy variables measuring whether the importing state is part of the NPT or Nuclear Suppliers Group (NSG), respectively, in year *t*-1. To classify membership in these institutions I consult lists compiled by the Center for Nonproliferation Studies (du Preez 2006).

Finally, contagion effects could influence nuclear assistance. In particular, a state might be more likely to demand nuclear assistance when its neighbors receive aid because they learn from the experiences of states around them or as a result of relative gains considerations (e.g., Waltz 1979). To control for this possibility, I create a dummy variable and code it 1 if a state's neighbor imports nuclear technology in year *t*-1 and 0 otherwise.[20]

Method of analysis

Since the dependent variable is dichotomous, I use logistic regression analysis (logit) to estimate the effect of the independent variables on the probability of peaceful nuclear assistance. All independent variables are lagged one year to control for endogeneity. I employ clustering across dyads to control for heteroskedastic error variance and use white robust estimation to correct the standard errors for spatial dependence. Additionally, I introduce a variable measuring the number of years since 1950 that lapse without a dyad signing a NCA and three cubic splines to control for autocorrelation in the dependent variable (Beck *et al.* 1998).

Results

Table 5.2 contains the initial results. Models 1–5 each include only one of the respective explanatory variables and controls for temporal dependence. Model 6 includes all five variables operationalizing my argument while Model 7 adds the controls for economic factors, nuclear nonproliferation, and contagion effects. To calculate the substantive effects produced by the independent variables I calculate the relative risk, which is the probability of an event in a treatment group divided by the probability of the same event in the control group. For dichotomous variables, I calculate the probability of nuclear aid in a given year when the variable equals 1, divided by the probability of nuclear aid when the variable equals 0, *ceteris paribus*. For continuous variables, the control treatment values are the mean and 1 standard deviation above the mean, respectively. Based on the relative risk, I calculate the percentage change in the likelihood of nuclear cooperation produced by each of the explanatory variables. These results are displayed in Table 5.3.

Some interesting results emerge from this analysis. A military alliance has a positive and statistically significant effect on the probability of a dyad signing a NCA in a particular year. The substantive effect produced by the military alliance variable is also quite significant. As Table 5.3 indicates, a military alliance increases the probability that two countries will sign a NCA in a particular year by 133 percent, all other things being equal. This is the strongest substantive effect produced by any of the explanatory variables. These results lend support to my argument that supplier states

Table 5.2 Effects of independent variables on nuclear cooperation agreements

	(1) Alliance	(2) Conflict	(3) Shared Enemy	(4) Superpower Enemy	(5) Joint Democracy	(6) Explanatory Variables	(7) Full Model
Supplier's Strategic Interests							
Alliance	1.875*** (0.091)	–	–	–	–	1.330*** (0.093)	0.862*** (0.093)
Militarized Conflict	–	–0.686* (0.394)	–	–	–	–0.849** (0.384)	–1.150*** (0.411)
Shared Enemy	–	–	1.503*** (0.104)	–	–	0.670*** (0.103)	0.202* (0.106)
Superpower Enemy	–	–	–	1.399*** (0.081)	–	1.042*** (0.083)	0.684*** (0.094)
Joint Democracy	–	–	–	–	1.169*** (0.083)	0.762*** (0.077)	0.454*** (0.078)
Economic Incentives							
Supplier's GDP	–	–	–	–	–	0.000*** (0.000)	0.000*** (0.000)
Recipient's GDP	–	–	–	–	–	0.000*** (0.000)	0.000*** (0.000)
Distance	–	–	–	–	–	–0.000*** (0.000)	–0.000*** (0.000)
Nonproliferation							
Nuclear Weapons	–	–	–	–	–	–	0.731*** (0.111)
NPT	–	–	–	–	–	–	–0.213*** (0.073)
NSG	–	–	–	–	–	–	0.881*** (0.097)
Contagion Effects							
Regional NCAs	–	–	–	–	–	–	1.006*** (0.088)
Constant	–3.153*** (0.091)	–2.608*** (0.093)	–2.833*** (0.082)	–2.960*** (0.087)	–3.174*** (0.091)	–3.746*** (0.087)	–4.272*** (0.107)
Observations	161,492	161,492	161,492	161,492	161,492	161,492	156,166

Notes

* significant at 10%; ** significant at 5%; *** significant at 1%. Robust standard errors in parentheses. Results for years passing without signing of nuclear cooperation agreement and 3 cubic splines are not reported in the interest of space.

Table 5.3 The substantive effects of independent variables on the probability of NCAs

Variable	Pr(Treatment)	Pr(Control)	Relative Risk	Percentage Change
Alliance	0.0128	0.0055	2.33	133
Conflict	0.0019	0.0058	0.33	–67
Shared Enemy	0.0070	0.0057	1.23	23
Superpower Enemy	0.0106	0.0054	1.96	96
Joint Democracy	0.0082	0.0052	1.58	58
Supplier's GDP	0.0071	0.0058	1.22	22
Recipient's GDP	0.0062	0.0058	1.07	7
Distance	0.0046	0.0058	0.79	–21
Nuclear Weapons	0.0112	0.0054	2.07	107
NPT	0.0053	0.0065	0.82	–18
NSG	0.0130	0.0054	2.41	141
Regional NCAs	0.0107	0.0039	2.74	174

Notes
All probabilities are generated using the estimates in Model 7, Table 5.2. For dichotomous variables, predicted probabilities are calculated when their value is shifted from 0 (control) to 1 (treatment) and all other variables are set to their mean. For continuous variables, predicted probabilities are calculated when their value is shifted from the mean (control) to one standard deviation above the mean. Relative risk is calculated by dividing Pr(Treatment) by Pr(Control). To calculate the percentage change, I subtract 1 from the relative risk and multiply that figure by 100.

use nuclear assistance to strengthen their allies and their alliances. Part of my argument regarding alliances is that suppliers also discriminate against their adversaries to make discrimination in favor of their allies more meaningful. The results support this expectation as well. The coefficient on the variable measuring whether the exporting and importing states are involved in militarized conflict is negative and statistically significant.[21] Substantively, the presence of militarized conflict reduces the likelihood of nuclear assistance by 67 percent.

The coefficient on the variable measuring whether the supplier and importer share a common enemy is positive and statistically significant, suggesting that states are statistically more likely to engage in nuclear cooperation with states with which they share a common enemy. The results indicate that countries are 23 percent more likely to assist the nuclear programs of enemies of enemies. This is the most modest effect produced by any of the explanatory variables, but these results still provide substantive and statistically significant support to my argument that states use civilian nuclear cooperation as a means to constrain the capabilities of their enemies. A related hypothesis is that states are likely to provide civilian nuclear assistance to those that are enemies of superpowers. The coefficient on the variable measuring whether the importing state is a superpower enemy is positive and statistically significant, indicating that suppliers are more likely to supply nuclear technology to those that are enemies of the most powerful states in the system. Being a superpower enemy also has a substantively significant effect on nuclear cooperation; it increases the probability that a supplier state will provide nuclear technology by 96 percent. Of the explanatory variables, only a military alliance has a stronger effect. Collectively, these two results lend support to my argument that civilian nuclear cooperation is a form of "soft balancing" (e.g., Pape 2005) that suppliers employ to strengthen partnerships aimed at countering the influence of threatening states.

I find that whether the supplier and recipient states are both democracies affects nuclear cooperation.[22] The joint democracy variable has a positive and statistically significant effect across model specifications. From a substantive standpoint, joint democracy increases the probability of nuclear assistance by 58 percent. This lends support to my argument that democratic states use nuclear aid to strengthen other democracies in ways that promote their strategic interests.

Turning to the controls, the economic variables behave largely as expected. The supplying and importing states' GDP and nuclear-related resources have positive and statistically significant effects on the probability of civilian nuclear cooperation. The substantive effects of these variables are weak, however, when compared to the effects produced by the explanatory variables. Increases in the value of the supplier's and recipient's GDP increase the likelihood of nuclear assistance by 22 percent and 7 percent, respectively. The coefficient on the variable measuring the distance between the supplier and importer has a statistically significant and negative effect, as expected. Substantively, increasing the distance between two countries from its mean (4,540 miles) to 1 standard deviation above its mean (8,154 miles) reduces the likelihood of nuclear cooperation by 21 percent. Thus, none of the economic variables produce effects as strong as the strategic variables.

The results dealing with the nonproliferation-related controls are especially interesting. The coefficient on the variable measuring whether the importing state is exploring nuclear weapons is *positive* and statistically significant, suggesting that states with weapons programs are more likely to be on the receiving end of nuclear cooperation agreements.[23] Countries exploring nuclear weapons are 107 percent more likely to receive nuclear aid for peaceful purposes. NSG membership has a positive and significant effect on the probability of nuclear cooperation but NPT membership has a negative effect on this probability, contrary to expectations.[24] NSG members are 141 percent more likely to receive nuclear assistance, which is a relatively strong effect, but NPT members are 18 percent *less* likely to receive aid. These findings challenge the conventional wisdom regarding the effect of normative considerations on the nuclear marketplace. They are, however, consistent with my argument that states provide nuclear assistance primarily to obtain strategic benefits. I will revisit the theoretical and practical implications of these findings in the conclusion.

Turning to the contagion effects argument, the regional NCA variable has a positive and statistically significant effect on the likelihood of nuclear assistance. When one of its neighbors receives nuclear assistance, a country is 174 percent more likely to do so. It is noteworthy that this is the strongest substantive effect produced by any of the variables in the model. The inclusion of this variable, however, does not affect the salience of strategic considerations relevant to my argument.

Temporal variation?

To further test the robustness of my results, I explore possible temporal variation in the determinants of civilian nuclear cooperation agreements.[25] These results are depicted in Table 5.4. I limit the analysis to: the complete Cold War period (column 1); the period prior to the creation of the nuclear nonproliferation regime (column 2); the Cold War period following the establishment of the nonproliferation regime (column 3); the entire period following the creation of the nonproliferation regime (column 4); and the post-Cold War period (column 5).[26]

Many of the results are consistent across model specifications. In the Cold War (1950–1991) and post-nonproliferation regime (1970–2000) periods, all five explanatory variables have statistically significant effects in the expected direction. There are a few noteworthy differences. In the pre-nonproliferation regime period (1950–1969) suppliers appear to be less inclined to use atomic aid to forge partnerships with enemies of enemies. In the post-Cold War period, the results do not lend support to my shared enemy, alliance, and joint democracy hypotheses. This may be due to system polarity. With the collapse of the international system's bipolar structure, states' nuclear trade policies are less influenced by international security, perhaps because there is less of a strategic need to link trade and security in a multi-polar world (Gowa 1994; Skålnes 2000). In spite of the differences, it is important to emphasize that I find empirical support for many of my hypotheses in the pre-regime and post-Cold War periods. Particularly striking is the finding that states use civilian nuclear cooperation as a means to constrain superpowers even after the collapse of the Soviet Union, suggesting that such behavior is not an artifact of the Cold War.

Conclusion

The findings presented above support my argument that the strategic interests of nuclear suppliers are salient in explaining civilian nuclear commerce. In particular, I find strong empirical support for my contention that countries offer nuclear assistance to strengthen their allies and alliances, to forge partnerships with enemies of enemies, and to strengthen existing democracies (if the supplier is also a democracy). My analysis

Table 5.4 Temporal breakdown of logit analysis on the effects of independent variables on nuclear cooperation agreements

	(1) Cold War, 1950–1991	(2) Cold War & Pre-Regime, 1950–1969	(3) Cold War & Post-Regime 1970–1991	(4) Post-Regime 1970–2000	(5) Post-Cold War 1992–2000
Supplier's Strategic Interests					
Alliance	0.971*** (0.100)	1.312*** (0.114)	0.566*** (0.116)	0.534*** (0.102)	-0.142 (0.160)
Militarized Conflict	-1.219** (0.549)	-1.542** (0.767)	-1.165 (0.777)	-1.136** (0.517)	-1.456** (0.576)
Shared Enemy	0.527*** (0.122)	0.250 (0.165)	0.550*** (0.142)	0.190* (0.112)	0.159 (0.164)
Superpower Enemy	0.394*** (0.107)	0.039 (0.149)	0.513*** (0.130)	0.832*** (0.105)	0.888*** (0.203)
Joint Democracy	0.591*** (0.078)	0.420*** (0.102)	0.669*** (0.094)	0.442*** (0.088)	-0.182 (0.134)
Economic Incentives					
Supplier's GDP	0.000*** (0.000)	0.000*** (0.000)	0.000*** (0.000)	0.000*** (0.000)	0.000*** (0.000)
Recipient's GDP	0.000*** (0.000)	0.000*** (0.000)	0.000*** (0.000)	0.000*** (0.000)	0.000*** (0.000)
Distance	-0.000*** (0.000)	-0.000*** (0.000)	-0.000*** (0.000)	-0.000*** (0.000)	0.000* (0.000)
Nonproliferation					
Nuclear Weapons	0.786*** (0.113)	1.008*** (0.148)	0.583*** (0.130)	0.529*** (0.124)	0.448** (0.198)
NPT	0.029 (0.079)	–	0.000 (0.102)	-0.273*** (0.091)	-0.900*** (0.193)
NSG	0.595*** (0.107)	–	0.631*** (0.103)	0.971*** (0.098)	2.435*** (0.174)
Contagion Effects					
Regional NCAs	1.097*** (0.091)	0.999*** (0.104)	1.043*** (0.113)	0.893*** (0.101)	0.380*** (0.131)
Constant	-4.406*** (0.107)	-5.105*** (0.162)	-3.948*** (0.155)	-3.877*** (0.142)	-4.376*** (0.248)
Observations	118,055	41,002	77,054	115,165	38,111

Notes
* significant at 10%; ** significant at 5%; *** significant at 1%. Robust standard errors in parentheses. Results for years passing without signing of nuclear cooperation agreement and 3 cubic splines are not reported in the interest of space.

reveals that these strategic considerations trump nonproliferation-related factors when it comes to civilian nuclear cooperation. States that are exploring nuclear weapons are actually *more* likely to receive civilian nuclear assistance. I find no support for the argument that NPT membership increases the likelihood that states will receive nuclear technology.

This chapter offers a number of theoretical and practical contributions. In a general sense, it sheds light on the factors motivating states to engage in civilian nuclear cooperation, which is something that was scantily understood prior to this study. To reiterate a point I made in the introduction, one of the reasons that it is important to understand civil nuclear assistance is that this can enhance our understanding of how nuclear weapons spread. Not only does atomic aid increase the probability that a country will acquire the bomb; receiving assistance also raises the risk that it will begin a nuclear weapons program (Furhmann 2009, 2010). Given these findings, this chapter tells us that nuclear weapons spread, in part, because supplier countries continually use nuclear assistance as a means to pursue their strategic interests. This insight adds to our understanding of the supply side of nuclear proliferation.

My findings that strategic considerations are more salient than nonproliferation concerns in explaining civilian nuclear assistance speaks to important debates in international relations. The NPT has been hailed as the "most successful treaty ever devised" (Williams and Wolfsthal 2005). It has earned this title in large part because the number of states that possess nuclear weapons today is much fewer than the number predicted by many observers prior to the creation of the NPT. In the early 1960s, President Kennedy famously warned that 15 or 20 nations would have nuclear weapons by 1970. Since Kennedy's warning only six additional countries crossed the nuclear weapons threshold – China (1964), Israel (1967), India (1988), South Africa (1982), Pakistan (1990), and, arguably, North Korea (2006) (Rauchhus, Kroenig and Gartzke, this volume). The NPT has also been considered to be successful due to the number of states that have signed on to the treaty; today only India, Israel, Pakistan, and North Korea remain outside the NPT. In judging the success of the NPT, however, its proponents have not adequately considered the two "grand bargains" of the treaty. The first bargain is that in exchange for giving up the pursuit of nuclear weapons, the five nuclear powers will make "good faith efforts" to move towards complete nuclear disarmament. The second is that states who forgo the nuclear option are entitled to nuclear technology for "peaceful purposes." Specifically, Article IV of the NPT states that: "Parties to the Treaty in a position to do so shall also co-operate in contributing ... to the further development of the applications of nuclear energy for peaceful purposes, especially in the territories of non-nuclear-weapon States Party to the Treaty."

My study suggests that the Article IV compromise has, on average, been a failure. Those who sign the treaty are no more likely than those that do not to receive nuclear technology for peaceful use. In fact, in some cases NPT signatories are actually less likely to receive nuclear aid. This raises cause for concern from a policy standpoint because it suggests that the nuclear weapons states (China, France, Russia, the United Kingdom, and the United States) are not living up to their commitment to supply nuclear technology for "peaceful purposes" to states that sign the NPT. This finding also speaks to a general debate in international relations regarding whether treaties and other institutional commitments matter (e.g., Chayes and Chayes 1993; Mearsheimer 1994/95; Downs *et al.* 1996). Although NPT membership may reduce the likelihood that states pursue nuclear weapons (Jo and Gartzke 2007), my results suggest that it does not make states more likely to receive nuclear technology for peaceful use. This casts some doubt on the argument that international commitments change state behavior and/or that states maintain the commitments they make, although we should be cautious about reading too much into this finding.

I mentioned in the introduction that the United States agreed to assist India's civil nuclear program in 2005 and has been widely criticized for doing so because New Delhi possesses nuclear weapons and refuses to sign the NPT. Statements from President Bush, Secretary Rice, and Undersecretary Burns make clear that the deal is intended to strengthen American relations with India, forge a partnership aimed partially and countering the rising influence of China in Asia, and strengthen an existing democracy (see Burns 2005; Rice 2006). Despite desperate attempts by Bush administration officials to justify the agreement on nonproliferation grounds, civil nuclear assistance to India flies in the face of nonproliferation norms. Many scholars have gone so far as to assert that the India nuclear deal threatens the existence of the nuclear nonproliferation regime (e.g., Perkovich 2005). What my analysis reveals is that there is less new about US behavior in the India case than most scholars imply. For decades, nuclear suppliers have been willing to export technology to states with poor nonproliferation records if doing so allows them to achieve strategic objectives such as strengthening their alliances or countering the influence of threatening states.

Notes

1 I thank Jeff Berejikian, Gary Bertsch, Matt Bunn, Jon Caverley, Erica Chenoweth, Alex Downes, Bryan Early, Aaron Hoffman, Erik Gartzke, Matt Kroenig, James Keeley, Quan Li, Andrew Long, Marty Malin, Steve Miller, Jon Monten, Alex Montgomery, T.V. Paul, Doug Stinnett, Jaroslav Tir, and participants in research seminars at Harvard University for helpful comments. I also thank the Belfer Center for Science and International Affairs at Harvard University and the Center for International Trade and Security and the University of Georgia for generous financial support.
2 The terms "nuclear cooperation," "nuclear assistance," "atomic assistance," and "nuclear trade" are used interchangeably throughout this chapter.

3 My analysis captures only state-sanctioned nuclear cooperation. Illegal nuclear activities not approved by the state are excluded, although these occurrences are fairly rare since states keep a close eye on nuclear-related activities. Even the A.Q. Khan network, which is often referred to as an illicit network, had at least tacit approval from the Pakistani government. My analysis does include covert activities if they are state sanctioned. For example, the Soviet Union covertly exported nuclear technology to China in the 1950s but these transactions are part of my analysis since Moscow signed agreements authorizing them.

4 NPT membership decreases the likelihood that states will have nuclear weapons programs but this does not necessarily imply that change in behavior is attributable to treaty membership (Jo and Gartzke 2007: 13).

5 While countries value civil nuclear programs in part because of their relationship to nuclear weapons, it is important to reiterate that suppliers almost never use peaceful cooperation as an explicit strategy to spread nuclear weapons.

6 This might also make the common enemy more likely to initiate a nuclear weapons program, which could undermine the supplier's security. Suppliers calculate, however, that this risk is relatively small so it does not offset the possible benefits they obtain from soft balancing against threatening states.

7 I make two modifications to Potter's (1990) list. I exclude Taiwan because it is not generally recognized as a sovereign country and is not eligible to join nonproliferation treaties or arrangements such as the NPT and NSG. I also add North Korea, which became a nuclear supplier of concern subsequent to Potter's work. The results are unchanged if I remove North Korea as a supplier from the analysis.

8 There is variation among the abilities of the countries listed in Table 5.1 to supply nuclear technology. As a robustness check in the online appendix (jcr. sagepub.com/supplemental), I only include major nuclear suppliers (United States, Soviet Union, Canada, United Kingdom, France, Italy, and Germany) in the sample and the results are virtually identical.

9 Keeley excludes the following: (1) agreements that are explicitly defense-related; (2) financial agreements; (3) agreements dealing solely with agricultural or industrial agreements not related to nuclear power; (4) agreements dealing with the leasing of nuclear material; (5) liability agreements; and (6) multilateral agreements. There are a few key exceptions to the latter point; agreements involving the European Atomic Energy Community (EURATOM) and the Belgo-Luxembourg Economic Union are included.

10 NCAs that involve EURATOM or the Belgo-Luxembourg Economic Union are classified as bilateral agreements between each state party to these arrangements and the other party to the NCA.

11 Online databases such as the Country Profiles maintained by the Nuclear Threat Initiative (NTI) are often useful in providing this additional information. See: www.nti.org/e_research/profiles/index.html.

12 This occurs in the first year subsequent to 1950 that suppliers acquire a nuclear engineering or uranium production capability. To determine when this occurred, I consult data on nuclear production capabilities compiled by Jo and Gartzke (2007). These data include latent nuclear weapon production capability estimates for 192 countries between 1938 and 2002 based on seven components.

13 If a dyad signs more than one NCA in the same year, only the first agreement is included.

14 Note that the number of 1s is greater than the number of NCAs because many agreements involve reciprocal supply. Additionally, some deals are multilateral (e.g., those involving EURATOM).

15 Klein, Goertz, and Diehl (2006: 335–340) consider two states in a dyad to be rivals if they experience at least three militarized interstate disputes over the period 1816–2001 that are fought over related issues.

16 Seven has been identified as a "natural cutpoint" on the Polity scale and it has become fairly standard to use this threshold (Reiter 2001).

17 These data are supplied by EUGene (Bennett and Stam 2000).

18 GDP is measured in current US dollars. These data were obtained by consulting Gleditsch (2002).

19 Border countries are coded as one mile (Fitzpatrick and Modlin 1986). These data were acquired using the EUGene program (Bennett and Stam 2000).

20 A neighbor is a state within 150 miles. Distance data are obtained using EUGene (Bennett and Stam 2000).

21 I substituted variables measuring whether the states in the dyad were involved in a militarized interstate dispute that resulted in a least one fatality or were involved in a rivalry using definitions offered by Thompson (2001) and Klein, Goertz, and Diehl (2006). The fatal MID modification produces identical results; the rivalry substitutions do not change the results and themselves do not have statistically significant effects. I also included a variable measuring the dyad's S-Score (Signorino and Ritter 1999), since the compatibility of states' foreign policy interests could be a proxy for the likelihood of future conflict. Including this variable also does not change the results.

22 I estimated Models 5–7 in Table 5.2 with only democratic suppliers in the sample and this did not affect any of my core findings. The joint democracy variable still had a statistically significant and positive effect on nuclear cooperation and the other explanatory variables also behaved as expected.

23 To further assess the robustness of this finding, I substituted variables measuring whether the recipient country was pursuing or had acquired nuclear weapons, as defined by Singh and Way (2004). These modifications produce identical results.

24 This may be because some states sign the NPT with no intention of developing a civil nuclear program. To determine whether this is affecting the NPT result, I include a variable measuring the size of the recipient state's existing nuclear program based on nuclear weapons production data compiled by Jo and Gartzke (2007). This does not change the results. The results also do not change when a variable measuring whether *both* the supplier and importer are members of the NPT is substituted for the current measure. A similar substitution for the NSG variable also leaves that result unchanged.

25 I conduct a variety of other robustness checks. In particular, I add additional control variables to the model, remove safety-related agreements from the dependent variable, and remove non-major suppliers from the sample. These changes do not affect the results in significant ways. The results of these robustness checks are included in the online appendix.

26 I choose these cut-off points since the end of the Cold War and the creation of the NPT could affect patterns of civilian nuclear cooperation.

Bibliography

Achen, Christopher (2005) "Let's put garbage can regressions and garbage can probits where they belong," *Conflict Management and Peace Science* 22(4): 327–339.

Anderson, James (1979) "A theoretical foundation for the gravity equation," *American Economic Review* 69(1): 106–115.

Beardsley, Kyle and Victor Asal (This Book) "Winning with the bomb."

Beardsley, Kyle and Kristian Gleditsch (2003) *Polity IVd Dataset*, University of Maryland.

Beck, Nathaniel, Jonathan Katz, and Richard Tucker (1998) "Taking time seriously in binary time-series–cross-section analysis," *American Journal of Political Science* 42(4): 1260–1288.

Bennett, D. Scott and Alan Stam (2000) "EUGene: A conceptual manual," *International Interactions* 26(2): 179–204.

Bliss, Harry and Bruce Russett (1998) "Democratic trading partners: the liberal connection, 1962–1989," *The Journal of Politics* 60(4): 1126–1147.

Boardman, Robert and James Keeley (eds) (1983) *Nuclear Exports and World Politics*, New York: St Martins.

Bratt, Duane (2006) *The Politics of CANDU Exports*, Toronto: University of Toronto Press.

Bunn, Matthew (2001) *Civilian Nuclear Energy and Nuclear Weapons Programs: The Record*, Cambridge, MA: Belfer Center for Science and International Affairs.

Burns, Nicholas (2005) "The U.S. and India: an emerging entente? Testimony before the House International Relations Committee," Washington, DC, September 8.

Chayes, Abram and Antonia Handler Chayes (1993) "On compliance," *International Organization* 47(2): 175–205.

Corera, Gordon (2006) *Shopping for Bombs: Nuclear Proliferation, Global Insecurity, and the Rise and Fall of the AQ Khan Network*, Oxford, UK: Oxford University Press.

Donaghy, Greg (2007) "Nehru's reactor: the origins of Indo-Canadian nuclear cooperation, 1955–1959," in C.S. Raj and A. Nafey (eds) *Canada's Global Engagements and Relations with India*, New Delhi: Manak.

Downs, George W., David M. Rocke, and Peter N. Barsoom (1996) "Is the good news about compliance good news about cooperation?," *International Organization* 50(3): 379–406.

Doyle, Michael (1983) "Kant, liberal legacies, and foreign affairs," *Philosophy and Public Affairs* 12(3): 205–235.

Eisenhower, Dwight D. (1953) "Address by Mr. Dwight D. Eisenhower, President of the United States of America, to the 470th Plenary Meeting of the United Nations General Assembly," December 8. Available at: www.iaea.org/About/history_speech.html.

Erickson, Jennifer and Christopher Way (This Book) "Membership has its privileges: conventional arms and influence within the Nuclear Non-Proliferation Treaty."

Fitzpatrick, Gary L. and Marilyn J. Modlin (1986) *Direct-line Distance*, Metuchen, NJ: The Scarecrow Press.

Fuhrmann, Matthew (2008) "Exporting mass destruction: the determinants of dual-use trade," *Journal of Peace Research* 45(5): 633–652.

Fuhrmann, Matthew (2009) "Spreading temptation: proliferation and peaceful nuclear cooperation agreements," *International Security* 34(1): 7–41.

Fuhrmann, Matthew (2010) "Atomic assistance: the causes and consequences of peaceful nuclear cooperation," Unpublished book manuscript.

Fuhrmann, Matthew and Sarah E. Kreps (2010) "Targeting nuclear programs in war and peace: a quantitative empirical analysis, 1941–2000," *Journal of Conflict Resolution* 54(6): 831–859.

Gartzke, Erik and Dong-Joon Jo (This Book) "Bargaining, nuclear proliferation, and interstate disputes."

Gelpi, Christopher (1999) "Alliances as instruments of intra-allied control," in Helga Haftendorn, Robert O. Keohane, and Celeste A. Wallander (eds) *Imperfect Unions: Security Institutions over Time and Space*, Oxford: Oxford University Press, pp. 107–139.

Ghosn, Faten, Glenn Palmer, and Stuart Bremer (2004) "The MID3 data set, 1993–2001: procedures, coding rules, and description," *Conflict Management and Peace Science* 21: 133–154.

Gibler, Douglas and Meredith Sarkees (2004) "Measuring alliances: the correlates of war formal interstate alliance data set," *Journal of Peace Research* 41(2): 211–222.

Gleditsch, Kristian (2002) "Expanded Trade and GDP Data," *Journal of Conflict Resolution* 46(5): 693–711.

Gowa, Joanne (1994) *Allies, Adversaries, and International Trade*, Princeton, NJ: Princeton University Press.

Horowitz, Michael (This Book) "The spread of nuclear weapons and international conflict: does experience matter?"

Hufbauer, Gary Clyde, Jeffrey Schott, and Kimberly Elliott (1990) *Economic Sanctions Reconsidered*, Washington, DC: Institute for International Economics.

Hymans, Jacques (2006) *The Psychology of Nuclear Proliferation: Identity, Emotions, and Foreign Policy*, Cambridge: Cambridge University Press.

Ikenberry, G. John and Anne-Marie Slaughter (2006) *Forging a World of Liberty under Law: U.S. National Security in the 21st Century*, Princeton, NJ: The Woodrow Wilson School of Public and International Affairs, p. 8.

Jo, Dong-Joon and Erik Gartzke (2007) "Determinants of nuclear weapons proliferation," *Journal of Conflict Resolution* 51(1): 1–28.

Keeley, James (1985) "Coding treaties: examples from nuclear cooperation," *International Studies Quarterly* 29(1).

Keeley, James (2003) "A list of bilateral civilian nuclear cooperation agreements," University of Calgary, Strategic Studies Program.

Kessler, Glenn (2007) *The Confidante: Condoleezza Rice and the Creation of the Bush Legacy*, New York: St Martin's Press.

Klein, James, Gary Goertz, and Paul Diehl (2006) "The new rivalry dataset: procedures and patterns," *Journal of Peace Research* 43(3): 331–348.

Kroenig, Matthew (2009) "Exporting the bomb: why do states provide sensitive nuclear assistance?," *American Political Science Review* 103(1).

Kroenig, Matthew (This Book) "Importing the bomb: sensitive nuclear assistance and nuclear proliferation."

Leeds, Brett Ashley and David Davis (1999) "Beneath the surface: regime type and international interaction, 1953–78," *Journal of Peace Research* 36(1): 5–21.

Leeds, Brett Ashley, Andrew Long, and Sarah McLaughlin Mitchell (2000) "Reevaluating alliance reliability: specific threats, specific promises," *Journal of Conflict Resolution* 44(5): 686–699.

Lester, Richard (1982) "U.S.–Japanese nuclear relations: structural change and political strain," *Asian Survey* 22(5): 417–433.

Lowrance, William (1976) "Nuclear futures for sale: to Brazil from West Germany, 1975," *International Security* 1(2): 147–166.

Mastanduno, Michael (1992) *Economic Containment: Cocom and the Politics of East–West Trade*, Ithaca, NY: Cornell University Press.

Mearsheimer, John (1994/95) "The false promise of international institutions," *International Security* 19(1): 5–49.

Montgomery, Alexander (2005) "Ringing in proliferation: how to dismantle an atomic bomb network," *International Security* 30(2): 153–187.

Morgenthau, Hans (1962) "A political theory of foreign aid," *American Political Science Review* 56(2): 301–309.

Pape, Robert (2005) "Soft balancing against the United States," *International Security* 30(1): 7–45.

Paul, T.V. (2000) *Power versus Prudence: Why Nations Forgo Nuclear Weapons*, Montreal: McGill University Press.

Paul, T.V. (2003) "Chinese–Pakistani nuclear/missile ties and the balance of power," *The Nonproliferation Review* 10(2): 1–9.

Paul, T.V., James Wirtz, and Michael Fortmann (eds) (2004) *Balance of Power: Theory and Practice in the 21st Century*, Stanford, CA: Stanford University Press.

Perkovich, George (2005) *Faulty Promises: The US-India Nuclear Deal*, Washington, DC: Carnegie Endowment for International Peace.

Poneman, Daniel (1982) *Nuclear Power in the Developing World*, Winchester, MA: Allen and Unwin.

Potter, William (ed.) (1990) *International Nuclear Trade and Nonproliferation: The Challenge of the Emerging Suppliers*, Lexington, MA: Lexington Books.

Preez, Juan du (2006) "Inventory of international nonproliferation organizations and regimes," Monterey, CA: Center for Nonproliferation Studies.

Rauchhaus, Robert (This Book) "Evaluating the nuclear peace hypothesis: a quantitative approach."

Rice, Condoleezza (2006) "The U.S.–India civilian nuclear cooperation agreement. Testimony before the Senate Foreign Relations Committee, Washington, D.C., April 5." Available at: www.state.gov/secretary/rm/2006/64136.htm.

Reiter, Dan (2001) "Does peace nurture democracy?," *Journal of Politics* 63(3): 935–948.

Sabrosky, Alan (1980) "Interstate alliances: their reliability and the expansion of war," in J. David Singer (ed.) *The Correlates of War II: Testing some Realpolitik Models*, New York: Free Press, pp. 161–198.

Sagan, Scott (1996/97) "Why do states build nuclear weapons? Three models in search of a bomb," *International Security* 21(3): 54–86.

Schweller, Randall (1994) "Bandwagoning for profit: bringing the revisionist state back in," *International Security* 19(1): 72–107.

Signorino, Curtis and Jeffrey Ritter (1999) "Tau-b or not tau-b: measuring the similarity of foreign policy positions," *International Studies Quarterly* 43(1): 115–144.

Singer, J. David, Stuart Bremer, and John Stuckey (1972) "Capability distribution, uncertainty, and major power war, 1820–1965," in Bruce Russett (ed.) *Peace, War, and Numbers*, Beverly Hills, CA: Sage.

Singh, Sonali and Christopher Way (2004) "The correlates of nuclear proliferation: a quantitative test," *Journal of Conflict Resolution* 48(6): 859–885.

Singh, Yogendra (2007) *India-Vietnam Relations: The Road Ahead*, New Delhi: Institute of Peace and Conflict Studies.

Skålnes, Lars (2000) *Politics, Markets, and Grand Strategy*, Ann Arbor, MI: University of Michigan Press.

Solingen, Etel (2007) *Nuclear Logics: Contrasting Paths in East Asia and the Middle East*, Princeton, NJ: Princeton University Press.

Sprecher, Christopher and Volker Krause (2006) "Alliances, armed conflict, and cooperation: theoretical approaches and empirical evidence," *Journal of Peace Research* 43(4): 363–369.

Thompson, William (2001) "Identifying rivals and rivalries in international politics," *International Studies Quarterly* 45(4): 557–586.

United States, National Security Council (1960) *U.S. Policy toward Japan. NSC 6008.* May 20.

Walt, Stephen (1987) *The Origins of Alliances*, Ithaca, NY: Cornell University Press.

Waltz, Kenneth (1979) *Theory of International Politics*, New York: McGraw-Hill.

Waltz, Kenneth and Scott Sagan (1995) *The Spread of Nuclear Weapons: A Debate*, New York: W.W. Norton.

Way, Christopher and Karthika Sasikumar (2007) "Leaders and laggards: when and why do countries sign the NPT?," Paper presented at the American Political Science Association, Chicago, August 29–September 2.

Williams, Joshua and Jon Wolfsthal (2005) "The NPT at 35: a crisis of compliance or a crisis of confidence," *UNA-USA Policy Brief* 7 (April 29). Available at: www.unausa.org/atf/cf/%7B49C555AC-20C8-4B43-8483-A2D4C1808E4E%7D/Policy%20Brief%20No%207.pdf.

6 A bargaining model of nuclear weapons

Development and disarmament[1]

Brett V. Benson and Quan Wen

Introduction

In a speech to the UN in September 2009, President Obama outlined the urgency of the threat of nuclear proliferation and made known his goal for a world free from nuclear weapons. As steps toward that goal, the US recently agreed to a disarmament deal with Russia, hosted an international nuclear-security summit to prevent nuclear material from falling into the hands of terrorist threats, and pushed for new United Nations sanctions against Iran's nuclear programs. Whether these efforts will actually stem the spread of nuclear weapons remains to be seen, but the widespread attention paid to these matters underscores the gravity of the general issue of nuclear proliferation.

Nuclear proliferation remains one of the gravest international security concerns. In the four decades since the Nuclear Nonproliferation Treaty (NPT) came into force in 1970, the number of nuclear capable states has grown. Many states, which currently do not possess nuclear weapons, aspired or attempted to acquire nuclear capability at some point. And, states have clashed militarily and diplomatically over weapons and nuclear programs. These facts lead us to ask why governments continue to develop nuclear weapons. An equally important question is why many states do not choose to develop weapons, since the number of nuclear capable states has increased by only four since the NPT.

Many efforts to contain proliferation have focused on controlling, containing, and reducing the spread of nuclear materials and knowledge. Signatories to the NPT commit to the peaceful use of nuclear technology subject to the standards of the International Atomic Energy Agency, which monitors nuclear facilities and tracks the development and flow of fissile material. Academic centers and independent organizations focus research and outreach efforts on improving information and spreading norms about such counter-proliferation efforts.[2] Additionally, recent scholarship that examines the effectiveness of counter-proliferation focuses on controlling the spread of materials and technology. These studies find that external cooperation and provision of sensitive nuclear technology and material is a strong determinant of states' decisions to develop nuclear weapons (see Kroenig, this volume; Fuhrmann, this volume).

Working to deny nuclear aspirants the material and know-how to arm themselves is one aspect of nuclear counter-proliferation. Another side is strategic denuclearization and bargaining. Thomas Schelling pointed out that "the emphasis has to shift from physical denial and technology secrecy to the things that determine incentives and expectations" (Schelling 1976: 30; quoted in Solingen 2007: 7). Governments determined to arm themselves have shown their ability to acquire nuclear weapons technology in spite of the NPT (e.g., North Korea, India, and Pakistan). Yet, many technically sophisticated governments have chosen not to weaponize (e.g., Japan and Germany). Some governments have decided to abandon programs midstream (e.g., South Korea, Taiwan, and Libya) or even after they have already developed weapons capability (e.g., South Africa). And, some governments have shielded their programs behind a wall of ambiguity (e.g., Israel and North Korea pre-test). To understand why these strategies are adopted and when they are more or less effective, it is important to examine aspirants' incentives.

It is also critical to analyze these decisions within the context of denuclearization strategies, which counter-proliferators formulate in environments of limited information. Since the introduction of the NPT, denuclearization efforts have mostly involved powerful nuclear powers (counter-proliferators) targeting relatively weaker aspiring nuclear powers (aspirants) to prevent them from acquiring weapons. Because aspirants typically do not cooperate with the NPT, weaponization efforts are generally not verifiable. Nor are counter-proliferators certain about the motives and potential threat posed by an aspirant should it achieve nuclear weapons. Under such conditions of limited information, counter-proliferators have, at various times, adopted a range of denuclearization strategies including direct military strikes, sanctions, diplomatic condemnation and pressure, and concessions. In addition to these strategies, counter-proliferators have also sometimes stood by and watched aspiring nuclear powers develop nuclear weapons without making any meaningful effort to counter. Aspirants respond to these various strategies differently, sometimes capitulating and sometimes pushing forward with their nuclear designs. In this chapter, we study the strategic interaction between counter-proliferators and aspirants. In particular, we focus on four specific questions. Why do aspirants choose to develop nuclear weapons? Under what conditions will counter-proliferators resort to military force to prevent aspirants from arming? Why do aspirants sometimes develop weapons ambiguously? And, when will counter-proliferators find it optimal to make concessions in exchange for cooperation?

To address these questions, we develop a two-player bargaining model. There are few formal theories of nuclear proliferation and counter-proliferation. Baliga and Sjostrom (2008) is a recent stand-out. This model shows that nuclear ambiguity gives aspirants security benefits without their actually having to develop a verifiable nuclear deterrent. Our model concentrates on the bargaining aspects of nuclear armament and disarmament, in order to determine whether nuclear ambiguity is a useful strategy for extracting concessions from counter-proliferators.

Our analysis shows decisions to arm depend on the presence of security threats or overriding interests in possessing nuclear weapons. These predictions are well supported in the empirical literature. We analyze two different counter-proliferation measures: preventative military strikes and concessions. Preventative military measures will be taken when counter-proliferators believe proliferators are highly motivated to possess nuclear weapons, they feel threatened by proliferation, and their costs for undertaking preventative military strikes are relatively low. In analyzing the preventative military option, we identify a nuclear security dilemma, in which nuclear aspirants arm in response to the fear they will be attacked, but counter-proliferators threaten to attack in order to prevent aspirants from becoming armed and dangerous. As an alternative to military measures, governments can also grant inducements in exchange for verifiable disarmament. Counter-proliferators will offer concessions to gain cooperation when nuclear aspirants' motivations for acquiring weapons are not so high that the bribe is not cost-efficient.

We first describe the set-up of the model. Then we analyze aspirants' decisions to arm themselves with nuclear weapons. Next, we discuss when counter-proliferators might find it optimal to attack nuclear aspirants. Finally, we examine an ambiguity equilibrium in which aspirants' unpredictable behavior results in counter-proliferators offering inducements in exchange for verifiable denuclearization. We illustrate the intuition of these results with examples.

The model

There are two governments, A, the counter-proliferator, and B, the aspirant. Government A is the more powerful of the two. Initially, B is not armed with nuclear weapons, and A is interested in persuading B not to arm. Government B can invest in nuclear weapons at a cost of $\kappa > 0$. We assume that B successfully acquires weapons if it chooses to arm. If it chooses not to arm, then it incurs no costs and it does not acquire nuclear weapons. Government A cannot observe B's decision to arm, and its uncertainty about whether B has or has not armed gets resolved at the end of the game.

Government A decides whether to attack B or to make an offer to B in exchange for giving up its weapons and allowing external verification. Since A is stronger, we assume it will win a war against B, but attacking is costly. Government A pays c_A if it attacks an armed B and attacking an unarmed B costs c_{NA}. Since attacking an unarmed opponent is less

Table 6.1 Payoffs if player A attacks B

B is armed	B is unarmed
$1 - c_A, \gamma - \kappa - \beta$	$1 - c_{NA}, -\beta$

dangerous, we assume $c_A > c_{NA} > 0$. It is better for B to have weapons if it is attacked, since it can use its advanced technology in a war. Thus, B gets a benefit γ if it is attacked when it is armed, and B always pays a cost β to fight a war regardless of whether it is armed. We assume that $\gamma > \kappa$, which implies that in war the benefits of having advanced weapons outweighs the costs of developing them. If A attacks, the game ends, and payoffs are as described in Table 6.1.

As an alternative to attack, A can make an offer x to convince B to give up its weapon and allow external verification that it is not armed. In practice, an offer might include security assurances, normalized diplomatic relations, peaceful nuclear capability, or direct monetary transfers. Once an offer is made, B can either accept or reject the offer. Rejecting means B retains weapons if it is armed, or it gets nothing if it is not armed. Developing and keeping weapons can provide leaders with many benefits. Several studies have discussed leaders' motivations for developing nuclear weapons. Reasons for weaponizing include deterrence, domestic pressures, international prestige (Sagan 1996/1997), regime type, domestic economic factors, and considerations of political survival (Solingen 2007). Additionally, states may develop weapons because they are valuable bargaining chips for achieving concessions from counter-proliferators. Whatever their motivations, governments arm because they perceive they can derive direct or instrumental value from having nuclear weapons. In developing a general theory, we do not focus on any specific motivating reason, but instead we concentrate on how intensely governments want nuclear weapons. All else equal, a government which has moderate deterrence concerns may be less likely to acquire nuclear weapons than a government which faces intense domestic pressures for political survival, and vice versa. Thus, prospective proliferators in our model differ according to how much utility they receive from successfully acquiring nuclear weapons. Accordingly, government B's value of keeping weapons if it rejects an offer is δ_t, where t denotes government B's type. The higher δ_t, the more B values having nuclear weapons for whatever reason.

Since our model analyzes the interaction between a government which appears to aspire to achieve nuclear weapons and another government which does not want the aspirant government to be armed, then it must be that government A suffers some cost if B develops and keeps weapons. This cost, represented by the parameter w_t, represents the amount of A's worry or its perceived level of threat from government B possessing nuclear

Table 6.2 Payoffs if player A makes an offer to B

armed B accepts	unarmed B accepts	armed B rejects	unarmed B rejects
$1 - x, x - \kappa$	$1 - x, x$	$1 - w_t, \delta_t - \kappa$	$1, 0$

weapons. Worry can be tied to several factors including the direct threat posed by an adversary possessing nuclear weapons, the threat to allies, and political concerns about the impact on one's influence as a result of shifts in relative power. For example, China's nuclear test in 1964 increased the USSR and India's worry about the direct nuclear threat posed by China while the United States worried more about China's threat to its East Asian allies and to its own relative influence in the region (Burr and Richelson 2000/2001). India worried that China's transfer of nuclear materials to Pakistan in the 1990s would both pose a direct threat to India and also reduce its influence in Southeast Asia (Perkovich 1999). Our argument attempts to capture the intuition that counter-arming strategies are a function of how much a government worries about the threat posed by another state having nuclear weapons. Therefore, in the model, government A suffers w_t if B arms and rejects an offer. If A makes an offer to B, then payoffs are as described in Table 6.2.

Among nuclear powers and those attempting to develop nuclear weapons, there is clear variation across both δ_t and w_t. Governments vary both in terms of how motivated they are to have nuclear weapons and how much of a threat they pose to other states. It is reasonable to assume that Japan had lower δ_t than China since the end of WWII. There is and has been strong public opposition to nuclear weapons in Japan, it formally adopted a resolution committing not to possess or tolerate nuclear weapons in its territory, and is shielded by the US security umbrella from many security threats (Berger 1993; Hughes 2007). By contrast, China, which tested nuclear weapons for three decades after its first test in 1964, was motivated by its aspirations of increasing its influence in the Communist bloc and the East Asia region, being admitted to the UN and achieving recognition as a great power, and securing its defense from both nuclear superpowers – the US and the USSR (Halperin 1965; Lewis and Xue 1988). India, like China and unlike Japan, is another government that could be said to have high δ_t during the decades leading up to its 1998 nuclear tests. In addition to having a nuclear neighbor in China on its north border and a nuclear aspirant rival in Pakistan on its northwestern border, India also was driven by nationalist aspirations to achieve major power status and to buck the nonproliferation regime, which it perceived to be an unfair vestige of Western colonialism (Perkovich 1999).

There are also meaningful differences between the amount of threat posed by different states possessing nuclear weapons, which is the parameter

w_t for government A's worry or its perceived threat from an armed B. For example, it is reasonable to assume Israel is relatively unthreatened by North Korea having weapons, but it clearly believes a nuclear Iran is dangerous for its own security. Therefore, in interpreting the parameters in the model, aspirants like China or India have higher δ_t than Japan, and Israel would suffer higher w_t if Iran acquires nuclear weapons than if North Korea arms.

Government A does not know B's benefits from arming. Accordingly, government B has two possible types: motivated (type Z) or normal (type N). We call a government "motivated" if it is strongly motivated to acquire nuclear weapons. Government B has a prior probability p_Z of being motivated, and it is normal with probability $1 - p_Z$. Both governments' payoffs depend on B's type. A motivated type B derives more benefit from nuclear weapons than a normal type, and government A only worries if a motivated type has weapons since a normal type does not pose a threat. Thus, we make the following assumptions: $\delta_Z > \delta_N = 0$ and $w_Z > w_N = 0$. Table 6.3 summarizes these assumptions.

To summarize, we consider the following game of incomplete information, which is depicted in Figure 6.1:

1   Nature determines the type of B, Pr $(t = Z) = p_Z$ and Pr $(t = N) = p_N = 1 - p_Z$.
2   After knowing its type, B chooses to arm (at cost $\kappa > 0$) or not to arm (at no cost).
3   A does not observe B's type and action, A may either attack or offer some x to B.
   3.1 If A attacks, the game ends.
   3.2 If A offers x, B may accept or reject.

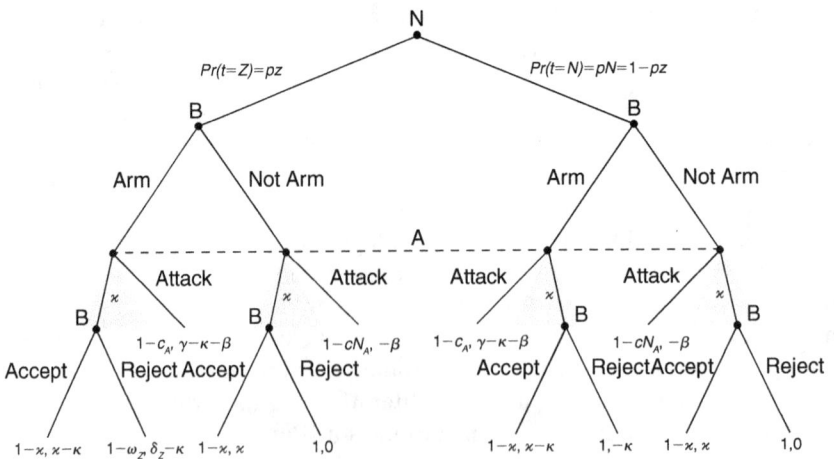

Figure 6.1 Nuclear bargaining game.

Table 6.3 Assumptions on parameters

A's parameters	B's parameters
$c_A > c_{NA} > 0$	$\delta_Z > \delta_N = 0$
$\delta_Z > \delta_N = 0$	$\gamma > \kappa > 0$

Developing nuclear weapons

In this section, we address the question about why governments choose to develop nuclear weapons. We can evaluate this problem by analyzing the pure strategy Nash equilibria of the bargaining game. There are three pure strategy equilibria. For simplicity, we label these equilibria: WAR, PEACE, and WMD. Formally, we have the following:

Proposition 1 *There are three possible types of pure strategy equilibria.*
1 *(WAR) There is a pure strategy equilibrium where both types arm and* A *attacks when* $c_A \leq \min\{p_Z w_Z, \delta_Z\}$, *i.e.,*

$$w_Z \geq c_A / p_Z \text{ and } \delta_Z \geq c_A \tag{1}$$

2 *(PEACE) There is a pure strategy equilibrium in which neither type arms, and* A *does not attack but also does not offer anything when* $\delta_Z \leq \kappa$.
3 *(WMD) There is a pure strategy equilibrium in which the motivated type arms while the normal type does not, and* A *does not attack but does not offer anything when*

$$w_Z \leq c^E / p_Z \text{ and } \delta_Z \geq \max\{p_Z w_Z, \kappa\}, \tag{2}$$

where $c^E = p_Z c_A + p_N c_{NA}$.

Proof. In Appendix. **QED**

These three pure strategy equilibria are illustrated in Figure 6.2 where *B*'s investment costs are greater than *A*'s war costs ($\kappa > c_A$). The WAR equilibrium occurs when the probability *B* is a motivated type is high, a motivated type's value for having nuclear weapons capability is high, and *A*'s worry about a motivated type having weapons is also high. In this equilibrium, both types of *B* will arm, because *B* expects *A* to attack. In the PEACE equilibrium, neither type of *B* arms and, consequently, *A* has no reason to attack. As can be seen in Figure 6.2, this equilibrium obtains when a motivated type's value for possessing nuclear weapons capability is lower than its costs for investing in them. The WMD equilibrium is a separating equilibrium, in which a motivated type arms, because its value for possessing a nuclear weapons capability is high. However, a normal type does not arm, because *A*'s belief and worry that *B* is a motivated type are low enough that it will not attack.

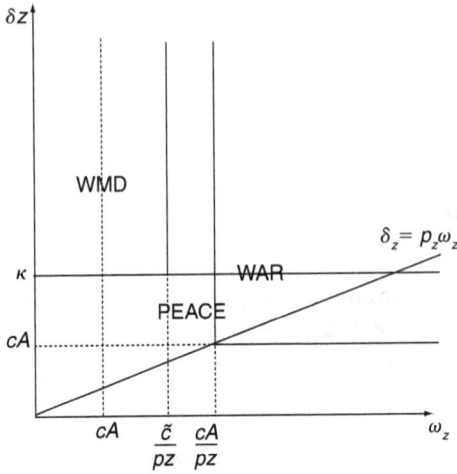

Figure 6.2 Pure strategy Nash equilibria.

Two implications are worth highlighting in greater detail. First, even though we have introduced a bargaining move to the model, there is not a pure strategy equilibrium in which government A offers positive concessions to B. Notice that armed B accepts A's offer if and only if $x \geq \delta_b$ and unarmed B accepts any offer $x \geq 0$. Since $\delta_z = 0$, government A does not make a positive offer to a normal type and offers an inducement $x \geq \delta_t$ only if it believes B is a motivated type. However, if A is going to make an offer, B is better off avoiding investment costs by not arming. But if B does not arm, then A offers nothing. Therefore, government A never offers concessions in pure strategy equilibrium. As a result, for aspirants, arming with certainty for the sake of extorting benefits from concerned counterproliferators in exchange for verifiable disarmament is not an equilibrium strategy. As we show below, government A is more likely to offer concessions when it is uncertain about B's decision to arm.

Second, the model identifies a nuclear security dilemma. A motivated type B will always arm if its value for possessing nuclear weapons is sufficiently high relative to its costs for investing in weapons. Otherwise, under peaceful circumstances, arming is too costly. However, a motivated type with higher investment costs than value for nuclear weapons will nevertheless arm if it believes A is likely to attack. A normal type government B does not have an incentive to arm in pure strategies *unless* it believes A is going to attack, in which case it is always better for B to arm. Hence, all types of aspirant government B will develop nuclear weapons when they expect government A to attack. Yet, the A in our model is not inherently aggressive. It will only attack if it believes B is motivated and it worries that

B having weapons is dangerous. Otherwise, it will not attack if it is certain *B* is a normal type or if it is not worried about a motivated type having nuclear weapons. Therefore, *A* attacks when it perceives *B* is likely to be armed and dangerous, and *B* arms when *B* fears *A* is going to attack.

This finding implies that nuclear weapons development pays when governments feel sufficiently threatened that having advanced weapons technology will benefit them in a war. Since *B* arms no matter what when *A* is a threat and *A* is a threat when it believes *B* is a threat, then rivalries should be strong empirical determinants of nuclear proliferation. This result is strongly supported in the quantitative literature. Singh and Way (2004) find that factors related to the external security environment are associated with states' decisions to acquire weapons. Participation in ongoing rivalries and the frequency of militarized disputes in the five years prior to acquisition strongly correlate with weapons development and acquisition. The analysis in Kroenig (this book) is consistent. Since *A* is more likely to attack and therefore threaten *B* when its costs for fighting are low, we should expect proliferation to be especially likely among states facing stronger powers. Jo and Gartzke (2007) show that states facing threats from states with significant conventional weaponry is the strongest determinant of nuclear proliferation. Interestingly, states facing nuclear powers are less likely to develop weapons. Nevertheless, the general prediction that states in threatening security environments are more likely to develop nuclear weapons is, therefore, relatively uncontroversial in the literature. Somewhat related is the finding in Fuhrmann (this book) that prospective proliferators are more likely to get support for their nuclear programs when they have a superpower enemy and their supplier shares that enemy. Common enemies often pose common security threats, and cooperation on nuclear development can neutralize the common threat both for the supplier and the recipient of nuclear cooperation.

In addition to these noteworthy points, the results described in Proposition 1 (Appendix) also explain other stylized facts about nuclear proliferation. The PEACE and WMD equilibria straightforwardly establish that unthreatened aspirants will not arm when the costs outweigh the benefits, but motivated types will arm when the benefits of weapons outweigh development costs even when they expect *A* is not a threat to their security. The majority of the quantitative empirical literature is devoted to testing this basic prediction. Scholars have argued that many factors increase an aspirant's benefit from nuclear weapons. Gartzke and Jo (this book) test a number of these claims. They find that democracies, which presumably create more pressure for leaders to acquire weapons, are more likely to acquire weapons once they have begun a nuclear program. The analysis also shows that major powers and regional powers are more likely to have weapons, which lends some support to the argument that governments' motivations for international prestige can drive them to proliferate. Factors that reduce the benefits from weapons include NPT membership and having a defense pact with a nuclear defender. In most cases, signing the NPT likely signals a government's lack of interest in weapons technology, and having a nuclear defender provides many benefits of nuclear weapons without governments actually having to incur the costs of development.

Of course, the other side of equation impacting decisions to proliferate contains the costs of development. Factors that reduce development costs include the wealth or economic capacity of a country and whether the country's industrial capacity to support a nuclear program includes domestically produced steel, electricity, uranium deposits, scientific experts, etc. When these cost-saving advantages are present, a government is more likely to develop nuclear weapons (Singh and Way 2004; Gartzke and Jo, this volume; Kroenig, this volume). As Kroenig (this book) shows, governments that have external suppliers who provide them with sensitive nuclear materials are dramatically more likely to proliferate. Not only does nuclear aid increase proliferation, but so does external assistance and cooperation (Fuhrmann, this volume). These short cuts to development provide a significant reduction in costs for aspirants and, therefore, increase their willingness to arm.

Preventative military strikes

The pure strategy equilibria also enable us to draw some conclusions about when we might expect a counter-proliferator to attack a nuclear aspirant. Consider why a counter-proliferator might allow an aspirant to acquire weapons. Condition (2) of the WMD equilibrium (Appendix) implies counter-proliferators will stand by and allow nuclear aspirants to acquire weapons for one of a few possible reasons. First, the costs of bribing aspirants with inducements to give up an incipient weapons program are too high (since aspirants are highly motivated to possess the weapons). Second, counter-proliferators' expected costs for striking and fighting against a motivated type are higher than their worry of allowing a motivated type to possess the weapon. Third, counter-proliferators do not believe the target state is a motivated type of aspirant. When these conditions fail to obtain, then A's decision to attack B to remove its weapons forcibly becomes an option. We should expect to observe strikes by counter-proliferators on aspirants when counter-proliferators believe B is a motivated type, A's threat from an armed motivated type is high, and A's costs for striking B are relatively low.

Arguments to use preventative military force to remove nuclear weapons or to halt their development have been framed in terms of these conditions. For example, at the present time, there is a debate about whether Israel will strike Iran to eliminate its nuclear program. Israel has resorted to military force before, wiping out Iraq's nuclear reactor in Osirak in 1981 and striking a nuclear reactor in Syria in 2007.

Former Israeli Defense Minister, Brigadier General Ephraim Sneh (2010) summarized the factors which will affect Israel's decision, and the calculation roughly tracks the equilibrium conditions for preventative strikes. In an op-ed piece in the Israeli left-wing daily, *Haaretz*, Sneh argues that disarming Iran is urgent for Israeli security, military strikes on Iran would "cripple [Iran's] nuclear project for a number of years," and "the retaliation against Israel would be painful, but bearable." Sneh's key point is that he believes Iran will soon be armed, a weaponized Iran is a significant threat to Israel, and the costs to Israel of attacking Iran are relatively low. This leads Sneh to conclude that, barring a change in these factors, Israel will likely attempt to remove forcibly Iran's nuclear program. Raas and Long lend some support to this conclusion. In a comparison of Israel's attack on Osirak in 1981 and a potential strike against Iran today, they conclude that even though Iran's nuclear sites are more difficult to attack than the reactor at Osirak, Israeli forces have improved since 1981 to the point that "The operation would appear to be no more risky than Israel's 1981 attack on Iraq's Osirak reactor, and it would provide at least as much benefit in terms of delaying Iranian development of nuclear weapons" (Raas and Long 2007: 24). If this assessment is correct, then the results of the model suggest Israel's threat to attack Iran is a definite possibility that depends on how costly a preventative war with Iran would be.

Levy (2008) argues that states' decisions to undertake preventative attacks are not as constrained by normative inhibitions or democratic institutions as once supposed. Instead, such decisions hinge on the kind of cost-benefit calculation we identify. According to Levy, the US decisions to attack in the 1990–1991 Persian Gulf War and 2003 Iraq War were built on public support for eliminating Iraq's threat of nuclear weapons. However, sometimes the costs of preventative strikes are too high, and counter-proliferators will decide against attacking after assessing the costs. During the 1993–1994 crises over North Korea's nuclear weapons, President Bill Clinton weighed the option of launching air strikes against North Korea's nuclear reactor at Yongbyon. Administration officials estimated the war would result in "52,000 US troops killed or wounded, 490,000 Republic of Korea military casualties, 'enormous' numbers of North Korean and civilian deaths, and a $61 billion cost, mostly to be paid by the US" (Levy 2008: 18; Oberdorfer 1997: 315; Sigal 1997: 211–212). This price was too high to pay, especially in contrast to the costs of the alternative strategy, which was to offer the inducements layed out in the 1994 Agreed Framework.

The United States made a similar calculation when deciding whether to attack China's nuclear weapons program in the early 1960s. Ultimately, the US decided against launching preventative strikes. However, the Kennedy administration seriously considered striking Chinese nuclear reactors at Lopnur and Lanzhou, and even explored a cost-sharing arrangement with the Soviet Union (Chang 1988). The US decision ultimately turned on those factors we identify. Initially, Kennedy ranked the prospect of China acquiring nuclear weapons among the gravest of US security concerns, calling it "intolerable" (Burr and Richelson 2000/2001: 96). The Kennedy administration ordered reports to determine the extent of China's threat to the US and the costs of preventative strikes. Both the Kennedy and Johnson administrations stepped up intelligence gathering efforts and weighed the available evidence prior to China's first test of a nuclear device in 1964. There was widespread agreement that the US would suffer psychological and political costs if China armed. In particular, China would increase its regional influence at the cost of US influence and would gain bargaining leverage with other countries. Leaders in the US also worried nuclear weapons in China might encourage India and Japan to counter with nuclear programs of their own, but they estimated such problems could be offset by increasing US assurances to their allies in the region (Burr and Richelson 2000/2001: 77). Moreover, analysts believed that the direct military threat to US security interests was low because of the asymmetry between the US and China's military capabilities. Consequently, the revised bottom line assessment concluded that China having nuclear weapons would be a set-back but not intolerable (Burr and Richelson 2000/2001: 97).

At the same time, the US government determined that the costs of a preventative action against China were high – too high, in fact, unless they could share costs with interested partners. Costs of a military strike included the complexity of an air attack deep into China, the infeasibility of a ground attack, and the compounding problem of uncertainty about the location of all of China's nuclear locations. Add to this the potential opprobrium of the international community and the possibility of Chinese retaliation against allies. To reduce the costs of preventative strikes, the US explored the possibility of joint strikes against China with the USSR (Chang 1988; Burr and Richelson 2000/2001). Decision-makers in Washington reasoned that partnering with the USSR would reduce its own costs by coordinating military efforts and eliminating international backlash. The USSR rebuffed US overtures, arguing that it believed nuclear weapons would only give China regional psychological and political benefits, neither of which adversely affected the USSR (Burr and Richelson 2000/2001: 67–70).

The US also explored the possibility of teaming with the Chinese Nationalists (Burr and Richelson 2000/2001: 72). According to the plan, the US would transport Nationalist forces from Taiwan to nuclear targets on the mainland. However, after careful consideration, Washington calculated it would be impossible to deny US involvement, and, therefore, concluded becoming involved with Chiang Kaishek in an offensive attack on China's mainland did not provide the US a sufficiently high savings in its own costs. Without a way to reduce the downsides of a preventative strike against China, the US decided to live with a nuclear China.

Ambiguous development and inducements

We now address the questions of why aspirants sometimes develop nuclear weapons ambiguously and why counter-proliferators sometimes offer inducements to ambiguous aspirants. There are several examples of ambiguous nuclear programs. Israel deliberately maintains ambiguity about its program. North Korea was ambiguous in the two decades prior to demonstrating its capability in its 2006 test of a nuclear device. The current status of Iran's nuclear program bears some similarity to North Korea during the 1990s. Iran has reportedly resumed and suspended its enrichment activities on again and off again since the early 2000s, and refuses to cooperate with the International Atomic Energy Agency to clarify the status of its programs. In 2006, US intelligence estimated Iran would have nuclear weapons capability within five to ten years (Sagan 2006). Latest US assessments estimate Iran will have weapons grade uranium within one year and the capability of assembling a nuclear weapon within two to five years (Sanger 2010). South Africa secretly developed nuclear weapons in the 1980s. Prior to India's nuclear tests in 1998, a debate raged about whether India should abandon two decades of nuclear ambiguity, along with its benefits, in exchange for the power and respect of being a transparent nuclear power (Perkovich 1999: 369). Michael Schrage (2003) claims Saddam Hussein "deliberately created ambiguity regarding the true nature of his regime's weapons programs" to deter his immediate threats (Kurds, Iranians, and Saudis) while simultaneously avoiding the ire of the West. As long as external verification of aspirants' nuclear programs is not possible, counter-proliferators are stuck formulating beliefs based upon best available information.

Baliga and Sjostrom (2008: 1025) refer to nuclear ambiguity as "deterrence by doubt." In their model, ambiguity obtains when aspirants refuse to allow weapons inspections, and they arm with some positive probability. They find that an equilibrium exists in which prospective aspirants will never permit inspections, which reduces incentives to proliferate. Ambiguity can deter aggression if there is a sufficiently high probability that the aspirant is really armed but not so high that it will insist on inspections.

Our model introduces a bargaining move and demonstrates that ambiguous aspirants can gain bargaining concessions from counter-proliferators as inducements for aspirants to submit to verifiable denuclearization. In our model, arming decisions are already unverifiable. We further refer to arming decisions as ambiguous if aspirants arm with mixed strategies. A player's mixed strategy affects its opponent's beliefs about which pure strategy it will choose. This yields an intuitive interpretation when thinking about decisions to arm with nuclear weapons. If an aspirant mixes its strategies, then the counter-proliferator is not entirely certain whether the aspirant arms. It believes the aspirant both arms and does not arm with positive probability.

Our model demonstrates two different sets of circumstances under which aspirants will be ambiguous about arming. First, an aspirant may develop ambiguously to extract concessions from the counter-proliferator. We pointed out above that government A will not offer concessions when B arms with certainty. However, when the aspirant develops ambiguously, offering an inducement to disarm verifiably can be better for the counter-proliferator than fighting a war with a potentially armed aspirant or living with the relatively high worry that the aspirant may be armed and dangerous. The formal conditions for this equilibrium that we label OFFER in Figure 6.3 are defined and proved in Proposition 4 in the Appendix. The second possible ambiguity outcome, which we refer to as NO OFFER in Figure 6.3, occurs when an aspirant expects the counter-proliferator might attack even if there is no chance the counter-proliferator will offer a concession. Corresponding conditions and proofs can be found in Propositions 5 and 7 in the Appendix.

Let us take a closer look at each equilibrium in turn. In the OFFER equilibrium, both types of government B will mix between arming and not arming and government A will mix between attacking and providing a concession in the amount of $\delta_z > 0$. This is the only equilibrium in the model in which A will offer concessions to B, which implies B's ambiguity is critical for extracting concessions. Why is this the case? Suppose the condition $\delta_z \leq p_z \, w_z$ is violated (see Proposition 4 in the Appendix). Then either a motivated type government B has high utility for arming, in which case A will have to increase the size of its concession to prevent a motivated type from arming with certainty, or the expected threat from a motivated type is low, which makes it more tolerable for A to live with an armed

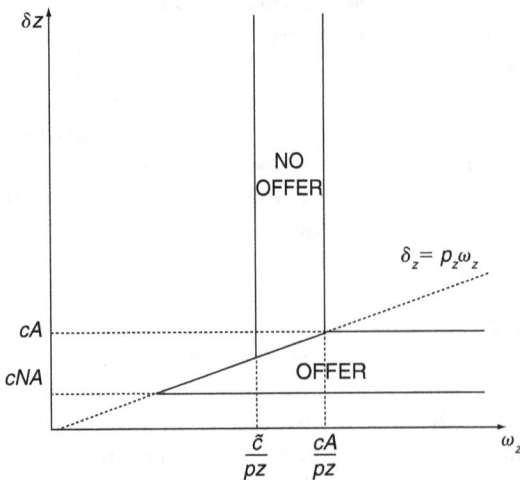

Figure 6.3 Ambiguity equilibria.

state B. If δ_Z is too high, it is not worthwhile for A to make any concessions at all. Both types would accept δ_Z, but A knows a normal type will accept nothing. Thus, if the expected threat of a motivated type is low (either because it is unlikely B is motivated or A's worry is low), then an offer of δ_Z is sub-optimal. In this case, a normal type will not arm with certainty because incurring the cost of investing in nuclear weapons is not worth getting nothing from A in return.

On the other hand, if δ_Z and w_Z are both high, so much so that $\delta_Z \geq c_A$ (thus violating the other condition of Proposition 4), then it is better for A to attack for sure instead of making such a large concession. Because the costs of concessions outweigh the costs of fighting with an armed B, A will attack, and, as we know from Proposition 1, when A attacks in pure strategies, both types of government B will arm. Therefore, regardless of B's type, being ambiguous about its nuclear program is only an effective bargaining chip if the likelihood of B being a motivated type is sufficiently high, a motivated type's benefits from having weapons are also not too high, and A's costs of striking B are relatively high. Normal type B states can seize on A's belief that B is likely motivated and pool on motivated government's type. Thus, strategic nuclear ambiguity occurs as a result of A both not being able to observe and verify B's action and its inability to distinguish between types in a mixed strategy equilibrium.

In the NO OFFER zone, government B will mix between arming and not arming, and government A will mix between attacking and offering B nothing. This follows when δ_Z is high. Concessions sufficiently high to induce B to abandon its weapons and submit to inspections are too expensive to make to a motivated type, and, therefore, a motivated type will reject any offer it gets. Note that for such high values of δ_Z, government A will live with the threat of an armed motivated government B when its worry w_Z is relatively low (WMD pure strategy equilibrium), which means A ignores B and normal types B are better off not incurring investment costs to arm. On the other hand, government A will attack if w_Z is sufficiently high (WAR pure strategy equilibrium), in which case it is better for normal types B to arm and defend themselves. For intermediate values of w_Z, where $c^E/p_Z \leq w_Z \leq c_A/p_Z$, government A is in between pure strategy equilibria. In this range, B's threat is moderate and the probability that B is a motivated type is relatively low. If A attacks for certain instead of mixing, then even normal types B will arm. Since there is a relatively good chance B is a normal type, then attacking with certainty makes A worse off than attacking with some positive probability. Yet, w_Z is not so low that A can forget about B altogether. Therefore, B mixes between attacking and offering nothing.

As can be seen by the diagonal line in Figure 6.3, a key distinction between the OFFER and NO OFFER outcomes is the relative values of δ_Z and $p_Z w_Z$. Suppose a counter-proliferator has the same level of worry for two different aspirants, both of whom share the same high probability of being a motivated type. If one of the aspirants values weapons more than the other, then the aspirant with the higher value of weapons could lie above the diagonal line while the other falls below it. The counter-proliferator will not concede an inducement to the aspirant above the line, but will make an offer to the one below. At the same level of worry and probability of being a motivated type, counter-proliferators are more likely to make offers to aspirants with lower values of possessing nuclear weapons. If δ_z is too high, then it becomes cost-prohibitive for a counter-proliferator to buy off the aspirant.

Now consider a scenario in which two aspirants, both of whom are equally likely to be a motivated type, have the same value for possessing nuclear weapons. One may lie above the diagonal line and the other beneath if the one beneath causes the counter-proliferator to worry more about the threat of allowing it to possess weapons. When the other parameters are fixed, higher levels of worry can result in a higher likelihood that an ambiguous aspirant gets awarded an inducement from the counter-proliferator.

Israel's policy of deliberate ambiguity about its nuclear program is a good example of a government in the NO OFFER zone, and uncertainty about North Korea's nuclear program prior to its nuclear test in 2006 nicely illustrates the OFFER equilibrium. For most counter-proliferators, especially the United States, Israel has been at least as motivated as North Korea to possess nuclear weapons, but the threat of nuclear weapons in North Korea's hands has always been more worrying. This suggests that a counter-proliferator like the US is more likely to offer inducements for verifiable disarmament to North Korea than Israel. As we discuss below, the US bargained with North Korea in an effort to end its weapons program and allow weapons inspections. By contrast, the US has not done the same with Israel. In fact, in a July 2010 meeting between US President Obama and Israeli Prime Minister Benjamin Netanyahu, Obama seemed to offer support to Israel's nuclear ambiguity, stating that Israel has "unique security requirements."[3] Israel's nuclear ambiguity deters prospective aggressors, since the probability of Israel possessing weapons is itself a deterrent. It also minimizes the chances for a regional arms race, which could result if it clarified its capability with a nuclear test. Finally, ambiguity gives Israel the advantage of avoiding international oversight of its nuclear programs, which obligation would follow should it join the NPT. Therefore, having a nuclear ambiguous program meets Israel's security needs, and counter-proliferators like the US, who have relatively low worry about Israel's motivations, do not have an incentive to pay the cost of inducements to get Israel to disarm.

On the other hand, nuclear ambiguity was an effective means for North Korea to extract concessions from counter-proliferators. While we know that North Korea partially detonated a nuclear device in 2006, there was a great deal of uncertainty about its nuclear intentions and the critical details of its enrichment activities during the time period prior to its test. North Korea's path to nuclear weapons was bumpy, and its signals along the way were unpredictable and confusing. It originally resisted joining the NPT, and then finally signed on in 1985. It resisted a safeguards agreement until 1992. It then announced its intention to quit the NPT in 1993, but then agreed to the 1994 Agreed Framework, in which the US offered substantial inducements in exchange for verifiable disarmament. The Agreed Framework collapsed in 2002, and North Korea kicked IAEA inspectors out and withdrew from the NPT. North Korea signed and reneged on other nuclear agreements too, including the 1991 Joint Declaration on the Denuclearization of the Korean Peninsula. Its mixed rhetoric was equally confusing. Sometimes it threatened to unleash a "sea of fire" against the United States, and at other times it has promised cooperation. For example, on September 19, 2005 North Korea agreed to give up its entire nuclear program and the US promised not to attack it. The following day, North Korea announced that it would not give up its nuclear program unless the US provided two light-water nuclear reactors. North Korea at various times denied weaponization and, in the next moment, claimed to possess or to be developing weapons (Saunders 2003; Lewis 2010). North Korea's erratic behavior has led scholars to question whether Kim Jung-il might be crazy (Cha and Kang 2003) or psychotic (Coolidge and Segal 2009). His apparent drive to develop a weapon and unpredictable behavior (neither consistently confirming nor denying having a weapons program) earned him a reputation for being random and caused uncertainty about his nuclear weapons program. Consistent with the predictions of the model, the US met North Korea's ambiguity with offers of concessions.

Scholars and policy-makers have debated about whether North Korea deliberately used its insipient nuclear program as a bargaining chip to exploit concessions from counter-proliferators (Saunders 2003). Historically, its demands have included more than just security guarantees. In fact, compared to contemporary fellow aspirants, who chose to abandon their nuclear weapons programs (e.g., Taiwan and South Korea), North Korea may have had relatively less need to develop a nuclear deterrent (Solingen 2007; Mitchell 2004). Yet, North Korea's program has given it extraordinary leverage to extract concessions from other governments both during the Kim Il-Song and Kim Jong-Il eras. North Korea routinely exported unconventional military technologies in exchange for oil, and made a deal with the Soviet Union in 1985 to sign the NPT in exchange for the Soviet Union giving North Korea a nuclear power plant and increased economic cooperation (Solingen 2007: 129). North Korea still held out on the IAEA safeguards agreement, so the US offered "the withdrawal of US tactical nuclear weapons from South Korea; suspension of the annual US–Republic of Korea military exercise, Team Spirit, in 1992; and a one-time diplomatic exchange with the North in New York in

January 1992" (Mazarr 1995: 95). The IAEA discovered inconsistencies with North Korea's program and demanded "special inspections" in 1993. North Korea threatened to withdraw from the NPT, and the US and North Korea cut another deal in the 1994 Agreed Framework which included a US promise not to use nuclear weapons against the North, improve diplomatic relations, two light-water nuclear reactors, and shipments of oil to North Korea in exchange for a freeze on North Korea's weapons program and unimpeded weapons inspections. After that deal fell apart in 2002, North Korea withdrew from the NPT and eventually tested a nuclear weapon. Victor Cha (2009), Director for Asian Affairs at the White House NSC from 2004–2007 and Deputy Chief of the US delegation to the six party talks on North Korea, claimed North Korea's strategy was to gain "energy and economic assistance, normalized relations with the US and a treaty ending the Korean War" as well as an agreement that permits North Korea to retain some nuclear power. Where nuclear disarmament has global currency, it appears that the threat of nuclear weaponization can serve as an effective bargaining instrument.

A comparison with India's nuclear program and the US response is illustrative. India's nuclear weapons program was also ambiguous prior to its test in 1998. While the US was bargaining and cutting deals with North Korea during the early to mid-1990s, the US apparently never offered any inducements to India during the same time period (Perkovich 1999: 345, 438). The US tried to pressure India not to test a nuclear weapon and signaled its preparedness to accept India's de facto nuclear program as long as the exact status of that program remained unverified (Perkovich 1999: 343). What accounts for the difference in US strategies towards North Korea and India prior to their nuclear tests? The differences can be seen by comparing the equilibria. In both the OFFER and NO OFFER scenarios, the probability the counter-proliferator attacks depends on the values of κ and γ. Government A attacks B with probability $q_A = \kappa/\gamma$, which implies that when B is ambiguous, the likelihood of A attacking increases the higher B's costs of investment in nuclear technology and the lower its benefits from using advanced weapons in a war with A. The lower the costs of investment and higher B's benefits from using advanced weapons, the more likely A will make concessions if it is in the OFFER equilibrium or offer nothing if it is in the NO OFFER equilibrium. By the 1990s, it is safe to assume India's costs of developing weapons were extremely low. US intelligence estimated it already possessed enough "weapon-grade fissile material for twenty to twenty-five nuclear weapons, several of which it could 'assemble within a few days' and deliver by aircraft" (Perkovich 1999: 340). Consequently, the probability the US would actually attack India was also low as to be a non-factor. However, the US also did not want to offer inducements to India, because it worried relatively little about the threat of India possessing nuclear weapons and India was highly motivated to possess weapons. In this respect, India and Israel are similar cases. By contrast, as we have seen, the US gave serious consideration to attacking North Korea, but instead offered inducements.

Why did the US offer nothing to India instead of offering it some positive inducement, and why did the US offer inducements to North Korea instead of just ignoring North Korea? India fits the NO OFFER equilibrium well. Like Israel, it stood to benefit a great deal from having weapons, because of the combination of threats from neighbors China and Pakistan. In India's case, it was also strongly motivated by nationalistic motivations to be on par with other nuclear states. Consequently, it had high δ_Z – so high that it was more cost-efficient for the US to attempt to freeze India's program than to try to roll it back with inducements. It also was less of a threat to the US than North Korea (lower w_Z). On the other hand, North Korea fits the OFFER equilibrium: the US was relatively worried about North Korea (higher w_Z), perceived that North Korea would accept an inducement, and found inducements to be cost-efficient because North Korea was not as motivated as India to keep nuclear weapons (δ_Z not too high).

Discussion

In this chapter, we develop a two-person bargaining model to understand why states develop nuclear weapons and why they sometimes do so ambiguously. We also analyze the model to understand when counter-proliferators will use preventative strikes versus inducements to prevent and disable insipient nuclear weapons programs. The results of the model show that a nuclear security dilemma is in play: aspirants arm when they think they are going to be attacked or when their benefits for possessing nuclear weapons outweigh the costs of development regardless of whether they face any serious security threats, and counter-proliferators attack aspirants when they believe aspirants are motivated types, their level of threat from an armed motivated type is high, and their costs for attacking the aspirant is relatively low.

We also show that ambiguous development can be an effective policy for extracting concessions from concerned counter-proliferators. Whether counter-proliferators offer inducements depend on how much motivated types want to keep nuclear weapons. In equilibrium, the probability counter-proliferators offer inducements depends on the costs to the aspirant of investing in weapons relative to its benefits of having weapons in a war. The less expensive aspirants' investment costs, the more likely counter-proliferators will make concessions to it. However, strategic ambiguity is not an effective strategy for gaining concessions when the benefit to the aspirant of acquiring weapons is high. When this is the case, then counter-proliferators may attack with certainty, offer nothing, or mix between these options depending on how much it worries about the aspirant's weapons threat.

The bargaining model we have developed is a useful baseline model to begin thinking about bargaining over nuclear weapons. The model can be extended in many different directions to advance our theoretical understanding of different aspects of nuclear bargaining. One promising direction would be to study the effects of verifiable arming on proliferation and counter-proliferation. In the current model, the counter-proliferator cannot observe B's move to arm, because there are no weapons inspections or other verification mechanisms. The model could be extended to include actions which are verifiable either because the aspirant permits weapons inspections or because it tests a nuclear weapon. The model could also be extended to evaluate the inclusion of sanctions as a possible counter-proliferation strategy. Sanctions accompany many decisions targeting nuclear aspirants, yet little is known about the reasons or effectiveness for such strategies. Other promising avenues include analyzing multilateral bargaining. North Korea preferred bilateral talks while the US preferred six-party talks. What affects governments' decisions to press for different negotiation environments? Also, how does uncertainty about the counter-proliferator's preferences affect bargaining? Finally, are democracies more vulnerable to making concessions in nuclear bargaining than autocracies because democratic audiences have higher worry?

Appendix

Proof of Proposition 1: We now verify each of these three possible pure strategy equilibria.

Case 1: Because A attacks, it is optimal for both types to arm due to $\gamma > \kappa$, which implies $\gamma - \kappa - \beta > - \beta$. It is straightforward that under the two inequality conditions of (1),

$$1 - c_A \geq \max\{1 - p_Z w_Z, 1 - \delta_Z\},$$

which implies that it is also optimal for A to attack.

Case 2: If neither type arms, it is optimal for A not to attack and not to offer anything because unarmed B accepts any $x \geq 0$. Note that both types prefer not to arm because of the high cost of investing in WMD, $\delta_N < \delta_Z \leq \kappa$.

Case 3: Given A's strategy, it is optimal for the motivated type to arm when $\delta_Z > \kappa$ by (2). The normal type does not arm due to $\kappa > 0 = \delta_N$. On the other hand, the two inequalities in (2) imply $1 - p_Z w_Z \geq \max\{p_Z(1 - c_A) + p_N(1 - c_{NA}), 1 - \delta_Z\}$, which means that A should offer $x = 0$, not attack, and not offer $\delta_Z > 0$. **QED**

Observe that $c^E = p_Z c_A + p_N c_{NA}$ in (c_{NA}, c_A) implies that $c_{NA}/p_Z < c^E/p_Z < c_A/p_Z$, and $c^E = p_Z c_A + p_N c_{NA} < p_Z c_A$ implies that $c_A < c^E/p_Z$.

Two remarks:
1 When $\kappa > c_A$, WAR and PEACE may coexist, as illustrated above.
2 When $\kappa \leq c_A$, these three types of equilibria generally do not coexist (except on a set of measure zero).

Now we argue that there is no other pure strategy equilibrium.
*   If the normal type arms but the motivated type does not, then country A would still offer $x = 0$. Then the normal type will not arm.
*   If both types arm and A offers 0, then the normal type will prefer not to arm.
*   If both types arm and A offers δ_Z, then both types will accept and will not arm (this is also the case even if A knows that B is motivated).

1 If A attacks, A's payoff will be

$$(p_Z\pi_Z + p_N\pi_N)(1 - c_A) + (1 - p_Z\pi_Z - p_N\pi_N)(1 - c_{NA}) =$$
$$1 - [(p_Z\pi_Z + p_N\pi_N)c_A + (1 - p_Z\pi_Z - p_N\pi_N)c_{NA}] = 1 - c^*.$$

2 If A offers x in $[0, \delta_Z) = [\delta_N, \delta_Z)$, only armed motivated type rejects and A's payoff is $p_Z\pi_Z(1 - w_Z) + (1 - w_Z)(1 - x) \leq p_Z\pi_Z(1 - w_Z) + (1 - p_Zw_Z) = 1 - p_Z\pi_Zw_Z$, which implies that offering any x in $(0, \delta_Z)$ is dominated by offering $x = \delta_N = 0$.
3 If A offers $x \geq \delta_Z$, B will accept and hence A's payoff is $1 - x \leq 1 - \delta_Z$, which implies that offering any $x > \delta_Z$ is dominated by offering $x = \delta_Z$.

In equilibrium a strategy of ambiguity is represented as a mixed strategy in which B arms with some probability and does not arm with probability $1 - \pi$, and A does not get to observe which action was taken. Government A will make concessions with some positive probability that depends on B's costs and benefits of arming.

First notice that during the last stage of the game where B's information set is a singleton, armed type t accepts A's offer if and only if $x \geq \delta_t$ and unarmed type t accepts any offer $x = 0$. Also observe that if A plays a pure strategy/action, then both types of B will play pure strategies as well. In other words, in any mixed strategy equilibrium, A must play a mixed strategy. There are four nodes in A's information set. Let π_Z be the probability that the motivated type is armed, and π_N be the probability that the normal type is armed.

To summarize, we obtain the following lemma:

Lemma 2 *In any mixed strategy equilibrium,* A *must mix among the following actions from which* A *has the same expected payoff:*
At this point, we cannot exclude any of these three actions. Unlike in any pure strategy equilibrium, we cannot exclude the possibility that A offers δ_Z to B.

Table 6.4

A's action	A's expected payoff
attack	$1 - c^*$
offer $x = 0$	$1 - p_Z \pi_Z w_Z$,
offer $x = \delta_Z$	$1 - \delta_Z$

Now we turn our attention to B's strategies. Suppose that A attacks with probability q_A, offers $x = 0$ with probability q_0, and offers $x = \delta_Z$ with probability $q_1 = 1 - q_A - q_0$.

Lemma 3 *In any mixed strategy equilibrium,*

1   *if $q_0 > 0$ and the normal type mixes, then the motivated type will arm.*
2   *if $q_0 = 0$ and the normal type mixes, then the motivated may also mix.*

Proof: If the normal type mixes, then we have

$$q_A (\gamma - \beta) + q_1 \delta_Z - \kappa = q_A(-\beta) + q_1 \delta_Z, \text{ equivalently } \kappa/\gamma \text{ in } (0, 1).$$

The motivated type has a higher payoff from being armed if $q_0 > 0$:

$$q_A (\gamma - \beta) + q_0 \delta_Z + q_1 \delta_Z - \kappa > q_A(-\beta) + q_1 \delta_Z.$$

In other words, if $\pi_N > 0$ and $q_0 > 0$ then $\pi_Z = 1$. **QED**

Proposition 4 *If $c_{NA} \leq \delta_Z \leq c_A$ and $\delta_Z \leq p_Z w_Z$, there is the following mixed strategy equilibrium:*

- *Type t arms with probability π_t in $[0, 1]$ such that*

$$p_Z \pi_Z + p_N \pi_N = (\delta_Z - c_{NA})/(c_A - c_{NA}) \text{ and } \pi_Z \geq \delta_Z/(p_Z w_Z), \tag{3}$$

- *Country A attacks with probability $q_A = \kappa/\gamma$ and offers δ_Z with $q_1 = 1 - \kappa/\gamma$. The expected payoff of country B (of either type) is*

$$q_A(-\beta) + (1 - q_A) \delta_Z = \delta_Z - \kappa(\delta_Z + \beta)/\gamma,$$

and country A's expected payoff is $1 - \delta_Z$

Proof: Suppose that A attacks with probability $q_A = \kappa/\gamma$, and does not offer $x = 0$. Then A must offer $x = \delta_Z$ with probability $q_1 = 1 - q_A = 1 - \kappa/\gamma$.
Since A does not offer $x = 0$, both types have the same payoffs from being armed and not armed. A is willing to mix if and only if it receives

the same expected payoff from attacking and offering $x = \delta_Z$, which is determined by $q = p_Z \pi_Z + p_N \pi_N$ (the probability that B is armed) by the following equation:

$$q(1 - c_A) + (1 - q)(1 - c_{NA}) = 1 - \delta_Z$$

$q^* = (\delta_Z - c_{NA})/(c_A - c_{NA})$ in $[0, 1]$ if and only if $c_{NA} \leq \delta_Z \leq c_A$.

For all $p_Z + p_N = 1$, there are (π_Z, π_N) in $[0, 1]^2$ such that

$$p_Z \pi_Z + p_N \pi_N = (\delta_Z - c_{NA})/(c_A - c_{NA}) \text{ in } [0, 1].$$

On the other hand, country A does not offer $x = 0$ if and only if

$$1 - \delta_Z \geq 1 - p_Z \pi_Z w_Z, \text{ equivalently } \pi_Z \geq \delta_Z/(p_Z w_Z).$$

The above inequality implies that $\delta_Z/(p_Z w_Z) \leq 1$ which is equivalent to $\delta_Z \leq p_Z w_Z$. Observe that $c_{NA} \leq \delta_Z \leq c_A$ and $\delta_Z \leq p_Z w_Z$ ensure the existence of well-defined mixed strategies (π_Z, π_N) in $[0, 1]^2$ that satisfy the two conditions in (3). **QED**

The mixed strategy equilibrium in Proposition 4 is our "interesting" ambiguity equilibrium because A will make concessions with positive probability. We describe it in greater detail below. For now, we assign values to our parameters to illustrate an example of this mixed strategy equilibrium. Suppose that $c_A = 0.3$, $c_{NA} = 0.1$, $p_Z = p_N = 0.5$, then

$$c_{NA} \leq \delta_Z \leq c_A \text{ iff } 0.1 \leq \delta_Z \leq 0.3, \qquad \delta_Z \leq p_Z w_Z \text{ iff } \delta_Z \leq 0.5 \, w_Z.$$

We now move to another mixed strategy equilibrium. This time A does not offer concessions in equilibrium. Suppose that $\pi_N > 0$ and $\pi_Z = 1$. In order for A to mix, we need

$$(p_Z + p_N \pi_N) c_A + (1 - p_Z - p_N \pi_N) c_{NA} = \min\{p_Z w_Z, \delta_Z\}.$$

We can state the following proposition:

Proposition 5 *If $\delta_Z \geq p_Z$ and*

$$c^E/p_Z \leq w_Z \leq c_A/p_Z, \tag{4}$$

there is a mixed strategy equilibrium in which the motivated type arms and the normal type arms with probability π_N where

$$(p_Z + p_N \pi_N) c_A + p_N(1 - \pi_N) c_{NA} = p_Z w_Z. \tag{5}$$

A attacks with probability $q_A = \kappa/\gamma$, offers $x = 0$ with probability

$$q_0 = 1 - q_A \text{ if } \delta_Z > p_Z w_Z,$$
$$q_0 \leq 1 - q_A \text{ if } \delta_Z = p_Z w_Z.$$

Country A's payoff is $1 - p_Z w_Z$, normal type B's payoff is $-\beta\kappa/\gamma$, motivated type B's payoff is

$$\kappa(\gamma - \beta)/\gamma + (1 - \kappa/\gamma)\delta_2 - \kappa = \delta_2 - \kappa(\delta_2 + \beta)/\gamma.$$

Proof: First observe that if $q_A = \kappa/\gamma$, the normal type is indifferent between arm and not arm. Lemma 3 implies that it is optimal for the motivated type to arm when $q_0 > 0$. Given B's strategies, (5) states that A has the same expected payoff to attack or to offer 0. Solving (5) yields

$$\pi_N = (p_Z w_Z - c_A p_Z - p_N c_{NA})/(p_N c_N - p_N c_{NA}) \text{ by (4)}.$$

To conclude, note that when $p_Z w_Z = \delta_Z$, A may mix between offering $x = 0$ and $x = \delta_Z$ arbitrarily. However, if A only mixes between attack and offering δ_Z, then the equilibrium is the same as the one characterized in Proposition 4. **QED**

The conditions in Proposition 5 describe a set of (w_Z, δ_Z) above line $\delta_Z = p_Z w_Z$. Except a measure-zero set, the last two propositions are mutually exclusive.

Consider the following example. Suppose that $c_A = 0.3$, $c_{NA} = 0.1$, $p_Z = p_N = 0.5$, then

$$\delta_Z \geq p_Z w_Z \text{ iff } \delta_Z \geq 0.5 \, w_Z$$
$$c^E/p_Z \leq w_Z \leq c_A/p_Z \text{ iff } 0.4 \leq w_Z \leq 0.6.$$

Lemma 6 *In any mixed strategy equilibrium,*
i   *if $q_0 > 0$ and the motivated type mixes, then the normal type will not arm.*
ii *if $q_0 = 0$ and the motivated type mixes, then the normal type may also mix.*

Proof: Suppose that A attacks with probability q_A, offers $x = 0$ with probability q_0, and offers δ_Z with probability $q_1 = 1 - q_A - q_0$. If the motivated type mixes, then

$$q_A(\gamma - \beta) + q_0 \delta_Z + q_1 \delta_Z - \kappa = q_A(-\beta) + q_1\delta_Z \text{ iff } q_A = \kappa/\gamma.$$

Because $\delta_Z > \delta_N = 0$, the normal type has higher payoff from not being armed if and only if $q_0 = 0$:

$$q_A(\gamma - \beta) + q_1 \delta_Z - \kappa = q_A(-\beta) + q_1\delta_Z.$$

Note that (ii) is the same as (ii) of Lemma 3. **QED**

Lemmas 3 and 6 assert that in any mixed strategy equilibrium, A must attack with probability $q_A = \kappa/\gamma$. This implies that if $\kappa \geq \gamma$, then there is no mixed strategy equilibrium.

Next, we focus on the possibility of a mixed strategy equilibrium where the motivated type mixes and the normal type does not arm, and A mixes between attack and offer $x = 0$ with probability $q_0 > 0$.

Proposition 7 *If there exists π_Z in $[0, 1]$ such that*

$$p_Z \, \pi_Z \, c_A + (1 - p_Z \, \pi_Z) \, c_{NA} = \min\{p_Z \, \pi_Z \, w_Z, \, \delta_Z\}, \tag{6}$$

there is a mixed strategy equilibrium where the normal type does not arm, the motivated type arms with probability π_Z, A attacks with probability $q_A = \kappa/\gamma$ in $(0,1)$, and offers $x = 0$ with

$q_0 = 1 - q_A > 0$ if $\delta_Z > p_Z \, \pi_Z \, w_Z$

$q_0 > 0$ if $\delta_Z = p_Z \, \pi_Z \, w_Z$

(if $p_Z \, \pi_Z \, w_Z = \delta_Z$, country A may mix between offering $x = 0$ and $x = \delta_Z$ arbitrarily).
Country A's payoff is $1 - p_Z \, \pi_Z \, w_Z$. Normal type B's payoff is $- q_A \, \beta = - \beta\kappa/\gamma$, motivated type B's payoff is $- \kappa\beta/\gamma + (1 - \kappa/\gamma) \, \delta_Z = \delta_Z - \kappa(\delta_Z + \beta)/\gamma$.

Proof: It is straightforward to verify such a mixed strategy equilibrium. Now we validate condition (6). Note that (6) implies that

$$\pi_Z = c_{NA}/(p_Z(w_Z + c_{NA} - c_A)) \text{ in } [0, 1] \text{ if } w_Z \geq c^E/p_Z.$$

Also, $p_Z \, \pi_Z \, w_Z = \min\{p_Z \, \pi_Z \, w_Z, \, \delta_Z\}$ requires that

$$\delta_Z \geq p_Z \, \pi_Z \, w_Z = c_{NA}w_Z/(w_Z + c_{NA} - c_A)$$

which is an increasing function of w_Z. **QED**

To illustrate, suppose that $c_A = 0.3$, $c_{NA} = 0.1$, $p_Z = 0.5$, then $w_Z \geq c^E/p_Z = 0.4$. The other condition is $\delta \geq c_{NA}w_Z/(w_Z + c_{NA} - c_A) = 0.1w_Z/(w_Z + 0.2)$.

Notes

1 This work was financially supported by the East–West Center through a POSCO Foundation Fellowship (Benson).
2 Examples of such efforts include the Nuclear Threat Initiative, which focuses on securing and reducing the spread of nuclear materials and technology, and the Harvard Belfer Center Project on Managing the Atom, which emphasizes the management and protection of fissile material. See, for example, Bunn (2010).
3 This meeting was widely reported in the press. A statement given by Assistant Secretary of State Andrew J. Shapiro addressing Obama's comments and the Obama administration's policy toward Israel can be found on the US Department of State webpage. See Shapiro (2010).

References

Baliga, Sandeep and Tomas Sjostrom (2008) "Strategic ambiguity and arms prolif-eration," *Journal of Political Economy* 116: 1023–1057.

Berger, Thomas U. (1993) "From sword to chrysanthemum: Japan's culture of anti-militarism," *International Security* 17(4): 119–150.

Bunn, Matthew (2010) *Securing the Bomb 2010*, Cambridge, MA and Washington, DC: Project on Managing the Atom, Harvard University, and Nuclear Threat Initiative.

Burr, William and Jeffrey T. Richelson (2000/2001) "Whether to 'strangle the baby in the cradle'," *International Security* 25(3): 54–99.

Cha, Victor (2009) "Up close and personal, here's what I learned," *The Washington Post*, June 14. Available at www.washingtonpost.com/wpdyn/content/article/2009/06/12/AR-2009061202685.html.

Cha, Victor D. and David C. Kang (2003) "The Korean crisis," *Foreign Policy* 136: 20–28.

Chang, Gordon (1988) "JFK, China, and the bomb," *The Journal of American History* 74(4): 1287–1310.

Coolidge, Frederick L. and Daniel L. Segal (2009) "Is Kim Jong-il like Saddam Hussein and Adolf Hitler? A personality disorder evaluation," *Behavior Sciences of Terrorism and Political Aggression* 1(3): 195–202.

Fuhrmann, Matthew (This Book) "Taking a walk on the supply side: the determi-nants of civilian nuclear cooperation."

Gartzke, Erik and Dong-Joon Jo (This Book) "Bargaining, nuclear proliferation, and interstate disputes."

Halperin, Morton (1965) "Chinese nuclear strategy," *The China Quarterly* 21: 74–86.

Hughes, Llewelyn (2007) "Why Japan will not go nuclear (yet)," *International Secur-ity* 31(4): 67–96.

Jo, Dong-Joon and Erik Gartzke (2007) "Determinants of nuclear weapons prolif-eration: a quantitative model," *Journal of Conflict Resolution* 51(1): 167–94.

Kroenig, Matthew (This Book) "Importing the bomb: sensitive nuclear assistance and nuclear proliferation."

Levy, Jack (2008) "Preventative war and democratic politics: Presidential address to the International Studies Association," *International Studies Quarterly* 52(1): 1–24.

Lewis, Jeffrey (2010) "How A.Q. Khan helped distort America's DPRK policy," March 29. Available at http://38north.org/2010/03/how-a-q-khan-helped-distort-america%E2%80%99s-dprk-policy.

Lewis, John W. and Xue Litai (1988) *China Builds the Bomb*, Stanford, CA: Stanford University Press.

Mazarr, Michael J. (1995) "Going just a little nuclear: nonproliferation lessons from North Korea," *International Security* 20(2): 92–122.

Mitchell, Derek J. (2004) "Taiwan's Hsin Chu program: deterrence, abandonment, and honor," in Kurt M. Campbell, Robert J. Einhorn, and Mitchell B. Reiss (eds) *The Nuclear Tipping Point*, Washington, DC: Brookings Institution Press.

Oberdorfer, Don (1997) *The Two Koreas: A Contemporary History*, Reading, MA: Addison-Wesley.

Perkovich, George (1999) *India's Nuclear Bomb: The Impact on Global Proliferation*, Berkeley and Los Angeles, CA: University of California Press.

Raas, Whitney and Austin Long (2007) "Osirak Redux? Assessing Israeli capabilities to destroy Iranian nuclear facilities," *International Security* 31(4): 7–33.

Sagan, Scott (1996/1997) "Why do states build nuclear weapons? Three models in search of a bomb," *International Security* 21(3): 54–86.

Sagan, Scott (2006) "How to keep the bomb from Iran," *Foreign Affairs* 85(5): 45–59.

Sanger, David E. (2010) "Officials say Iran could make bomb fuel in a year," *New York Times*, April 15: A14.

Saunders, Phillip C. (2003) "Confronting ambiguity: how to handle North Korea's nuclear program," *Arms Control Today*, March.

Schelling, Thomas C. (1976) "Who will have the bomb?," *International Security* 1(1): 77–91.

Schrage, Michael (2003) "No weapons, no matter. We called Saddam's bluff," *The Washington Post*, May 11: B2.

Shapiro, Andrew J. (2010) "The Obama administration's approach to US–Israel security cooperation: preserving Israel's qualitative edge," Remarks at the Brookings Center for Middle East Policy, Washington, DC, July 16. Available at www.state.gov/t/pm/rls/rm/144753.htm.

Sigal, Leon V. (1997) *Disarming Strangers: Nuclear Diplomacy with North Korea*, Princeton, NJ: Princeton University Press.

Singh, Sonali and Christopher R. Way (2004) "The correlates of nuclear proliferation: a quantitative test," *Journal of Conflict Resolution* 48(6): 859–885.

Sneh, Ephraim (2010) "When friends are mad at you," *Haaretz*, April 2. Available at www.haaretz.com/print-edition/opinion/when-friends-are-mad-at-you-1.283711.

Solingen, Etel (2007) *Nuclear Logics: Contrasting Paths In East Asia and the Middle East*, Princeton, NJ: Princeton University Press.

7 Nuclear politics

The political decision to acquire, sustain or discard a nuclear arsenal

James Wirtz

Most theorists believe that nuclear weapons are political weapons. Through their very existence, they influence the behavior of both domestic and international actors when it comes to issues of war and peace. Sometimes they moderate behavior. Optimists believe that a Nuclear Revolution, produced by a situation of Mutual Assured Destruction, helped keep the Cold War cold between the superpowers (Jervis 1989). Sometimes, they seem to exacerbate latent or nascent conflicts by emboldening decision-makers. Pessimists note that a stability–instability paradox can emerge as states try to capitalize on the fear and restraint created in the mind of the opponent when nuclear weapons are introduced into a dispute (Snyder 1964). They also shape perceptions of the general strategic landscape. Nuclear weapons can reassure policymakers and polities by pushing fears about existential threats into the background. By contrast, they also can create politically powerful anxieties about mass casualty terrorism and the threats posed by rogue states. Despite the fact that they have not been used in combat for nearly 70 years and a "taboo" against their use is said to exist in world politics (Paul 2009; Tannenwald 2008), nuclear weapons continue to have a profound influence on international affairs.

Scholars have concentrated on explaining the domestic politics of nuclear proliferation, the incentives and disincentives that shape political decisions to acquire nuclear weapons (Lavoy 2006; Hymans 2006; Sagan 1996/1997). By contrast, few studies explore the interaction between domestic politics and the decision to augment or maintain existing nuclear arsenals. This is surprising, given the fact that nuclear weapons are political weapons in all facets of the term. Nuclear weapons have to enjoy broad-based societal and institutional support or governments and the organizations within them will turn their attention to more pressing issues or more politically and bureaucratically popular programs. Nuclear weapons are political weapons because they reflect a national commitment to a certain type of defense and acceptance of the risks that are inherent in remaining a nuclear power. Maintenance or augmentation of a nuclear arsenal also requires political support in the sense that bureaucracies and other institutions must place sustaining a nuclear arsenal high on their agendas. Without this bureaucratic and societal support, the myriad decisions needed to maintain the arsenal, decisions that are taken by thousands of relatively independent military officers and policymakers, will not coalesce in a way that sustains nuclear weapons programs.

Several chapters in this volume also suggest that there is a link between nuclear weapons and domestic politics. Michael Horowitz, for example, notes that once states obtain nuclear weapons, they tend to moderate their behavior over time. The observation that a type of positive nuclear learning takes place once states acquire nuclear weapons opens up the possibility that this learning occurs in a domestic political setting. It is national governments that moderate their behavior, and these governments must present themselves to a domestic political audience. By noting that possessing nuclear weapons does not seem to influence the overall probability that a state will be involved in conflict, Erik Gartzke and Dong-Joon Jo also point to the possibility that domestic political arguments and forces play an important role in helping to justify an ongoing commitment to a nuclear arsenal. Policymakers have to explain the relevance of nuclear weapons despite their apparent lack of impact on national involvement in international conflict.

Variation in the size of nuclear arsenals or associated research, development and procurement activity should logically be associated with changes in the threat environment. When threats increase, budget, interest and political support should flow to the nuclear enterprise; when threats recede, sustaining a nuclear arsenal should wane as a priority. Yet, there have been occasions when proliferation and terrorism threats have been high and political interest in the US nuclear arsenal has evaporated. There also have been moments when threats have been well recognized but administrations have been slow to respond. The Harry S. Truman administration seemed hesitant to acquire fusion weapons even though it appeared highly unlikely that the Soviets would show similar restraint. The Jimmy Carter administration recognized the growing threat of Soviet military power and foreign initiatives and even bolstered defense spending, but the Ronald Reagan administration approached the issue of Soviet military power with much public zeal, which increased qualitative growth in the US nuclear arsenal. The fact that the United States expanded its nuclear enterprise when the Soviet Union posed a heightened nuclear threat and then reduced it at the end of the Cold War is clear in hindsight. But did officials and politicians see things as so cut and dry at the time, or did they believe that there was a distinct politics to nuclear procurement policy? Did they treat nuclear procurement questions as political questions?

In order to explore the relationship between domestic nuclear politics and nuclear arsenals, the chapter will first describe the logic behind nuclear politics by exploring the findings of the *Report of the Secretary of*

Defense Task Force on DoD Nuclear Weapons Management (Task Force on DOD Nuclear Weapons Management 2008, hereafter referred to as the Schlesinger Report). The overarching finding of this Blue Ribbon Commission is that maintenance of a credible nuclear deterrent requires an enterprise wide commitment, a commitment that is fundamentally political. In other words, the decision to acquire a nuclear weapon might be made by a small nexus of policymakers, but maintenance of a nuclear arsenal requires active participation of many organizations and programs. Political support in this context corresponds to a dominant societal belief that a robust arsenal or ongoing enhancements to the arsenal are necessary to national security. The chapter thus suggests that the effort to generate or channel political support is directly related to the success of efforts to procure new nuclear weapons systems or to sustain existing programs. Without a political or strategic narrative to help organize the whole gamut of activities involved in sustaining a nuclear arsenal, it is difficult to muster the political and budgetary support needed to sustain programs.

The chapter will then explore two key phases in the history of the US nuclear weapons program. It describes two critical events in the US nuclear buildup, National Security Policy Memorandum 68 often referred to as NSC-68, and the decisions made in the early 1980s by the Ronald Reagan administration to modernize the US nuclear arsenal. It will then explore two key moments in the "diminution" of US nuclear capability that followed the end of the Cold War: the 2001 and 2010 Nuclear Posture Reviews.

The political weapon

A critical observation about the buildup and reduction in the capability and size of the US nuclear arsenal is that they both occurred in the absence of a coherent or sustained planning process or a long-term strategic plan. Given changing administrations, continual organizational reform and reorganization, a changing threat environment, and the march of technology, it is not particularly surprising that the American system of government is not really capable of creating a five, ten or 20-year strategic plan. There are, of course, key turning points in the history of the US nuclear arsenal that had a major impact on its size and capabilities. In the early 1960s, for instance, Secretary of Defense Robert McNamara employed systems analysis to identify how the law of diminishing returns shaped the destructive power of the US nuclear arsenal, devising assured destruction criteria related to cost-benefit calculations (Wirtz 2006; Enthoven and Smith 1971). Whether or not the notion of assured destruction was actually related to US employment doctrine, however, remained a hotly debated topic among scholars until the end of the Cold War (Ball 1986). The McNamara Pentagon might have been largely responsible for "sizing" the US nuclear arsenal, but it was left up to subsequent planners and policymakers to match this force to various nuclear doctrines. In effect, one of the key decisions in the history of the US nuclear weapons program, deciding the general size of the US nuclear force, was based on solving the problem of the day (i.e., how to set a cap on Minuteman missile deployments), not some long-range strategic assessment or a well-developed strategic plan.

In the absence of a well-defined nuclear procurement and deployment plan, what factors shaped the size and composition of the US nuclear arsenal and associated delivery vehicles? Sometimes, technology seemed to push development of delivery capabilities and weapons in the absence of a clear strategic imperative. Multiple independently targeted re-entry vehicles (MIRV), for example, emerged with relatively little strategic fore-sight or analysis (Greenwood 1988). At other times, bureaucratic impera-tives seemed to dominate decisions about weapons procurement. For instance, despite the fact that the Jimmy Carter administration cancelled the B-1 bomber, that the Stealth B-2 bomber was under development, and that a bomber capable of both low and high-altitude operations was extremely expensive and technologically complex, supporters eventually managed to place a version of the bomber into production (Brown 1992). It is therefore not surprising that several explanations were offered during the Cold War to account for a "nuclear arms race" that had little to do with centralized decision-making. "Action–reaction phenomena," technological imperatives, bureaucratic politics, and the political efforts of a military–industrial complex were all identified as "non-strategic" factors that shaped US nuclear procurement and deployment doctrine (Evangelista 1988).

In hindsight, the quantitative and qualitative US nuclear buildup during the Cold War appears over-determined. Factors located at a variety of levels of analysis seemed to coalesce in a way that pushed the United States towards developing a robust nuclear capability. Mathew Evangelista, for instance, provides a compelling description of how forces found at several levels of analysis coalesced around the procurement of US tactical nuclear weapons:

> ...Internal factors figure prominently in the early stages, as scientists seek support for new technical ideas among their military associates ... During the middle stages, external factors – such as the identifica-tion of a foreign threat – serve to aid the process of consensus-building, as the supporters of new weapons seek funding from Congress. External events often provide a window of opportunity that enhances the prospects for a particular innovation ... During the later stages, arguments focused on the new weapon's cost-effectiveness, its desirability to NATO allies, or its usefulness as a bargaining chip with the USSR may come into play.
>
> (Evangelista 1988: 228)

Evangelista cautioned against concluding that "everything" plays a role when it comes time to adopt a new nuclear system, but it is difficult not to conclude that a variety of forces, actors and interests do in fact line up behind certain procurement programs.

Another way to explain this phenomenon is to suggest that there was a broad political consensus about maintaining a robust nuclear capability, and that this consensus sustained socially, bureaucratically and technologically complex nuclear systems. The B-1 program, for instance, was not preserved by the Carter administration, but by members of Congress and the military who believed that the bomber served as an important strategic hedge and technology demonstrator. The general political consensus that it was in US interests to maintain a robust nuclear capability, combined with narrower industrial, institutional and service interests, sustained the nuclear arsenal, making it difficult to eliminate high-profile programs or capabilities. There was widespread agreement within government that a robust nuclear capability was desirable, and this agreement sustained the nuclear program, especially when senior officials failed to anticipate key requirements. Because policymakers and planners could not anticipate every unforeseen development and unanticipated need when it came to maintaining a robust nuclear arsenal, it was left up to officers and officials throughout the government to work through the details and problems when it came to sustaining the nuclear arsenal, an objective that was deemed not only as acceptable, but desirable.

In the absence of this political consensus or interest, however, it becomes extraordinarily difficult to sustain a robust nuclear arsenal. Scores of organizations and hundreds of individual decision-makers have to place nuclear matters ahead of other individuals or organizational priorities because it is impossible ex ante to anticipate the myriad issues involved in maintaining an arsenal. Without interest and support, policymakers and military officers stop paying "attention to detail," and potentially dangerous mistakes are made. In August 2007, for instance, a B-52 strategic bomber stationed at Minot Air Force Base mistakenly transported a load of nuclear-tipped cruise missiles across the United States. Pentagon spokesmen stated that an "erosion" of weapons handling standards at the bases involved caused the incident (Baker 2007). In August 2006, the US government mistakenly delivered a shipment of "sensitive missile components" to the government of Taiwan, prompting Secretary of Defense Robert Gates to order the Secretary of the Navy and Air Force and the Director of the Defense Logistics Agency to launch a "comprehensive review and physical inventory of all nuclear weapons-related materials under their possession or custody" (Gates 2008). Incidents involving nuclear weapons and delivery systems occurred during the Cold War, but during periods of heightened political interest these incidents are more directly attributable to physical accidents (aircraft fires, accidental damage to systems) or normal accidents (unanticipated operator–machine interactions), not a gross failure to follow procedures or to knowingly ignore safeguards (Sagan 1993; Perrow 1999).

Without political support, the level of interest needed to maintain an effective nuclear arsenal begins to wither on the vine. The Schlesinger Report noted, for instance, that there is evidence of this lack of interest in nuclear matters in the top echelons of the US Defense Department:

> The Task Force found widespread fragmentation, dispersal of responsibility, and weakening authorities in the Office of the Secretary of Defense's (OSD) management of the nuclear mission and the nuclear mission area. The decline in management attention to nuclear matters is evidenced by a dramatically reduce workforce, fragmentation of nuclear policy and guidance responsibility across the office, dilution of organizational focus because of proliferating missions, and relegation of nuclear-focused organizations to positions of lower authority.
> (Task Force on DOD Nuclear Weapons Management 2008: v)

This sort of management "fragmentation" reduces opportunities for effective policy advocacy when it comes to budgetary and strategic decisions. In other words, there is no senior military or civilian official organization that can represent the needs or position of the nuclear enterprise when it comes to allocating resources or determining how best to integrate the nuclear arsenal into overall defense policy. Organizations that once focused solely on the nuclear mission, for example Strategic Air Command, have been replaced by commands with multiple functions that lack actual operational command over forces, for instance US Strategic Command. Without a powerful representative in budgetary debates, nuclear programs become a target for officials eager to find easy ways to recapture costs and redirect resources.

A lack of advocacy and focus at the top translates into a lack of attention and interest at lower levels in the chain of command. Competing priorities begin to exert pressures on nuclear programs and capabilities, leading subordinate commanders to make uncoordinated decisions that begin to degrade force structure. As incredible as it may sound, entire classes of weapons are effectively terminated without deliberate national level consideration. Schlesinger and his colleagues noted:

> Since the 1990s, there has been a shedding of nuclear capabilities by the Military Services. Such efforts are sometimes abetted by combatant commands and by service components in order to free up resources to use elsewhere. In some cases, the Services have perfected the art of starving a capability in order to justify shedding the associated mission ... For example, the criterion employed by some in the military for procuring a weapons system (specifically TLAM-N, ALCM, and

dual-capable aircraft, especially in NATO) is whether it is "militarily cost-effective." This ignores the weapon's political value, overlooking the crucial deterrence and assurance elements that these nuclear deployments and capabilities provide. Nuclear deterrence is inherently a national mission, and neither a military service nor a combatant commander should make unilateral decisions regarding whether to retain particular nuclear capabilities.

(Task Force on DOD Nuclear Weapons Management 2008: vi)

TLAM-N (Tomahawk Land-Attack Missile – Nuclear) was the last vestige of the US Navy's "tactical" nuclear delivery mission, a role that was virtually abandoned by the unilateral nuclear initiatives announced by President George H.W. Bush in September 1991 (Powaski 2000). Senior Navy officers supported the Bush decision to "de-nuclearize" the Navy, and worked tirelessly to minimize the resources devoted to maintaining even a vestige of a theater delivery capability.

In an interesting paradox, the absence of a "follow-on" program to TLAM-N also makes it difficult to sustain the existing TLAM-N capability (Task Force on DOD Nuclear Weapons Management 2008: 25). As a weapons system and associated infrastructure age, a follow-on program helps policymakers preserve parts of the existing system and industrial infrastructure important to sustaining the capability in the coming decades. New programs and requirements guide decisions to preserve hard to replace elements of the existing system or industrial infrastructure. Without a new program, there is little to guide decisions on preserving research and development and manufacturing capability, leading to erosion in the ability to field similar weapons systems. The lack of a "future" leaves an existing program without a metric of ongoing success or even failure. Should program managers sustain existing capabilities at all costs? Or should existing programs be liquidated completely, eliminating all costs by divesting resources and capabilities that could be used to reconstitute a similar program at a later date? The "future" helps to define the "present" because it helps to define metrics for current operations, maintenance, and redevelopment.

Without political support, a waning enterprise also fails to sustain itself along another important dimension, human resources. Few individuals are attracted to the study of the technical, operational and strategic aspects of nuclear weapons. Although political observers dubbed early 2010 as "the nuclear spring" and money flowed for scholars undertaking nonproliferation research at prominent think tanks, few see a job in the nuclear weapons complex as an attractive option. A career as a nuclear weapons designer or technician simply does not seem particularly promising or exciting. The fact that a lack of intellectual interest or employment prospects stands as a significant threat to the continuation of the US nuclear arsenal has been recognized for over a decade. In 1999, the Commission on Maintaining United States Nuclear Weapons Expertise noted that interest in seeking employment in the nuclear enterprise was sharply in decline:

> Our discussions with college students, placement officers, and department heads revealed several ... recruitment problems for the nuclear weapons complex. In most instances, undergraduates in the engineering and information technology fields are no longer knowledgeable of Department of Energy laboratories and production facilities. The many years without significant recruitment have left the labs and production facilities without reputations on campuses across the country – campuses where they once were very competitive recruiters. Further, where they are known, they do not have a reputation for offering challenging design and development opportunities.
>
> (Commission on Maintaining United States Nuclear Weapons Expertise 1999: 30)

An aging workforce, combined with the perspective that the US nuclear arsenal is a waning asset, are making it increasingly difficult to sustain the expertise needed to maintain a robust nuclear deterrent. And without political support, there are few personal or societal incentives to seek out a career in the nuclear enterprise.

Nuclear weapons are political weapons in that they require political support. When they enjoy widespread endorsement, nuclear capabilities will remain highly robust or increase, even in the absence of, or despite, specific policy decisions. Whey they lack political support, nuclear capabilities will wane, even if policymakers attempt to reinvigorate critical facets of the nuclear arsenal. People, organizations and institutions exercise a good deal of control over nuclear arsenals, and they can take matters into their hands when it comes to the parts of the nuclear arsenal they interact with.

The politics of nuclear politics

The notion that nuclear weapons require a political commitment is sometimes remembered and sometimes ignored by scholars and policymakers alike. But here too, a pattern also might be emerging. When political support for maintaining a nuclear arsenal is strong, politicians and strategists seem to have a keen appreciation for the salience of nuclear politics and the important role political support plays in sustaining a robust nuclear arsenal. The political and strategic implications of nuclear decisions take center stage in official pronouncements, providing strategic justifications for policy. When political support is waning, the domestic political dimensions of nuclear programs are given short shrift – nuclear decisions are treated as a narrow technical concern that involve only a small number of officials, officers and experts. The way policy decisions are framed pushes the link between political support and the nuclear enterprise further into the background.

The politics of a robust force: NSC-68 and the Reagan buildup

NSC-68, issued on April 14, 1950 (United States Objectives and Programs for National Security 1950, hereafter referred to as NSC-68), and the nuclear buildup launched by the Reagan administration in the early 1980s were both undertaken in crisis atmosphere. For the authors of NSC-68 – the State Defense-Policy Review Group Chaired by Paul Nitze – the emergence of a Soviet Union armed with fission weapons, and the prospect that the Soviets might soon produce a fusion warhead was the cause for alarm. These concerns became a source of political controversy in November 1949, when the Atomic Energy Agency recommended that the United States delay development of a fusion weapon, which set off a policy struggle between nuclear advocates and nuclear minimalists within the Harry S. Truman administration. "Public concern and press reports about this battle within the administration," according to Samuel Wells, "forced Truman to ... direct a special committee of the National Security Council to make a thorough review of the superbomb issue including political and military as well as technical factors" (Wells 1979: 118–119). On January 31, 1950 the special committee informed Truman that it favored an acceleration of the entire US nuclear program, including production of fusion weapons, but that this accelerated program required a "strategic review" of US defense policies. NSC-68 was the product of this strategic review.

The Reagan administration also was concerned about a negative shift in the balance of power between the United States and the USSR. During the 1976 and 1980 election campaigns and his first years in the White House, Reagan and his advisors repeatedly noted that a lack of political will to combat the Soviet Union had emerged in the American body politic. Often referred to as the "Vietnam syndrome," this collapse in will was reflected in a decline of American prestige and activism on the world stage. Ronald Reagan noted in 1976, for example, that:

> [a]ll I can see is what other nations the world over see: collapse of the American will and the retreat of American power ... The evidence mounts that we are number two in a world where it is dangerous, if not fatal, to be second best.
>
> (Kirkpatrick 1981: 33)

The Reagan administration also asserted that the Soviets had capitalized on this decline in US morale by increasing their military capabilities, especially their nuclear arsenal. According to Reagan, "We're already in an arms race, but only the Soviets are racing. They are outspending us in the military field by fifty percent, and more than double, sometimes triple in their strategic forces" (Pipes 1981: 41).

Members of both administrations thus recognized that a direct link existed between decisions to strengthen the US nuclear arsenal and politics and strategy writ large. Members of the Truman administration realized that their decision to develop fusion weapons could only be justified and implemented within a clearly articulated strategic context: NSC-68 would offer description of how the US nuclear arsenal would be integrated into an overall plan to contain the Soviet Union. In contrast, the Reagan administration believed that it would first be necessary to reinvigorate "American will" in the ongoing contest with the Soviet Union before it could move to bolster the US nuclear arsenal. In the words of Norman Podhoretz, one of the ideologues who helped shape Reagan's approach to international affairs, "A strategy ... centered on considerations of 'Realpolitik,' would be unable to count indefinitely on popular support. Sooner or later (probably sooner rather than later) it would succumb to a resurgence of isolationism...." (Podhoretz 1981: 41). For the Reagan administration, nuclear procurement decisions would falter without political support.

Although both administrations understood that a clear strategy was required to harness political support to facilitate procurement of a robust nuclear arsenal, they approached the task from opposite sides of the political–procurement divide. Nitze and his colleagues defined the deadly peril posed by the Soviet Union. Nitze suggested that given their competing political systems, the Soviets were better able to carry out their foreign policy with stealth, secrecy and speed. These Soviet advantages combined with their nascent nuclear capability created an obvious threat to the United States: America was in danger of suffering another "Pearl Harbor," only this time nuclear and possibly thermonuclear warheads would rain down on US cities and military installations. In the face of this nuclear threat, the sluggish American democracy could "compensate for its natural vulnerability," according to Nitze, "only if it maintains clearly superior overall power in its most inclusive sense" (United States Objectives and Programs for National Security 1950: 24). The United States, according to Nitze's analysis, had to acquire fusion weapons: "we should produce and stockpile thermonuclear weapons in the event they prove feasible and would add significantly to our net capability" (United States Objectives and Programs for National Security 1950: 39). The Truman administration believed that once they were armed with fusion weapons, the American public would have the political will to embrace the concept of containment as the guiding principle behind US foreign policy, a policy they saw as not without a clear risk of nuclear war.[1] The confidence generated by a robust nuclear capability would translate into political will to undertake an open-ended confrontation with the Soviets.

In contrast, the Reagan administration believed that the causal arrow, so to speak, pointed in the opposite direction. The US nuclear arsenal, along with the entire US military, required expansion and modernization in the face of the "Soviet military buildup" that occurred during and after the ebacle experienced by the United States in Southeast Asia. But the administration believed that efforts to start a nuclear modernization program would falter without political support. According to Richard V. Allen,

> The President seeks to have a consistent foreign policy that is believable ... the kind of foreign policy talk that ordinary people can understand and that can generate bipartisan support in Congress, and the restoration of the military capability of the US.
>
> (Allen 1981: 8)

What was first needed was an effort to renew the American ideological commitment to the Cold War battle against communism. The administration gave high priority to restating the threat posed by the Soviet Union.[2] Philip Nicolaides, the coordinator of Voice of America commentary and news analysis provided a summary of how the administration intended to portray the Soviet threat "as the last great predatory empire on earth, remorselessly enslaving its own diverse ethnic populations, crushing the legitimate aspirations of its captive nations, and ever seeking by all means ... to widen the area it subjugates" (Nicolaides, quoted in Getler 1981: 20). Reagan, the great communicator, repeatedly delivered the call to action to meet this threat. During his first years in office, Reagan repeatedly drew upon a speech he had first delivered during the 1964 Presidential campaign to explain the underlying basis of his foreign and defense policy to the American public:

> We are at war with the most dangerous enemy that has ever faced mankind in his long climb from the swamp to the stars ... and it has been said if we lose that war, and in so doing lose this freedom of ours, history will record with the greatest astonishment that those who had the most to lose did the least to prevent its happening ... You and I have a rendezvous with destiny. We will preserve for our children this, the last best hope for man on earth, or we will sentence them to take the last step into a thousand years of darkness.
>
> (Smith *et al.* 1980: 136)

Today, it is hard to imagine this sort of rhetoric being associated with the US nuclear weapons program. Nevertheless, the Reagan administration struck a political chord with the American public and Congress. Reagan presided over one of the largest military buildups in US history and today the US nuclear arsenal is made up largely of weapons and delivery systems developed and procured by his administration.

The politics of decline: the 2001 and 2010 Nuclear Posture Reviews

Although it is too early to assess the impact of the 2010 Nuclear Posture Review (NPR), it is clear that the 2001 NPR was highly controversial and largely ineffective, at least in terms of the portion of the review that actually dealt with revitalizing the US nuclear arsenal.[3] The vision of the US nuclear procurement, employment, deployment, and declaratory policy developed by the George W. Bush administration in 2001 was both logical and consistent, while offering a compelling description of how nuclear weapons would be combined with missile defense and conventional capabilities to create a new "strategic deterrent." But this technical and strategic virtuosity could not overcome the fact that the 2001 Nuclear Posture Review failed to account for nuclear politics. As a result, criticism of the NPR was immediate, overwhelming and shallow: critics never admitted that its logic was sound, its policies coherent, or that concerns about arms race and crisis instability were overblown when it came to deterring Iran, North Korea or al-Qaeda. Echoes of the logic inherent in the 2001 NPR continue to reverberate today (Lieber and Press 2009), but they are met with incredulity and renewed calls for nuclear disarmament (Lodal 2010).

The 2001 NPR began with the premise that with the collapse of the Soviet Union, the United States essentially had escaped a situation of Mutual Assured Destruction, especially if one believed that relations between the United States and Russia would improve over time.[4] Nevertheless, the United States still faced an emerging threat posed by nuclear terrorism and rogue states armed with chemical, biological, nuclear or radiological weapons. The authors of the Bush NPR, led by Keith Payne, believed that the US nuclear arsenal – essentially the Cold War surplus arsenal created by the Reagan defense buildup – was ill suited to this nascent threat. Existing warheads were too large and were nearing the end of their life expectancy. Missile defenses were rudimentary. Delivery systems were not designed to meet emerging threats. Many in the administration also believed that US nuclear deterrent threats appeared increasingly incredible to friend and foes alike. It was becoming increasingly difficult to assert that an American President would fire a submarine launched ballistic missile packed with warheads with a combined yield measured in multiple megatons in response to some attack by a rogue regime. The US nuclear arsenal had to be retooled to meet this changing threat environment (Wirtz and Russell 2002/2003).

The 2001 NPR called for a reduction in the role of nuclear weapons in the Russian–American strategic relationship and overall US deterrent policy. Instead, the US would create a new "strategic deterrent," based on a "new triad" of long-range conventional precision strike capabilities, missile defense, and a revitalized nuclear infrastructure. Additionally, new types of nuclear weapons would be developed – earth penetrating warheads, low yield nuclear warheads, "boutique" nuclear weapons that would offer variations in nuclear weapons effects – to better match emerging threats posed by proliferation of weapons of mass destruction into the hands of dangerous regimes or terrorist groups. Strategists would eventually possess a larger basket of capabilities to meet potential threats. Preventive war and pre-emptive options would increase against opponents armed with highly limited capabilities. Most importantly, deterrence would be bolstered because the United States could make threats that were proportional to the challenges posed by proliferators. The United States would possess an effective capability to defeat and, by implication, deter emerging threats.

Over the course of its eight years in office, the Bush administration enjoyed some success in terms of implementing its NPR. The size of the US nuclear arsenal was vastly reduced: the Bush administration cut the size of the US nuclear stockpile by nearly 50 percent (Kristensen 2010). In May 2002, the administration also signed a Strategic Offensive Reductions Treaty with the Russians, despite the fact that relations between Moscow and Washington were at times rocky (Treaty Between The United States of America and the Russian Federation on Strategic Offensive Reduction (SORT/Treaty of Moscow 2002). Progress was made in developing a "strategic deterrent" as national missile defenses were deployed and advances continued in developing a conventional global strike capability. The administration experienced absolutely no success, however, when it came to developing and deploying new types of nuclear weapons. The administration failed to even obtain funding for a feasibility and cost study related to the development of a Robust Nuclear Earth Penetrator. The administration then focused on development of the Reliable Replacement Warhead, which was intended to serve as a safe and easily maintained replacement for Reagan era weapons that were reaching the end of even their extended life expectancy. This program also failed to receive any funding from Congress (Medalia 2009). The failure to tie a highly technical program to any compelling political or strategic vision doomed the more ambitious elements of the 2001 NPR to political oblivion.

The Barack Obama administration benefitted from the Bush administration's experience: the 2010 Nuclear Posture Review is a public document that was released with much fanfare. The two documents share much in common. The Obama administration announced its commitment to the new strategic triad, while also reducing the role of nuclear weapons in US military strategy. The administration also intends to maintain strategic stability with Russia and to continue the arms control process. Additionally, the Obama administration has made a commitment to bolster the US nuclear infrastructure, operational forces, and command and control structure so that the United States can maintain a safe and effective nuclear deterrent for the foreseeable future. But in a political sense, the administration has laid down an important new benchmark for US nuclear policy: The United States has now apparently adopted nuclear abolition as the ultimate goal of US nuclear strategy. Nuclear deployment, employment, procurement, and declaratory policy will now be developed with this ultimate goal in mind.

Admittedly, the Obama administration is realistic about its proposed time frame for meeting this objective, i.e., not in the lifetime of anyone reading this chapter. It also is realistic about the political, strategic and technological conditions – basically the virtual elimination of even the prospect of significant conflict or nuclear "breakout" – that would have to be in place before the United States completely abandoned its nuclear arsenal. The administration, however, is apparently banking on the political support created by this objective for the backing it needs to maintain a nuclear infrastructure and force structure. With this force as a strategic hedge, and without a nuclear research and development program to monitor advances in the field of nuclear physics, the United States could find itself without the leverage or intelligence it needs to advance its disarmament agenda. Paradoxically, the administration has advanced disarmament as a justification for maintaining a viable nuclear arsenal, or at least prevent the US nuclear force from disintegrating over the next couple of decades. Whether or not the administration can pull off this political sleight of hand, while providing concrete evidence that the United States is slowly getting out of the nuclear business – termination of TLAM-N is a case in point – remains to be seen. Whether it can maintain a viable nuclear infrastructure without building new nuclear weapons seems highly unlikely.

Conclusion

Are the political and strategic statements developed by various administrations epiphenomenal? In other words, is it better to think of administration statements on nuclear weapons and strategy as reflecting rather than leading public and elite opinion? That is a difficult question to answer because administrations that championed successful nuclear programs were able to articulate clearly their strategic outlook in a way that corresponded to political realities. The above survey also suggests that Presidents have to either develop or harness political support for their programs. Nuclear programs that extend beyond the existing societal consensus are apparently doomed to failure: that is the dominant lesson drawn from the 2001 NPR. By tying US nuclear doctrine to nonproliferation and disarmament objectives, the Obama administration has chosen a plausible political argument for maintaining a safe and effective nuclear deterrent. Whether or not this vision of a future world devoid of nuclear weapons will work to strengthen the US nuclear enterprise over the short and medium-term, however, remains problematic. But the administration has taken an important first step by acknowledging political realities and by framing its nuclear doctrine in a politically acceptable manner.

Another question that was raised, but remains unanswered by this chapter is the impact of domestic nuclear politics on the Obama administration's foreign and defense policies that clearly focus on diminishing the US nuclear arsenal. So far, at least, nuclear politics are manifest in decisions related to the growth of the US arsenal, either serving to bolster or break efforts to improve qualitatively nuclear warheads and associated delivery systems. But will nuclear politics serve as a break on the downside, limiting administrative leeway in cutting critical programs? In other words, it is clear that the US public does not support qualitative improvements in its nuclear arsenal, but that does not mean it no longer supports the continued maintenance of a nuclear capability second to none. The Obama administration apparently recognizes this fundamental limitation to its disarmament objectives: it steadfastly avoided any reference to accepting vulnerability to Chinese nuclear forces. Recognizing, accepting or endorsing mutual societal vulnerability between the United States and the People's Republic of China would probably amount to political suicide. Nevertheless, the possibility that nuclear politics also bounds the limits of what is possible on the downside suggests that overly ambitious disarmament agendas are just as likely to be defeated by domestic opposition as they are to be frustrated by international actors that ignore nonproliferation norms.

Notes

1 According to the authors of NSC-68:

> There are risks in making ourselves strong. A large measure of sacrifice and discipline will be demanded of the American people. They will be asked to give up some of the benefits, which they have come to associate with their freedoms. Nothing could be more important than they fully understand the reasons for this. The risks of a superficial understanding or of an inadequate appreciation of the issues are obvious and might lead to the adoption of measures, which in themselves would jeopardize the integrity of our system. At any point in the process of demonstrating our will to make good our fundamental purpose, the Kremlin may decide to precipitate a general war, or in testing us, may go too far. These are the risks we will invite by making ourselves strong, but they are lesser risks than those we seek to avoid.
>
> (United States Objectives and Programs for National Security 1950: 36)

2 According to Richard Pipes:

> To frustrate Soviet global strategy, it is necessary, first and foremost, to acknowledge that it exists. We must get rid of the notion, that the Soviet Union acts out of fear, that its actions are invariably reactions to U.S. initiatives ... We are dealing with an adversary who is driven not by fear but by aggressive impulses.
>
> (Pipes 1981: 191)

3 The 2001 NPR remains classified. Excerpts from the classified version of the report were apparently published in the *New York Times* and *Los Angeles Times*. Most of the text is posted at http://globalsecurity.org/wmd/library/policy/dod/npr.htm. By contrast, the 2010 NPR is a public document (*Nuclear Posture Review*

Report 2010), see *Nuclear Posture Review Report,* April 2010, www.defense.gov/npr/docs/2010%20nuclear%20posture%20review%20report.pdf.

4 The possibility that Mutual Assured Destruction would not dominate strategic considerations opened the door for policymakers to reconsider pre-emptive war fighting options when it came to dealing with emerging threats. See Payne for a discussion of the history and logic behind this alternative nuclear strategy (Payne 2008).

References

Allen, Richard V. (1981) "Interview with *Business Week,*" *Selected Statements,* US Department of Defense, June 29.

Baker, Fred W. (2007) "Air Force relieves commanders involved in nuclear weapons incident." Available at Global Security.org www.globalsecurity.org/military/library/news/2007/10/mil-071019-afps078.htm.

Ball, Desmond (1986) "Development of the SIOP, 1960–1983," in Desmond Ball and Jeffrey Richelson (eds) *Strategic Nuclear Targeting,* Ithaca, NY: Cornell University Press.

Brown, Michael (1992) *Flying Blind: The Politics of the U.S. Strategic Bomber Program,* Ithaca, NY: Cornell University Press.

Commission on Maintaining United States Nuclear Weapons Expertise (1999) *Report of the Commission on Maintaining United States Nuclear Weapons Expertise.* Available at http://www.doeal.gov/llnlcompetition/reportsandcomments/chilesrpt.pdf.

Enthoven, Alain C. and Wayne K. Smith (1971) *How Much is Enough? Shaping the Defense Program 1961–1969,* New York: Harper and Row.

Evangelista, Mathew (1988) *Innovation and the Arms Race: How the United Sates and the Soviet Union Develop New Military Technologies,* Ithaca, NY: Cornell University Press.

Gates, Robert M. (2008) Correspondence, Secretary of Defense to The Honorable James R. Schlesinger, June 12, regarding Establishment of Task Force on Nuclear Weapons Management.

Getler, Michael (1981) "ICA plans Poland TV Spectacular," *Washington Post,* January 28.

Greenwood, Ted (1988) *Making the MIRV: A Study of Defense Decision Making,* Lanham, MD: University Press of America.

Hymans, Jacques (2006) *The Psychology of Nuclear Proliferation: Identity, Emotions, and Foreign Policy,* Cambridge: Cambridge University Press.

Jervis, Robert (1989) *The Meaning of the Nuclear Revolution,* Ithaca, NY: Cornell University Press.

Kirkpatrick, Jeane (1981) "U.S. security & Latin America," *Commentary* 71.

Kristensen, Hans M. (2010) "United States discloses size of nuclear weapons stockpile," FAS Strategic Security Blog, May 3. Available at www.fas.org/blog/ssp/2010/05/stockpilenumber.php.

Lavoy, Peter R. (2006) "Nuclear proliferation over the next decade," *NonProliferation Review* 13: 433–454.

Lieber, Keir and Daryl Press (2009) "The nukes we need," *Foreign Affairs* 88(2).

Lodal, Jan (2010) "The counterforce fantasy," *Foreign Affairs* 90(2).

Medalia, Jonathan (2009) "The reliable replacement warhead program: background and current developments," *CRS Report for Congress* RL32929, Congressional Research Service, July 27. Available at www.fas.org/sgp/crs/nuke/RL32929.pdf.

Nuclear Posture Review Report (2010). Available at www.defense.gov/npr/docs/2010%20nuclear%20posture%20review%20report.pdf.

Paul, T.V. (2009) *The Tradition of Non-use of Nuclear Weapons*, Stanford, CA: Stanford University Press.

Payne, Keith B. (2008) *The Great American Gamble: Deterrence Theory and Practice from the Cold War to the Twenty-first Century*, Fairfax, VA: National Institute Press.

Perrow, Charles (1999) *Normal Accidents: Living with High-risk Technologies*, Princeton, NJ: Princeton University Press.

Pipes, Richard (1981) *U.S.–Soviet Relations in the Era of Détente*, Boulder, CO: Westview Press.

Podhoretz, Norman (1981) "The future danger," *Commentary* 71.

Powaski, Ronald (2000) *Return to Armageddon*, Oxford: Oxford University Press.

Sagan, Scott D. (1993) *The Limits of Safety*, Princeton, NJ: Princeton University Press.

Sagan, Scott D. (1996/1997) "Why do states build nuclear weapons? Three models in search of a bomb," *International Security* 21(3): 54–86.

Smith, Hedrick, Adam Clymer, Leonard Lilk, Robert Lindsey and Richard Burt (1980) *Reagan, the Man, the President*, New York: Macmillan Publishing Company.

Snyder, Glenn (1964) "The balance of power and the balance of terror," in Paul Seabury (ed.) *The Balance of Power*, San Francisco, CA: Chandler.

Tannenwald, Nina (2008) *The Nuclear Taboo*, Cambridge: Cambridge University Press.

Task Force on DOD Nuclear Weapons Management (2008) *Report of the Secretary of Defense Taskforce on DoD Nuclear Weapons Management, Phase II: Review of the DoD Nuclear Mission (Schlesinger Report)*.

Treaty Between The United States of America and the Russian Federation on Strategic Offensive Reduction (SORT/Treaty of Moscow), May 24, 2002. Available at http://cns.miis.edu/inventory/pdfs/sort.pdf.

United States Objectives and Programs for National Security (NSC-68) (1950) *Report to the President Pursuant to the President's Directive of January 31, 1950*, National Security Council.

Wells, Samuel F. (1979) "Sounding the toscin: NSC-68 and the soviet threat," *International Security* 4(2).

Wirtz, James J. and James A. Russell (2002/2003) "A quiet revolution: nuclear strategy for the 21st century," *Joint Forces Quarterly*. Available at www.dtic.mil/doctrine/jel/jfq_pubs/0433.pdf.

Wirtz, James J. (2006) "System Analysis," in Peter Karsten (ed.) *Encyclopedia of War and American Society*, Thousand Oaks, CA: Sage.

8 Bargaining, nuclear proliferation, and interstate disputes

Erik Gartzke[1] *and Dong-Joon Jo*

Introduction

Since the advent of the nuclear age, speculation has raged about whether taming the atom inflames or pacifies world politics. Optimists claim that nuclear weapons deter, and therefore stabilize the politics of nations (Mearsheimer 1984, 1993; Waltz 1981, 1990). Pessimists see nuclear weapons as inciting fear, hubris, and misperception (Jervis 1984, 1988, 1989a; Sagan 1989). A third, somewhat neglected possibility is that both arguments are right, and wrong. Diplomatic bargains tend to dampen the observable impact of nuclear weapons, even as contrasting tendencies tend to cancel each other out. To the degree that nuclear weapons influence the concessions proliferators are likely to obtain in lieu of force, proliferation does much less to account for behavioral conflict.

Possession of nuclear weapons increases the risks to opponents that choose to fight. In general, military advantages can be used to discourage an opponent from attempting to shift the status quo in the opponent's favor (deterrence) or to encourage an opponent to accept a shift that favors the advantaged state (compellence). A tradeoff thus exists between efforts to secure the status quo, and seeking to procure new prerogatives or benefits. Pressing for concessions raises the risk of war. Failing to press an opponent reduces the benefits available to a state. If opponents are more inhibited by nuclear weapons than nuclear states are emboldened, then deterrence prevails, as optimists suggest. If instead opponents are less cowed by nuclear weapons than proliferators are encouraged, conflict will tend to spiral, as pessimists warn. Where ambition roughly equals inhibition, nuclear weapons will not appear to make much difference as to whether states fight.

Even if only some of the substantial increase in lethality from "going nuclear" can be converted into political leverage, nuclear capable nations are bound to increase their influence in international affairs. Greater influence amounts to getting what states want without having to use force. To the degree that nuclear capabilities lead to bargains that approximate the outcomes states expect from fighting, aggression becomes less appealing and the anxieties of opponents are reduced. Diplomacy serves as a tool for smoothing the bumpy road of world politics.

The decision to proliferate is also endogenous to conflict. Nations are not assigned nuclear weapons at random, but select into nuclear status despite high costs, long delays in development, and international opprobrium. Countries with significant security problems or responsibilities, and substantial governmental resources are more prone to seek nuclear weapons (Jo and Gartzke 2007). These same nations fight more often, not because they possess a nuclear arsenal, but because the causes of conflict also prompt states to proliferate. Nations with few enemies, modest resources, limited technology, or little dissatisfaction about world affairs are unlikely to pursue nuclear capabilities and also are less inclined to fight. Thus, nominal nuclear status probably overstates the empirical effect of proliferation in propagating interstate disputes.

This does not mean that nuclear proliferation is "consequence free." On the contrary, as other studies in this issue demonstrate, nuclear weapons status heavily influences the distribution of conflict behavior. Nuclear capable countries have more minor disputes, but fewer wars (Rauchhaus, this volume). Opponents of nuclear powers are less likely to escalate during crises, though nuclear status does not appear to be an important determinant of selection into crises (Beardsley and Asal, this volume). The introduction of nuclear weapons also front-loads conflict. While new nuclear nations have more disputes, the effect decays as older nuclear powers have slightly fewer disputes (Horowitz, this volume). Proliferation seems to matter most for the quality, not the quantity of conflict.

After reviewing the relevant literature, we develop hypotheses from the optimist and pessimist perspectives, as well as our own theory about the consequences of proliferation. We then instrument for the tendency of some nations to acquire a nuclear arsenal. Nuclear weapons do not have a significant effect on conventional disputes once the impetus to proliferate is taken into account. Instead, proliferators prosper by becoming influential diplomatically. Nuclear weapons thus appear to matter more for who gets what in the world than for who fights whom.

Nuclear security scholarship

The preeminent concern of early research on nuclear security – after fear of the consequences if these weapons were used – was how to use these weapons (Freedman 1981). Diplomats and scholars understood that world politics occurs in the shadow of force (Clausewitz 1976[1832]; Nicolson 1960). The prospect of military violence generates influence which in turn often obviates the need to fight. With nuclear weapons, however, the scale of ensuing carnage ensures that many threats are incredible (Powell 1990). If threats lack credibility, then nuclear weapons have no foreign policy utility and are only useful when used. Strategists grappled with ways to make the unthinkable plausible (Brodie 1946, 1959; Kahn 1960; Kissinger 1957; Schelling 1960, 1966), not out of a desire for annihilation, but because of the need for diplomatic leverage.

Whether or to what degree efforts by advocates to engineer credibility succeeded, and what effect these efforts had on the Cold War, are subjects of considerable debate (Gaddis 1989; LeFeber 2002; Lebow and Stein 1995). Strategies like brinkmanship were perceived to be useful by some participants, while others practiced détente, presumably also out of a sense that this was in the national interest (Gaddis 1983). Part of the ambiguity may result from a false rhetoric of Cold War politics. Kennan's (1947) influential notion of containment enshrined the status quo as the nominal US strategic objective (Gaddis 2005).[2] The Soviets pushed and the US resisted. Yet, Kennan's conception and most discussions of deterrence ignore a more dynamic reality in which the United States, protected by its nuclear umbrella, was able to pursue ambitious revisions of the international order. Nations that opposed US interests were forced to decide whether they were willing to play chicken with a nuclear power in advancing preferred objectives. The United States probably was not willing to risk nuclear war over many policies, but opponents were similarly constrained. Few could credibly threaten the United States in more than a peripheral manner when a direct attack meant nuclear retaliation. Nuclear weapons thus provided a cushion permitting the freer exercise of conventional force and contained conflict to distant places.

Dichotomy prompts dialectic: optimists and pessimists

While some scholars worked on ways to make nuclear weapons more potent politically, others focused on the hazards posed by proliferation. Pessimists emphasize the consequences of nuclear war, accidents, and the risk that the possession of nuclear weapons may cause politicians, or publics, to become more aggressive (Dunn and Kahn 1976; Betts 1977b; Barnaby 1993; Sagan 1996).[3] Concerns about nuclear proliferation can be clarified by distinguishing between the number of nuclear weapons available to states, and the number of countries that possess nuclear weapons. Existing nuclear powers could easily address the global supply of nuclear weapons by reducing their own arsenals. The number of nuclear-equipped nations is of more concern, but if the fear of nuclear war is based on likely casualties, destruction, and environmental damage, then some metric exists linking the probability of wars involving nuclear weapons with the intensity of an exchange, should one occur. Increasing the potential for nuclear war is not necessarily worse than increasing the anticipated scale of a nuclear contest. Nor is proliferation inherently harmful to the proliferator, even if adding members to the nuclear club raises the risk of nuclear war. Pessimists thus conceive of proliferation as a collective action problem in which individual-level benefits from proliferating are seen as more intense than the social bad of one more nuclear nation.

If proliferation is a collective action problem, however, many more states should have proliferated in the six-odd decades of the nuclear era. Given available evidence, we must conclude either that nuclear weapons are not all that appealing to most nations, or that the normative efforts to counter proliferation have been effective. Previous research suggests that pressure from the international community and from major powers has had a limited effect (Singh and Way 2004; Jo and Gartzke 2007). Instead, what appears to have kept most nations from proliferating is that nuclear weapons are: (1) extremely expensive and difficult to develop or acquire, and (2) their utility is relatively limited. The exercise or threat of nuclear war is only practical when touching on national survival. Most nations, if not content, are secure enough in their sovereign status to rate the possibility of conquest as small. Even insecure nations often possess protection from major powers. Countries that fear overthrow from abroad, or other similar major security problems are more likely to consider proliferation prudent. Countries with ambitious foreign policies – designed either to maintain or significantly alter the status quo – may also find nuclear proliferation appealing if their opponents are much stronger materially, or if they possess large conventional capabilities, so that there are declining margins from further investments in existing military structures. For most of the world's nations, too poor to buy a significant conventional capability, and not unhappy or optimistic enough to believe that major change is possible and beneficial, nuclear weapons are not a practical option. Where pessimists fear conflict resulting from nuclear proliferation, optimists see the opportunity to promote stability. Precisely because nuclear contests promise to inflict unprecedented trauma, nuclear war is unlikely to occur. A looming risk of nuclear conflagration will tend to deter conventional forms of international violence, given the risk of escalation faced by nuclear powers.[4] Waltz (1990) argues that the chilling effect of nuclear weapons means that proliferation among "stable powers" is bound to promote peace. Mearsheimer (1984, 1990) suggests that proliferation generally is defensible and that the desire for nuclear weapons is understandable. Jervis (1989b) claims that nuclear deterrence can be credited with the lack of major war since 1950. Was it not nuclear weapons that kept the United States and the Soviet Union at bay during the Cold War?[5]

Existing arguments thus offer contradictory conclusions about nuclear proliferation and its effects on conventional conflict. At least some sources of the dialectic lie in differing (and incomplete) theoretical frameworks. Optimists, who focus on the deterrent effect of nuclear weapons, ignore psychological and informational aspects of proliferation. Pessimists are more attuned to the role of perception in international affairs, but fail to differentiate the stochastic and equilibrium consequences of claims. Work in other contexts notes that contrasting conclusions about cause and effect in international competition derive from different, typically implicit, assumptions about risk propensity (Bueno de Mesquita 1981). The nuclear dialectic appears also to hinge on contrasting claims about human behavior, with optimists arguing that fear inhibits, while pessimists emphasize that anger may spiral into aggression. At the same time, both perspectives assume that, while capabilities evolve, policy positions do not. Shifts in military potential brought about by nuclear proliferation almost certainly alter the balance of power, but whether capability shocks increase or decrease the likelihood of militarized disputes depends on how diplomats respond to these evolving conditions. Leaders might err on the side of caution or recklessness in estimating relative power. Citizens could become apprehensive or enraged by new strategic threats. But whether these reactions lead to war or to peace depends, in large part, on what diplomatic bargains nations fashion in the shadow of fear, anger, and nuclear weapons.

Empirical analysis of nuclear status and conflict

The paucity of nuclear conflict makes meaningful empirical inferences about the consequences of proliferation difficult. Nevertheless, several studies attempt to draw conclusions from samples of conventional disputes (Geller 1990; Huth 1990; Sample 1998, 2002; Gibler *et al.* 2005).[6] The rationale for studying non-nuclear contests is twofold. First, these disputes are of interest in their own right. Knowledge of how proliferation influences conventional conflicts affects evaluation of the overall consequences of proliferation. Insights also enrich our understanding of war. Second, divergent claims about nuclear proliferation carry over to the study of conventional conflict.

One group of studies claims that nuclear weapons reduce the likelihood of militarized contests by dissuading challengers from precipitating violence. The cost of nuclear war can be seen as a deterrent to conflict regardless of whether nuclear contests result from cumulative and unplanned actions of states or are waged by defenders after performing rational calculations (Schelling 1980: 187–203; Morgan 1977: 42–45; Powell 1990: 110; Sagan and Waltz 2003: 34). Several studies support the claim that nuclear weapons deter conventional conflict (Bueno de Mesquita and Riker 1982; Betts 1977a; Russett 1989; Huth and Russett 1993).

Another group of studies argues that nuclear weapons do not have any significant effect on conventional contests. Use of nuclear weapons is proscribed by international and domestic norms. A "nuclear taboo" makes these weapons impotent in both military or political terms (Osgood and Tucker 1967; Blainey 1988[1973]; Snyder and Diesing 1977; Blechman and Kaplan 1978). Because nuclear threats are not credible, they must be ineffective as well (Huth and Russett 1988; Paul 1995). Earlier studies support the claim that there is no deterrent effect of nuclear weapons in the outbreak of militarized contests (Organski and Kugler 1980; Kugler

1984). Huth and Russett show that nuclear weapons have no significant impact on extended deterrence (Huth and Russett 1984, 1988; Huth 1988; Russett 1989). Huth (1990) assesses an interaction between nuclear weapons status and conventional capabilities. Nuclear weapons matter most in deterrence situations where the conventional capabilities of the nuclear state are relatively weak; they matter least when the nuclear power possesses significant conventional forces.

Theory: Goldie Locks and Dale Carnegie

We add three elements to the study of nuclear politics. First, while optimists and pessimists each make valid points, their claims tend to work in opposite directions; if both views are (partially) correct, then the net effect is to diminish observable results of either perspective. Second, to the degree that nuclear weapons matter politically, they should tend to yield different self-enforcing settlements, regardless of whether nations fight or not. The effects of proliferation on influence and on conflict are then substitutes. Finally, variable incentives to proliferate imply that nations that "go nuclear" are more prone to fight, with or without nuclear weapons. This endogeneity tends to inflate the apparent impact of proliferation on conflict. The first two items are discussed below, while the third item (endogeneity) is presented in the subsequent empirical section.

Goldie Locks and the three theories of nuclear porridge

In the old fairy tale, Goldie Locks samples three bowls of purloined porridge. One is too cold. Another is too hot. But the third bowl of porridge is just right, and so she eats it all up. The effect of proliferation on conventional disputes is like a bowl of porridge, but which one? The optimistic view is that proliferation is cold. Nations will avoid conflict if there exists a sufficient hazard of unacceptable costs or risks. Possession of nuclear weapons dampens the ardor of nations for war by making fighting prohibitively costly. The status quo prevails as challenges are less likely.

Deterrence is a special case of coercive foreign policy in which the demand the deterring nation makes is the status quo. The claims of proliferation optimists hinge on the assertion that nuclear nations do not expand their objectives as they increase their capabilities. Yet, proliferators face incentives to do just this. While often couched in terms of deterrence, brinkmanship involves an attempt by at least one nation to challenge and alter the status quo. If a challenger is equipped with nuclear weapons, then either this capacity is not being exercised, or the challenger is using its nuclear status to seek to compel, not deter. Scholars generally agree that compellence does not reduce the risk of conflict. It follows that the risk of war is contingent on what is being demanded by both sides, and that what is being demanded is in turn subject to the expectations of competitors. Countries with a nuclear advantage must choose between spending some or all of this advantage on security (freedom from harm), or influence (discretion over outcomes). The bounded nature of any budget means that a country cannot increase its security and influence with the same increment of power. A country that only sought to deter could lower the probability of experiencing a dispute, but to do so, the country must refrain from pursuing any changes in the status quo that might be opposed by other nations. Countries with nuclear weapons that want to alter the status quo have the potential to do so, but again only by increasing opposition, and in turn the risk of conflict. Nuclear nations may prefer security to influence, but this is a more idiosyncratic claim than the assertion that nuclear status deters. There is a case to be made on either side of the debate. Not all nations proliferate. Those that do must be different in some way from those that do not. One way that proliferators might differ from non-proliferators is in their valuation for influence. The pessimist view sees proliferation porridge as hot. Nuclear weapons may feed a political appetite that exceeds the national grasp, exacerbating instability and encouraging conflict. Proliferation might also cause other countries to underestimate the nuclear country's capabilities or resolve. Disagreements about the efficaciousness of nuclear weapons, rapid changes in the balance of power brought about by nuclear weapons, or secrecy could lead nations to misperceive. Finally, nuclear weapons could encourage leaders to act precipitously or without consulting with opponents.

While it is reasonable to be concerned that nuclear weapons may lead to recklessness, it is no less plausible that proliferation encourages restraint. To get the proliferation story "just right," requires mixing elements of both stories. The ardor for war among some leaders may diminish in the face of nuclear weapons. Anecdotes from the Cold War, and from crises in the Indian subcontinent suggest that leaders are well aware of the tremendous dangers posed by escalating in the face of nuclear capabilities. At other times, the presence of nuclear weapons might inflame hostilities. Efforts by nuclear powers to use force appear to be encouraged by their security from retaliation under a nuclear umbrella. If nuclear weapons deter in some instances, and spiral at other times, then these two forces will tend to cancel one another out. Even if one tendency occurs more often, the overall relationship is weakened by the countervailing tendency.

"Just right" could result from mixing "too hot" and "too cold." Yet, there are tremendous incentives for leaders to correctly gauge strategic conditions. Proliferation almost certainly alters the balance of power. States that acquire nuclear weapons see their military capabilities change, increasing dramatically the ability of these states to inflict harm. Nuclear nations and competitors will benefit most if they adjust diplomatic bargains in response to evolving strategic conditions, rather than choosing to fight costly and unnecessary battles. Whether leaders judge circumstances correctly, or err in some manner, is key to assessing the consequences of proliferation.

What evidence is there that leaders err in equilibrium? War is rare. Even perennial rivals, with both means and motive, typically interact through words rather than force. Many purported precursors are omnipresent. At the very least, the timing of conflicts remains unclear. Conflicts should be more common, if factors that are regularly present are the cause. If instead disputes result from misperception, then it must be that the errors that precipitate disputes occur relatively infrequently, implying that states regularly identify mutually acceptable bargains, and that the presence of nuclear weapons is not sufficient for war. It is easier to explain the infrequent, episodic nature of warfare if leaders' estimates and initiatives usually match empirical conditions.

Finally, both optimists and pessimists imply a roughly uniform reaction to proliferation. If instead nuclear weapons can be used to shape global politics through influence, then what a nation wants is highly relevant to whether and to what extent another state approves/disapproves of attempts to proliferate. Powerful countries clearly pick favorites and targets when it comes to nuclear proliferation (Kroenig 2009a; Fuhrmann 2009). Capturing the effects of interest on proliferation ultimately requires that theories address differences in national objectives, but getting the overall relationships "about right" may be achieved by balancing the effects of "too hot" conceptions of nuclear pessimists with the "too cold" perspective of optimists:

Hypothesis 1 Optimist ("Too Cold"): States with nuclear weapons are less likely than non-nuclear states to be targets of conventional disputes.

Hypothesis 2 Pessimist ("Too Hot"): States with nuclear weapons are more likely than non-nuclear states to initiate conventional disputes.

Hypothesis 3 Balanced ("Just Right"): States with nuclear weapons are about as likely as non-nuclear states to initiate, or be the targets of, conventional disputes.

How to win friends or influence countries

Dale Carnegie, the business self-help guru, offered to make people popular and powerful at the same time. It may be more difficult in international politics to obtain friends and influence simultaneously. Winning friends involves doing things that other nations like, or at least not getting in the way of other nations as they pursue their objectives. A nation with limited aims and a strong defense is likely to be the optimal candidate for successful deterrence. In contrast, attempts to generate influence impinge on the interests of other countries. Having one's way in a conflict means denying others their ideal policies. The need often to concede influence for security, or vice versa, impacts the utility of military capabilities of any kind. It is a truism that diplomacy involves the politics of the possible. By proscribing what is possible, nuclear weapons arguably alter what nations contemplate in calling for, or resisting, change. Proliferation limits the influence of existing nuclear states and other powers by shifting the conditions that all states prefer to fighting. Countries intent on charting a different course in world affairs (pariah or rogue states),[7] and regional or major powers find it particularly valuable to proliferate. If warfare results disproportionately from uncertainty about power relations (Blainey 1988[1973]; Fearon 1995), and if nuclear capability shocks are relatively easily apprehended, then nuclear weapons should not have much impact on whether states fight. Even if nuclear weapons have the cognitive effects that proliferation partisans predict, changes in the probability of warfare only occur if competitors remain unresponsive to these changes. Bringing diplomacy "back in" to the study of nuclear politics implies little or no observable deterrent effect. Instead, we expect that nuclear status significantly influences a nation's status as well as success in diplomatic wrangling.

Hypothesis 4: States with nuclear weapons are more likely to receive diplomatic missions from other states than states without nuclear weapons.

Hypothesis 5: States with nuclear weapons are likely to receive higher level diplomatic missions from other states than states without nuclear weapons.

Hypothesis 6: States with nuclear weapons are more likely to obtain preferred policies peacefully.

Research design and data

We employ the directed dyad unit-of-analysis to test six hypotheses about the effect of nuclear weapons status on the initiation of militarized disputes, on influence, and on the settlement of conflicts. Directed dyads make it possible to differentiate between the behavior of initiators and targets, revealing additional information about causal processes (Bennett and Stam 2000). We use probit and ordinal probit, "White" standard errors to correct for the effects of spatial dependence on statistical significance, and cluster on the dyad to address heteroskedastic error variance. We also correct for temporal dependence using "peace years" and splines (Beck *et al.* 1998).

Nuclear weapons may be endogenous to conflict. Proliferation might effect, or reflect, power relations or patterns of interstate dispute behavior. The result would be to bias the size, or significance, of key coefficients. We examine this endogeneity by constructing an instrument for nuclear weapons status based on previous research (Jo and Gartzke 2007). The instrument is produced by estimating the effect of determinants of conventional conflict on nuclear weapons status in a dataset of country-years. Both datasets cover the period 1945 to 2001.[8] All variables rely on data from EUGene (Bennett and Stam 2001), with additional changes as noted.

Dependent variables

The main conflict variable is from the Correlates of War (COW) Militarized Interstate Dispute (MID) dataset (Gochman and Maoz 1984; Jones *et al.* 1996; Ghosn *et al.* 2004). MID Initiation is coded "1" if the potential challenger initiates a MID against its counterpart and "0" otherwise.[9]

We operationalize influence in two ways. Each is flawed, but hopefully together they lend some credibility to our claims. First, the COW Diplomatic Exchange Dataset (Bayer 2006) lists directed bilateral deputations at the chargé d'affaires, ministerial, or ambassadorial level. These data are not coded annually.[10] Formal recognition reflects attention from (to) other nations (Small and Singer 1973). While diplomatic ties result from many factors, our argument about nuclear status as influence implies that proliferation will increase diplomatic recognition.

Second, we examine variables from the Issue Correlates of War (ICOW) project (Hensel and Mitchell 2007). ICOW data code issues (territory, river, maritime) over which nations disagree. These data are unusual in capturing the distribution of stakes in a conflict, not just the presence or absence of violent behavior. ICOW also code information about settlement attempts. We focus on whether any attempt is made to resolve an ICOW issue in a given year (ATTNONE), whether attempts are peaceful (ATTANYP), and which side obtains concessions (RESOLVED).

Independent variables

The possession of nuclear weapons is both a dependent and independent variable in our analysis. Nuclear status is coded dichotomously (presence or absence of nuclear weapons by a country in a given year). The directed dyadic analysis distinguishes between a potential Nuclear Initiator and a Nuclear Target. We use the consensus list of dates for nuclear status adopted by all participants in this book, though our results do not depend on this coding.[11] In addition to actual nuclear status, we generate predicted probabilities of possessing nuclear weapons, Pr.(Nuclear Initiator) and Pr.(Nuclear Target), based on work by Jo and Gartzke (2007) and detailed in an appendix to this study. An appropriate instrument should: (1) correlate with the key predicting variable (i.e., the nuclear weapons dummies), (2) not correlate with the error term, and (3) act on the outcome indirectly, through other predicting variables. Our instrument reflects latent nuclear production capacity, regime type, economic and military capabilities, and conventional and nuclear threat.

Nuclear and conventional capabilities could be substitutes or complements. We rely on the COW Composite Index of National Capability (CINC) to measure a country's power. Since the analysis involves directed dyads, we can assess the impact of capability separately for each state. Enduring rivalries are widely used to identify states or dyads facing important national security challenges (Bennett 1996; Diehl and Goertz 2000). Dyadic Rivalry is a dummy variable coded "1" when the members of a dyad are considered rivals with each other (Klein *et al.* 2006). States that are not rivals may nevertheless experience greater hostility due to diffusion. Nuclear status is especially likely to matter when one or both members of the dyad proliferate to address security concerns with third-party states. Once armed, nuclear nations may act more aggressively toward any partner. We thus add a dummy variable for each state's monadic Rivalry Status.[12]

Alliance is a dummy variable coded for whether dyad members share an alliance.[13] Most researchers agree that allies should be less likely to fight each other (Morrow 2000; Kimball 2006). In contrast, Bueno de Mesquita (1981) argues that allies are more dispute prone. Others see the effect of alliances as contingent on other factors (Bremer 1992; Bearce *et al.* 2006).

Regime type is widely viewed as a determinant of conflict behavior (Doyle 1997; Russett 1993; Russett and Oneal 2001). Previous research finds that democracies are more likely to develop nuclear weapons (Jo and Gartzke 2007). We construct three variables using Polity IV data (Gurr *et al.* 1989; Jaggers and Gurr 1995; Marshall and Jaggers 2002). To measure the regime type of each state, we take the difference between Polity DEMOC and AUTOC indexes, add ten, and then divide by two. This produces a regime score with an interval [0, 10] that matches the domain of the component variables. We use the product of monadic regime scores, since it is the interaction of democracies that is said to make them different (Oneal and Russett 1999; Oneal *et al.* 2003).

Neighbors fight more often than distant states (Boulding 1962; Bremer 1992; Gleditsch 2003). Contiguity is an ordinal variable identifying national proximity based on the COW six-point scale.[14] Since contiguity may capture both opportunity and willingness, it makes sense also to include a metric measure of geographic proximity. Distance is coded as the log transformed great circle distance between capital cities of countries in a given directed dyad year.

Though not reviewed below, we examined many other variables. We use Gleditsch's (2002) dataset of economic variables to determine whether dyadic trade interdependence or monadic openness alters our basic findings. Economic ties have a moderate effect on conflict (McMillan 1997; Mansfield and Pollins 2001).[15] Economic integration may also condition a state's motivation (Fuhrmann, this volume), or ability to proliferate (Kroenig 2009b). We also assess economic development, measured as gross domestic product per capita (GDPPC). Prosperous countries may be more satisfied, while wealthy nations can fund capable militaries (Boehmer 2001). While the economic variables do significantly influence conflict behavior, our findings remain unchanged.

Studies of interstate conflict often include COW major power dummies. Unfortunately, the coding criteria for these data are subjective. More problematic for our purposes, the COW list appears to have been influenced by nuclear weapons status. We prefer not to include major power dummies in the main statistical tests, since the list overlaps closely with early proliferators.[16]

Results

Table 8.1 lists the coefficient estimates and standard errors of two probit models relating nuclear weapons status and other variables to the likelihood of a MID in the period 1945 to 2000. The exogenous model codes the actual presence or absence of nuclear weapons. The endogenous model uses the probability that a state possesses nuclear weapons as an instrument for nuclear status, based on the model outlined in the appendix.[17] Military capabilities, regime type, rivalry status, and alliances have two possible avenues for influencing conflict. Each variable directly affects whether states fight, and also impacts conflict indirectly, through proliferation.

The effect of nuclear status on conflict does appear to be conditioned by the causes of proliferation. In the first (exogenous) model, having nuclear weapons significantly increases the chances of initiating a militarized dispute. The situation changes after incorporating the indirect effect of causal variables on MIDs. Substituting the instrument for nuclear proliferation reveals that relatively little of the effect of nuclear weapons on conflict behavior is attributable to the weapons themselves. Instead, countries with security problems, greater interest in international affairs, or significant military capabilities are simultaneously more likely to fight and proliferate.

While reported significance thresholds are adequate to reject hypotheses involving a relationship between nuclear weapons and MID initiation, assessing the hypothesis that nuclear weapons do not affect dispute behavior requires that we reverse the bias in significance testing. Our null is that some relationship exists between nuclear proliferation and

Table 8.1 The effect of nuclear weapons on MID initiation (probit, directed dyads, 1945–2000)

DV: MID initiation	Exogenous model		Endogenous model	
	Coeff.	(SE)	Coeff.	(SE)
Nuclear Weapons A	0.260***	(0.070)	−0.003	(0.234)
Nuclear Weapons B	−0.001	(0.077)	−0.033	(0.239)
Nuke A × Nuke B	−0.212	(0.135)	−0.255	(0.198)
Rivalry Status A	0.293***	(0.032)	0.285***	(0.031)
Rivalry Status B	0.157***	(0.030)	0.157***	(0.030)
Dyadic Rivalry	1.113***	(0.051)	1.122***	(0.038)
CINC A	0.778	(0.707)	2.353	(1.474)
CINC B	1.589†	(0.829)	1.782	(1.518)
CINC A × CINC B	0.207	(15.833)	−1.536	(20.308)
Democracy A	0.023***	(0.006)	0.025***	(0.006)
Democracy B	0.041***	(0.006)	0.041***	(0.005)
Dem. A × Dem. B	−0.005***	(0.001)	−0.005***	(0.001)
Contiguity	−0.137**	(0.044)	−0.139***	(0.022)
Distance (ln)	−0.050†	(0.026)	−0.047***	(0.013)
Alliance	0.043	(0.040)	0.016	(0.033)
Intercept	−2.308***	(0.081)	−2.297****	(0.061)
N	1,051,218		1,016,102	
Log-likelihood	−6008.249		−5823.235	
$\chi^2_{(19)}$	6,942.134		8,643.780	

Notes
Significance levels: † = 10%; * = 5%; ** = 1%; *** = 0.1%. Spline coefficients and SEs suppressed.

interstate conflict. Taking the standard errors of the coefficient estimate for Nuclear Weapons A in the endogenous equation and using a 95 percent threshold, we obtain a 5 percent confidence interval around the estimated coefficient, or [−0.0091609, 0.0025291]. Since this interval overlaps zero, we can reject the null that the estimated coefficient is statistically different from zero with 95 percent confidence.[18]

Neither of the coefficient estimates for Nuclear Weapons B are statistically significant. This appears disappointing for deterrence theory, but if we are correct, nuclear weapons have a larger deterrent effect than is reflected in these findings. Nuclear nations may be converting some or all of the conflict-diminishing effects of deterrence into bigger demands on other nations, or may be "trading" security for influence (Morrow 1991). Nations protected by a nuclear umbrella may be more assertive, in turn diminishing the observable deterrent effect of nuclear capabilities.

The lack of statistical significance for jointly nuclear dyads in the endogenous model may result from small sample size, but an interpretation consistent with the non-findings for the component nuclear status variables is again that nuclear states attempt to compel as often as they seek to deter. Nuclear status may help avoid disputes over certain issues, but these issues are probably also less important, and thus may fail to justify proliferation. Nuclear dyads may be less likely to fight over a given set of differences than non-nuclear dyads, but perhaps they also face more, or more serious, differences. This can result, as Rauchhaus (this book) argues, in an increase in low-level conflict, but fewer major disputes, as nuclear powers play chicken (Snyder 1965).

Results for most of the remaining independent variables in Table 8.1 corroborate previous empirical findings. Rivals are more likely to fight one another, even as monadic rivalry separately correlates with conflict. Disputes increase with the capability scores of each state in the dyad, though these relationships are generally not statistically significant. Interestingly, the monadic effect of regime type is positive and significant, while the interaction of regime scores operates as anticipated (Maoz and Russett 1993; Rousseau *et al.* 1996).[19] Contiguity and Distance are both negative and significant, while alliance ties fail to influence dispute initiation.

If nuclear weapons do not alter the probability of conventional conflict, perhaps nuclear nations are primarily interested in symbolic payoffs, such as prestige (O'Neill 2006). Countries might also be led by delusional leaders whose motives bear no semblance to empirical fact (Jervis 1988; Bush 2002). Yet, if force remains a means to an end, we must also look to the ends to understand when certain means are appealing, and when they are not. Relatively little attention has been focused on measuring the allocation of benefits or prerogatives in international politics. Research on treaties is promising, but is still evolving (Koremenos 2001; Leeds 2003; Neumayer 2005; Simmons and Hopkins 2005). The International Crisis Behavior (ICB) dataset codes data about bargains reached by states during crises. Beardsley and Asal (this book) use these data to show that nuclear powers tend to obtain concessions from crisis opponents. These findings support the thesis that nuclear capabilities tend to translate into better bargains for proliferators. However, we still cannot say whether nuclear status matters for the bargains nations obtain in lieu of crises.

We look at diplomatic recognition to assess whether proliferation allows states to obtain more of what they want. Nations with demands need to be recognized before those demands can be satisfied. If countries with nuclear weapons are recognized more often than countries that lack nuclear weapons, then at least nuclear powers are being listened to, if not actually obeyed.

Table 8.2 presents two regressions that report the effects of nuclear status on the likelihood that State B recognizes State A. There is no need for a structural equations approach, as the effect of nuclear status does not appear to hinge the other exogenous variables. States that recognize one another also do not appear to be more likely to acquire nuclear weapons. Countries that are not yet recognized may consider proliferating, but those with recognition no doubt find the extra leverage useful as well. Thus, nuclear status should effect, but not reflect, the dependent variable.

Table 8.2 Nuclear weapons and diplomatic recognition (probit, directed dyads, 1945–2000)

DV: Diplomatic recognition (State B recognizes State A)	Dichotomous		Ordinal	
	Coeff.	*(SE)*	*Coeff.*	*(SE)*
Nuclear Weapons A	0.168***	(0.033)	0.232***	(0.028)
Nuclear Weapons B	0.116***	(0.033)	0.252***	(0.029)
Nuke A × Nuke B	−0.241	(0.186)	0.071	(0.155)
Rivalry Status A	0.250***	(0.010)	0.139***	(0.009)
Rivalry Status B	0.260***	(0.010)	0.137***	(0.009)
Dyadic Rivalry	−0.757***	(0.073)	−0.561***	(0.055)
CINC A	9.566***	(0.485)	5.432***	(0.354)
CINC B	12.311***	(0.542)	6.471***	(0.386)
CINC A × CINC B	9.173	(63.830)	−96.018***	(16.082)
Democracy A	0.035***	(0.002)	0.008***	(0.002)
Democracy B	0.043***	(0.002)	0.011***	(0.002)
Dem. A × Dem. B	0.002***	(0.000)	0.002***	(0.000)
Contiguity	−0.196***	(0.050)	−0.396***	(0.041)
Distance (ln)	−0.200***	(0.007)	−0.158***	(0.005)
Alliance	0.652***	(0.021)	0.146***	(0.016)
Lagged DV			0.780***	(0.003)
Intercept	0.830***	(0.057)		
_cut1			0.467***	(0.044)
_cut2			0.573***	(0.044)
_cut3			0.575***	(0.044)
N	213,451		187,394	
Log-likelihood	−79093.293		−64753.548	
$\chi^2_{(14, 20)}$	44,041.069		69,850.369	

Notes
Significance levels: †=10%; * = 5%; ** = 1%; *** = 0.1%. Spline coefficients and SEs suppressed.

Rather than attempt to interpolate missing values of the COW diplomatic recognition data, we chose to rely on the existing intervals. This reduces the sample size from roughly 1,000,000 cases to a little over 200,000. The difference should not matter for these analyses. A more serious concern is how to deal with temporal dependence. For the model with a dichotomous dependent variable, we construct standard Beck, Katz, and Tucker (1998) splines.[20] Addressing temporal dependence in the ordinal analysis is problematic. We lag the dependent variable (previous observation, not always the same time interval). Recognition trends strongly. A given diplomatic relationship in one period tends to persist in subsequent periods.

Nuclear capable states are more likely to be recognized by, and to formally recognize other nations. The effect of nuclear status on recognition intensifies when we use the ordinal dependent variable for the level of diplomatic mission, since this contains more information. The coefficient estimates for the Nuclear Weapons variables grow larger, while the standard errors associated with these estimates decrease. The finding is robust to the effects of other determinants of diplomatic recognition. Dyadic Rivalry is negative and significant, while states with rivalries are more likely to recognize, and be recognized by, other states. Countries with high CINC scores are more likely to send and receive diplomatic recognition. Capable countries are particularly likely to recognize one another. Democracies are more active diplomatically, again particularly with each other. Distant nations are less likely to recognize one another. Contiguous states are less likely to recognize each other and are less likely to have higher-level embassies.

For additional evidence of the diplomatic impact of nuclear status, we turn to ICOW data on settlement attempts of contentious issues. Table 8.3 contains two regressions of the effects of nuclear weapons status and other variables on attempts to settle ICOW disputes. In a separate regression (not reported), we find that states with nuclear weapons are more likely to obtain settlements of ICOW issues. Here, we examine whether nuclear weapons status affects the nature and content of settlement attempts. The first regression in Table 8.3 evaluates whether there is any attempt to settle

Table 8.3 Nuclear weapons and ICOW settlement attempt (probit, directed dyads, 1945–2000)

DV: ICOW settlement (State A targets State B)	Settlement attempt		Peaceful attempt	
	Coeff.	*(SE)*	*Coeff.*	*(SE)*
Nuclear Weapons A	0.090	(0.212)	0.108	(0.156)
Nuclear Weapons B	−0.602***	(0.189)	0.550***	(0.116)
Salience to Challenger			−0.080	(0.058)
Salience to Target			0.127†	(0.076)
Rivalry Status A	0.216	(0.132)	−0.115	(0.087)
Rivalry Status B	0.016	(0.120)	−0.071	(0.085)
Dyadic Rivalry	−0.607***	(0.158)	0.250*	(0.115)
CINC A	−2.936†	(1.568)	0.357	(1.186)
CINC B	3.335	(2.388)	−1.295	(1.692)
CINC A × CINC B	−115.467	(223.152)	127.719	(183.545)
Democracy A	−0.016	(0.027)	0.022	(0.023)
Democracy B	−0.032	(0.020)	0.030	(0.019)
Dem. A × Dem. B	0.000	(0.003)	−0.001	(0.003)
Contiguity	0.396*	(0.188)	−0.287**	(0.109)
Distance (ln)	0.058**	(0.021)	−0.050***	(0.013)
Alliance	−0.069	(0.119)	0.077	(0.079)
Intercept	0.875**	(0.285)	−0.545*	(0.225)
N	3,233		3,233	
Log-likelihood	−1502.776		−1248.575	
$\chi^2_{(14, 20)}$	66.823		537.608	

Notes
Significance levels: †=10%; *=5%; **=1%; ***=0.1%. Spline coefficients and S.E.'s suppressed.

an ICOW issue in a given year. The variable is coded inversely; a "1" implies no settlement attempt of any kind. As is clear from the results, nuclear challengers are no more or less likely to seek to initiate a settlement. However, nuclear targets are much more likely to be the recipients of overtures. Other states seek to resolve differences with nuclear powers over ongoing ICOW issues, even while nuclear powers are no more prone to seek settlements with other states.

Use of the ICOW data requires some changes to the model specification. The interaction term between nuclear status is excluded from the model since its zero values perfectly determine zero values of the dependent variable. Rivalry may also correlate strongly with ICOW issues, since rivals are by definition facing ongoing tensions. We ran regressions with and without the rivalry variables without noticeable changes. We also included ICOW variables for issue salience, but found that the salience issues do not confound our results. Finally, the temporal dependence variables are highly co-linear. Several of these variables often drop out of these models.

The second regression in Table 8.3 examines the determinants of peaceful settlement attempts. Again, nuclear challengers behave much as non-nuclear challengers, but the opponents of nuclear targets appear more willing to pursue peaceful settlements. This does not mean that disputes are less likely to occur when states have nuclear weapons, since nuclear powers themselves may become less tractable in negotiations.

Table 8.4 assesses whether nuclear weapons make states more or less tractable. Here, each regression uses different portions of the ICOW Resolved variable. In the first regression in Table 8.4, the dependent variable is coded "1" if ICOW records an issue as being "dropped by the challenger" or "renounced by the challenger." As these results reveal, the nuclear status of the target is a significant determinant of whether challengers concede issues. Similarly, if it is the target which is conceding, then the nuclear status of the challenger is salient (but not that of the target). In sum, opponents of nuclear powers are more willing to accommodate nuclear states, while nuclear states are not more willing to pursue peaceful accommodation with their opponents.

Conclusion

For nuclear weapons to inhibit conventional conflict, proliferation must discourage aggression from other states, without at the same time encouraging the nuclear state to become more aggressive. For nuclear weapons to increase conventional dispute behavior, states with nuclear weapons must become more aggressive without their opponents responding by becoming more circumspect. Predictions from both perspectives hinge on partial equilibria frameworks in which one actor adjusts its behavior in response to the nuclear capability shock, while other actors do not.

Table 8.4 Nuclear weapons and ICOW resolution (probit, directed dyads, 1945–2000)

DV: ICOW resolution (State A targets State B)	Challenger concedes		Target concedes	
	Coeff.	(SE)	Coeff.	(SE)
Nuclear Weapons A	−0.026	(0.316)	2.054**	(0.652)
Nuclear Weapons B	0.715**	(0.274)	0.622	(0.616)
Rivalry Status A	0.043	(0.241)	−4.807***	(0.373)
Rivalry Status B	0.344	(0.257)		
Dyadic Rivalry	−0.085	(0.272)	5.430	(0.000)
CINC A	4.542	(3.045)	−71.536**	(24.844)
CINC B	−3.541	(3.388)	−38.485	(46.400)
CINC A × CINC B	−1794.496†	(1089.284)	−25178.662	(41311.316)
Democracy A	0.095*	(0.044)	0.406	(0.268)
Democracy B	0.090†	(0.052)	0.508*	(0.240)
Dem. A × Dem. B	−0.023***	(0.006)	−0.017†	(0.028)
Contiguity	−6.058***	(1.235)		
Distance (ln)	−0.812***	(0.158)		
Alliance	−0.346†	(0.201)	−0.102	(0.400)
Intercept	3.349**	(1.233)	−7.018**	(2.460)
N	3,233		3,233	
Log-likelihood	−152.776		−32.888	
$\chi^2_{(14, 20)}$	70.355			

Notes
Significance levels: †=10%; *=5%; **=1%; *** = 0.1%. Spline coefficients and SEs suppressed.

Instead, both nuclear nations and their opponents may adjust roughly simultaneously to the presence of nuclear capabilities. States with nuclear weapons become more ambitious, while their counterparts become more tractable. Indeed, if both powerful nations and pariahs proliferate in large part to gain greater influence, then nuclear capable countries are particularly likely to seek to realize increased influence through mechanisms that are more diplomatic than military. The spread of nuclear weapons is neither pacific nor chaotic, but reflects an evolution of the struggle for influence that has always characterized world affairs. The largest impact of nuclear weapons is likely to be in terms of what nations bring to the bargaining table, and what they take home.

Our analysis offers some evidence that nuclear weapons matter less for war and peace than is generally presumed. Nuclear capable states do not appear to differ significantly in terms of their dispute propensity once we address the tendency of states to proliferate. Instead, it is in the realm of diplomatic wrangling and bargained settlements that we observe a significant shift associated with nuclear weapons. Our analysis of diplomatic recognition shows that nations with nuclear weapons are more likely to garner attention from other countries. Similarly, opponents of nuclear states are more likely to attempt to settle ongoing conflicts, and to settle them peacefully.

If the acquisition of nuclear weapons is costly and time-consuming, then proliferation should appeal disproportionately to the most insecure countries or those with the biggest defense budgets. Nations facing major threats may find that proliferation is an avenue to secure primary interests, while affording greater freedom to pursue broader objectives, such as aiding allies or wielding influence in the face of powerful opponents. The richest states have more flexibility in designing national defense. While nuclear weapons are less fungible than conventional forces, countries with substantial conventional capabilities may find that the declining marginal value of additional conventional defense effort reduces the opportunity cost of building nuclear weapons. In contrast, nations with friendly neighbors, limited budgets, or that are satisfied with their lot in the world system are unlikely to proliferate. While nuclear weapons may have little impact on the potential for conventional contests, our "middle path" argument suggests that nuclear weapons significantly affect the international status quo. One need not draw a sword to make its presence felt. If diplomacy involves the politics of the possible, then proliferation changes the possibilities. It is the parallel between shifts in relative power brought about by nuclear weapons and the diplomatic response that helps to explain the apparent non-impact of nuclear weapons.

Constructing an instrument for nuclear weapons status

Our instrument for nuclear status is based on previous research (Jo and Gartzke 2007) and on the specific needs of the current study. The determinants of nuclear proliferation fall into three categories loosely based on opportunity and willingness: latent national capacity (nations that cannot build the bomb, do not), threat or interest (nations that can build the bomb but that have no need to, will not), and institutional or normative factors (audience costs in democracies).

Since there is no market in nuclear arms, the ability to build the bomb is an important choke point in the proliferation process.[21] Jo and Gartzke (2007) offer an index of latent national nuclear capacity, based on the size or availability within a country of seven key inputs (uranium deposits, metallurgists, chemical engineers, nuclear engineers/physicists/chemists, nitric acid production capacity, electronic/explosive specialists, electricity production capacity). In addition, countries that are generally powerful, populous, or rich are better able to allocate scarce resources to nuclear weapons development, and to compensate for any lack of latent capacity. We use energy consumption per capita as a proxy for economic development. Energy consumption correlates closely with gross domestic product, and these data are available with fewer missing values. We also use the Correlates of War CINC score to measure a country's material power.

Nations with large military arsenals may care more about the policies of other nations than countries with smaller investments in arms. Nations that have no rivals probably have less interest in proliferating. To see whether proliferation is diffused by concerns about balancing, or by nuclear threats in particular, we look at whether a country has a rivalry with a nuclear capable nation. Discussions of a "nuclear umbrella" imply that rivals with nuclear protectors are also a threat. We include a dummy variable for whether a rival is allied with a nuclear capable state.

States facing large conventional threats may seek nuclear weapons to compensate for a conventional imbalance. In contrast, nuclear capable partners have less need to proliferate if other states are already providing protection. We examined variables measuring whether a state has a nuclear capable ally and the largest or the sum of conventional threats from rivals. We omit these variables, as no version proved statistically significant in preliminary analysis.

Domestic political structure and international institutions impact the decision to proliferate. Previous research reveals that democracies are more likely to acquire nuclear weapons. Democratic willingness to proliferate may reflect the premium democracies place on public goods provision, greater risk aversion on the part of democratic leaders, or because citizens punish leaders for failed programs. It is tempting to also include a variable to measure membership in the Nuclear Non-Proliferation Treaty (NPT). However, NPT membership is closely aligned with a decision not to proliferate. In effect, NPT status is a proxy for nuclear status or aspirations among all states subsequent to the original five nuclear powers. For this reason, we omit a measure of NPT status.

While consistent with Jo and Gartzke (2007), we found several ways to streamline or improve the model. First, the original model includes both regime type and political instability as separate variables. Strikes, riots, and other forms of unrest in a country correlate strongly with regime type. Indeed, recent research shows that the Polity scale subsumes political instability (Gates *et al.* 2006). For this reason, we omit a measure of domestic unrest. Second, major and regional power status variables correlate strongly with nuclear status and were omitted. Third, we omit a measure of diplomatic recognition, as this is one of the dependent variables. Fourth, we remove the nuclear contagion variable, since this correlates strongly with temporal processes.

Table 8.5 details results of a probit regression of the independent variables just described on nuclear status. The unit-of-analysis is the country-year, covering the same time period as the sample for the main regression (1945–2000). As expected, Latent National Capacity, CINC, and Rivalry Status are all highly significant and increase the likelihood that a country will produce nuclear weapons. Democracy and per capita energy consumption are significant at the 5 percent level and operate in the expected direction. Overall, this model does correlate strongly as an instrument, accounting for almost 64 percent of the variance in annual national nuclear weapons status.

Table 8.5 Nuclear weapons status (probit, country years, 1945–2000)

DV nuclear status	Coeff.	(SE)
Latent National Capacity	0.525**	(0.181)
Energy Cons. Per Cap.	0.041*	(0.018)
Democracy	0.084*	(0.040)
CINC	24.110***	(4.312)
Rivalry Status	1.113**	(0.400)
Nuclear Rival	–0.030	(0.429)
Rival has Nuclear Ally	–0.295	(0.386)
Intercept	–6.736***	(1.187)
N	7,723	
Log-likelihood	–484.3	
$\chi^2_{(7)}$	85.424	

Notes
Significance levels: † = 10%; * = 5%; ** = 1%; *** = 0.5%.

An instrument requires both exogenous and endogenous variables. The endogenous variables are those that appear in the main conflict equation as well as in the instrument equation. These are CINC, Rivalry Status, and Democracy. The exogenous variables include Latent National Capacity, Energy Cons. Per Cap., Nuclear Rival, and Rival with Nuclear Ally.

Notes

1 For helpful comments on earlier versions of this chapter, the author would like to thank the authors in this special issue, Bruce Russett, and two anonymous reviewers. Replication data and an online appendix are available at http://jcr.sagepub.com/supplemental.

2 Deterrence theory implies the moral superiority of the status quo over other available bargains, and thus privileges established powers over challengers (cf. United Nations 1995). This is particularly problematic for realists (Grieco 1990; Mearsheimer 2001). Given anarchy, it is not clear why the status quo is objectively different from other bargains.

3 Arguing more forcefully that some nations should lack a nuclear deterrent has the effect of bolstering Western interests. It may be true that nuclear weapons proliferation in India and Pakistan will increase the likelihood of crises, accidents, terrorism, and nuclear war (Sagan 2001), but surely these problems exist in other places as well.

4 The claim that nuclear deterrence has some redeeming value really rests on the assertion that nuclear weapons decrease conventional conflict, since nuclear war can be averted simply by not proliferating.

5 Mueller (1988) argues that nuclear weapons had little salience for the "long peace" during the Cold War.

6 Geller and Sample inquire whether nuclear weapons inhibit escalation, not initiation or onset. Huth studies extended immediate nuclear deterrence, also selecting on the dependent variable (Fearon 1994).

7 Caprioli and Trumbore (2005) find that "rogue states" are no more dispute prone than other states. Instead, rogue status has more to do with attempts by revisionists to thwart the policy interests of status quo powers.

8 Analysis of the entire 1816–2001 period covered by most COW datasets produces comparable results.

9 More restrictive (fatal MIDs), and less restrictive codings (MIDs begun by either state) yield similar results.

10 Values are coded intermittently, usually at five-year intervals, but there are gaps in the nineteenth century.

11 We examined eleven different codings, ranging from narrow (publicly declared nuclear status, detonated a nuclear device) to broad (temporarily "inherited" nuclear weapons). Results are the same, with the exception that the interaction term between nuclear powers in the exogenous model is sometimes significant.

12 Attempts to measure latent conflict include inductive techniques, such as a lag model of previous disputes (Crescenzi and Enterline 2001), or deductive approaches intended to capture interests (Bueno de Mesquita 1981; Bueno de Mesquita and Lalman 1992; Gartzke 1998). With little consensus about what comprehensive models of conflict motives should include, we adopt a conservative approach of measuring past behavior.

13 Comparable results can be obtained using a dummy variable coded "1" exclusively for defense pacts.

14 States with contiguous colonies are contiguous. Results are similar using other measures of contiguity.

15 For studies challenging the view that interdependence is pacific, see Beck *et al.* (1998), Barbieri (2003).

16 Small and Singer (1982) acknowledge that "the criteria for differentiation between major powers and others are not as operational as we might wish." They note particular concerns "for the period since 1965." We conducted tests using COW dummies and an "objective" measure based on Schweller's definition of a "pole" as a state with "at least half of the resources of the most powerful state in the system" (Schweller 1998: 46).

17 The endogenous model uses the IVPROB procedure in STATA, which implements Amemiya's Generalized Least Squares estimator with endogenous regressors. Equations for the estimator are from Newey (1987).

18 The estimated coefficient for State A is just short of being indistinguishable from zero at the 1 percent threshold.

19 Quackenbush and Rudy (2006) find that democracy has opposing effects on conflict in monads and dyads.

20 There is a risk that the splines might bias the results, since not all time intervals are of the same five-year duration. Our findings are unchanged when removing the splines or using a lagged dependent variable.

21 No nation has ever bought (or sold) the bomb. However, as Kroenig (2009b) and Fuhrmann (2009) demonstrate, trade in nuclear components and know-how is a significant contributor to proliferation success.

References

Barbieri, Katherine (2003) *The Liberal Myth*, Ann Arbor, MI: University of Michigan Press.

Barnaby, Frank (1993) *How Nuclear Weapons Spread: Nuclear-Weapon Proliferation in the 1990s*, New York: Routledge.

Bayer, Resat (2006) *Diplomatic Exchange Data Set*, Correlates of War Project. Available at http://correlatesofwar.org (accessed on December 10).

Bearce, David H., Kristen M. Flanagan, and Katherine M. Floros (2006) "Alliances, Internal Information, and Military Conflict Among Member States," *International Organization* 60: 595–625.

Beardsley, Kyle and Victor Asal (This Book) "Winning with the Bomb."

Beck, Nathaniel, Jonathan Katz, and Richard Tucker (1998) "Taking Time Seriously: Time-series–Cross-section Analysis with a Binary Dependent Variable," *American Journal of Political Science* 42: 1260–1288.

Bennett, D. Scott (1996) "Security, Bargaining, and the End of Interstate Rivalry," *International Studies Quarterly* 40: 157–184.

Bennett, D. Scott and Allan Stam (2000) "Research Design and Estimator Choices in the Analysis of Interstate Dyads: When Decisions Matter," *Journal of Conflict Resolution* 44: 653–685.

Bennett, D. Scott and Allan Stam (2001) "EUGene: Expected Utility and Data Management Program, version 2.250," Computer Program, The Pennsylvania State University and Dartmouth University.

Betts, Richard (1977a) *Nuclear Blackmail and Nuclear Balance*, Cambridge: Harvard University Press.

Betts, Richard (1977b) "Paranoids, Pygmies, Pariahs & NonProliferation," *Foreign Policy* 26: 157–183.

Blainey, Geoffrey (1988[1973]) *The Causes of War*, New York: Free Press.

Blechman, Barry M. and Stephen S. Kaplan (1978) *Force Without War: US Armed Forces as a Political Instrument*, Washington, DC: Brookings Institution.

Boehmer, Charles (2001) "Economic Growth, Strategic Interaction, and Interstate Conflict," Paper presented at the International Studies Association, February 20–25.

Boulding, Kenneth (1962) *Conflict and Defense*, New York: Harper & Row.

Bremer, Stuart (1992) "Dangerous Dyads: Conditions Affecting the Likelihood of Interstate War," *Journal of Conflict Resolution* 36: 309–341.

Brodie, Bernard (ed.) (1946) *The Absolute Weapon: Atomic Power and World Order*, New York: Harcourt, Brace & Co.

Brodie, Bernard (1959) *Strategy in the Missile Age*, Princeton, NJ: Princeton University Press.

Bueno de Mesquita, Bruce (1981) *The War Trap*, New Haven, CT: Yale University Press.

Bueno de Mesquita, Bruce and David Lalman (1992) *War and Reason: Domestic and International Imperatives*, New Haven, CT: Yale University Press.

Bueno de Mesquita, Bruce and William H. Riker (1982) "An Assessment of the Merits of Selective Nuclear Proliferation," *Journal of Conflict Resolution* 26: 283–306.

Bush, George W. (2002) *The National Security Strategy of the United States of America*, The White House.

Caprioli, Mary and Peter F. Trumbore (2005) "Rhetoric versus Reality: Rogue States in Interstate Conflict," *Journal of Conflict Resolution* 49: 770–791.

Clausewitz, Carl von (1976[1832]) *On War*, indexed edn, Princeton, NJ: Princeton University Press.

Crescenzi, Mark J.C. and Andrew J. Enterline (2001) "Time Remembered: A Dynamic Model of Interstate Interaction," *International Studies Quarterly* 45: 409–431.

Diehl, Paul F. and Gary Goertz (2000) *War and Peace in International Rivalry*," Ann Arbor, MI: University of Michigan Press.

Doyle, Michael (1997) *Ways of War and Peace: Realism, Liberalism, and Socialism*, New York: Norton.

Dunn, Lewis A. and Herman Kahn (1976) *Trends in Nuclear Proliferation, 1975–1995*, Croton-on-Hudson, NY: Hudson Institute.

Fearon, James D. (1994) "Signaling Versus the Balance of Power and Interests: An Empirical Test of the Crisis Bargaining Model," *Journal of Conflict Resolution* 38: 236–269.

Fearon, James D. (1995) "Rationalist Explanations for War," *International Organization* 49: 379–414.

Freedman, Lawrence (1981) *The Evolution of Nuclear Strategy*, New York: St Martin's Press.

Fuhrmann, Matthew (2009) Taking a Walk on the Supply Side: The Determinants of Civilian Nuclear Cooperation." *Journal of Conflict Resolution* 53(2): 181–208.

Gaddis, John Lewis (1983) "The Rise, Fall, and Future of Détente," *Foreign Affairs* 62: 354–377.

Gaddis, John Lewis (1989) *The Long Peace: Inquiries into the History of the Cold War*, Oxford: Oxford University Press.

Gaddis, John Lewis (2005) *Strategies of Containment: A Critical Appraisal of American National Security Policy During the Cold War*, New York: Oxford University Press.

Gartzke, Erik (1998) "Kant We All Just Get Along?: Motive, Opportunity, and the Origins of the Democratic Peace," *American Journal of Political Science* 42: 1–27.

Gates, Scott, Håvard Hegre, Mark P. Jones, and Håvard Strand (2006) "Institutional Inconsistency and Political Instability: Polity Duration, 1800–2000," *American Journal of Political Science* 50: 893–908.

Geller, Daniel S. (1990) "Nuclear Weapons, Deterrence, and Crisis Escalation," *Journal of Conflict Resolution* 34: 291–310.

Ghosn, Faten, Glenn Palmer, and Stuart Bremer (2004) "The MID 3 Data Set, 1993–2001: Procedures, Coding Rules, and Description," *Conflict Management and Peace Science* 21: 133–154.

Gibler, Douglas M., Toby J. Rider, and Marc L. Hutchinson (2005) "Taking Arms Against a Sea of Troubles: Conventional Arms Races During Periods of Rivalry," *Journal of Peace Research* 42: 131–147.

Gleditsch, Kristian (2002) "Expanded Trade and GDP Data," *Journal of Conflict Resolution* 46: 712–724.

Gleditsch, Kristian (2003) *All Politics is Local: The Diffusion of Conflict, Integration, and Democratization*, Ann Arbor, MI: University of Michigan Press.

Gochman, Charles S. and Zeev Maoz (1984) "Militarized Interstate Disputes, 1816–1976: Procedure, Patterns, and Insights," *Journal of Conflict Resolution* 28: 585–615.

Grieco, Joseph M. (1990) *Cooperation Among Nations: Europe, America, and Non-Tariff Barriers to Trade*, Ithaca, NY: Cornell University Press.

Gurr, Ted Robert, Keith Jaggers, and Will H. Moore (1989) "Polity II: Political Structures and Regime Change, 1800–1986," Computer File, Boulder, CO: Center for Comparative Politics, Ann Arbor, MI: Inter-University Consortium for Political and Social Research.

Hensel, Paul R. and Sara McLaughlin Mitchell (2007) "Issue Correlates of War Project: User Manual for ICOW Data, V. 1.1," The Issue Correlates of War (ICOW) Project. Available at www.paulhensel.org/icow.html (accessed on March 20, 2008).

Horowitz, Michael (This Book) "The Spread of Nuclear Weapons and International Conflict: Does Experience Matter?"

Huth, Paul K. (1988) *Extended Deterrence and the Prevention of War,* New Haven, CT: Yale University Press.

Huth, Paul K. (1990) "The Extended Deterrent Value of Nuclear Weapons," *Journal of Conflict Resolution* 34: 270–290.

Huth, Paul K. and Bruce Russett (1984) "What Makes Deterrence Work?: Cases from 1900 to 1980," *World Politics* 36: 496–526.

Huth, Paul K. and Bruce Russett (1988) "Deterrence Failures and Crisis Escalation," *International Studies Quarterly* 32: 29–45.

Huth, Paul K. and Bruce Russett (1993) "General Deterrence Between Enduring Rivals: Testing Three Competing Models," *American Political Science Review* 87: 61–73.

Jaggers, Keith and Ted R. Gurr (1995) "Transitions to Democracy: Tracking Democracy's 'Third Wave' with the Polity III Data," *Journal of Peace Research* 32: 469–482.

Jervis, Robert (1984) *The Illogic of American Nuclear Strategy,* Ithaca, NY: Cornell University Press.

Jervis, Robert (1988) "The Political Effects of Nuclear Weapons: A Comment," *International Security* 13: 80–90.

Jervis, Robert (1989a) "Rational Deterrence: Theory and Evidence," *World Politics* 42: 183–207.

Jervis, Robert (1989b) *The Meaning of the Nuclear Revolution: Statecraft and the Prospect of Armageddon,* Ithaca, NY: Cornell University Press.

Jo, Dong-Joon and Erik Gartzke (2007) "Determinants of Nuclear Proliferation: A Quantitative Model," *Journal of Conflict Resolution* 51: 167–194.

Jones, Daniel, Stuart Bremer, and J. David Singer (1996) "Militarized Interstate Disputes, 1816–1992: Rationale, Coding Rules, and Empirical Patterns," *Conflict Management and Peace Science* 15: 163–213.

Kahn, Herman (1960) *On Thermonuclear War,* Princeton, NJ: Princeton University Press.

Kennan, George F. (1947) "The Sources of Soviet Conduct," *Foreign Affairs* 25: 566–582.

Kimball, Anessa L. (2006) "Alliance Formation and Conflict Initiation: The Missing Link," *Journal of Peace Research* 43: 371–389.

Kissinger, Henry (1957) *Nuclear Weapons and Foreign Policy,* New York: Harper.

Klein, James P., Gary Goertz, and Paul F. Diehl (2006) "The New Rivalry Dataset: Procedures and Patterns," *Journal of Peace Research* 43: 331–348.

Koremenos, Barbara (2001) "Loosing the Ties that Bind: A Learning Model of Agreement Flexibility," *International Organization* 55: 289–326.

Kroenig, Matthew (2009a) "Exporting the Bomb: Why States Provide Sensitive Nuclear Assistance," *American Political Science Review* 103(1).

Kroenig, Matthew (2009b) "Importing the Bomb: Sensitive Nuclear Assistance and Nuclear Proliferation." *Journal of Conflict Resolution* 53(2): 161–180.

Kugler, Jacek (1984) "Terror Without Deterrence: Reassessing the Role of Nuclear Weapons," *Journal of Conflict Resolution* 28: 470–506.

Lebow, Richard Ned and Janice Gross Stein (1995) *We All Lost the Cold War,* Princeton, NJ: Princeton University Press.

Leeds, Brett Ashley (2003) "Alliance Reliability in Times of War: Explaining State Decisions to Violate Treaties," *International Organization* 57: 801–827.

LeFeber, Walter (2002) *America, Russia, and the Cold War, 1945–2002*, Ithaca, NY: Cornell University Press.

McMillan, Susan (1997) "Interdependence and Conflict," *Mershon International Studies Review* 41: 33–58.

Mansfield, Edward D. and Brian Pollins (2001) "The Study of Interdependence and Conflict: Recent Advances, Open Questions, and Directions for Future Research," *Journal of Conflict Resolution* 45: 834–859.

Maoz, Zeev and Bruce Russett (1993) "Normative and Structural Causes of the Democratic Peace, 1946–1986," *American Political Science Review* 87: 624–638.

Marshall, Monty and Keith Jaggers (2002) "Polity IV Project: Political Regime Characteristics and Transitions, 1800–2002. Version p4v2002e," Computer File, College Park, MD: Center for International Development and Conflict Management, University of Maryland. Available at www.cidcm.umd.edu/inscr/polity/index.htm (accessed on May 20, 2004).

Mearsheimer, John J. (1984) "Nuclear Weapons and Deterrence in Europe," *International Security* 9: 19–46.

Mearsheimer, John J. (1990) "Back to the Future: Instability in Europe After the Cold War," *International Security* 15: 5–56.

Mearsheimer, John J. (1993) "The Case for a Ukrainian Nuclear Deterrent," *Foreign Affairs* 72: 50–66.

Mearsheimer, John J. (2001) *The Tragedy of Great Power Politics*, New York: W.W. Norton.

Morgan, Patrick M. (1977) *Deterrence: A Conceptual Analysis*, Los Angeles, CA: Sage.

Morrow, James (1991) "Alliances and Asymmetry: An Alternative to the Capability Aggregation Model of Alliances," *American Journal of Political Science* 35: 904–933.

Morrow, James (2000) "Alliances: Why Write Them Down?," *Annual Review of Political Science* 3: 63–83.

Mueller, John (1988) "The Essential Irrelevance of Nuclear Weapons: Stability in the Postwar War," *International Security* 13: 55–79.

Neumayer, Eric (2005) "Do International Human Rights Treaties Improve Respect for Human Rights?," *Journal of Conflict Resolution* 49: 925–953.

Newey, Whitney (1987) "Efficient Estimation of Limited Dependent Variable Models with Endogenous Explanatory Variables," *Journal of Econometrics* 36: 231–250.

Nicolson, Harold George (1960) *Diplomacy*, USA: Oxford University Press.

Oneal, John R. and Bruce Russett (1999) "The Kantian Peace: The Pacific Benefits of Democracy, Interdependence, and International Organizations," *World Politics* 52: 1–37.

Oneal, John R., Bruce Russett, and Michael L. Berbaum (2003) "Causes of Peace: Democracy, Interdependence, and International Organizations," *International Studies Quarterly* 47: 371–393.

O'Neill, Barry (2006) "Nuclear Weapons and National Prestige," *Cowles Foundation Discussion Paper* 1560.

Organski, A.F.K. and Jacek Kugler (1980) *The War Ledger*, Chicago, IL: University of Chicago Press.

Osgood, Robert E. and Robert W. Tucker (1967) *Force, Order, and Justice*, Baltimore, MD: Johns Hopkins University Press.

Paul, T.V. (1995) "Nuclear Taboo and War Initiation in Regional Conflicts," *Journal of Conflict Resolution* 39: 696–717.

Powell, Robert (1990) *Nuclear Deterrence Theory: The Search for Credibility*, Cambridge: Cambridge University Press.

Quackenbush, Stephen L. and Michael Rudy (2006) "Evaluating the Monadic Democratic Peace," typescript, Columbia, MO: University of Missouri.

Rauchhaus, Robert W. (This Book) "Evaluating the Nuclear Peace Hypothesis: A Quantitative Approach."

Rousseau, David L., Christopher Gelpi, Dan Reiter, and Paul K. Huth (1996) "Assessing the Dyadic Nature of the Democratic Peace, 1918–1988," *American Political Science Review* 90: 512–533.

Russett, Bruce (1989) "The Real Decline in Nuclear Hegemony," in Ernst-Otto Czempiel and James N. Rosenau (eds) *Global Changes and Territorial Challenges: Approaches to World Politics for the 1990s*, Lexington, MA: Lexington Books, pp. 177–193.

Russett, Bruce (1993) *Grasping the Democratic Peace: Principles for a Post-Cold War World*, Princeton, NJ: Princeton University Press.

Russett, Bruce and John R. Oneal (2001) *Triangulating Peace: Democracy, Interdependence, and International Organizations*, New York: Norton.

Sagan, Scott D. (1989) *Moving Targets: Nuclear Strategy and National Security*, Princeton, NJ: Princeton University Press.

Sagan, Scott D. (1996) "Why Do States Build Nuclear Weapons?: Three Models in Search of a Bomb," *International Security* 21: 54–86.

Sagan, Scott D. (2001) "The Perils of Proliferation in South Asia," *Asian Survey* 41: 1064–1086.

Sagan, Scott D. and Kenneth N. Waltz (2003) *The Spread of Nuclear Weapons: A Debate*, New York: Norton.

Sample, Susan G. (1998) "Military Buildups, War, and Realpolitik: A Multivariate Model," *Journal of Conflict Resolution* 42: 156–175.

Sample, Susan G. (2002) "The Outcomes of Military Buildups: Minor States vs. Major Powers," *Journal of Peace Research* 39: 669–691.

Schelling, Thomas C. (1960) *The Strategy of Conflict*, Cambridge: Harvard University Press.

Schelling, Thomas C. (1966) *Arms and Influence*, New Haven, CT: Yale University Press.

Schelling, Thomas C. (1980 [1960]). The Strategy of Conflict. 2nd Ed. Cambridge, MA: Harvard University Press.

Schweller, Randall (1998) *Deadly Imbalances: Tripolarity and Hitler's Strategy of World Conquest*, New York: Columbia University Press.

Simmons, Beth A. and Daniel J. Hopkins (2005) "The Constraining Power of International Treaties: Theory and Methods," *American Political Science Review* 99: 623–631.

Singh, Sonali and Christopher Way (2004) "The Correlates of Nuclear Proliferation," *Journal of Conflict Resolution* 48: 859–885.

Small, Melvin and J. David Singer (1973) "The Diplomatic Importance of States, 1816–1970: An Extension and Refinement of the Indicator," *World Politics* 25: 577–599.

Small, Melvin and J. David Singer (1982) *Resort to Arms*, Beverly Hills, CA: Sage.

Snyder, Glenn H. (1965) "The Balance of Power and the Balance of Terror," in Paul Seabury (ed.) *The Balance of Power*, San Francisco, CA: Chandler.

Snyder, Glenn H. and Paul Diesing (1977) *Conflict Among Nations: Bargaining,*

Decision-Making, and System Structure in International Crises, Princeton, NJ: Princeton University Press.

United Nations (1995) "Charter of the United Nations," in United Nations (ed.) *The United Nations and Human Rights 1945–1995,* New York: Department of Public Information, United Nations.

Waltz, Kenneth N. (1981) "The Spread of Nuclear Weapons: More May be Better," *Adelphi Papers 171,* London: International Institute for Strategic Studies.

Waltz, Kenneth N. (1990) "Nuclear Myths and Political Realities," *American Political Science Review* 84: 731–745.

9 The spread of nuclear weapons and international conflict

Does experience matter?

Michael C. Horowitz[1]

Does the fact that new nuclear states lack experience in dealing with nuclear weapons influence they way they behave and the way they are treated by potential adversaries? This question is highly relevant for both academics and policy makers. In the United States, the proliferation of weapons of mass destruction (WMD), and especially nuclear weapons, has been at the top of the foreign-policy agenda for decades.

Given that nuclear weapons have not been used in war since 1945, that modern biological weapons have arguably never been utilized in warfare, and that the risk of chemical weapons is often considered exaggerated, one might think preventing the proliferation of WMDs is not a critical policy issue. However, the proliferation of new weapons systems can have a profound impact on international politics even at levels short of war. The impact on the coercive power of states and the potential for actual use make nuclear weapons potentially destabilizing in the international security environment.

This chapter presents a quantitative test of the belief in policy circles and one of the central arguments of this special journal issue (Gartzke and Kroenig, this volume) that nuclear weapons increase the coercive bargaining power of the states that possess them. While it is almost certainly true that nuclear weapons affect the balance of power between states, it is also possible that variations in experience with nuclear weapons are relevant for international politics. Specifically, the length of time countries have nuclear weapons may influence both the way they think about how to use their arsenal to achieve national goals and they way they are perceived by adversaries; nuclear learning may occur. The results of this project provide strong initial evidence that nuclear states and their opponents behave differently over time in dispute situations. New nuclear states, with a nascent arsenal and lack of experience in nuclearized disputes, play the "nuclear card" significantly more often than their more experienced nuclear counterparts, making them more likely to reciprocate militarized disputes. Perhaps counter-intuitively, more experienced nuclear states also reciprocate disputes less frequently, which suggests perhaps that opponents learn over time about how to calibrate their challenges against nuclear powers.

The results have both academic and policy relevance. The successful coercion of a state in situations short of war becomes much more difficult in the years immediately following a state's acquisition of nuclear weapons. Nuclear proliferation, therefore, may risk more dangerous militarized disputes, or opponents of new nuclear states may back down and make concessions to avoid conflict.

International relations theory, nuclear weapons, and time

Many scholars have written that, for reasons related to their magnitude relative to conventional weapons, nuclear weapons have changed the character of warfare (Betts 1987; Brodie and Brodie 1973; Jervis 1989a; Mueller 1989). Both Waltz and Sagan, for example, agree that nuclear weapons are unique in their destructive capacity, causing significant changes in the calculations of costs and benefits by nation-states – mostly for Waltz – and the way military organizations will develop routines and conduct planning – for Sagan (Sagan and Waltz 1995).

Slantchev focuses on actions like military maneuvers that he argues send clear implicit signals to adversaries, even in the absence of explicit threats about what a state will do with the recently maneuvered forces. He also emphasizes that bluffing can be effective in conditions of incomplete information, but the logic of his argument applies to inherent capabilities as well (Slantchev 2005). If bluffing works because the false nature of successful bluffs is never revealed, then inherent capabilities, to the extent they signal the ability to coerce at relatively lower cost, can deter action absent an explicit threat (Ikle 1964; Powell 1990).[2]

Betts (1987) argues that inherent nuclear capabilities played precisely this sort of coercive role during the Cold War, which influenced crisis situations. It was something inherent to nuclear weapons, given their destructive power, rather than the specificity of the threats involved that mattered. As Betts writes:

> Any sort of nuclear threat in the midst of crisis, which is by definition an unstable situation, ought to be considered serious business. However indirect or tentative it may be, such a threat must be intended to raise by some degree the danger that disastrous escalation might result, and any degree is worrisome at that level of stakes.
>
> (Betts 1987: 9)

Some theoretical models focusing more directly on nuclear proliferation have come to relatively inconclusive outcomes (Brito and Intriligator 1996). However, empirical research on the causes of proliferation shows the importance of both security and economic factors in predicting proliferation (Singh and Way 2004; Jo and Gartzke 2007). More recently, scholars have investigated the role of civilian nuclear power and nuclear transfers in determining proliferation patterns, finding that civilian nuclear cooperation agreements are often made for strategic reasons and that the prominence of international nuclear transfers in many cases highlights the importance of approaching nuclear proliferation from a supply-side perspective (Kroenig, this volume; Fuhrmann, this volume).

Research by Huth and Russett (1984), Huth (1988, 1990), Fearon (1994), Danilovic (2002), and Signorino and Tarar (2006) has come to varying conclusions about the impact of nuclear weapons on deterrence failure. Other work on the effect of nuclear weapons on international politics suggests that nuclear weapons influence the success of states in international disputes as well as whether or not conflicts escalate (Simon 1999). Recent work by Gartzke and Jo (this book) endogenizes a model of the consequences of proliferation by substituting whether or not states have nuclear weapons for predicted values drawn from a model of proliferation. The endogenized model shows that in general, nuclear weapons states are not necessarily more likely to either initiate disputes or face challenges. However, general estimation equation models of conflict involving nuclear states show that they do appear more likely to end up in low-level disputes, although those disputes are less likely to escalate and become major wars (Rauchhaus, this volume). Finally, examining behavior in international crisis, rather than militarized disputes, Beardsley and Asal (this book) highlight how the asymmetric possession of nuclear weapons in a dispute dyad increases the probability of a favorable outcome.

However, little work to date has analyzed whether or not the length of time countries possess nuclear weapons influences their behavior and the way other states respond. Do the experiences states have over time change the way they behave in subsequent interactions? Most generally, learning is a process by which actors adapt (or do not adapt) their behavior over time as they gather more information from a variety of inputs: experiences, descriptions of experiences, and/or other sources (Levy 1994).

There is growing evidence that prior experiences influence how actors think about the international security environment (Khong 1992; Leng 2000; Reiter 1996). In some cases, through information diffusion, actors can also learn from events they did not directly experience. Multiple actors can also learn together if they have a shared interpretation of a key historical event. For example, Knopf shows how Argentina and Brazil developed a mutual understanding of risk, as well as the link between bilateral tension and the failures of economic integration in the late 1980s, which contributed to bilateral tension reduction in the early 1990s (Knopf 2003). Additionally, once a weapon, product, or concept has existed for a while, late adopters may have a faster learning curve because of vicarious learning.

Theorizing the relationship between nuclear weapons possession and time

The crux of the relationship between nuclear proliferation and international stability is whether nuclear weapons matter only because of the technologies involved – because a nuclear war would likely be so much more destructive than a conventional conflict – or whether there is something about proliferation that alters, perhaps temporarily, existing expectations about capabilities and resolve. The indeterminacy of much of the deterrence literature highlights the importance of rigorous testing (Downs 1989; George and Smoke 1989; Jervis 1989b). Scholars have disagreed, extensively, over how states in deterrence crises calculate the costs and benefits of different actions (Huth and Russett 1990: 466). Many scholars argue that nuclear proliferation is likely to lead to more international conflict, although some disagree. Waltz, for example, argues that nuclear weapons deter challengers and take escalation off the table, making disputes less likely. The balance of threat from nuclear escalation outweighs issue-specific calculations of interests. According to Waltz, the risk of nuclear escalation trumps any uncertainty generated by nuclear acquisition, making post-proliferation conflicts less likely (Waltz 1995: 5–8).

A simple measurement problem limits existing research on nuclear war; all observations after 1945 are censored and end in a condition of no nuclear war. However, it is possible to empirically evaluate the relevance of nuclear weapons in military disputes short of war. In disputes like some of the US–Soviet clashes in the Cold War, the issue of nuclear proliferation intersects with broader questions of learning and information.

Learning as states gain experience with nuclear weapons is complicated. While to some extent nuclear acquisition might provide information about resolve or capabilities, it also generates uncertainty about the way an actual conflict would go – given the new risk of nuclear escalation – and uncertainty about relative capabilities. Rapid proliferation may especially heighten uncertainty given the potential for reasonable states to disagree at times about the quality of the capabilities each possesses.[3] What follows is an attempt to describe the implications of inexperience and incomplete information on the behavior of nuclear states and their potential opponents over time. Since it is impossible to detail all possible lines of argumentation and possible responses, the following discussion is necessarily incomplete. This is a first step.

The acquisition of nuclear weapons increases the confidence of adopters in their ability to impose costs in the case of a conflict and the expectations of likely costs if war occurs by potential opponents. The key questions are whether nuclear states learn over time about how to leverage nuclear weapons and the implications of that learning, along with whether actions by nuclear states, over time, convey information that leads to changes in the expectations of their behavior – shifts in uncertainty – on the part of potential adversaries.

Learning to leverage?

When a new state acquires nuclear weapons, how does it influence the way the state behaves and how might that change over time? Although nuclear acquisition might be orthogonal to a particular dispute, it might be related to a particular security challenge, might signal revisionist aims with regard to an enduring dispute, or might signal the desire to reinforce the status quo.

This section focuses on how acquiring nuclear weapons influences both the new nuclear state and potential adversaries. In theory, systemwide perceptions of nuclear danger could allow new nuclear states to partially skip the early Cold War learning process concerning the risks of nuclear war and enter a proliferated world more cognizant of nuclear brinksmanship and bargaining than their predecessors. However, each new nuclear state has to resolve its own particular civil–military issues surrounding operational control and plan its national strategy in light of its new capabilities. Empirical research by Sagan (1993), Feaver (1992), and Blair (1993) suggests that viewing the behavior of other states does not create the necessary tacit knowledge; there is no substitute for experience when it comes to handling a nuclear arsenal, even if experience itself cannot totally prevent accidents. Sagan contends that civil–military instability in many likely new proliferators and pressures generated by the requirements to handle the responsibility of dealing with nuclear weapons will skew decision-making toward more offensive strategies (Sagan 1995). The questions surrounding Pakistan's nuclear command and control suggest there is no magic bullet when it comes to new nuclear powers making control and delegation decisions (Bowen and Wolvén 1999).

Sagan and others focus on inexperience on the part of new nuclear states as a key behavioral driver. Inexperienced operators, and the bureaucratic desire to "justify" the costs spent developing nuclear weapons, combined with organizational biases that may favor escalation to avoid decapitation – the "use it or lose it" mindset – may cause new nuclear states to adopt riskier launch postures, such as launch on warning, or at least be perceived that way by other states (Blair 1993; Feaver 1992; Sagan 1995).[4]

Acquiring nuclear weapons could alter state preferences and make them more likely to escalate disputes once they start, given their new capabilities.[5] But their general lack of experience at leveraging their nuclear arsenal and effectively communicating nuclear threats could mean new nuclear states will be more likely to select adversaries poorly and find themselves in disputes with resolved adversaries that will reciprocate militarized challenges.

The "nuclear experience" logic also suggests that more experienced nuclear states should gain knowledge over time from nuclearized interactions that help leaders effectively identify the situations in which their nuclear arsenals are likely to make a difference. Experienced nuclear states learn to select into cases in which their comparative advantage, nuclear weapons, is more likely to be effective, increasing the probability that an adversary will not reciprocate.

Coming from a slightly different perspective, uncertainty about the consequences of proliferation on the balance of power and the behavior of new nuclear states on the part of their potential adversaries could also shape behavior in similar ways (Schelling 1966; Blainey 1988). While a stable and credible nuclear arsenal communicates clear information about the likely costs of conflict, in the short term, nuclear proliferation is likely to increase uncertainty about the trajectory of a war, the balance of power, and the preferences of the adopter.

Through interactions over time, opponents learn what the new nuclear state is likely to do with its arsenal, and the new nuclear state learns how to most efficiently leverage its capabilities. Interactions provide information that reduces uncertainty. Therefore, when states first acquire nuclear weapons, adversaries may reciprocate their challenges more often since there is still uncertainty about the implications. The results of dispute reciprocation provide important information. This logic also explains some of the selection problems that new nuclear states may face. Declining uncertainty about the likely behavior of a nuclear state over time may also help more experienced nuclear states credibly signal resolve in disputes. Adversaries have to take seriously the possibility of nuclear escalation because the experienced nuclear state has demonstrated a responsible pattern of behavior with nuclear weapons, meaning threats represent an accurate barometer of intentions. Moreover, non-nuclear states, initially on edge when dealing with new nuclear powers, may become less concerned with raw power grabs by experienced nuclear states, since they trust that the more experienced nuclear states will not shift the coercive goalposts. This makes reciprocation less likely.

Hypothesis 1: For initiators, newer nuclear states will have their militarized dispute initiations reciprocated *more* often than older nuclear states.

Both of these arguments, however, are mostly about nuclear-armed challengers. What about the flip side, when a state initiates a militarized dispute against a nuclear-armed actor? The reduction over time in uncertainty about the behavior of nuclear states should also affect nuclear-armed defenders. In defending situations, the inexperience of new nuclear states means it is possible that they will conceptualize their interests differently than more experienced nuclear states in ways that make reciprocation more likely. New nuclear states might place the highest emphasis on the importance of nuclear weapons, meaning they will recip-rocate more than experienced nuclear states with a better idea of how nuclear bargaining works.[6] Basic deterrence logic would suggest nuclear states in general should experience fewer challenges since their new cap-abilities will deter many potential challengers from even initiating dispute. However, as Fearon argues, non-nuclear states that initiate against nuclear states are likely to be highly resolute, since they select into the conflict with knowledge of the nuclear capabilities of the defender, meaning those disputes should be more likely to escalate (Fearon 1994).

Learning could cut both ways, especially for defenders. Experience over time with nuclear weapons, combined with a more stable arsenal, could also cause a shift in how older nuclear states defend themselves. Older nuclear states might not reciprocate low-level military actions due to faith that their nuclear arsenal will function to deter escalation at higher levels, consistent with the findings of Rauchhaus (this book). More experienced nuclear states learn that their nuclear arsenals represent a de facto guar-antor of national survival. Nuclear states can make small-scale concessions with confidence, knowing their nuclear arsenal will always represent a credible threat in the case of a challenge to core national interests. But this may be knowledge acquired over time, rather than something under-stood inherently upon possession.[7]

Hypothesis 2: For defenders, newer nuclear states will reciprocate mili-tarized dispute initiations *more* often than older nuclear states.

Another plausible alternative worth mentioning is the idea that experi-enced nuclear states may be viewed as more responsible in dealing with nuclear issues – too responsible. Older nuclear states' safe experience with nuclear weapons may undermine their ability to credibly leverage nuclear capabilities in militarized disputes, especially in disputes involving nonvital areas of interest. Adversaries will discount the possibility of nuclear escala-tion if the issue does not impact the vital interests of the nuclear state. Nuclear experience could therefore lead to the opposite result as that hypothesized above.[8] However, the logic of experience drawn from Sagan and the information provided to all sides after dispute participation by new nuclear states would seem to suggest that nuclear learning should help experienced nuclear powers more effectively leverage their weapons, which will also influence adversary perceptions rather than undermine their credibility.

Finally, it is important to recognize that these concepts are somewhat indeterminate. The logics of experience and uncertainty are not the only way to think about nuclear learning, and they could also be drawn out to come to very different conclusions. As a first cut at the question, the point of the empirical tests that follow is precisely to test these extrapolations of some of the deterrence literature and generate initial insights about the relationship between the amount of time a state has nuclear weapons, its behavior, and the behavior of its potential opponents.

Research design

This chapter uses the Militarized Interstate Dispute (MIDs) 3.02 dataset created by the Correlates of War (COW) project to test the 1946–2002 period (Ghosn and Bennett 2003). The data are set up in directed-dispute dyads, meaning they describe the interaction of pairs of states, where Side A refers to the challenger, the state that originally initiated the dispute by threatening, deploying, or using military force against another state, and Side B refers to the defender.[9] A directed-dyads approach is necessary since the hypotheses depend on the specific capabilities of the challenger or the defender. The dependent variable is whether or not a defender reciprocates an initial militarized action by a challenger or if the defender backs down (Schultz 1999). The decision to respond to a militarized action with a militarized action – the joining of the dispute by the defender – moves a dispute beyond its initial stages, although there are still many other escalatory steps before a dispute reaches war. Given the specificity of the arguments to the way variations in nuclear capabilities affect the decisions by challengers and defenders, the actions taken by the defender in response to dispute initiation represent a valid way to operationalize the arguments above.[10]

Measuring the independent variables of interest: nuclear weapons acquisition and possession over time

The first set of independent variables of interest is whether or not each side in a dyad has nuclear weapons, *Side A nuclear* and *Side B nuclear*.[11] Each side in the dyad is coded a 0 if a state does not have nuclear weapons and 1 if it does. While often the possession of nuclear weapons is considered a relatively simple question – either a state has a nuclear weapon or does not – recent research by Singh and Way (2004) points to the importance of being careful in nuclear weapons coding decisions. There are some differences in the way scholars have coded the nuclear arsenals of states over the last 50 years (Jo and Gartzke 2007; Singh and Way 2004). For example, while some have coded Israel as acquiring nuclear weapons in 1966, others say 1972 or even 1973. While some argue India acquired nuclear weapons capabilities in 1974 when it exploded a peaceful nuclear device, others say it was not until 1988, 1990, or even 1998 that India finally acquired nuclear weapons. To measure nuclear proliferation, I draw on the list of dates of nuclear proliferation provided by Gartzke and Kroenig (this book).[12]

The second set of independent variables of interest is the number of years a country has possessed nuclear weapons, *Side A nuclear age* and *Side*

B nuclear age. A counter measures the number of years since a country acquired nuclear weapons, with year one counted as the first year a country has had prior experience with nuclear weapons, or the second year in which a country possesses nuclear weapons.[13]

Other factors that influence militarized dispute success

Isolating the relative importance of nuclear weapons requires differentiating the impact of nuclear weapons possession from the influence of other factors on the probability of militarized dispute reciprocation.[14] Given that the most prominent existing research on signaling and credibility focuses on domestic political regimes, *Side A democracy* and *Side B democracy* were created to measure domestic political regime type using the Polity IV dataset (Jaggers and Gurr 1995). Regimes with a combined polity score of eight or more, meaning their democracy score (−10 to 10) minus their autocracy score (−10 to 10) was equal to or greater than eight, were coded 1, with all other states defined as non-democracies and coded 0.[15]

Two additional variables deal with the relationship between the two states in a dyad. The first, *Dyadic satisfaction*, generated using the Signorino and Ritter "S" – score, measures the satisfaction of both states in the dyad based on their alliance portfolios. The variable, modified as suggested by Bennett and Stam, runs from 0 to 1 (as opposed to −1 to 1), with 0 indicating dissatisfaction and 1 showing satisfaction (Bennett and Stam 2004; Signorino and Ritter 1999).[16] Since this chapter starts from the theoretical position that military capabilities matter for international politics, a measure of the conventional balance of forces was also included. Using relative national power scores (combining measures of economic, demographic, and military power) as coded by the COW dataset, the balance of power control measures the gap between the relative power of Side A and Side B.[17]

Finally, the chapter also includes controls for the particular issue involved in the dispute with three variables: territory, regime/government change, and policy (Bueno de Mesquita and Siverson 1997; Schultz 1999). Issue type matters in this case because, given the potentially existential threat posed by nuclear weapons, the stakes of the issue may be important in determining the credibility of a threat, and therefore how to respond. Some issues, such as territorial control, are often valued more than simple policy changes. The MID data for each dispute include a four-tiered variable for both Side A and Side B measuring whether each state has revisionist demands and the type of demand: the issue categories are territory, regime/governmental change, policy, and other.[18]

Results

The hypotheses above are compared to a null hypothesis predicting no effect between time and behavior. Given the dichotomous nature of the dependent variable, the most appropriate statistical model is logistic regression.[19] These tests include Huber-White robust standard errors and control for the possibility of fixed time effects with peace year splines (Beck *et al.* 1998).[20] Table 9.1 presents initial statistical representations of the relationship between MID reciprocation and the possession of nuclear weapons, building from a simple model without any control variables to larger models including relevant controls. The results show a clear and consistent statistically significant impact to learning over time with nuclear weapons.

The control variables behave in the predicted directions. As Schultz finds, reciprocation is less likely when a challenger is democratic. Interestingly, as the relative power of Side A in a dispute increases, reciprocation appears more likely. This suggests that the general relationship between power and dispute reciprocation is not necessarily linear. Neither the dyadic satisfaction variable nor the joint nuclear possession variable, measuring whether both sides have nuclear weapons, is significant.[21] In general,

Table 9.1 Relationship between nuclear weapons possession, time of possession, and militarized dispute reciprocation

	Simple logit model	Full logit model	Full logit model with US and Russia control[32]
	Coefficient (Robust Standard Error)	Coefficient (Robust Standard Error)	Coefficient (Robust Standard Error)
Side A Nuclear	−0.246 (0.302)	0.156 (0.355)	0.466 (0.374)
Side B Nuclear	0.733 (0.302)**	1.063 (0.364)***	1.034 (0.390)***
Side A Nuclear Age	−0.0217 (0.011)**	−0.024 (0.012)**	−0.026 (0.012)**
Side B Nuclear Age	−0.034 (0.012)***	−0.024 (0.013)*	−0.028 (0.014)**
Joint Nuclear		−0.688 (0.570)	−0.527 (0.607)
Conventional Balance of Forces		0.618 (0.286)**	0.666 (0.292)**
Dyadic Satisfaction		−0.028 (0.288)	0.017 (0.287)
Side A Democracy		−0.511 (0.230)**	−0.757 (0.242)***
Side B Democracy		−0.049 (0.158)	−0.050 (0.164)
Territorial Dispute		2.026 (0.476)***	2.038 (0.489)***
Regime/Government Change		1.782 (0.551)***	1.686 (0.560)***
Policy		0.415 (0.464)	0.389 (0.476)
United States			0.668 (0.348)*
Russia			−0.936 (0.372)**
Constant	−0.436 (0.087)***	−1.717 (0.581)***	−1.742 (0.591)***

Notes
Splines Suppressed: Simple Model − *N*: 1,057, Wald chi2(7): 60.12, Prob > chi2: 0, Pseudo R2: 0.0649, Log pseudo likelihood: −611.4322. Full Logit Model − *N*: 1,036, Wald chi2(15): 151.21, Prob > chi2: 0, Pseudo R2: 0.1519, Log pseudo likelihood: −547.829. Full Model with US and Russia controls − *N*: 1,036, Wald chi2(17): 161.35, Prob > chi2: 0, Pseudo R2: 0.1626, Log pseudo likelihood: −540.976: * $p < .10$ ** $p < .05$ *** $p < .01$.

the significance of the Side B nuclear weapons variable suggests there is something inherent about nuclear capabilities that influences militarized behavior, although the nuclear variable for Side A is not significant. However, the results show that nuclear experience matters as well. The Side A nuclear experience variable is –0.024 and significant at the 0.05 level. Given the caveats above about the indirect nature of these tests, the nuclear learning argument seems clearest in explaining the results for challengers. The negative and significant coefficient for Side A shows that the challenges of older nuclear states are reciprocated significantly less than the challenges of younger nuclear and non-nuclear states.

The results for defenders, although a bit less clear, are potentially even more interesting. The longer the defending side (Side B) possesses nuclear weapons, the less likely it is to reciprocate a militarized dispute. This is the opposite of the coefficient for the possession of nuclear weapons by the defending state in general. Possession of nuclear weapons by the defending state, all other things being equal, makes the defending state more likely to reciprocate a militarized challenge with militarized activity of its own.[22]

The results for defenders could represent a reversion to the mean as nuclear states gain experience. There are other alternatives as well. It is possible that other states learn about experienced nuclear powers and selectively challenge nuclear powers on issues in which they are likely to succeed, which are often issues that do not involve the territory or regime of the nuclear power. Alternatively, it is also possible that threats by more established nuclear powers lack credibility since attackers know the state is unlikely to escalate to the nuclear level. For example, North Korea is the classic example of a small, beleaguered state confronted by a large coalition of states led by a major nuclear power. Even before North Korea tested a nuclear weapon in 2006, analysts expected enormous costs if a conventional war on the Korean peninsula erupted. Knowledge that the United States did not want to pay those costs and was very unlikely to escalate to the nuclear level – the only way to eliminate the North Korean threat without paying the costs of conventional war – likely made it harder for the United States and its allies to influence North Korean behavior.[23]

However, there is some simple statistical evidence that suggests that nuclear defenders decide whether or not to reciprocate challenges on the basis of threats to core national security issues – they are more efficient in when they decide to respond to challenges. There are 136 cases in the data in which Side B has nuclear weapons but Side A does not. When the issue involves policy or "other" demands, Side B backs down 75 percent of the time (75 of 100). However, when the issue involves territorial demands or regime change, the probabilities reverse: Side B reciprocates 75 percent of the time (27 of 36).[24] Side B backs down in only 25 percent of the cases. More evidence for this interpretation of the data is the average nuclear experience of nuclear-armed defenders in these situations. Older nuclear-armed defenders, those with nuclear experience levels above the tenth percentile of average ages for all nuclear-armed defenders, only reciprocate policy or "other" challenges 22 percent (22 of 100) of the time. In contrast, the probability that older nuclear-armed defenders will reciprocate on territorial or regime change issues is 56 percent (20 of 36). Moreover, nuclear-armed defenders facing regime change challenges, the most serious possible threat, are extremely unlikely to make concessions, with 80 percent (4 of 5) reciprocating and an average nuclear experience age of 16.5. In comparison, in those cases where Side A possesses an asymmetric nuclear advantage (186 cases), Side B reciprocates 22 percent of the time in general and 26 percent of the time when the issue involves territorial or regime change issues.

This evidence is somewhat disconcerting since it suggests that experienced nuclear states may become targets. However, the effect might just represent a regression to the mean if new nuclear states feel more confident in their capabilities immediately after acquiring nuclear weapons and reciprocate challenges even if they are not about critical national security issues like territory or the regime. The combination of a fear that nuclear weapons might be "unusable" for a variety of international political and domestic reasons but knowledge that they are an important coercive chip may influence Side B, which shifts as Side B gains more experience with nuclear weapons.

In general, these results provide clear evidence demonstrating that nuclear experience matters, although the contours are a bit less clear. The experience countries have with nuclear weapons influences both the way they behave and the way states respond to them. Initial analysis shows fairly robustly the significance of the nuclear age variables. The models also reaffirm Schultz's (1999) conclusion that democratic challenges are significantly less likely to be reciprocated.

Marginal effects are generated to ensure the statistical results are not an artifice of the large number of non-nuclear states, meaning the negative sign on the nuclear experience coefficient refers to non-nuclear states rather than less experienced nuclear states. The marginal effects further highlight the way altering the balance of nuclear capabilities within a dyad (both the possession of nuclear weapons by each state and the experience each side has with nuclear weapons) influences the probability of dispute reciprocation. Based on model 2 in Table 9.1, Figure 9.1 compares the probability of dispute reciprocation when Side A has asymmetrical possession of nuclear weapons within a dyad to a situation in which Side B has asymmetrical possession of nuclear weapons within a dyad. In both cases, the longer a country has nuclear weapons, the lower the probability of dispute reciprocation. As Side A gains experience with nuclear weapons, the probability of dispute reciprocation by Side B drops from 0.30 the first year Side A has nuclear weapons to 0.11 in year 56. In contrast, as Side B gains experience with nuclear weapons, it becomes increasingly likely to not reciprocate militarized challenges. The probability of reciprocation drops from 0.53 the first year Side B has nuclear weapons to 0.23 in year 56. As noted above, on territorial and regime change issues, Side B is still likely to reciprocate even if it is an experienced nuclear state. While there is a decline in the probability of reciprocation over time, the predicted probability of reciprocation by Side B on regime change issues in year 56 is still 0.44 and it is 0.50 on territorial issues. This compares very favorably with a reciprocation probability of just 0.16 on policy issues in year 56.[25]

A final comparison involves varying the experience both sides have with nuclear weapons to highlight the way risk calculations may shift as the experience each side has with nuclear weapons changes. A situation in which neither side has nuclear weapons is compared to several "scenarios," or balances of nuclear capabilities between both sides. Table 9.2 shows the difference between the relative risk of MID reciprocation when a side does not have nuclear weapons versus when it is a new nuclear state, meaning the nuclear age variable is 0, versus gradually increasing levels of nuclear experience based on averages for Side A and Side B described below. This setup also helps deal with the nonmonotonic effect caused by the pooling of zeroes.

The biggest relative risks are consistent with nuclear learning. If both sides have nuclear weapons but have had them for a relatively short period of time, Side A will not have built up credibility over time with its nuclear arsenal and Side B will not have learned to focus more on existential security risks. The nuclear-experience theory would predict a higher

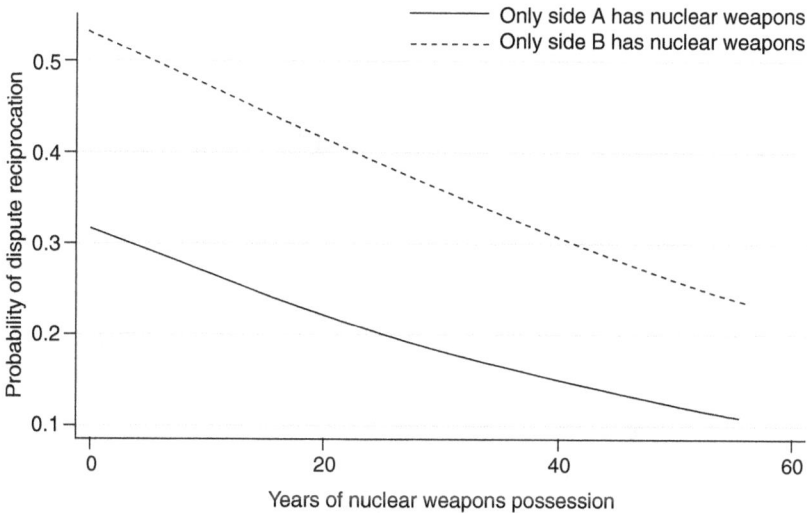

Figure 9.1 Substantive relationship between years of nuclear weapons possession and militarized dispute reciprocation.

Table 9.2 Substantive impact of different levels of dyadic nuclear experience

	Probability of Reciprocation	First Difference with No Nuclear Weapons	Relative Risk (%)	Odds Ratio
No Nuclear Weapons	0.287	0.000	0.00	1.000
Side A "New"	0.281	−0.006	−1.94	1.028
Side A "Medium"	0.191	−0.096	−33.43	1.704
Side A "Experienced"	0.122	−0.165	−57.41	2.890
Side B "New"	0.491	0.205	71.37	0.416
Side B "Medium"	0.367	0.080	28.07	0.693
Side B "Experience"	0.245	−0.042	−14.57	1.239
Both "New"	0.480	0.193	67.49	0.435
Both "New-Medium"	0.379	0.093	32.34	0.657
Both "Medium"	0.253	−0.033	−11.67	1.185
Both "Experienced"	0.101	−0.185	−64.64	3.563
Side A "Medium" Side B "New"	0.362	0.075	26.20	0.709
Side B Medium Side A "New"	0.359	0.072	25.08	0.719
Side A "Experienced" Side B "Medium"	0.166	−0.121	−42.06	2.018
Side B "Experienced" Side A "Medium"	0.161	−0.126	−43.85	2.095
Side B "Experienced" Side A "New"	0.241	−0.046	−16.08	1.269
Side A "Experienced" Side B "New"	0.250	−0.036	−12.73	1.204

Notes
New/Medium/Very Experienced are derived from the summary data for the nuclear age variables. New – 5th percentile: Side A – 3, Side B – 1. Medium – Mean: Side A – 25.3, Side B – 23.6. Very Experienced – 95th percentile: Side A – 51, Side B – 48. Results generated using Clarify (King et al. 2000; Tomz et al. 2003). Odds ratios reversed in table.

relative risk for this situation, an expectation verified by the actual relative risk increase of 67 percent compared to a situation in which neither side has nuclear weapons. In contrast, if both sides have extensive experience with nuclear weapons, Side A will be believed to have high credibility with its nuclear challenges while Side B will likely view the issue as not essential to its credibility, which explains the 65 percent decreased relative risk of dispute reciprocation. Similarly, if Side A has had nuclear weapons for a few decades but Side B is a new nuclear state, Side A will have some nuclear credibility built for its challenges, but Side B will be especially likely to select into the dispute because of its nuclear arsenal, which explains the 26 percent increase in the relative risk of dispute reciprocation. In contrast, if Side A is a very experienced nuclear state and Side B has a "medium" level of nuclear experience, the relative risk of reciprocation drops 42 percent.

One problem with the results from the dyadic models is that a selection process might be at work since Side A initiates a dispute with knowledge of the nuclear capabilities of Side B. The variables significantly related to militarized-dispute reciprocation may just reflect the decision-making of dispute initiators, which biases the results.

If the selection argument were true, one would expect to see nuclear-armed defenders only challenged when Side A is especially resolute, so they will not be deterred by nuclear capabilities. However, more than 75 percent of the challenges to nuclear-armed defenders in the dataset occur over policy issues, not territorial or regime change issues in which, presumably, Side A would be more resolute. While the issue-specific data for dyads in which only Side B has nuclear weapons are relatively inconclusive, it does slightly tilt against this particular selection argument. Of the 136 total challenges against nuclear-armed defenders when only the defender has nuclear weapons, 23 percent are over territorial issues, 72 percent over policy issues, and 4 percent are over regime change issues. In comparison, when Side B does not possess nuclear weapons, 25 percent of challenges occur over territorial issues and 6 percent over regime change issues, while 66 percent are over policy issues. So, Side B is marginally more likely to be challenged on policy issues, as opposed to territorial or regime change issues, when Side B possesses nuclear weapons.

To more effectively test for the presence of selection effects that might inaccurately make the nuclear-experience argument appear more powerful than it actually is, a series of models were estimated to look at MID initiation and the link between initiation and reciprocation. These can also help shed light on the potential applicability of the arguments presented in this chapter to questions of initiation. The dataset is all MID dyads and 10 percent of nondispute dyads from 1946 to 2002, a rare events selection model (King and Zeng 2001). There are two probit models presented that mimic models 2 and 3 from Table 9.1, following by a bivariate probit selection model, since MID reciprocation is dependent on MID initiation, and a censored probit model that just looks at reciprocation given initiation. The dependent variable in the selection equation is MID initiation, and the dependent variable in the outcome equation is reciprocation. The results are presented below in Table 9.3.[26]

The results provide some limited support for the nuclear experience argument that reinforces the dyadic results above. Interestingly, in the pure initiation equation, adding the same controls used above makes both nuclear-experience variables insignificant. While the nuclear-possession variables are both significant, combined with the work by Gartzke and Jo (this book), these results suggest the relationship between nuclear possession and initiation is more complicated than initially thought.

However, in the censored probit selection model, the nuclear-age variable for Side A is significant and positive in the selection equation, which means that as states gain experience with nuclear weapons, they become significantly more likely to initiate disputes. The nuclear-age variable for Side B is not significant. In the outcome equation, the nuclear-experience variable is significant for side B in the same direction as the initial censored dyadic analysis, while the Side A experience variable falls just short of significance (P>absval(z) = 0.107 in a two-tailed test). However, there are limits to selection models in international relations, since there are no instances of the outcome (reciprocation) without the treatment (initiation). Therefore, we turn to the censored model, where the results are actually stronger than in Table 9.2. Accounting for initiation, increasing levels of nuclear experience on the part of challengers make their challenges less likely to be reciprocated. Similarly, while inexperienced nuclear states are extremely likely to reciprocate when they are militarily challenged, the effects fade over time as states gain experience with nuclear weapons.

Discussion

These results are consistent with variants of the nuclear-experience hypotheses presented above. The nuclear experience is not immutable – there are changes over time in the behavior of nuclear states. It is hard to untangle the different causal mechanisms or logics that govern the learning process, but some initial findings stand out. First, nuclear learning seems to occur especially for challengers, as more experienced nuclear states more efficiently challenge and succeed in militarized disputes. Second, new nuclear states appear the most "risky" from the perspective of low-level militarized disputes, with a higher probability of reciprocation than either experienced nuclear states or even non-nuclear states. One possible explanation is that nuclear defenders learn over time to differentiate those challenges worth pursing and those not worth the effort. The nuclear card cannot be played every time – otherwise the defender is exposed as a likely bluffer, making

Table 9.3 Relationship between nuclear weapons possession, time of possession, militarized dispute initiation, and militarized dispute reciprocation

	Probit: MID initiation	Probit: MID initiation with controls	Selection model: MID initiation	Selection model: MID reciprocation	Censored probit: reciprocation (censored on MID initiation)
Side A Nuclear	0.611 (0.064)***	0.512 (0.068)***	0.634 (0.064)***	−0.341 (0.153)**	0.493 (0.225)**
Side B Nuclear	0.705 (0.063)***	0.610 (0.066)***	0.715 (0.07)***	0.026 (0.185)	0.704 (0.253)***
Side A Nuclear Age	0.008 (0.002)***	0.002 (0.002)	0.008 (0.002)***	−0.01 (0.005)	−0.016 (0.007)**
Side B Nuclear Age	0.002 (0.002)	−0.003 (0.002)	0.002 (0.002)	−0.014 (0.006)**	−0.019 (0.009)**
Joint Nuclear		0.249 (0.108)**	0.176 (0.118)	−0.193 (0.22)	−0.57 (0.501)
Conventional Balance of Forces	0.221 (0.029)***	0.221 (0.029)***	0.218 (0.035)***	−0.09 (0.117)	0.346 (0.18)*
Dyadic Satisfaction	0.134 (0.042)***	0.153 (0.042)***	0.99 (0.058)***		0.106 (0.181)
Side A Democracy	−0.188 (0.029)***	−0.173 (0.030)***	−0.202 (0.029)***	0.024 (0.081)	−0.337 (0.142)**
Side B Democracy	0.136 (0.026)***	0.143 (0.026)***	0.146 (0.026)***	−0.218 (0.068)***	−0.069 (0.102)
Territorial Dispute					1.172 (0.274)***
Regime/Government Change					0.948 (0.323)***
Policy					0.176 (0.265)
United States		0.473 (0.063)***			0.408 (0.217)*
Russia		0.427 (0.063)***			−0.646 (0.228)***
Constant	−2.069 (0.039)***	−2.090 (0.040)***	−2.45 (0.039)***	1.247 (0.276)***	−1.103 (0.343)***

Notes

All splines suppressed: Initial Probit – N: 108,694, Wald chi2(11): 1581.97, Prob > chi2: 0, Pseudo R2: 0.1509, Log pseudo likelihood: −6738.0045. Add controls – N: 108,694, Wald chi2(14): 1777.78, Prob > chi2: 0, Pseudo R2: 0.1556, Log pseudo likelihood: −6700.4332. Selection Model – N: 108,694, Censored Obs: 107,189, Uncensored Obs: 1,505, Wald chi2(11): 101.39, Prob > chi2: 0, Log likelihood: − 7591.311, LR Test of Independent Equations: chi2(1): 10.59, Prob > chi2: 0.0011. Censored Probit – N: 936, Wald chi2(17): 151.32, Prob >chi2: 0, Pseudo R2: 0.1581, Log pseudo likelihood: −479.37.

brinkmanship by initiators increasingly likely in repeated games. Third, if nothing else, the results suggest nuclear weapons increase the influence of proliferators. Acquiring nuclear weapons makes a state harder to leverage, at least initially. This is consistent with the findings elsewhere in this book, especially by Beardsley and Asal.

US and Soviet learning during the Cold War demonstrates the plausibility of the nuclear-experience argument. Experience over time with civil–military relations and command authority for launching nuclear weapons created shared US–Soviet knowledge about the risk of nuclear war and led to a mutual appreciation of the costs and the condition of incomplete information in which nuclear escalation would likely occur (George 1983; Nye 1987).

One example of the willingness of new nuclear states to brandish their nuclear arsenals is the way the United States responded during the first Berlin Airlift crisis (1948–1949). According to Kohler, the US chargé in the Soviet Union, American possession of the atomic bomb allowed the US to stand firm. Soviet apprehension about fighting a nuclear-armed adversary, especially in a war over Berlin, a territory some thought Stalin did not consider worth a conventional or nuclear war, influenced the US decision (United States Department of State 1973: 1196; United States Department of State 1974: 920). The relative strength of the US atomic arsenal allowed the US to oppose Soviet actions (Druks 1967: 167–168; Halperin 1987: 7).

As the Cold War went on, both sides gained experience in crisis situations and with different deployment strategies. These experiences provided information that, although imperfectly aggregated into national policy over time, led to shifts both in micro-level decisions such as doctrine and in more macro-level decisions about strategy (George 1983). Even while critiquing reforms and pointing out areas where learning was incomplete, Sagan writes that the American military extensively studied the 1962 nuclear alert during the Cuban Missile Crisis, seeking to improve its procedures to enhance both effectiveness and safety. The October 1973 alert then demonstrated learning through the institutionalization of previously ad-hoc procedures during the 1963 Cuban Missile Crisis, such as placing nuclear warheads on test missiles at Vandenberg and not dispersing nuclear-armed bombers when DEFCON 3 was instituted (Sagan 1993: 219–224). The fact of learning, whether effective or not, shows that the logic described above is a plausible way to think about nuclear strategy over time.

Some argue that, because nuclear war has not happened since 1945, nuclear weapons lack importance for international politics because threats to use them are not credible (Geller 1990). In contrast, the evidence presented in this chapter suggests that nuclear weapons do have some degree of inherent credibility. Even if a state never makes an explicit nuclear threat, the mere presence of nuclear weapons may exert a powerful coercive role in low-level militarized disputes.[27]

Another alternative explanation for the results is that more experienced nuclear states have larger and more sophisticated arsenals, and those factors drive the shifting behavior of nuclear states over time. The Natural Resources Defense Council (NRDC) has collected systematic data on the arsenal sizes of nuclear states from 1945–2001 (Natural Resources Defense Council 2007).[28] A control run that added a variable measuring the nuclear-arsenal size of each nuclear state in a given year was estimated to test this theory but did not change the results. To further control for differences in nuclear arsenals, using the NRDC Nuclear Databook and other sources, I generated a nuclear-sophistication variable. It is coded 1 if a country has a deliverable nuclear weapon, 2 if a country has both air and land-based missile delivery systems, and 3 if a country has a sea-based delivery system as well.[29] Including this variable did not change the results either. So, while arsenal size and the nuclear balance of power are obviously important factors governing the behavior of nuclear states in militarized disputes against each other, the theory is more focused on asymmetrical nuclear interactions.[30]

One could further argue that the results are driven by states' actual participation in militarized disputes, meaning militarized incidents, not experience, really drive change. However, control runs with MID participation did not produce significant changes. Even if MID participation shifts how countries think about nuclear weapons and how opponents evaluate resolve, however, it still demonstrates a learning process that contradicts static understandings of the impact of nuclear weapons on politics.

Finally, it is possible that the results are just an artifact of a changing international system since 1945, especially as knowledge about nuclear weapons has spread. As Knopf, Reiter, and others describe, learning does not just happen on a direct basis but through the vicarious observation of others. If it is shifts over time that matter, meaning new nuclear states now learn "faster" than their predecessors, it is consistent with the broad argument made in this chapter. Time-based effects still demonstrate that possessing nuclear weapons is not an immutable characteristic, but is subject to a learning process.

From a measurement perspective, the problem is that "time" is already captured to a large extent in the nuclear-age variables, making it difficult to add an independent time variable without running into correlation problems. A pure calendar-time variable would also suffer from problems of interpretation, since it would not be clear whether the variation it explained was caused by changes in beliefs about nuclear weapons or other facets of the international system. A variable just counting the number of nuclear weapons states is similarly hard to interpret, since it linearly increases with the nuclear-age variables, excluding when South Africa drops out of the nuclear club in 1990.[31]

Conclusion

This chapter finds that there are important consequences for international politics as states gain experience with nuclear weapons. The initial
evidence, while tentative, suggests that new nuclear states are especially
risky – their challenges are reciprocated more often, while their desire to
demonstrate their nuclear clout makes them substantially less likely to
concede when facing a challenge. However, it is difficult to tell whether it
is the logic of inexperience or the logic of uncertainty driving the results.
The behavior of defending states over time is harder to unravel. One possibility is that as defending states gain experience with nuclear weapons,
they reconceptualize the way they think about national security. Instead of
viewing all challenges as potentially risky for the survival of the state,
nuclear-armed defenders come to rely on their nuclear arsenals as guaran-
tors of security, making it more acceptable to make concessions on issues
unrelated to core national interests. However, the evidence does not yet
support going that far. These results indicate that nuclear learning is an
issue worth studying both in academic and military settings. More detailed
tests building on this research are necessary to clarify this issue and determine the actual reasoning driving nuclear learning, keeping in mind that
learning may work differently for different states at different times. As we
consider how possession of nuclear weapons affects the capabilities and
resolve of states involved in crisis-bargaining situations, learning over time
may be an important part of the process.

Notes

1 Replication data available at the *JCR* web page.
2 Nuclear weapons are also interesting because once a demonstration occurs,
   they have some degree of inherent credibility. In the current security environment, many new potential nuclear proliferators are already relatively dissatisfied with the international system, which means their arsenals may send signals
   to existing powers like the United States absent explicit threats.
3 In cases of slow proliferation, adaptation can more easily occur as states anticipate new capabilities and adjust accordingly.
4 On the other hand, inexperienced operators in new nuclear states might be
   especially cautious. A lack of experience and the costs expended in arsenal
   development could lead leaders to be especially conservative in the brandish-
   ing of their new nuclear arsenal. States are often reluctant to risk their most
   prized military assets – with German reticence to deploy its fleet for most of
   World War I representing just one example.
5 There could also be a selection effect in which knowledge of those new capabilities leads to fewer challenges.
6 This follows from Sartori's (2005) understanding of crisis bargaining, in which
   behavior in past crises influences the way states are perceived in future crises.
7 Alternatively, as states learn how to leverage their nuclear arsenal they might
   become more confident and likely to reciprocate challenges. An example of an
   older power not escalating a potential military dispute is the American non-
   response to frequent threats emanating from North Korea.

8 Another potential alternative argument might concern a growing nuclear taboo. However, since this chapter is concerned with coercion at levels below war, the taboo argument is less applicable, although a taboo might influence the credibility of nuclear threats.

9 For an explanation of the merits of using dyad years, see Bennett and Stam (2004) and Gleditsch and Hegre (1997).

10 One could argue that the theory presented above also applies to dispute initiation. However, this chapter focuses on reciprocation for several reasons. First, the theory is specific to the way states behave when they get into disputes – how inexperience and uncertainty influence the way nuclear states and their opponents respond. While the theoretical logic may apply to initiation, modeling dispute initiation is much more complicated. I limited the core tests to reciprocation since this is a first attempt to examine the role of nuclear experience. Future work could certainly refocus on the initiation question. Second, states often acquire nuclear weapons in part because of security concerns, so we should not necessarily expect to see an effect on dispute initiation – it may be endogenous to nuclear weapons acquisition. The disputes already exist. It is the way states behave within those disputes that change. Moreover, as Gartzke and Jo (this book) point out, endogenizing predictions about nuclear proliferation into the study of MID initiation shows that nuclear weapons may not be related to initiation. Finally, tests conducted using nonendogenized models (in the language of Gartzke and Jo) show that the probability of dispute initiation does increase when states get nuclear weapons, although it seems to increase with time (results generated from model 1, Table 9.3, using Clarify and available upon request). Therefore, bracketing the caveats, new nuclear states appear somewhat more prone to initiate disputes and to face initiations than non-nuclear states, but more experienced nuclear states are even more likely to initiate.

11 Nuclear state coding is consistent with the rest of the chapters in this volume. There is a sample size question, since the total number of nuclear weapons states is so small. However, since the unit of analysis is the dyad year, each nuclear weapons state is counted each time it gets into a dispute. Since the chapter tests whether the way nuclear states behave changes as they gain experience with nuclear weapons, having multiple observations per nuclear state does not bias the results. Of 1,057 total conflict dyads, once the revisionist-variable corrections are made, only Side A has nuclear weapons in 18 percent of cases, only Side B has nuclear weapons in 13 percent of cases, and both have nuclear weapons in 4 percent of cases.

12 The post-Soviet states are excluded (Gartzke and Kroenig, this volume). Including them does not substantively change the results.

13 The results that follow are robust even when run on different nuclear-possession codings.

14 These variables were generated using EUGene (Bennett and Stam 2000).

15 Adding an interaction term between democracy and the nuclear weapons did not significantly influence the results.

16 All results are consistent whether using S scores or Bueno de Mesquita's Tau-B scheme (Bueno de Mesquita and Lalman 1992).

17 The equation used to produce the relative power variable was cap_1/(cap_1+cap_2). Using alternative conventional capability measures (military spending and personnel) or adding an arms-race variable did not significantly change the results.

18 The "other" revisionist issue variable was forcibly dropped due to extremely high collinearity. Of 1,706 post-1945 dyadic MIDs, set up with Side A as the initiator, 142 (8 percent) are dyads in which Side B, not Side A, had revisionist aims. In another 279 cases (16 percent) both sides had types of revisionist aims.

If Side A is not revisionist or if both sides are revisionist, it will influence state behavior in different ways by changing the nature of the stakes to both sides. So the paper drops the problematic cases for the main data runs but also conducts analyses that do not include the revisionist-types variables at all.

19 Selection and fixed-effects models are estimated below to capture any omitted strategic interaction effects.

20 Adding a peace-years-count variable (time since the last MID) had no impact on the results.

21 This is also likely because only a small fraction of the cases, 39 of 1,057, come from interactions between two nuclear states and because, excluding the United States and Soviet case, the nuclear balance of power within nuclear dyads has been relatively constant.

22 This result was also consistent in two fixed-effects models, one pooling on nuclear states and the other on dyadic interactions.

23 For more on leveraging North Korea, see Horowitz (2005).

24 In the opposite situation, when Side A possesses an asymmetric nuclear advantage over Side B, only 10 percent of total challenges (19 of 187) involve territorial or regime change issues.

25 Marginal effects controlling for issue type available upon request.

26 The results are consistent using bivariate probit and seemingly unrelated bivariate probit models as well.

27 For example, the placement of American bombers on alert in 1958 after a coup in Iraq apparently influenced Soviet behavior despite the lack of an explicit statement or threat (Betts 1987: 66–68).

28 While some of the sizes are only estimates given opacity about the arsenals of some countries, the NRDC data are arguably the best available public source on nuclear arsenal sizes and a source frequently cited by scholars interested in the topic.

29 Thanks to an anonymous reviewer for suggesting multiple delivery mechanisms as a metric. Since submarine-launched missiles are generally considered the most survivable delivery vehicle, the presence of sub-launched missiles is considered the highest level of sophistication. Alternative specifications did not change the results.

30 A nuclear second-strike variable was not added because it is not relevant for most smaller nuclear powers and because of measurement problems. The total of 39 joint nuclear cases occurs because of the exclusions given the revisionist-issue variables.

31 Despite these, I tried adding a calendar-time variable and a "number of nuclear states" variable (each in a separate model) and reestimated the core models of Table 9.2, interacting the nuclear-age variables with the time variable in question. The results are hard to interpret, since there is already a tacit relationship between the nuclear-weapons-possession and nuclear-age variables. However, in a control run with the other key controls – arsenal size and sophistication – there was a significant interaction between time and nuclear experience on the part of Side A.

32 Given the small number of nuclear powers, it is important to make sure the results are not an artifact of just one or two countries. Models excluding countries as opposed to controlling for them did not alter the results.

Bibliography

Albright, David (1994) "South Africa and the affordable bomb," *Bulletin of the Atomic Scientists* 50: 37–47.

Beardsley, Kyle and Victor Asal (This Book) "Winning with the bomb."

Beck, Nathaniel *et al.* (1998) "Taking time seriously: time-series–cross-section analysis with a binary dependent variable," *American Journal of Political Science* 42: 1260–1288.

Bennett, D. Scott and Allan C. Stam (2000) "EUGene: a conceptual manual," *International Interactions* 26: 179–204.

Bennett, D. Scott and Allan C. Stam (2004) *The Behavioral Origins of War*, Ann Arbor, MI: University of Michigan Press.

Betts, Richard K. (1987) *Nuclear Blackmail and Nuclear Balance*, Washington, DC: Brookings Institution.

Blainey, Geoffrey (1988) *The Causes of War*, New York: Free Press.

Blair, Bruce G. (1993) *The Logic of Accidental Nuclear War*, Washington, DC: Brookings Institution.

Bowen, Clayton P. and Daniel Wolvén (1999) "Command and control challenges in South Asia," *The Nonproliferation Review* 6: 25–35.

Brito, Dagobert L. and Michael D. Intriligator (1996) "Proliferation and the probability of war: a cardinality theorem," *Journal of Conflict Resolution* 40: 206–214.

Brodie, Bernard and Fawn McKay Brodie (1973) *From Crossbow to H-bomb*, revised and enlarged edn, Bloomington, IN: Indiana University Press.

Bueno de Mesquita, Bruce and Randolph M. Siverson (1997) "Nasty or nice? Political systems, endogenous norms and the treatment of adversaries," *Journal of Conflict Resolution* 41: 175–199.

Cohen, Avner (1998) *Israel and the Bomb*, New York: Columbia University Press.

Danilovic, Vesna (2002) *When the Stakes are High: Deterrence and Conflict among Major Powers*, Ann Arbor, MI: University of Michigan Press.

Downs, George W. (1989) "The rational deterrence debate," *World Politics: A Quarterly Journal of International Relations* 41: 225–237.

Druks, Herbert (1967) *Harry S. Truman and the Russians, 1945–1953*, New York: R. Speller.

Farr, Warner D. (1999) *The Third Temple's Holy of Holies: Israel's Nuclear Weapons*, The Counterproliferation Papers – Future Warfare Series – No. 2, Maxwell Air Force Base, Alabama: USAF Counterproliferation Center, Air University.

Fearon, James D. (1994) "Signaling versus the balance of power and interests: an empirical test of a crisis bargaining model," *Journal of Conflict Resolution* 38: 236–269.

Feaver, Peter (1992) *Guarding the Guardians: Civilian Control of Nuclear Weapons in the United States, Cornell Studies in Security Affairs*, Ithaca, NY: Cornell University Press.

Fuhrmann, Matthew (This Book) "Taking a walk on the supply side: the determinants of civilian nuclear cooperation."

Gartzke, Erik and Dong-Joon Jo (This Book) "Bargaining, nuclear proliferation, and interstate disputes."

Gartkze, Erik and Matthew Kroenig (This book) A strategic approach to nuclear proliferation.

Geller, Daniel S. (1990) "Nuclear weapons, deterrence, and crisis escalation," *Journal of Conflict Resolution* 34: 291–310.

George, Alexander L. (1983) *Managing U.S.–Soviet Rivalry: Problems of Crisis Prevention*, Boulder, CO: Westview Press.

George, Alexander L. and Richard Smoke (1989) "Deterrence and foreign policy," *World Politics: A Quarterly Journal of International Relations* 41: 170–182.

Ghosn, Faten and D. Scott Bennett (2003) *Codebook for the Dyadic Militarized Interstate Incident Data, version 3.0* [cited January 20, 2006]. Available at http://cow2. la.psu.edu/COW2%20Data/MIDs/Codebook%20for%20Dyadic%20MID%20 Data.pdf.

Gleditsch, Nils Petter and Havard Hegre (1997) "Peace and democracy: three levels of analysis," *Journal of Conflict Resolution* 41: 283–310.

Halperin, Morton H. (1987) *Nuclear Fallacy: Dispelling the Myth of Nuclear Strategy*, Cambridge, MA: Ballinger Publishing Co.

Horowitz, Michael (2005) "Who's behind that curtain? Unveiling potential leverage over Pyongyang," *Washington Quarterly* 28: 21–44.

Horton, Roy E. (2000) *Out of (South) Africa: Pretoria's Nuclear Weapons Experience*, *ACDIS Occasional Paper*, Champaign, IL: ACDIS University of Illinois.

Huth, Paul K. (1988) *Extended Deterrence and the Prevention of War*, New Haven, CT: Yale University Press.

Huth, Paul K. (1990) "The extended deterrent value of nuclear weapons," *Journal of Conflict Resolution* 34: 270–290.

Huth, Paul K. and Bruce Russett (1984) "What makes deterrence work? Cases from 1900 to 1980," *World Politics: A Quarterly Journal of International Relations* 36: 496–526.

Huth, Paul K. and Bruce Russett (1990) "Testing deterrence theory: rigor makes a difference," *World Politics: A Quarterly Journal of International Relations* 42: 466–501.

Ikle, Fred Charles (1964) *How Nations Negotiate*, 1st edn, New York: Harper & Row.

Jaggers, Keith and Ted Robert Gurr (1995) "Tracking democracy's third wave with the Polity III data," *Journal of Peace Research* 32: 469–482.

Jervis, Robert (1989a) *The Meaning of the Nuclear Revolution: Statecraft and the Prospect of Armageddon, Cornell Studies in Security Affairs*, Ithaca, NY: Cornell University Press.

Jervis, Robert (1989b) "Rational deterrence: theory and evidence," *World Politics: A Quarterly Journal of International Relations* 41: 183–207.

Jo, Dong-Joon and Erik Gartzke (2007) "Determinants of nuclear weapons proliferation," *Journal of Conflict Resolution* 51: 167.

Khong, Yuen Foong (1992) *Analogies at War: Korea, Munich, Dien Bien Phu, and the Vietnam Decisions of 1965*, Princeton, NJ: Princeton University Press.

King, Gary and Langche C. Zeng (2001) "Explaining rare events in international relations," *International Organization* 55: 693–715.

King, Gary *et al.* (2000) "Making the most of statistical analyses: improving interpretation and presentation," *American Journal of Political Science* 44: 347–361.

Knopf, Jeffrey W. (2003) "The importance of international learning," *Review of International Studies* 29: 185–207.

Kroenig, Matthew (This Book) "Importing the bomb: sensitive nuclear assistance and nuclear proliferation."

Leng, Russell J. (2000) *Bargaining and Learning in Recurring Crises: the Soviet–American,*

Egyptian–Israeli, and Indo-Pakistani rivalries, Ann Arbor, MI: University of Michigan Press.

Levy, Jack S. (1994) "Learning and foreign policy: sweeping a conceptual mine-field," *International Organization* 48: 279–312.

Mueller, John E. (1989) *Retreat from Doomsday: The Obsolescence of Major War,* New York: Basic Books.

Natural Resources Defense Council (2007) *Table of Global Nuclear Weapons Stockpiles, 1945–2002,* NRDC Nuclear Program, [cited January 30, 2007]. Available at www. nrdc.org/nuclear/nudb/datab19.asp.

Nizamani, Haider K. (2000) *The Roots of Rhetoric: Politics of Nuclear Weapons in India and Pakistan,* Westport, CT: Praeger.

Norris, Robert S. (1994) *British, French, and Chinese Nuclear Forces: Implications for Arms Control and Nonproliferation, PRAC paper 11,* College Park, MD: University of Maryland at College Park.

Nuclear Weapon Archive (2006) *France's Nuclear Weapons 2001* [cited January 20, 2006]. Available at http://nuclearweaponarchive.org/France/FranceArsenal-Dev.html.

Nye, Joseph S. Jr (1987) "Nuclear learning and U.S.–Soviet security regimes," *International Organization* 41: 371–402.

Perkovich, George (1999) *India's Nuclear Bomb: The Impact on Global Proliferation,* Berkeley, CA: University of California Press.

Powell, Robert (1990) *Nuclear Deterrence Theory: The Search for Credibility,* Cambridge; New York: Cambridge University Press.

Rauchhaus, Robert (This Book) "Evaluating the nuclear peace hypothesis: a quantitative approach."

Reiter, Dan (1996) *Crucible of Beliefs: Learning, Alliances, and World Wars,* Cornell Studies in Security Affairs, Ithaca, NY: Cornell University Press.

Sagan, Scott D. (1993) *The Limits of Safety: Organizations, Accidents, and Nuclear Weapons,* Princeton, NJ: Princeton University Press.

Sagan, Scott D. (1995) "More will be worse," in S.D. Sagan and K.N. Waltz (eds) *The Spread of Nuclear Weapons: A Debate,* New York: W.W. Norton.

Sagan, Scott D. and Kenneth N. Waltz (1995) *The Spread of Nuclear Weapons: A Debate,* 1st edn, New York: W.W. Norton.

Sartori, Anne E. (2005) *Deterrence by Diplomacy,* Princeton, NJ: Princeton University Press.

Schelling, Thomas C. (1966) *Arms and Influence,* New Haven, CT: Yale University Press.

Schultz, Kenneth A. (1999) "Do democratic institutions constrain or inform? Contrasting two institutional perspectives on democracy and war," *International Organization* 53: 233–266.

Signorino, Curt S. and Ahmer Tarar (2006) "A unified theory and test of extended immediate deterrence," *American Journal of Political Science* 50: 586–605.

Signorino, Curt S. and Jeffrey M. Ritter (1999). "Tau-b or not Tau-b: Measuring the similarity of foreign policy positions," *International Studies Quarterly* 43: 115–144.

Simon, Michael W. (1999) "Asymmetric nuclear acquisition and international conflict," Ph.D., The University of Iowa, Iowa City.

Singh, Sonali and Christopher R. Way (2004) "The correlates of nuclear proliferation: a quantitative test," *Journal of Conflict Resolution* 48: 859–885.

Slantchev, Branislav L. (2005) "Military coercion in interstate crises," *American Political Science Review* 99: 533–547.

Tomz, Michael *et al.* (2003) *CLARIFY: Software for Interpreting and Presenting Statistical Results* (2.1) Harvard University, January 5 [cited January 20, 2006]. Available at http://gking.harvard.edu.

United States Department of State (1973) *Germany and Austria Vol. II, Foreign Relations of the United States of America*, Washington, DC: United States Government Printing Office.

United States Department of State (1974) *Eastern Europe; the Soviet Union Vol. IV, Foreign Relations of the United States of America*, Washington, DC: United States Government Printing Office.

Waltz, Kenneth N. (1995) "More may be better," in S.D. Sagan and K.N. Waltz (eds) *The Spread of Nuclear Weapons: A Debate*, New York: W.W. Norton.

10 Evaluating the nuclear peace hypothesis

A quantitative approach

Robert Rauchhaus[1]

> It may be that we shall by a process of sublime irony have reached a stage in this story where safety will be the sturdy child of terror, and survival the twin brother of annihilation.
>
> Winston Churchill

From the vantage point of 1946, few were optimistic about the stability of emerging postwar order and the long-term prospects for peace. The inter-war period (1918–1939) had shown the ineffectiveness of collective secur-ity, the fragility of the international political economy, and the danger of nascent democracies. As the wartime alliance between the United States and USSR deteriorated and each side implemented new strategic doc-trines, many suspected that another great military contest was inevitable (Lippmann 1947). The fear of another world war was only compounded by the splitting of the atom and the spread of nuclear weapons.

Although the Cold War was often fierce, especially in the developing world where it frequently played out, it never managed to escalate to World War III. Indeed, with the benefit of hindsight, this has prompted some to argue that Cold War is better thought of as the "Long Peace" (Gaddis 1986, 1987; Kegley 1991).[2] Despite the worries of some, the col-lapse of the Soviet Union and the end of bipolarity has not, or at least has not yet, undermined the Long Peace. Although violence has mutated into other forms (e.g., civil wars and terrorism), it is with great fortune that we can point to a long-term decline in deaths from interstate war (Human Security Report 2005; Lacina *et al.* 2006).[3]

What is responsible for the absence of major wars among great powers over the last six decades? The three main approaches to international rela-tions (IR) have each offered answers to this question.[4] The most widely cited explanation is that of neo-liberals. Building on Kant's Perpetual Peace (1795), modern liberals point to democracy (Maoz and Russett 1993), trade (Keohane and Nye 1977), and international organizations (Keohane 1984) as key causes of peace. Similarly, constructivism views democracy, trade, and international organizations as important factors, but it parts company with neo-liberalism by attributing the root cause of the Long Peace to evolving norms and the social construction of identity (Katzenstein 1996; Wendt 1992, 1999).[5] Neo-realism, in contrast, is fundamentally at odds with both approaches and rejects the importance of the Kantian Tripod and evolving norms. Instead, the Long Peace during the Cold War is attributed to bipolarity and nuclear deterrence (Waltz 1979, 1990).[6]

In recent years, neo-liberal explanations of the Long Peace have received the most rigorous empirical scrutiny.[7] Realist explanations including the distribution of power, system polarity, and alliance systems have also received considerable attention.[8] Surprisingly, the nuclear peace hypothesis – one of the central tenants of realist explanations for the Long Peace – has received relatively little quantitative scrutiny. Scholars have employed case studies, counter-factual analysis, and formalized their arguments with game theory, but, with the exception of this issue (Gartzke and Jo; Horowitz; Beardsley and Asal, this volume), only a handful of studies have attempted to quantitatively evaluate the effects of nuclear weapons (Bueno de Mesquita and Riker 1982; Geller 1990; Asal and Beardsley 2007). Moreover, previous quantitative studies have exclusively focused on the relationship between nuclear weapons and crises, or between nuclear weapons and dispute escalation. The relationship between nuclear weapons and the probability of war remains quantitatively untested.

The central purpose of this chapter is to offer an empirical answer to the question: do nuclear weapons reduce the probability of war? To answer this question, this project borrows heavily from the last 15 years of work on Democratic Peace Theory (DPT). Beginning with Maoz and Russett (1993), the dyadic DPT research design has been reproduced in dozens of articles and survived peer review in nearly every leading journal of political science and international relations. Building on Pevehouse and Russett (2006) and using the same key "control" variables, this study incorporates new data that allow for the quantitative evaluation of the nuclear peace hypothesis.

The results presented below indicate that the impact of nuclear weapons is more complicated than is conventionally appreciated. Both proliferation optimists (Waltz 1981) and proliferation pessimists (Sagan 1994) find confirmation of some of their key claims. As proliferation optimists contend, when two states possess nuclear weapons, the odds of war drop precipitously. However, in most other respects, proliferation pessimists find vindication of their position. In disputes where only one of two parties possess nuclear weapons, there is an increased chance of war. Moreover, nuclear weapons are generally associated with higher likelihoods of crises, uses of force, and conflicts involving lower levels of casualties. The findings of this chapter are consistent with the larger themes of this volume, demonstrating that nuclear possession can enhance the security of their possessors by shifting conflict to the lower end of the intensity spectrum.

What explains these results? For disputes between two nuclear powers, Snyder's (1965) seminal essay provides a possible answer: the stability–instability paradox identifies a link between strategic nuclear stability and more conflict at lower levels of escalation. The results reported in this study provide empirical support for this view. For disputes between a nuclear power and non-nuclear power, we have results in need of an explanation. Unfortunately, here the scholarly literature on nuclear deterrence is of considerably less value because it is largely confined to situations of nuclear symmetry. Currently the field lacks a coherent theory (or theories) of nuclear asymmetry.

Along with contributing to our understanding of crisis diplomacy, nuclear deterrence theory, and the stability–instability paradox, this study has relevance for several ongoing policy debates. What are the likely consequences of nuclear proliferation? How do nuclear weapons affect crises at different levels of escalation? In addition to the continuing concern for nuclear proliferation, the United States government and other nuclear states will face tough choices stemming from aging nuclear stockpiles. A lively debate is already emerging between the proponents of force modernization and those who are calling for the United States to take steps toward Non-Proliferation Treaty (NPT) commitments. A better understanding of the effects of nuclear deterrence will aid in assessing the costs and benefits of various policies.

This study is divided into five parts. The first section briefly overviews previous work on this subject. Section two lays out the logic of nuclear deterrence theory and deduces a number of testable hypotheses. Section three describes the research design, dataset, coding, and testing procedures. The fourth section reports and interprets the findings. The final section offers a brief summary and discusses next steps in this research program.

Previous quantitative work

Unlike the proliferation of both formal and informal analytic work on nuclear deterrence, there are only a few efforts to statistically evaluate the nuclear peace hypothesis. Considering the importance of this question, the availability of new datasets and modern statistical software, and the trends in other areas of international relations and political science, it is surprising that this literature has generally not transitioned to more rigorous forms of empirical analysis. This is particular striking when one considers the recent flurry of work on the democratic peace.

Geller (1990) and Asal and Beardsley (2007) represent two important exceptions to this trend. Geller's study, which uses the Correlates of War Interstate Disputes dataset, concludes that crises are more likely to escalate to higher levels when one or both parties possess nuclear weapons (Geller 1990: 301). His study made good use of the data and methods that were available at the time, but the *t*-tests and cross-tabs of previous decades are now viewed with skepticism. The same can be said of earlier studies that quantitatively explore the effects of nuclear proliferation (Bueno de Mesquita and Riker 1982).

Making use of improved datasets and recent advances in statistical methods and software, Asal and Beardsley (2007: 139) examine the "relationship between the severity of violence in crises and the number of involved states with nuclear weapons." Using the International Crisis Behavior (ICB) dataset for the 1918–2001 period, the study concludes that nuclear weapons tend to decrease the likely level of violence in a crisis (Asal and Beardsley 2007: 152). This is the opposite conclusion of the one reached by Geller.

Although not primarily focused on the issue of nuclear deterrence, Gartzke (2007) also weighs in on this debate. In the appendix of his study on the "liberal peace," he includes a broad array of control variables, including whether one or both parties to dispute (dyad) possess nuclear weapons. In contrast to the aforementioned studies, Gartzke finds no significant effect, neither positive nor negative.

Considering the importance of this subject and the existence of equivocal empirical results, clearly more work is needed. The research design employed in this study improves on earlier work in two key ways. First, this study directly explores the relationship between nuclear weapons and the probability of war. In contrast, previous quantitative work has tended to explore the relationship between nuclear weapons and militarized disputes or crises. Second, the results presented below control for potential selection effects that may be present in earlier studies. By focusing on year-by-year dyadic relations including non-events (e.g., no crisis or dispute), the results allow for direct estimation of the relationship between nuclear weapons, crisis, and war.

Theory and hypotheses

From the early days of the nuclear revolution, proponents of nuclear deterrence have argued that atomic weapons have the capacity to reduce the probability of conventional war (Brodie 1946, 1947). Reflecting on the Cold War, some scholars argue that this is indeed what happened: despite dozens of crises and several proxy wars, the United States and USSR avoided a direct military conflict because each feared that matters might escalate to nuclear war (Gaddis 1986, 1987; Waltz 1990, 1993, 2000). Unlike conventional deterrence in previous eras, nuclear deterrence is extremely robust because even irrational or unintelligent leaders are likely to recognize the exceedingly high cost of nuclear war. Thus, proponents of nuclear deterrence claim with a high degree of confidence that "the probability of major war among states having nuclear weapons approaches zero" (Waltz 1990: 740).

Scholars who are critical of nuclear deterrence have generally avoided questioning whether nuclear weapons make war less likely. Instead, they usually take one of two approaches. "Safety critics" warn that the nuclear weapons pose a danger because of accidental detonations and inadvertent escalation (Sagan 1993). In contrast, "moral critics" argue that nuclear weapons should be eliminated because they violate international law, are immoral, or both (Falk and Lifton 1991). Oddly enough, neither safety critics nor moral critics tend to question whether nuclear weapons deter war. To the contrary, some critics have assumed that nuclear weapons do indeed reduce the chance of conflict, but argue instead that their deterrent value is outweighed by safety concerns and the prospects of more proliferation (Sagan 1994).

Scholars have also examined the theoretical underpinnings of nuclear deterrence from a number of other perspectives. Using game theory and other formal methods, scholars have examined crisis stability, various deterrent strategies, the credibility of threats, and the consequences of proliferation (Berkowitz 1985; Brito and Intriligator 1996; Bueno de Mesquita and Riker 1982; Harvey and James 1996; Intriligator and Brito 1981; Langlois 1991; Nalebuff 1988; Powell 1985, 1987, 1988, 1989a, 1989b, 1990; Schelling 1960, 1966; Wagner 1991; Zagare and Kilgour 2000). Others have scrutinized the psychological underpinnings of deterrence and the assumption of rationality (Jervis 1984, 1989; Jervis *et al.* 1985). Despite the potential problems associated with nuclear deterrence, the pacifying effects of nuclear weapons are seldom challenged. In these and other studies, the concern is generally for the potential failure of nuclear deterrence, not for the irrelevance of nuclear deterrence. Thus, with only a few caveats and exceptions, the literature on nuclear deterrence makes a rather unambiguous prediction.[9]

Hypothesis 1: The probability of major war between two states will decrease if both states possess nuclear weapons.

For levels of conflict short of war, there is much more ambiguity in the literature. Beginning with Snyder's (1965) seminal essay on what was later dubbed the stability–instability paradox, scholars have widely recognized that while nuclear weapons might reduce the chance of major war, it is unclear what they mean at lower levels of escalation, in proxy wars, or other contests that do not challenge vital national interests or state survival. While Snyder's essay was the first to give the stability–instability paradox detailed treatment, he was certainly not the first to recognize its existence. B.H. Liddell Hart (1954), for example, speculated that the effects of nuclear weapons might prevent another world war, but might nevertheless generate more local aggression and small conflicts. Waltz

(1959: 236) also warned that while nuclear weapons might reduce the chance of major war between nuclear powers, they could produce "a spate of smaller wars." The difficulty of predicting the effects of strategic nuclear stability on lower levels of conventional conflict also received extensive treatment by Jervis (1984, 1989). Building on Snyder, Jervis and other proponents of the stability–instability paradox, we can readily deduce a hypothesis for lower levels of conflict.

Hypothesis 2: The probability of crisis initiation and limited uses of force between two states will increase when both states possess nuclear weapons.

Next let us turn to situations where only one of two disputants has nuclear weapons. What are the effects of nuclear asymmetry? Unfortunately, the literature on nuclear deterrence is virtually silent on this point. The Cold War era focus on US–Soviet relations and Mutually Assured Destruction (MAD) largely crowded out discussions of nuclear asymmetry. Might we extrapolate or tease out predictions for nuclear asymmetry from theories that examine nuclear symmetry? Doing so is difficult. Most theories contain enough ambiguity and porousness that, depending on the additional assumptions, one could readily deduce hypotheses that make antithetical predictions. This is clearly an area that would benefit from more research, particularly from formalization. In lieu of a solid theory or theories of nuclear asymmetry, this study uses the basic intuition of formal rational choice to generate the following two hypotheses:

Hypothesis 3: The probability of major war between two states will decrease or remain constant if one state possesses nuclear weapons.

The same can be said of lower levels of escalation:

Hypothesis 4: The probability of lower level conflicts will decrease or remain the same if one state possesses nuclear weapons.

These two hypotheses are generated by considering what formal rational choice theory generically has to say about the relationship between the probability of war and (1) the distribution of power and (2) the costs of war. First, the basic intuition behind these hypotheses is that changes in the distribution of power will lead to subsequent changes in what states demand or are willing to accept when bargaining in the shadow of war. Thus, within the context of strategic interaction, changes in the distribution of power will lead disputants to make mutually offsetting demands and concessions that leave the probability of war unchanged. This prediction is consistent with Wittman's (1989) seminal study, and mirrors later work such as Fearon's (1995) exposition of formal rationalist explanations of war, and Powell's (1996) explanation of why studies have historically yielded equivocal results when examining the relationship between the distribution of power and the probability of war.

When evaluating the effects of nuclear weapons on the costs of fighting, the predictions – although different – are equally unambiguous. The use of nuclear weapons will drive up the costs of fighting for one or both players. It is difficult to imagine a situation where nuclear weapons would reduce the net costs of fighting.[10] Thus, if nuclear weapons impact the expected cost of fighting, one can conservatively deduce that nuclear asymmetry should make crises and wars less likely. Needless to say, with different assumptions about preferences over outcomes, information, or the structure of a game, one could certainly deduce alternative hypotheses. Therefore the tests performed below are not intended to "prove" or "disprove" the rationalist paradigm – they should merely generate further discussion. When the game of chicken was found to be a poor fit for explaining nuclear brinksmanship, Schelling did not abandon game theory, but instead invented one of the key concepts in rational deterrence theory (Schelling 1960, 1966). While the field has developed a deep understanding of nuclear symmetry, our understanding of nuclear symmetry remains in the world of 2x2 games.

Research design

The research design employed in this study follows in the footsteps of studies on the democratic peace. More than two centuries after its publication, Kant's Perpetual Peace (1795) continues to inspire scholars working in this area.[11] Kant's contention that democracies are less war prone has been proved false, but a variation of the democratic peace is now widely accepted. In its third and most recent incarnation, the democratic peace holds that democracies are less likely to fight one another.[12] According to one leading scholar, the current version of the democratic peace is "the closest thing we have to a law in international politics" (Levy 1988: 653).[13]

Beginning with work by Babst (1964, 1972) and Small and Singer (1976), the quantitative DPT research program has generated dozens of books and hundreds of articles. This study especially benefits from the line of research started by Maoz and Russett (1993), which has grown to include nearly a dozen studies that add independent variables (e.g., trade and international organization membership), broaden the time span (1885–1992), and use more rigorous statistical methods.[14] This study modifies one of the more recent studies (Pevehouse and Russett 2006) with new data on nuclear weapons.

There are a number of reasons why this research design is a good fit for evaluating the nuclear peace. First, the questions are analogous. Asking whether two democratic states are less likely to fight one another is very similar to asking whether two nuclear states are less likely to fight one another. The dyadic structure of the dataset allows us to examine the effects of nuclear symmetry and nuclear asymmetry. Second, this research design is extremely well vetted. Scholars know a great deal about the research design, data and statistical models. Third, the results presented in this study are easy to compare with earlier work. The problem of two studies potentially "talking past" one another is avoided because variables are operationalized in the same way. Finally, this research design has advanced neo-liberal explanations of the "Long Peace." If neo-realist and rational deterrence theory find empirical support from a research design developed by neo-liberal scholars, then this represents somewhat of a hard test – it certainly mitigates against the concern that the research design was purposely created to privilege the hypotheses being tested.

Dataset

This study uses cross-section, time-series data. The unit of analysis is the dyad-year. The basic dataset is generated using EUGene v.3.203, which integrates Correlates of War data (Small and Singer 1982, 1982; Sarkees 2000), Militarized Interstate Disputes data (MIDs) (Jones *et al.* 1996) and a MIDs update (Maoz 2005).[15] The dataset used is this study is largely consistent with Pevehouse and Russett (2006) and contains 611,310 dyad-years.[16] It should be noted that this includes "all dyads," not just "politically relevant" ones. This is especially important for the purposes of this study, because the subset of politically relevant dyads would represent a biased sample in which approximately 75 percent of the dyads would include at least one nuclear power.

As in Pevehouse and Russett (2006), dyad-years are drawn from the 1885–2000 period. While nuclear weapons did not exist before 1945, the 1885–1944 period is included so that readers can compare these findings with previous studies and know that the results differ only because of the addition of variables that measure the presence of nuclear weapons. Tests performed on a dataset restricted to the 1946–2000 period did not noticeably alter the statistical or substantive effects of nuclear weapons.

Dependent variables

The dependent variable in this study is conflict. In the field of international relations, there is no generally accepted definition for conflict, or for its opposite, peace. Conflict can mean as little as an innocuous policy disagreement over fisheries to as much as thermonuclear war. Similarly, peace can mean as little as the absence of violence, or it can be defined as something much more stringent, such as the resolution of underlying grievances and complete concord between parties. To avoid this conceptual quagmire, the dependent variable is operationalized in four ways. As Figure 10.1 illustrates, each definition becomes more restrictive in terms of level of fatalities.[17]

MID is one of the two dependent variables used in Pevehouse and Russett (2006). It is a binary variable that equals one during the first year of a dispute in which one or both parties use or threaten to use force. FATAL is a binary variable that equals one during the first year of a dispute in which there are any fatalities. FORCE is a new variable included in this study. It is a binary variable that equals one when one or both parties have used military force. I include the new indicator to capture a broader set of conflicts. Force includes all of the cases of fatalities, but captures a number of instances where a state uses force that, either by accident or design, does not result in any battle deaths.

For theoretical, methodological, and substantive reasons, this study also adds a fourth dependent variable. WAR is a binary variable that equals one if a dispute escalates to war, which the Correlates of War project measures as 1000 military fatalities (sustained battle deaths) between regular combat forces (Small and Singer 1972). The 1000 deaths cutoff is the conventional threshold for this literature. While some criticize the 1000 deaths cutoff as arbitrary, and one might want to lower or raise the threshold in the future, the main point here is to focus attention on war as opposed to MIDs or limited uses of force.[18]

For theoretical reasons, it is very important to directly evaluate the relationship between nuclear deterrence and war. Most studies of nuclear

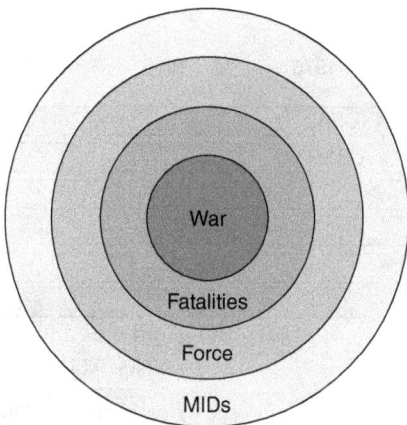

Figure 10.1 Operationalizing conflict.

deterrence focus specifically on war, not on lower levels of conflict. The methodological reason for including war is that it avoids potential selection effects posed by "easy" cases. For example, nuclear weapons may reduce the number of crises that emerge between dyads, or reduce the number of crises that lead to minor uses of force, but have no impact on preventing escalation to full-scale wars. Thus, the other three indicators may be registering easy cases. The main substantive reason for including war is the obvious point that policymakers, analysts, and the public are especially concerned about events that cause large numbers of fatalities.

Independent variables

This study includes ten independent variables. AYSMNUKE is a binary variable that equals one if one of the states in a dyad has nuclear weapons. SYMNUKE is a binary variable that equals one if both states in a dyad have nuclear weapons. Information on states with nuclear weapons was drawn from Gartzke and Kroenig (this issue). Figure 10.2 describes the years that states acquired and in some cases abandoned nuclear weapons. Since there is some ambiguity in assessments of what year states acquire nuclear weapons, tests were performed using alternative proliferation dates. Neither the statistical nor substantive results were affected by these alternative specifications.

All of the remaining variables and coding is consistent with Pevehouse and Russett, which can be consulted for a more detailed discussion of the data. DISTANCE is a continuous variable that measures the natural logarithm of the distance between capitals of two states, or for large states, the distance between nearest ports. CONTIG is a binary variable that equals one if the two states are contiguous. This includes being directly connected by land, or indirectly connected by less than 150 miles across water. Contiguity also includes contact with other states through colonial

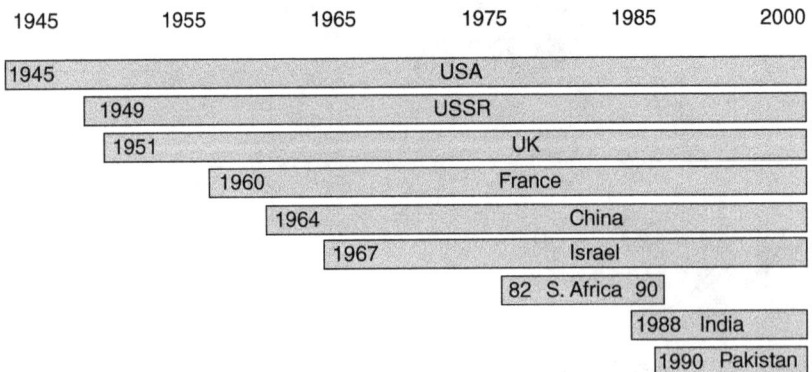

Figure 10.2 Nuclear weapons states.

possessions. The dataset includes three variables that are intended to evaluate realist concerns. The variable MAJPOW equals one if one or both of the states in the dyad are major powers. ALLIANCE equals one if the two parties have a formal military alliance or non-aggression pact. CAPRAT measures relative distribution of power between states.

Three independent variables evaluate neo-liberal hypotheses. To control for the effects of regime type, DEMOC uses a scale that ranges from −10 (autocracy) to +10 (democracy). Each state's autocracy score is subtracted from its democracy score, and the least constrained state's score is included.[19] The effects of economic interdependence are measured by INTERDEP. All of the data used for the period post World War II period are from Gleditsch (2002). Earlier data are collected through a variety of historical sources and estimating procedures (Russett *et al.* 2003: 377; Pevehouse and Russett 2006). IGOMEM measures shared membership in intergovernmental organizations (Pevehouse and Russett 2006).

Testing method

The relationship between nuclear weapons and conflict is evaluated with a generalized estimating equation (GEE) regression model (Liang and Zegar 1986).[20] GEE is a population-averaged method that was developed specifically for panel data. It makes full use of both cross-sectional and temporal information. For all of the tests performed in the next section, time dependency and autocorrelation are controlled for with first-order auto-regression (AR1) and robust standard errors.

Similar to studies on the democratic peace, this study faces a number of difficulties because of data limitations. When using dyad-year data, of particular concern is time dependency: what happens between two states in period *t* is likely to affect *t* +1. There are a number of methods for controlling for time dependency. Techniques used in the Democratic Peace Theory (DPT) literature include fixed effects models, models with distributed lags, and GEE. For the purposes of this study, GEE is selected because it allows us to deal with the problem of perfect separation. While states with nuclear weapons have engaged in MIDs and wars with non-nuclear states, and nuclear states have engaged in MIDs with one another, the dataset does not include any instances of two nuclear states engaging in war with one another.[21] Thus, there is a perfect correlation between the absence of war and dyads where both states possess nuclear weapons. In fixed effects, random effects, and distributed lag models, the perfect correlation causes the symmetric nuclear variable to be dropped from the analysis. The intuition behind the math is that the coefficient is essentially negative infinity, which cannot be estimated, and the variable is therefore dropped. GEE overcomes this problem by using population averaging.[22] Instead of generating a unique slope for each observation, GEE creates a simple pooled model with a single intercept.

How reliable and robust is GEE? Fortunately, there is a side-by-side comparison of the three methods with a similar research design and data (Russett and Oneal 2001b).[23] The three sets of results, although not identical, show strong similarity. All three testing methods produce coefficients with the same sign for each independent variable. Moreover, major power status, alliances, contiguity, and democracy report nearly the same substantive effect for each method. Interdependence and capabilities all have the same sign, but the ratios between their coefficients and standard errors vary and leave some of the variables below the statistical significance threshold. Nevertheless, the overall similarity of the results allows Russett and Oneal (2001b: 471) to conclude that "the three techniques produce robust, statistically significant evidence in support of the liberal peace." For another study that applies GEE and Logit to the liberal peace, and thereby allows for comparison of the two methods, see Gartzke (2007).

Findings

The results of the general estimating equation are presented in Table 10.1. Let us first turn our attention to the effects of nuclear weapons. As the results clearly indicate, nuclear weapons have statistically significant effects on the chance of conflict. This is true for both symmetric nuclear dyads where both states possess nuclear weapons, as well as for asymmetric dyads where only one of the states possesses nuclear weapons. The results are also substantively significant. For a more detailed substantive interpretation of the data, all of the coefficients can be converted into odds ratios. For our purposes here, it is worth noting the sign of coefficients and the relative impact of the variables.

Substantively, all of the coefficients for asymmetric nukes and symmetric nukes are positive except for one. When two states have nuclear weapons, the negative coefficient indicates that they are less likely to go to war with one another. This coefficient has the strongest substantive effect of all the measures of nuclear deterrence, and the statistical significance is at the $p < .001$ level. In all other instances but this one, the coefficients are positive which indicates that states with nuclear weapons are more likely to engage in militarized disputes (crises), to use force, and to be involved in uses of force that result in fatalities. This is true for situations of nuclear symmetry as well as asymmetry, although the effect is more pronounced when both states possess nuclear weapons.

How do these empirical results mesh with the hypotheses derived in section three? The hypotheses on nuclear symmetry find strong empirical support. The probability of major war between two states is indeed found to decrease when both states possess nuclear weapons (Hypothesis 1). Similarly, the probability of crisis initiation and limited uses of force between two states is found to increase when both states possess nuclear weapons (Hypothesis 2). When combined, these results suggest that the

Table 10.1 Results*

	MID (I)	FORCE (II)	FATAL (III)	WAR (IV)
SYMNUKE	1.94*** (0.50)	2.07*** (0.43)	2.06*** (0.41)	−14.81*** (0.53)
ASYMNUKE	0.71*** (0.16)	0.81*** (0.18)	0.85*** (0.23)	0.90 (0.53)
CONTIG	2.59*** (0.18)	3.20*** (0.23)	2.29*** (0.26)	2.94*** (0.62)
DISTANCE	−0.58*** (0.07)	−0.48*** (0.08)	−0.74*** (0.10)	−0.69*** (0.15)
CAPABIL	−0.30*** (0.05)	−21*** (0.05)	−0.41*** (0.06)	−0.64*** (0.19)
ALLIANCE	−31* (0.15)	−0.35* (0.17)	−0.35*** (0.20)	−0.44 (0.37)
MAJPOW	1.81*** (0.18)	1.25*** (0.20)	1.53*** (0.25)	2.35*** (63)
DEMOC	−0.06*** (0.01)	−0.04*** (0.01)	−0.06*** (0.02)	−0.08* (0.03)
INTERDEP	−50.18*** (12.33)	−43.69*** (14.70)	−112.79*** (27.93)	−118.63* (54.76)
IGOMEM	−0.01** (0.00)	−0.01** (0.005)	−0.02*** (0.01)	−0.02* (0.02)
CONSTANT	−1.49*** (0.58)	−3.11*** (0.67)	−1.09*** (0.86)	−3.85*** (1.57)
Wald Chi 2	2164.59	1855.44	1178.62	2109.10
$p<$	0.00	0.00	0.00	0.00

Notes

Columns I though IV include information on each of the dependent variables. Rows include information on each of the independent variables. Statistically significant coefficients are indicated by asterisks (= $p < .05$, ** = $p < .01$, *** = $p < .001$). Robust standard errors appear within parentheses below the coefficients.

stability–instability paradox is reality, as opposed to a mere thought experiment. In contrast to the hypotheses on nuclear symmetry, the hypotheses on nuclear asymmetry perform poorly. Not only do the hypotheses on nuclear asymmetry find no empirical support in these results, the statistically significant coefficients have the opposite sign than is expected. For examples, dyads in which one state has nuclear weapons are associated with an increased chance of war. This is the opposite of what Hypothesis 3 predicts. Similarly, Hypothesis 4 misses the mark in that asymmetric dyads are more prone to be involved in militarized disputes and conflicts that involve force or limited numbers of fatalities.

Although the main focus of this analysis is on nuclear weapons, it is worth noting that the results for the other independent variables in this analysis are largely consistent with Pevehouse and Russett (2006) and other work on DPT. The model for general MIDs and MIDs restricted to fatalities produces results with approximately the same statistical and substantive significance. Note, however, alliances now have statistically significant effects for MIDs and not for fatalities, where in their study, the opposite is true. The results for MIDs restricted to uses of force are similar to MIDs with fatalities, with the exception that alliances now register statistically significant results.

The story is much different for war. Here the substantive impact of variables is quite different. The effect of realist variables including relative capabilities, alliances, and the major power status is much more pronounced. Neo-liberal variables have more mixed results. The positive effects of IGO membership on wars is greater than for MIDs, MIDs with uses of force, and MIDs with fatalities, but democracy does not fare as well, a finding that is consistent with Gartzke (2007). The effects of interdependence increase substantially, but of all the variables that are included, the interpretation of this variable requires some caution. Scholars worry about potential selection effects, the direction of causation, and the shadow that future wars may cast on trade relations.[24]

Conclusion

As many have noted, Jervis (1984: 31) provides one of the clearest definitions of Snyder's (1965) stability–instability paradox: "To the extent that the military balance is stable at the level of all-out nuclear war, it will become less stable at lower levels of violence." A number of studies have sought to qualitatively test the stability–instability paradox. To date, these studies have generated equivocal results. Even when addressing the same case study, scholars have drawn opposite conclusions (Krepon 2003; Kapur 2005; Ganguly and Wagner 2004; Sagan and Waltz 2003). The results presented in this study represent one of the first efforts to quantitatively evaluate the relationship between strategic nuclear stability and conflicts at lower levels of escalation.

As the results presented in the previous section indicate, both proliferation optimists and proliferation pessimists find validation for some of their key claims. Kenneth Waltz and other proponents of nuclear deterrence find strong empirical support for their claims that nuclear powers are less likely to fight one another – nuclear weapons may indeed help explain the Long Peace. Nevertheless, Scott Sagan and other proliferation pessimists find support for their concerns. At lower levels of escalation, nuclear symmetry does not appear to have a pacifying effect. Worse yet, nuclear asymmetry is generally associated with a higher chance of crises, uses of force, fatalities, and war. On balance, however, these findings support the broader themes of this issue. Nuclear weapons do not affect the frequency of conflict, but they do affect the timing, intensity, and outcome of conflict. This study demonstrates that nuclear weapons tend to shift the intensity of disputes toward the lower end of the conflict scale.

The results presented in this study also point to an area that has been seriously neglected. In a post-Cold War world where mutually assured destruction between superpowers is no longer the main concern, it is time for the field to more fully explore the effects of nuclear asymmetry. Clearly the effects of nuclear asymmetry are more complicated than is conventionally appreciated.

Notes

1 For helpful comments on earlier versions of this chapter, the author would like to thank the authors in this special issue, Bruce Russett, and two anonymous reviewers. Replication data and an online appendix are available at http://jcr.sagepub.com/supplemental.

2 For a critique of the Long Peace thesis, see Siverson and Ward (2002). Also see Brecher and Wilkenfeld (1991) and Ray (1991) in Kegley's edited volume.

3 Although battlefield deaths from interstate war have been in decline since World War II, this is not true for most other forms of violence. Extra-state (colonial) wars increased sharply during the period of decolonization, then declined. Similarly, civil wars increased exponentially immediately after the end of the Cold War, and have since steadily declined. Deaths caused by terrorism have steadily increased since 1970s. See the Human Security Report (2005) for more details.

4 For a review of this debate, see Jervis (2002).

5 For a proto-constructionist view on how changing identities may facilitate peace, see Deutsch *et al.* (1957). While not usually lumped under the heading of constructivism, Mueller (1988, 1989) makes a forceful argument that is completely consistent with this school.

6 While classical realists disagreed about what type of polarity was most war prone, there was broad consensus among neo-realists that bipolar systems were less war prone than multipolar systems. Concerning unipolarity and the post-Cold War era, however, there is little consensus. Prior to Charles Krauthammer's (1990/1991, 2002/2003) coining of the term unipolarity, this constellation of power was not really considered. Most neo-realists expect unipolarity will be unstable, or at least short lived (Layne 1993, 2006; Waltz 1993, 2000). Gilpin's (1981) analysis of hegemony might lead one to believe that unipolarity is more stable than bipolarity.

7 For quantitative work on the Democratic Peace Theory (DPT), see Babst (1964), Babst (1972), Pevehouse and Russett (2006), Gartzke (1998, 2000), Lake (1992), Russett and Oneal (1997), Russett and Oneal (2001a), Russett and Oneal (2001b), Maoz (1997, 1998), Oneal *et al.* (1996), Risse-Kappen (1995), Russett (1993), and Singer and Small (1976). For a review of the literature, see Ray (1998) and Morrow (2002). For critiques of the democratic peace, see Gowa (1999), Layne (1994), Spiro (1994), Thompson (1996), and Thompson and Tucker (1997). Note also that the DPT has recently evolved into an evaluation of the Kantian Tripod, and therefore includes data on interdependence and international organizations. See Russett, Oneal, and Berbaum (2003), Pevehouse and Russett (2006), and Russett, Oneal and Davis (1998). For other recent work evaluating the relationship between war and trade, see Barbieri (1996, 2002), Gartzke (2003), Gartzke *et al.* (2001) Gowa (1994), and Mansfield (1995).

8 See, for example, Bueno de Mesquita (1981), Bueno de Mesquita and David Lalman (1994), Deutsch and Singer (1964).

9 As later hypotheses make clear, there are some caveats to this claim. There is no consensus on the effects of nuclear weapons on lower levels of escalation. Hence this hypothesis does not say war in general, but restricts the claim to *major* wars. There is also debate as to the requirements of deterrence. This study adopts the stance of nuclear minimalism in keeping with Waltz (1980, 1990). While there is a general consensus among international relations scholars that nuclear weapons reduce the probability of *major* war, there are some scholars that categorically reject the deterrent value of nuclear weapons (Mueller 1988, 1989; Vasquez 1991). For example, Mueller's central argument is that while "nuclear weapons may have substantially influenced political rhetoric, public discourse, and defense budgets and planning," they have not "had a significant impact on the history of world affairs since World War II" (1989: 56). Mueller's view is that the costs of World War II, new norms, and changes in identity have made major war obsolete. The Long Peace was therefore overdetermined and would have happened even without nuclear weapons. In other words, nuclear weapons have no deterrent value because there is nothing to deter – no one wants to fight a large war.

10 When one takes account of the costs of developing and fielding nuclear weapons, along with the likely political costs associated with their use, it is difficult to imagine a situation where they would reduce the costs of fighting in absolute terms. Perhaps thinking of costs in relative terms (i.e., opportunity cost compared to conventional war) might yield different results.

11 For the essays that relaunched this debate, see Doyle (1983a, 1983b).

12 The first democratic peace thesis – democracies are more pacific than autocracies – survived from ancient times to the 1980s. The second democratic peace thesis, advanced during the 1980s and 1990s, held that democracies *never* fight one another. This version was short lived. Historical examples and ongoing events at the time (e.g., Kargil, Kosovo, Ethiopia) showed that the claim was too strong. Some initially modified the democratic peace thesis to hold that *liberal democracies* have never fought one another, but most scholars moved toward the "*less likely*" formulation.

13 For critiques of the democratic peace, see fn. 6. It is worth noting that Levy stated the democratic peace is the *closest* thing that we have to a law. He is frequently misquoted as saying it is our only law.

14 See fn. 7 for more recent studies by Oneal, Maoz, Russett and other scholars involved in this research program.

15 EUGene stands for the Expected Utility Generation and Data Management Program, which is available from www.eugenesoftware.org. For published documentation on an earlier version of EUGene, see Bennett and Stam (2000).

16 Consistent with previous studies, data with missing values are dropped. See Russett, Oneal and Berbaum (2003) for a detailed discussion of case selection.

17 Note that for statistical purposes, it may be problematic to treat conflict as a series of discrete categories with ordinal rankings. Many would argue that conflict is best thought of as a multi-dimensional concept with only nominal categories. In some situations fatalities may be normatively worse than force because it involved loss of life. In other cases, force or MIDs may be worse than fatalities because an event like the Cuban Missile Crisis is more significant than the seizure of a fishing vessel that results in a few fatalities.

18 Future studies may want to raise or lower the 1000 deaths threshold, or perhaps treat the number of fatalities at the dependent variable.

19 This is called the weakest link constraint. The logic is that the democratic peace will rest on the least democratically constrained state.

20 All tests are performed using the STATA/IC (v.10).

21 Kargil, Sino-Soviet border disputes, etc., register under FATAL and FORCE, but not under WAR because of the limited number of casualties.

22 For a broader discussion of the problem of perfect correlation and separation, see Zorn (2005).

23 Also see Hu *et al.* (1998) for a similar effort in epidemiology. For a critique of fixed effects models and a plea not to use them in the DPT literature because of dichotomous dependent variables, see Beck and Katz (2001).

24 As Jervis (2002: 6) notes, critics "worry that interdependence may be more an effect than a cause, more the product than a generator of expectations of peace and cooperation." Despite efforts to control for this effect, such as Russett and Oneal's (2001b) decision to lag the trade variable by one year, Jervis notes that they may not "get to the heart of the matter since trade the year before could be a product of expectations of future good relations" (Jervis 2002: 6). Indeed, in considering the Long Peace, trade may be a security externality that is a result of the Cold War (Gowa 1994).

Bibliography

Asal, Victor and Kyle Beardsley (2007) "Proliferation and international crisis behavior," *Journal of Peace Research* 44: 139–155.

Babst, Dean V. (1964) "Elective governments – a force for peace," *The Wisconsin Sociologist* 3: 9–14.

Babst, Dean V. (1972) "A force for peace," *Industrial Research* 55–58.

Barbieri, Katherine (1996) "Economic interdependence: a path to peace or source of interstate conflict?," *Journal of Peace Research* 33: 29–49.

Barbieri, Katherine (2002) *The Liberal Illusion: Does Trade Promote Peace?*, Ann Arbor, MI: University of Michigan Press.

Beck, Nathaniel and Jonathan Katz (2001) "Throwing out the baby with the bath water: a comment on Green, Yoon and Kim (with N. Beck)," *International Organization* 55: 487–498.

Bennett, D. Scott and Allan Stam (2000) "EUGene: a conceptual manual," *International Interactions* 26: 179–204.

Berkowitz, Bruce D. (1985) "Proliferation, deterrence, and the likelihood of nuclear war," *The Journal of Conflict Resolution* 29: 112–136.

Brecher, Michael and J. Wilkenfeld (1991) "International crises and global instability: the myth of the long peace," in Charles W. Kegley Jr (ed.) *The Long Postwar Peace: Contending Explanations and Projections*, New York: HarperCollins.

Brito, Dagobert L. and Michael D. Intriligator (1996) "Proliferation and the probability of war: a cardinality theorem," *Journal of Conflict Resolution* 40: 6–214.

Brodie, Bernard (ed.) (1946) *The Absolute Weapon: Atomic Power and World Order*, New York, NY: Harcourt.

Brodie, Bernard (1947) *Strategy in the Missile Age*, Princeton, NJ: Princeton University Press.

Bueno de Mesquita, Bruce (1981) *The War Trap*, New Haven, CT: Yale University Press.

Bueno de Mesquita, Bruce and David Lalman (1994) *War and Reason*, New Haven, CT: Yale University Press.

Bueno de Mesquita, Bruce and William H. Riker (1982) "An assessment of the merits of selective nuclear proliferation," *The Journal of Conflict Resolution* 26: 283–306.

Deutsch, Karl and J. David Singer (1964) "Multipolar power systems and international stability," *World Politics* 16: 390–406.

Deutsch, Karl W. *et al.* (1957) *Political Community and the North Atlantic Area: International Organizations in the Light of Historical Experience*, Princeton, NJ: Princeton University Press.

Doyle, Michael W. (1983a) "Kant, liberal legacies, and foreign affairs, part I," *Philosophy and Public Affairs* 12: 205–235.

Doyle, Michael W. (1983b) "Kant, liberal legacies, and foreign affairs, part II," *Philosophy and Public Affairs* 12: 323–353.

Falk, Richard and Robert Jay Lifton (1991) *Indefensible Weapons: The Political and Psychological Case against Nuclearism*, New York, NY: Basic Books.

Fearon, James D. (1994) "Signaling vs. balance of power and interests," *Journal of Conflict Resolution* 38.

Fearon, James D. (1995) "Rationalist explanations for war," *International Organization* 49: 393–397.

Gaddis, John Lewis (1986) "The long peace: elements of stability in the postwar international system," *International Security* 10: 99–142.

Gaddis, John Lewis (1987) *The Long Peace*, Oxford: Oxford University Press.

Ganguly, Sumit and R. Harrison Wagner (2004) "Indian and Pakistan: bargaining in the shadow of nuclear war," *The Journal of Strategic Studies* 27: 479–507.

Gartzke, Erik (1998) "Kant we all just get along? Motive, opportunity, and the origins of the democratic peace," *American Journal of Political Science* 42: 1–2.

Gartzke, Erik (2000) "Preferences and the democratic peace," *International Studies Quarterly* 44: 191–212.

Gartzke, Erik (2003) "War, peace, and the invisible hand: positive political externalities of economic globalization," *International Studies Quarterly* 47: 561–586.

Gartzke, Erik (2007) "The capitalist peace," *American Journal of Political Science* 51: 166–191.

Gartzke, Erik, Quan Li, and Charles Boehmer (2001) "Investing in the peace: economic interdependence and international conflict," *International Organization* 55: 391–438.

Geller, Daniel S. (1990) "Nuclear weapons, deterrence, and crisis escalation," *Journal of Conflict Resolution* 3: 291–310.

Giles, Jim (2005) "Internet encyclopaedias go head to head," *Nature* 438: 900–901.

Gilpin, Robert (1981) *War and Change in World Politics*, Cambridge: Cambridge University Press.

Gleditsch, Kristian Skrede (2002) "Expanded trade and GDP data," *Journal of Conflict Resolution* 46: 712–24.

Gowa, Joanne (1994) *Allies, Adversaries, and International Trade*, Princeton, NJ: Princeton University Press.

Gowa, Joanne (1999) *Ballot and Bullets: The Search for the Elusive Democratic Peace*, Princeton, NJ: Princeton University Press.

Harvey, Frank P. and Patrick James (1996) "Nuclear crisis as a multi-stage threat game: toward an agenda for comparative research," *International Political Science Review* 17: 197–214.

Hu, Frank B., Jack Goldberg, Donald Hedeker, Brian R. Flay, and Mary Ann Pentz (1998) "Comparison of population-averaged and subject-specific approaches for analyzing repeated binary outcomes," *American Journal of Epidemiology* 147: 694–703.

Human Security Report (2005) *War and Peace in the 21st Century*, Oxford, UK: Oxford University Press.

Intriligator, Michael D. and Dagobert L. Brito (1981) "Nuclear proliferation and the probability of nuclear war," *Public Choice* 37: 247–260.

Jervis, Robert (1984) *The Illogic of American Nuclear Strategy*, Ithaca, NY: Cornell University Press.

Jervis, Robert (1989) *The Meaning of Nuclear Revolution*, Ithaca, NY: Cornell University Press.

Jervis, Robert (2002) "Theories of war in an era of leading-power peace, *Presidential Address*," *American Political Science Review* 96: 1–14.

Jervis, Robert, Richard Ned Lebow, and Janice Gross Stein (1985) *Psychology and Deterrence*, Baltimore, MD: The Johns Hopkins University Press.

Jones, Daniel M., Stuart A. Bremer, and J. David Singer (1996) "Militerized interstate disputes, 1816–1992: rationale, coding rules, and empirical patterns," *Conflict Management and Peace Science* 15.

Kant, Immanuel (1795) *Perpetual Peace: A Philosophical Sketch.*

Kapur, Paul S. (2005) "India and Pakistan's unstable peace: why nuclear South Asia is not like Cold War Europe," *International Security* 30: 127–152.

Katzenstein, Peter J. (1996) *The Culture of National Security: Norms and Identity in World Politics*, New York: Columbia University Press.

Kegley, Charles W. Jr (ed.) (1991) *The Long Postwar Peace: Contending Explanations and Projections*, New York: Harper Collins.

Keohane, Robert O. (1984) *After Hegemony: Cooperation and Discord in the World Political Economy*, Princeton, NJ: Princeton University Press.

Keohane, Robert O. and Joseph S. Nye (1977) *Power and Interdependence: World Politics in Transition*, Boston, MA: Little, Brown and Company.

Krauthammer, Charles (1990/1991) "The unipolar moment," *Foreign Affairs*, winter.

Krauthammer, Charles (2002/2003) "The unipolar moment revisited," *The National Interest* 70.

Krepon, Michael (2003) *The Stability–Instability Paradox, Misperception, and Escalation Control in South Asia*, Washington, DC: Henry L. Stimson Center.

Lacina, Bethany, Nils Petter Gleditsch, and Bruce Russett (2006) "The declining risk of battle death," *International Studies Quarterly* 50: 673–680.

Lake, David (1992) "Powerful pacifists: democratic states and war," *American Political Science Review* 86: 24–37.

Langlois, Jean-Pierre (1991) "Rational deterrence and crisis stability," *American Journal of Political Science* 35: 801–832.

Layne, Christopher (1993) "The unipolar illusion: why new great powers will rise," *International Security* 17(4): 5–51.

Layne, Christopher (1994) "Kant or cant: the myth of the democratic peace," *International Security* 19: 5–49.

Layne, Christopher (2006) *The Peace of Illusions: International Relations Theory and American Grand Strategy after the Cold War*, Ithaca, NY: Cornell University Press.

Lebow, Richard Ned and Janice Gross Stein (1995) "Deterrence and the Cold War," *Political Science Quarterly* 110: 157–181.

Levy, Jack S. (1988) "Domestic politics and war," *Journal of Interdisciplinary History* 18: 653–673.

Liang, Kung-Yee and Scott Zeger (1986) "Longitudinal data analysis using general linear models," *Biometrika* 73: 13–22.

Liddell Hart, B. H. (1954) *Strategy*, London: Faber and Faber.

Lippmann, Walter (1947) *The Cold War: A Study in U.S. Foreign Policy*, New York: Harper.

Mansfield, Edward D. (1995) *Power, Trade, and War*, Princeton, NJ: Princeton University Press.

Maoz, Zeev (1997) "The controversy over the democratic peace: rearguard action or cracks in the wall?," *International Security* 22: 162–198.

Maoz, Zeev (1998) "Realist and cultural critiques of the democratic peace: a theoretical and empirical re-assessment," *International Interactions* 24: 1–89.

Maoz, Zeev (2005) Dyadic MID Dataset (version 2.0): http://psfaculty.ucdavis.edu/zmaoz/dyadmid.html

Maoz, Zeev and Bruce M. Russett (1993) "Normative and structural causes of the democratic peace, 1946–1986," *American Political Science Review* 87: 624–638.

Morrow, James D. (2002) "International conflict: assessing the democratic peace and offense-defense theory," in Ira Katznelson and Helen V. Milner (eds) *Political Science: The State of the Discipline*, New York: W.W. Norton and Company.

Mueller, John (1988) "The essential irrelevance of nuclear weapons: stability in the postwar world," *International Security* 13: 55–79.

Mueller, John (1989) *Retreat from Doomsday: The Obsolescence of Major War*, New York, NY: Basic Books.

Nalebuff, Barry (1988) "Minimal nuclear deterrence," *Journal of Conflict Resolution* 32: 411–425.

Oneal, John R. and Bruce M. Russett (1997) "The classical liberals were right: democracy, interdependence, and conflict, 1950–1985," *International Studies Quarterly* 41: 267–293.

Oneal, John R., Frances H. Oneal, Zeev Maoz, and Bruce M. Russett (1996) "The liberal peace: interdependence, democracy, and international conflict, 1950–85," *Journal of Peace Research* 33: 11–28.

Pevehouse, Jon C. and Bruce Russett (2006) "Democratic IGOs cause peace," *International Organization* 60: 969–1000.

Powell, Robert (1985) "The theoretical foundations of strategic nuclear deterrence," *Political Science Quarterly* 100: 75–96.

Powell, Robert (1987) "Crisis bargaining, escalation, and MAD," *American Political Science Review* 81: 717–736.

Powell, Robert (1988) "Nuclear brinkmanship with two-sided incomplete information," *American Political Science Review* 82: 155–178.

Powell, Robert (1989a) "Crisis stability in the nuclear age," *The American Political Science Review* 83: 61–76.

Powell, Robert (1989b) "Nuclear deterrence and the strategy of limited retaliation," *American Political Science Review* 83: 503–519.

Powell, Robert (1990) *The Nuclear Revolution and the Problem of Credibility*, Cambridge, MA: Cambridge University Press.

Powell, Robert (1996) "Stability and the distribution of power," *World Politics* 48.

Ray, James Lee (1998) "Does democracy cause peace?," *Annual Review of Political Science* 1: 27–46.

Risse-Kappen, Thomas (1995) *Cooperation Among Democracies: The European Influence on U.S. Foreign Policy*, Princeton, NJ: Princeton University Press.

Russett, Bruce M. (1993) *Grasping the Democratic Peace: Principles for a Post-Cold War World*, Princeton, NJ: Princeton University Press.

Russett, Bruce M. and John Oneal (2001a) *Triangulating Peace: Democracy, Interdependence, and International Organizations*, New York: W.W. Norton.

Russett, Bruce M. and John Oneal (2001b) "Clear and clean: the fixed effects of the liberal peace," *International Organization* 55: 469–485.

Russett, Bruce M., John Oneal, and Michael Berbaum (2003) "Causes of peace: democracy, interdependence, and international organizations, 1885–1992," *International Studies Quarterly* 47: 371–393.

Russett, Bruce M., John R. Oneal, and David R. Davis (1998) "The third leg of the Kantian tripod for peace: international organizations and militarized disputes, 1950–1985," *International Organization* 52: 441–468.

Sagan, Scott D. (1993) *The Limits of Safety: Organizations, Accidents, and Nuclear Weapons*, Princeton, NJ: Princeton University Press.

Sagan, Scott D. (1994) "The perils of proliferation," *International Security* 18: 66–107.

Sagan, Scott D. and Kenneth Waltz (2003) *The Spread of Nuclear Weapons: A Debate Renewed*, New York, NY: W.W. Norton.

Sarkees, Meredith Reid (2000) "The correlates of war data on war: an update to 1997," *Conflict Management and Peace Science* 18: 123–144.

Schelling, Thomas (1960) *The Strategy of Conflict*, Cambridge, MA: Harvard University Press.

Schelling, Thomas (1966) *Arms and Influence*, New Haven, CT: Yale University Press.

Siverson, Randolph M. and Michael D. Ward (2002) "The long peace: a reconsideration," *International Organization* 56: 679–691.

Small, Melvin and J. David Singer (1976) "The war proneness of democratic regimes, 1816–1965," *Jerusalem Journal of International Relations* 1: 50–69.

Small, Melvin and J. David Singer (1982) *Resort to Arms: International and Civil Wars, 1816–1980*, Beverly Hills, CA: Sage Publications.

Snyder, Glenn (1965) "The balance of power and the balance of terror," in Paul Seabury (ed.) *Balance of Power*, San Francisco, CA: Chandler.

Spiro, David E. (1994) "The insignificance of the liberal peace," *International Security* 19: 50–86.

Thompson, William R. (1996) "Democracy and peace: putting the cart before the horse?," *International Organization* 50: 141–174.

Thompson, William R. and Richard M. Tucker (1997) "A tale of two democratic peace critiques," *Journal of Conflict Resolution* 41: 428–454.

Vasquez, John (1991) "The deterrence myth: nuclear weapons and the prevention of nuclear war," in Charles W. Kegley (ed.) *The Long Postwar Peace: Contending Explanations and Projections*, New York: HarperCollins.

Wagner, R. Harrison (1991) "Nuclear deterrence, counterforce strategies, and the incentive to strike first," *American Political Science Review* 85: 727–749.

Waltz, Kenneth N. (1959) *Man, the State, and War*, Columbia, NY: Columbia University Press.

Waltz, Kenneth N. (1979) *Theory of International Politics*, Reading, MA: Addison-Wesley.

Waltz, Kenneth N. (1981) "The spread of nuclear weapons: more may be better," *Adelphi Papers* 171: 1–39.

Waltz, Kenneth N. (1990) "Nuclear myths and political realities," *American Political Science Review* 84: 731–745.

Waltz, Kenneth N. (1993) "The emerging structure of international politics," *International Security* 18: 44–79.

Waltz, Kenneth N. (2000) "Structural realism after the Cold War," *International Security* 25: 5–41.

Wendt, Alexander (1992) "Anarchy is what states make of it: the social construction of power politics," *International Organization* 46.

Wendt, Alexander (1999) *Social Theory of International Politics*, Cambridge: Cambridge University Press.

Wittman, Donald (1989) "Why democracies produce efficient results," *Journal of Political Economy* 97: 1395–1424.

Zagare, Frank C. and D. Marc Kilgour (2000) *Perfect Deterrence*, New York: Cambridge University Press.

Zorn, Christopher (2005) "A solution to separation in binary response models," *Political Analysis* 13: 157–170.

11 Winning with the bomb

Kyle Beardsley and Victor Asal[1]

Introduction

Nuclear weapons are destructive instruments created to coerce other states. Indeed, the Manhattan Project was launched, in part, out of fear that Hitler would develop the bomb first en route to global domination, and the first uses of atomic weapons in combat were attempts to precipitate a Japanese surrender. States endure considerable risks and costs to develop nuclear weapons, presumably to enhance their bargaining leverage toward getting a larger share of the global resource pie, or, at a minimum, better holding onto the resources already possessed.

Use of atomic weapons, however, has not been attempted since 1945 and they are rarely explicitly threatened (Betts 1987). Whether they can be credibly threatened as coercive devices remains in question because the potential costs to the user are prodigious, especially against another nuclear state. A substantial literature exists attempting to explain how nuclear weapons can be useful for coercive diplomacy in light of such credibility issues (e.g., Schelling 1966; Powell 1987, 1988, 1990; Snyder and Diesing 1977). Such studies tend to only explain how nuclear weapons can be used in deterrence, with the ability to compel left in doubt. Zagare and Kilgour (2000) have also pointedly observed that much of this "classical deterrence" literature uses irrational constructs to explain how rational actors threaten higher risk of escalation to make a foe back down.

In line with an overarching argument of this volume, this chapter considers whether nuclear proliferators actually reap benefits from their weapons. We specifically address whether nuclear states are better able to succeed in crisis bargaining. While there has been a great deal of attention to conflict initiation in the international relations literature, scholars less often focus on the bargained outcomes of conflicts (Werner 1998: 322). Some researchers have suggested that capability distribution is a key causal factor in determining who wins (Desch 2002), while others point out the importance of strategic choices (Arreguín-Toft 2005; Gartner and Siverson 1996), or domestic politics (Reiter and Stam 2002). Others have suggested that the political outcomes are a product of original war aims (Werner

1998) or similarly the resolve of the sides and their willingness to suffer (Maoz 1983). Stam (1996) has integrated many of these approaches in the most comprehensive account thus far to demonstrate that both third-image and second-image characteristics can explain war outcomes. Gelpi and Griesdorf (2001) specifically assess international crises in their analysis of how domestic institutions impact the prospects for victory.

One issue that is generally missing from the literature on victory and failure in conflict is the impact of nuclear weapons. Stam (1996) predicts almost the same results for victory during the nuclear period as before; and Gelpi and Griesdorf (2001) include nuclear weapons as a control variable and reveal mixed findings about their effects. Other work suggests that nuclear weapons have an important impact on strategic interaction in conflicts and crises, as evident in assessments of direct deterrence (Geller 1990; Asal and Beardsley 2007; Beardsley and Asal 2009; Rauchhaus, this volume: chapter 10) and extended deterrence (Fearon 1994; Huth 1988, 1990; Huth and Russet 1988; Signorino and Tarar 2006). None of these studies systematically unpack how nuclear weapons affect an actor's ability to achieve better bargains. We are interested in how states benefit from the bomb even when they do not actually use it.

Theoretical framework

The question of what effects nuclear weapons have on successful coercive diplomacy is in part a function of how nuclear weapons change an opponent's perceived crisis costs. Classical deterrence theorists such as Schelling (1966), Snyder and Diesing (1977), Jervis (1989), Waltz (1990, 2003), Gaddis (1986), Intriligator and Brito (1981, 1984) and Powell (1987, 1988, 1990), while disagreeing on other matters, tend to argue that the potential costs of nuclear attack are so great that restraint from opponents of nuclear states follows. Even Zagare and Kilgour (2000), using perfect deterrence theory to demonstrate that nuclear weapons are probably not as stabilizing as the classical deterrence scholars expect, contend that nuclear weapons have the potential to increase the costs of conflict of their opponents and enhance their success in coercive diplomacy.

We cannot, however, take as given that nuclear weapons actually increase the expected costs of conflict. While this is something that has often been argued, there are few systematic empirical tests for whether the observed world conforms to what one would expect if nuclear weapons do increase costs of conflict. Some scholars discount the role that nuclear weapons have played in increasing an opponent's costs of conflict and stabilizing peace. Mueller (1988) has argued that nuclear weapons are actually irrelevant, as they can never credibly be threatened. Geller (1990) has also argued that nuclear weapons are generally irrelevant against non-nuclear actors, and finds that nuclear weapon states are unable to deter non-nuclear states from aggression. Proliferation pessimists like Sagan

(2003) argue that some decision makers, particularly military leaders, will not weigh the costs the same way as civilian leaders.

We argue that nuclear weapons could have two competing effects. When states face nuclear opponents, the cost of all-out, unrestrained war is certainly going to be prodigious. At the same time, the probability of such unrestricted war decreases when an actor faces a state with nuclear weapons. In this vein, Jervis (1989: 3) notes that difficulties in understanding the impact of nuclear weapons "stem in part from the fact that the trade-off between the chance of war and the consequences of war is an extremely painful one, the kind that people try to avoid facing." Without an *a priori* expectation of whether the costs of unlimited war change as much as the probability of such a war, there can be no strong expectation about whether opponents of nuclear weapon states face higher expected costs in crisis than if they faced a non-nuclear state.

The puzzle thus becomes an empirical question of whether or not states behave as if the expected conflict costs are a function of the other side's nuclear capabilities. Since the analyst is not an omniscient observer, those expected costs cannot be directly measured. Instead, we derive some hypotheses that would be consistent with what should occur if the world were such that opponents of nuclear states faced higher expected costs of engaging in a crisis. If the expected costs of conflict rise, opponents of nuclear states will be more eager to settle and settle in as short a time as possible. By testing the hypotheses, an empirical analysis of international crisis behavior provides substantial support for the notion that states do indeed face higher expected costs when confronting a nuclear state.

Competing effects of nuclear weapons

The approach here focuses on the expected costs of conflict, conceived as a weighted average of the costs of all the potential scenarios that could occur in conflict. Nuclear weapons influence those expected costs of conflict via both the costs of certain scenarios and the probability of those scenarios. The maximum-escalation scenarios in this setup should obviously entail enormous damage when involving a nuclear state.

While the costs of the maximum-escalation scenarios will increase in the shadow of nuclear weapons, the associated probabilities should decrease. The size of these weapons, and their clumsy inability to not cause horrific damage even when used in a limited sense, make them an unlikely option in war. Against a nuclear opponent, especially one with second-strike capabilities, the risk to the using state would likely be in the form of a catastrophic response. Such a threat of retaliation from a nuclear adversary is obvious, but there are also substantial risks to using nuclear weapons against a non-nuclear state. The use of nuclear weapons can hinder the using state from pursuing some of its strategic objectives, such as winning the support of an adversary's domestic population or even gaining control of a disputed area that becomes irradiated. Beyond these instrumental incentives, Tannenwald (1999, 2005) has traced the development of a nuclear taboo, in which there are substantial normative costs to a first-strike nuclear attack. Once the nuclear taboo is established, decision makers may never consider using a nuclear first strike because it simply always lies outside of the range of possible appropriate actions, or they risk sanction from the greater international or domestic communities for violating a deeply rooted norm.

The probability of full escalation is lower in the shadow of nuclear weapons, but the costs are greater. The previous theoretical work on nuclear deterrence is ambiguous as to the rate of increase or decrease in the costs and probability of nuclear use. In Zagare and Kilgour's (2000) work on perfect deterrence theory, they effectively show that deterrence success decreases with the credibility of a threat such as nuclear use but increases with the costs that it would impose on the other side. Because they have no prior assumptions about how nuclear weapons specifically affect their variables, they are only able to show that nuclear deterrence *can* fail, but not whether it fails more or less often than under conventional deterrence. This is the essence of the puzzle considered. Nuclear weapons may not alter the *expected* costs of conflict because of the competing effects on the costs and probabilities of full-escalation scenarios.

If nuclear weapons were to increase the expected costs of conflict, what should we observe? While the impact of nuclear weapons on bargaining behavior has thus far been treated as an empirical question, we use the view that nuclear weapons do increase an opponent's expected crisis costs, consistent with Jervis (1989) and Waltz (2003), as the basis for postulating falsifiable hypotheses. If it is true that opponents of a nuclear state face higher expected costs of crisis, we should first observe that they are more willing to concede to the nuclear state's demands, or at least back down from their own demands. We would expect nuclear states to realize divisions of the disputed goods that are higher than if they did not have nuclear weapons. The logic is that opponents facing higher costs of conflict will find more alternatives that are preferable to fighting – there is more room for concession and there is less incentive to push their own demands at risk of greater escalation.

The central argument is thus that we should observe nuclear weapon states prevail in their coercive diplomacy – where prevailing is defined as either gaining concessions or having an opponent back down from their demands – if the weapons actually increase the expected costs of an opponent's crisis. The reasoning is necessarily a bit complicated because concessions are defined relative to the status quo, and the argument has not made any assumptions about the positioning of the status quo. From a purely probabilistic standpoint, however, we posit that as an actor's costs of conflict increase, there is a higher probability that a given outcome which gives the actor less than the status quo will be preferable to fighting.

So, when an actor finds more concessionary outcomes preferable to war, the probability, by no means a guarantee, that those concessions are realized will increase. Achieving concessions, however, is not the only means for states to prevail in their crises. When the nuclear states are the status quo actors that are satisfied and merely hoping to hold onto what they have, successful coercive diplomacy entails not making concessions. That is, if nuclear weapons increase an opponent's expected conflict costs, then nuclear states will face fewer challengers unwilling to back down because the challengers' expected outcomes from fighting will more rarely be superior to the status quo.

There are a number of caveats that should be considered when empirically testing this argument. First, since states expecting concessions should make greater demands, this necessitates that the operational definition of bargaining gains not be too contingent upon the endogenous demands and goals. For example, a definition of victory that hinges on realizing the demands made will be problematic because nuclear states may demand more going into a crisis, which raises the bar of achieving victory. Second, we will need to be wary of self-selection bias because it is possible that opponents of nuclear states may concede more *prior* to a crisis, which leaves a special subset of opponents that are reluctant to concede as those that actually enter into a crisis. Related, those opponents of nuclear states demanding a change from the status quo might only make such demands if they are truly dissatisfied and resolved to not back down. The methods section describes how we account for such potential problems of endogenous demands and self-selection bias.

Hypothesis 1: Nuclear weapon states are more likely to prevail in either gaining concessions or convincing an opponent to back down in their crises than non-nuclear weapon states.

Actors facing higher costs of engagement will not only want to concede *more*, but they will also want to concede *faster*. If nuclear weapons increase the costs of the full-escalation scenarios in each conflict period more than they decrease the probability of such scenarios, then opponents of nuclear states have a greater incentive to resolve the crisis sooner rather than later. Because of the per-period expected costs, opponents of nuclear states will be less willing to patiently wait for a better bargain. If the probability of nuclear use increases as a crisis endures and escalates, then the weapons' effects on the conflict costs will be especially pronounced at later escalation phases. Opponents of nuclear states will thus have incentives to exit their crises before the expected costs of conflict increase beyond acceptable levels.

Hypothesis 2: Opponents of nuclear weapon states are more likely to end crises sooner than opponents of non-nuclear weapon states.

Thus far, the discussion has centered on a non-nuclear opponent facing a nuclear state. While much of the previous literature has focused solely on the dynamics within symmetric nuclear dyads, we distinguish between nuclear and non-nuclear protagonists. When nuclear states square off against each other, extant research on nuclear deterrence suggests that the probability of full escalation should be at its lowest. That is, if Mutually Assured Destruction adheres, then nuclear use becomes almost unthinkable for each side. While the probability of full escalation most closely approaches zero for actors in symmetric nuclear dyads, the costs of a full-escalation scenario to each side should be similar for both nuclear and non-nuclear actors facing a nuclear opponent. In both cases, full escalation entails mass devastation. Taking into account both the probability and costs of full escalation, the per-period *expected* costs of crisis will be lower for nuclear states facing a nuclear opponent than for non-nuclear states facing a nuclear opponent. The logic dictates that nuclear actors will fare better in their bargaining outcomes against non-nuclear states than against fellow members of the nuclear club.

Hypothesis 3: Nuclear weapon states in symmetric dyads are less likely to prevail in their crises than those in asymmetric dyads.

Hypothesis 4: Opponents of nuclear weapon states in symmetric dyads are less likely to end their crises sooner than those in asymmetric dyads.

One additional implication follows from the proposed logic. The actors themselves have control over the probability of each escalation scenario. Actors that go into a crisis, presumably over a lesser issue, with absolutely no intention of escalating past a certain point should not be expected to have a probability of full escalation greater than zero. Since states rarely threaten nuclear use, it would be a tenuous assertion to say that all crises involving nuclear actors have some lingering implicit threat. As a result, the effect of nuclear weapons should be contingent on the saliency of the crisis to the actors involved. In low-salient conflicts that an actor has no intention to escalate if needed, nuclear weapons should have no bearing. In more salient crises, where the probability of full escalation is greater than zero – though still presumably small – if nuclear weapons do have an impact on crisis outcomes it will be in these situations.

Hypothesis 5: Nuclear weapon states will be more prone to prevail and to face shorter crises when saliency is high.

Analysis

To test these hypotheses, data are used from the International Crisis Behavior (ICB) data project, in conjunction with numerous other sources of data detailed below. The appropriate level of analysis is the crisis actor, and since crisis actors often face multiple opponents, we use directed crisis dyads from 1945 to 2002. The dyads are directed in the sense that A's actions toward B are different than B's actions toward A. They are defined according to Hewitt (2003), and updated to be consistent with version 8 of the ICB data.[2] Brecher and Wilkenfeld (2000) define an ICB crisis as an interstate dispute that threatens at least one state's values, has a heightened probability of military escalation, and has a finite time frame for resolution. The benefit of using ICB crises is that they comprise a useful set of cases in which bargaining failure could occur and lead to escalation but is not a necessary condition.[3]

Dependent variables

The two dependent variables from the hypotheses are an indicator of whether an actor prevails and the duration of the conflict. For the former, the framework defines crisis success as either gaining a better share of the bargain or convincing an opponent to back down. Two different measures are used to capture crisis victory. An existing ICB variable categorizes outcomes according to whether an actor was victorious in realizing all of its goals, reached a compromise to realize some of its crisis goals, or faced stalemate or defeat to not achieve any of its goals. For one dichotomous measure of crisis success, we use the first category of this existing variable, following Gelpi and Griesdorf (2001). States that avoid compromise, stalemate or defeat are definitely victorious and successful in their crises.

We also use another measure of crisis success because we suspect that a crisis actor's goals are endogenous. If the expected costs felt by a crisis actor are greater when facing a nuclear state, then we should simply expect that the nuclear state would increase its demands and expectations of what it can get from the opponent. As a result, the bar would be higher for the nuclear actor to achieve all of its goals, so the probability of victory defined in this way might not change even if nuclear weapons do improve a state's bargaining position. In light of this potential problem, we adopt another measure that better accounts for endogenous demands because it is less restrictive on what prevailing in crisis entails. Clearly an actor still prevails if it is coded as victorious, and it does not succeed if it only reaches a stalemate or fails in defeat. For those actors that reach a compromise, this could indicate a slightly better bargain, maintenance of the status quo, or a slightly worse bargain. To distinguish between these potential scenarios, we use another variable that codes the satisfaction of the crisis actors. We contend that if an actor reaches a compromise and expresses satisfaction with the outcome, this is an indication that the actor succeeded in either gaining concessions or not acceding to an opponent's demands.[4] In sum, an actor is coded as winning in this second measure if it is victorious in achieving all of its goals, or if it is demonstrably satisfied with a compromise.

Turning to the duration of conflict, the ICB data code a variable that counts the number of days between a crisis actor's trigger date and the actor's termination date. The first and last days of crisis are rarely the same for both actors in a dyad, as the crisis is usually perceived first by one actor, and then the other actor only perceives a crisis after the other responds, usually days or weeks later. A directed dyad approach remains valid because this outcome measure varies between the A to B and B to A directed dyads, although the analyses will take care to account for the interdependence of the AB and BA observations.

Independent variables

Dichotomous indicators for whether each state in a directed dyad has nuclear weapons are included as the most important explanatory variables. Table 11.1 presents the dates used, which are consistent with other chapters in this volume. Of the 1,218 crisis actors in these data, 221 (18 percent) have nuclear weapons.[5]

Degree of salience also plays an important role in the hypotheses. We measure salience using a dummy variable that combines two threat severity indicators: the stakes involved and the presence of violence.[6] In terms of

Table 11.1 Dates of weapon states

Country	Nuclear Weapons	
	Start	End
United States	1945	>2001
Soviet Union/Russia	1949	>2001
United Kingdom	1952	>2001
France	1960	>2001
China	1964	>2001
Israel	1967	>2001
India	1988	>2001
South Africa	1982	1990
Pakistan	1990	>2001
North Korea	>2001	>2001

stakes, nuclear weapons will be most credible when addressing a clear security threat. The ICB data code the gravity of a crisis, and the highest two values for this variable – a threat of grave damage and a threat to existence – are the most clear indicators of a core value being threatened. So, one component of high salience in our coding scheme is thus whether the crisis obtains one of these two values. Having some minimal level of violence should also be required for a crisis to be salient and for nuclear weapons to have relevance. Violent crises are not limited probes that have no intention of escalating even a modest amount. The ICB data have a four-point indicator of violence experienced in a crisis, and we only code crises as highly salient if there is some minimal level of violence. In sum, highly salient crises are those involving a severe threat, as defined by: (1) gravity at least at the level of a threat of grave damage; and (2) some minimal level of violence.[7]

The models implement a combination of control variables. One of the most frequently used variables in analyses of conflict outcomes is the balance of military capabilities within a dyad (see Stam 1996; Reiter and Stam 2002; Gelpi and Griesdorf 2001; Gartner and Siverson 1996). Actors with nuclear weapons are likely to have relatively large amounts of conventional capabilities, which may shape escalation behavior in ways that are independent of the possession of nuclear weapons. We include the ratio of the actor's level of capability (CINC) to the sum capability of the dyad from the Correlates of War National Military Capabilities 3.01 index (Singer *et al.* 1972; Singer 1987).[8] Related, the models also control for whether an actor is a superpower. This variable is used to see if the results hold for all nuclear actors, or just for the US and Soviet Union/Russia. There could be something distinctive about those two actors that would not be captured by simple measures of capability ratios.

Controlling for violence level is important, as the use of brute force by a nuclear state to attain victory is not the same as using tacit threats to achieve a desired outcome. By including violence in the models, the effects of nuclear status can be considered independently from the levels of violence used on the way to the ultimate outcome. Violence level is measured as a four-point categorical variable from the ICB data.

As Jo and Gartzke (2007) contend, states choose to pursue nuclear weapons strategically.[9] They find that states with high levels of external threats are more likely to proliferate (see also Sagan 1997; Singh and Way 2004). The presence of external threats might also dictate how well a state performs in its crises, as having previously unresolved issues indicates the tendency for crises to stalemate. Unless we control for a state's external security concerns, a nuclear weapons variable may be picking up any correlation between rivalry and outcomes instead of the relationship between the weapons and the outcomes. As a result, we include a variable that, for each year, counts the number of preceding crises that a state has been in since 1918 and then averages over the years since 1918 or the state's entrance into the system.

Finally, we control for whether a state is a target of aggression. A distinction between compellence and deterrence is often made, often in respect to the balance of interests (Schelling 1966; Jervis 1989; Betts 1987). The argument is typically that actors will be better able to use nuclear coercive diplomacy in defense of a value or resource instead of in trying to acquire something from another actor. Controlling for whether a state is on the defensive resolves a restriction of the directed dyad approach, in which both actors, regardless of which initiated the crisis, are assumed to have equal outcome tendencies. We define a targeted state in a dyad as an actor which perceived the crisis first and that perceived the other actor in the dyad as its primary source of threat according to the ICB data.[10] The states in a dyad that perceive a crisis first are, by definition of a crisis, the first to experience a threat and are thus considered to be targeted by the source of threat. Actors that perceive a crisis later typically are experiencing the threat of a response.

Models

Estimation of the impact of nuclear weapons on bargaining outcomes and crisis duration requires two different classes of models. For the models of outcomes, we rely on probit models. For duration, the data are single-observation survival time, and we rely on Cox proportional hazard estimation for many of our analyses because it does not assume a certain shape of the hazard function.[11]

The analyses are subject to potential selection bias, as states strategically select themselves in and out of crises, not wanting to fight when they are likely to lose. Taking selection effects seriously, we demonstrate robustness using simultaneous-equation estimation of the selection and outcome processes. In estimating the selection equation, the base set of cases is the set of dyad years, consistent with Rauchhaus (this book: chapter 10). For the models of bargaining outcomes, we use a censored probit model, which is a special case of a bivariate probit model and is often referred to as a "Heckman probit" model (see Dubin and Rivers 1989; Reed 2000). For the duration models, we use Boehmke's (2005; Boehmke et al. 2006) estimator to account for selection effects. The selection equation of each of these models includes the independent variables described above, a measure of contiguity and a measure of similarity of alliance portfolios, from the Eugene 3.1 software. Since the selection equations in these models involve binary longitudinal data with a probit link, we include time since the previous crisis among the dyadic actors, its square and cube to account for temporal dependence (Carter and Signorino 2010; Beck *et al.* 1998).

While we demonstrate robustness with the selection models, we rely on the more conventional models for our interpretations of the magnitudes of the effects. Any lingering concerns of selection effects might be dispelled by noting that because entrance into a low-level crisis does not require significant costs or risks, strategic selection will be much less of a problem when dealing with a set of crises than a set of violent conflicts. In addition, the potential selection effects likely bias the observed impact of nuclear weapons status toward zero – if there is non-random selection of more resolved types that participate in crises despite the disadvantage of facing nuclear states – which means that significant relationships should only become stronger if crisis selection were random.

Since it is rare for both actors in a directed dyad to prevail[12] and common for each actor to have similar duration times, the observations are not independent of each other. Observations from the same crisis will be interdependent. In effect, this inflates the number of observations and thus deflates the estimated standard errors. To correct for this, all models use robust standard errors, clustered on each non-directed crisis dyad pair.

Results

Nuclear status and bargaining gains

Table 11.2 presents the probit results of whether crisis actors are effectively able to succeed in gaining concessions, or at least in not yielding to demands. Model 1 uses the less restrictive measure of victory, to better account for endogenous demands, while Model 2 uses the more conventional measure directly from the ICB outcome variable. Models 3 and 4 include the indicator of a severe threat and its interaction with the nuclear status variable to test Hypothesis 5.

The first two models demonstrate that, in comparison to non-nuclear actors, nuclear states have an increased probability of prevailing against non-nuclear opponents. The coefficient on the nuclear status of the opponent also provides some support, as it is negative in both models and statistically significant in Model 2. The most direct test of Hypothesis 1 is whether a nuclear state tends to gain more often, but we might also expect that opponents of nuclear states would be less able to succeed in their crises. A corollary to Hypothesis 1 would expect this variable to be negative, as non-nuclear states will find their chances of winning concessions diminished in the face of high expected costs of crisis against a nuclear opponent. Model 5 provides a more direct test of this corollary hypothesis by using defeat, taken directly from the ICB data, as the dependent variable. From the results of this model, non-nuclear opponents of nuclear states are more likely to face defeat, while nuclear states are less likely to realize defeat in their crises against non-nuclear states.

The results also provide some support for Hypothesis 3, as the bargaining advantage of nuclear weapons only appears to hold against non-nuclear states. A linear combination test reveals that states in symmetric nuclear dyads are less likely to prevail than nuclear states in asymmetric

Table 11.2 Probit models of crisis outcomes

	(1) Victory	(2) Victory (restrictive)	(3) Victory	(4) Victory (restrictive)	(5) Defeat	(6) Defeat
Nuclear A	0.346** (0.141)	0.247* (0.142)	0.052 (0.162)	-0.008 (0.167)	-0.560** (0.186)	-0.475* (0.205)
Nuclear B	-0.150 (0.121)	-0.288** (0.133)	-0.056 (0.149)	-0.260* (0.156)	0.575** (0.122)	0.366** (0.151)
Nuclear A&B	-0.166 (0.222)	-0.362* (0.207)	-0.181 (0.223)	-0.346* (0.205)	-0.292 (0.228)	-0.246 (0.231)
Salience			0.030 (0.092)	-0.252** (0.096)		-0.225* (0.104)
Nuclear A* Salience			0.807** (0.231)	0.645** (0.214)		-0.320 (0.284)
Nuclear B* Salience			-0.245 (0.217)	-0.078 (0.236)		0.529** (0.216)
Capability Share	0.239 (0.147)	-0.001 (0.154)	0.290* (0.149)	0.032 (0.157)	0.106 (0.161)	0.066 (0.164)
Super Power A	0.102 (0.155)	0.481** (0.156)	0.109 (0.161)	0.490** (0.157)	0.300 (0.202)	0.317 (0.208)
Target A	0.436** (0.078)	0.516** (0.084)	0.426** (0.081)	0.473** (0.085)	-0.322** (0.096)	-0.335** (0.098)
Previous Crisis A	0.233 (0.201)	0.245 (0.219)	0.271 (0.203)	0.281 (0.219)	-0.434* (0.217)	-0.468* (0.219)
Violence	0.070* (0.030)	0.007 (0.032)	0.037 (0.038)	0.037 (0.037)	-0.025 (0.033)	0.014 (0.039)
Constant	-0.643** (0.140)	-0.855** (0.148)	-0.592** (0.144)	-0.851** (0.151)	-0.606** (0.154)	-0.593** (0.157)
Observations	1,218	1,218	1,218	1,218	1,218	1,218

Notes

Robust standard errors in parentheses, clustered on each non-directed dyad.

*Significant at 5%; **significant at 1% in a one-tailed test.

dyads, and this difference is statistically significant ($p < 0.001$ in a one-tail test) in Model 2 and approaching significance ($p < 0.07$) in Model 1. That is, nuclear states are less likely to achieve concessionary gains, or force an opponent to back down, against another nuclear state than against a non-nuclear state. Moreover, in Model 5, a linear combination test reveals that non-nuclear opponents of nuclear states are significantly more likely to experience defeat than nuclear opponents, again demonstrating that nuclear states have less of a bargaining advantage in symmetric dyads.

The ongoing inability for other nuclear powers to push North Korea into an agreement – or keep it to an agreement – illustrates the limitations for nuclear states to use their weapons for general bargaining strength against other nuclear states. Also demonstrative of this point is the dispute between Russia/USSR and China over territorial claims along the Ussuri River, which nearly escalated to war in 1969 and only recently realized a compromise settlement. While nuclear weapons may have had some influence in tempering escalation dynamics in this conflict, it does not appear that they helped either side attain their preferred outcome in an expedited fashion.

Hypothesis 5 expected the relationship between weapon status and crisis outcome to be weaker at low levels of intensity because it simply is less believable to expect nuclear weapons to have an influence over crises with relatively minor salience. In support, we see that an interaction between the high intensity indicator and weapons status of the crisis actor is positive and statistically significant in Models 3 and 4. It is worth noting that the nuclear status constitutive term is not statistically significant in these two models. That is, when the salience dummy variable is zero, the relationship between nuclear status and victory is not statistically significant. At high intensity, nuclear states are more likely to have enhanced bargaining leverage when compared to non-nuclear states.[13] Model 6 provides additional confirmation to Hypothesis 5, as non-nuclear opponents of nuclear states are especially more likely to experience defeat in highly salient crises.

The censored probit models, which adjust for nonrandom selection into a crisis, are given in Table 11.3. Models 7 and 8 demonstrate the robustness of the findings. When accounting for the nonrandom selection into mediation, nuclear states still are more likely to succeed in achieving their demands, and getting the opponent to back down, against non-nuclear states.[14] Moreover, that relationship is much stronger in high-salience cases than in ones without a substantial threat involved. It is interesting that, in the selection equations, the possession of nuclear weapons has a statistically significant and positive relationship with crisis involvement, consistent with the findings in Rauchhaus (this book: chapter 10) that symmetric and asymmetric nuclear dyads are more likely to experience militarized interstate disputes. Although the rho statistic is statistically significant, we use the non-censored probit models for substantive interpretations because the results are quite similar in the regular probit models.

Table 11.3 Selection Models

	(7) Victory 1	(8) Victory 1	(9) Duration	(10) Duration
Outcome Equations				
Nuclear A	0.308* (0.154)	0.00201 (0.164)	0.286* (0.149)	0.123 (0.172)
Nuclear B	-0.120 (0.134)	-0.0472 (0.165)	0.329** (0.125)	0.132 (0.142)
Nuclear A&B	-0.188 (0.202)	-0.209 (0.190)	-0.475 (0.319)	-0.476 (0.311)
Salience		0.0101 (0.103)		-0.406** (0.117)
Nuclear A * Salience		0.838** (0.268)		0.438** (0.155)
Nuclear B * Salience		-0.178 (0.253)		0.544** (0.160)
Capability Share	0.237 (0.170)	0.288* (0.171)	0.0166 (0.0426)	0.00774 (0.0416)
Super Power A	0.115 (0.159)	0.124 (0.166)	-0.0160 (0.150)	0.00338 (0.147)
Target A	0.470** (0.0927)	0.462** (0.0926)	0.0370 (0.0741)	-0.0197 (0.0729)
Previous Crisis A	0.462* (0.246)	0.523* (0.240)	0.0220 (0.180)	0.0151 (0.178)
Violence	0.069* (0.0371)	0.0358 (0.0460)	-0.174** (0.0442)	-0.118** (0.0486)
Constant	-0.930** (0.214)	-0.904** (0.223)	-4.446** (0.212)	-4.440** (0.205)
Selection Equations				
Nuclear A	0.00601 (0.0674)	0.00609 (0.0674)	-0.0110 (0.0350)	-0.0109 (0.172)
Nuclear B	0.411** (0.0531)	0.411** (0.053)	0.220** (0.0276)	0.220** (0.0276)
Nuclear A&B	-0.160 (0.140)	-0.159 (0.140)	-0.0803 (0.0889)	-0.0807 (0.0888)
Capability Share	-0.118** (0.0103)	-0.118** (0.0103)	-0.0682** (0.00440)	-0.0682** (0.00439)
Super Power A	0.282** (0.0788)	0.282** (0.0788)	0.145** (0.0442)	0.146** (0.0442)
Previous Crisis A	1.303** (0.0447)	1.302** (0.0447)	0.763** (0.0289)	0.763** (0.0289)
Contiguity	0.986** (0.0649)	0.986** (0.0650)	0.544** (0.0340)	0.544** (0.0340)
S-score	-0.189 (0.127)	-0.189 (0.127)	-0.0651 (0.0643)	-0.0651 (0.0644)
Enduring Rivalry	1.428** (0.113)	1.427** (0.113)	1.096** (0.0830)	1.098** (0.0832)
Peace Years	-0.0666** (0.00932)	-0.0667** (0.00932)	-0.0356** (0.00469)	-0.0356** (0.00469)
Peace Years^2	0.00218** (0.000448)	0.00218** (0.000448)	0.00117** (0.000226)	0.00117** (0.000226)
Peace Years^3	-2.06e-05** (6.00e-06)	-2.06e-05** (6.00e-06)	-1.11e-05** (3.02e-06)	-1.11e-05** (3.02e-06)
Constant	-2.919** (0.113)	-2.919** (0.113)	-1.873** (0.0575)	-1.873** (0.0575)
Rho	0.0899* (0.0474)	0.100* (0.0495)	-0.163** (0.0102)	-0.152** (0.0136)
P			0.914** (0.0268)	0.927** (0.0259)
Observations	1,077,737	1,077,737	1,077,737	1,077,737

Notes
Robust standard errors in parentheses, clustered on each non-directed dyad.
*Significant at 5%; **significant at 1% in a one-tailed test.

Returning to Model 1 in Table 11.2, we derive some predictions about the impact of nuclear weapons, given different levels of intensity and holding all control variables at their median values. Table 11.4A presents the predicted probabilities of an actor reaching a beneficial outcome, calculated using CLARIFY (King *et al.* 2000; Tomz *et al.* 2003). When evaluating all crises, non-weapon states have about a 40 percent probability of prevailing in their crises. This probability increases to 54 percent for nuclear states in asymmetric dyads and drops back to 41 percent in a symmetric dyad. The positive impact of nuclear weapons in asymmetric dyads is even more stark in high-salience crises, where the probability of success is about 74 percent, as compared to 44 percent for non-nuclear states and 66 percent for nuclear states in symmetric dyads. The starker effects of nuclear status in the third column compared to the second one again confirms the conditioning effect of salience.

Nuclear status and crisis duration

Turning to the hypotheses concerning the duration of crises, we also see substantial support for Hypothesis 2 and qualified support for Hypothesis 4. Table 11.5 presents the duration models. All the coefficients in these models are in terms of the non-exponentiated coefficients, where positive coefficients indicate a higher likelihood of early termination.

Model 11 presents the basic model for crisis duration. We find that nuclear states and opponents of nuclear states face significantly shorter crises. Recall that the logic behind Hypothesis 2 is that opponents of nuclear states will be eager to end a crisis because the expected costs are higher on average. As a result, the most direct test of this hypothesis is the coefficient on the nuclear status of the opponent (NUCLEAR B). Opponents of nuclear states will tend to shorten their crises by removing

Table 11.4A Probability of victory

	All crises	*Low salience*	*High salience*
Non-weapon state	0.399 (0.018)	0.369 (0.028)	0.443 (0.024)
Assymetric dyad	0.535 (0.053)	0.418 (0.070)	0.736 (0.077)
Symmetric dyad	0.411 (0.082)	0.282 (0.086)	0.658 (0.154)

Table 11.4B Expected crisis duration, in days

	All crises	*Low salience*	*High salience*
Non-weapon state	163.38 (12.05)	120.64 (11.53)	246.07 (25.27)
Assymetric dyad	111.39 (14.94)	105.42 (1966)	115.69 (18.46)
Symmetric dyad	147.79 (33.14)	145.86 (41.35)	114.49 (36.30)

Table 11.5 Duration models of crisis length

	(11) Cox	*(12) Cox*
Nuclear A	0.302** (0.112)	0.149 (0.137)
Nuclear B	0.311** (0.099)	0.145 (0.119)
Nuclear A&B	–0.525* (0.241)	–0.499* (0.228)
Salience		–0.369** (0.097)
Nuclear A* Salience		0.395** (0.136)
Nuclear B* Saliene		0.450** (0.137)
Capability Share	0.016 (0.037)	0.010 (0.037)
Super Power A	–0.020 (0.133)	–4.08e-04 (0.132)
Target A	0.019 (0.060)	–0.026 (0.058)
Previous Crisis A	–0.107 (0.142)	–0.082 (0.142)
Violence	–0.142** (0.037)	–0.087* (0.043)
Observations	1,218	1,218

Notes
Robust standard errors in parentheses, clustered on each non-directed dyad.
*Significant at 5%; **significant at 1% in a one-tailed test.

themselves early. The coefficient on the nuclear status of the crisis actor (NUCLEAR A) also examines Hypothesis 2, although it is perhaps not as direct a test because the logic is that nuclear states are the beneficiaries of shorter crises and not the actors that are actually responsible for early termination. Regardless, the results confirm that nuclear states and their non-nuclear opponents are more likely to be in shorter crises.

While the NUCLEAR A and NUCLEAR B coefficients are positive and statistically significant, the symmetric-dyad term is negative and statistically significant. When comparing states in symmetric nuclear dyads to opponents of nuclear states in asymmetric dyads, a linear combination test reveals that the former are prone to have longer crises, as expected in Hypothesis 4, but the difference is not statistically significant. That is, the results indicate with a high degree of confidence that non-nuclear opponents of nuclear states will tend to have shorter crises than states in non-nuclear dyads, but we do not have high confidence that they will tend to have shorter crises than states in symmetric nuclear dyads.

Model 12 assesses the role of crisis salience in making nuclear weapons more relevant to crisis duration. The interaction between a severe threat and the nuclear status of the opponent is positive and statistically significant. This provides further evidence in support of Hypothesis 5, as crises are even shorter when actors face nuclear opponents and there is both a threat of great damage and some violence. The interaction involving the nuclear status of the actor under observation is also positive and statistically significant. Note again that the coefficients on the nuclear status constitutive terms are not statistically significant with the interactions included. When the salience variable is zero, there is no statistically significant relationship between nuclear status and duration. Only in the salient cases do we observe nuclear weapons having a meaningful dampening effect on crisis length. So, the presence of a severe threat is needed for nuclear weapons to have a statistically significant shortening effect on international crises. Nuclear weapons are much less relevant when there is minimal salience.

Israel's conflicts with its Arab neighbors illustrate the conditional effect of nuclear weapons on both the probability of victory and crisis length. Notable conflicts that ended with compromises or stalemates tend to have occurred either when Israel did not yet have nuclear weapon capability – as during the Sinai incursion crisis and the War of Attrition – or when the relative salience was low – as in the Lebanese interventions which had much lower stakes than other conflicts with either existential threats or global geopolitical implications (Ben-Yehuda 2001). These crises also tended to drag on especially when compared to many of the crises involving a nuclear Israel and high salience, as in the Six Day War, October War and preventive strikes against the Iraqi and Syrian nuclear weapons programs, all of which also had relatively definitive outcomes.

Models 9 and 10 of Table 11.3 again demonstrate the robustness of the findings. In simultaneous equation models that adjust for correlation in the disturbances of the crisis selection and outcome processes, nuclear weapons still shorten the crises for nuclear states and their non-nuclear opponents. It does not appear that the non-random selection produces biased inferences in these models even though the correlations between the selection and outcome equations are statistically significant.

Table 11.4B gives the expected length of crisis for these different types of actors. Most notably, in the high-intensity crises where nuclear weapon status matters most, nuclear weapon states are expected to only last 116 days in crisis against a non-nuclear state. This is substantially less than the 246 days that a non-nuclear state is expected to last against a non-nuclear opponent. Note, however, that the average length of crisis for nuclear states in symmetric dyads is nearly the same as those in asymmetric dyads, indicating that all opponents of nuclear states, nuclear and non-nuclear, are less willing to endure a crisis when the stakes are high. The conditioning effect of salience is again evident, as there is much less of an effect of nuclear status in the low-salience cases.

Alternative explanations

The connection between nuclear weapons and the ability to prevail lends itself to alternative explanations that would call into question whether nuclear weapons themselves actually cause states to perform better in coercive diplomacy. In particular, many of the nuclear states tend to be allies of the US or permanent members of the UN Security Council. Such states represent the status quo arrangement of power in the international system, as they have better access to leverage – via the hegemon or the

UN – by which they can shape the system in their favor peacefully. Consequently, they are likely to be more content about their geopolitical position and perceive a higher level of security. With less of a need to use coercive means to change their security environment, these "status quo" states are freer to selectively choose to enter those crises in which there is a high likelihood of gaining more concessions. To address this alternative explanation for the relationship between nuclear status and crisis success, we run a model that controls for whether a state has a defense pact with the US – using the ATOP data coded by Leeds *et al.* (2002) – or is a P-5 member. In Models 13 and 14 of Table 11.6, we observe that the relationship between nuclear status and gaining concessions remains relatively unchanged.

Michael Horowitz, in Chapter 9, demonstrates the importance of considering how the impact of nuclear weapons on coercive diplomacy might change depending on how long a state has had the capability. New nuclear states may be more dissatisfied than mature nuclear states because the weapons give them a boost in their power status and thus an incentive to restructure the terms of their existing arrangements. If states that initiate crises – the dissatisfied states – tend to be the ones that win, then we might expect only new nuclear states to prevail more. While the previous models control for whether a state was the target of a crisis, we attempt to gain additional leverage on this argument by checking to see if "young" nuclear states that have developed their capability in the previous ten years – and that are thus prone to be dissatisfied – are more apt to win in their crises than more "mature" nuclear states that have had an opportunity to restructure their bargaining positions. As Models 15 and 16 demonstrate, we observe that both types of nuclear states fare well in gaining concessions, although the relationship between new nuclear states and crisis success is only statistically significant in Model 15. Mature nuclear states tend to win just as well as, if not more than, new nuclear states still adapting to their new bargaining position.

Conclusion

Why do states proliferate? Nuclear weapons and the programs necessary to create them are expensive. They are dangerous. Other countries may attack a state while it is trying to create a nuclear arsenal and there is always the risk of a catastrophic accident. They may help generate existential threats by encouraging first strike incentives amongst a state's opponents. This chapter has explored the incentives that make nuclear weapons attractive to a wide range of states despite their costly and dangerous nature. We have found that nuclear weapons provide more than prestige, they provide leverage. They are useful in coercive diplomacy, and this must be central to any explanation of why states acquire them.

Since August 9, 1945 no state has used a nuclear weapon against another state, but we find evidence that the possession of nuclear weapons

Table 11.6 Robustness checks

	(13) Victory	(14) Victory (restrictive)	(15) Victory	(16) Victory (restrictive)
Nuclear A	0.523** (0.154)	0.298* (0.151)	−0.152 (0.121)	−0.289* (0.133)
Nuclear B	−0.149 (0.122)	−0.271* (0.133)	−0.168 (0.222)	−0.366* (0.208)
Nuclear A&B	−0.193 (0.233)	−0.378 (0.207)	0.234 (0.148)	−0.006 (0.155)
Capability Share	0.275* (0.147)	0.012 (0.154)	0.082 (0.157)	0.469** (0.159)
Super Power A	0.398* (0.208)	0.644** (0.215)	0.432** (0.079)	0.512** (0.085)
Target A	0.438** (0.078)	0.520** (0.084)	0.230 (0.201)	0.242 (0.219)
Previous Crisis A	0.347 (0.213)	0.325 (0.230)	0.070* (0.030)	0.007 (0.032)
Violence	0.063* (0.031)	0.008 (0.032)		
P-5 State	−0.501** (0.192)	−0.205 (0.198)		
US Defense Ally	0.003 (0.105)	0.143 (0.107)		
New Nuclear State		0.396** (0.168)	0.295* (0.168)	0.202 (0.170)
Mature Nuclear State			0.285* (0.168)	
Constant	−0.653** (0.149)	−0.914** (0.160)	−0.638** (0.141)	−0.850** (0.149)
Observations	1218	1218	1218	1218

Notes
Robust standard errors in parentheses, clustered on each non-directed dyad.
*Significant at 5%; **significant at 1% in a one-tailed test.

helps states to succeed in their confrontations with other states even when they do not "use" them. Conflict with nuclear actors carries with it a potential danger that conflict with other states simply does not have. Even though the probability of full escalation is presumably low, the evidence confirms that the immense damage from the possibility of such escalation is enough to make an opponent eager to offer concessions. Asymmetric crises allow nuclear states to use their leverage to good effect. When crises involve a severe threat – and nuclear use is not completely ruled out – the advantage that nuclear actors have is substantial. Nuclear weapons help states win concessions quickly in salient conflicts. Consistent with the other papers in this volume, we report that nuclear weapons confer tangible benefits to the possessors. These benefits imply that there should be a general level of demand for nuclear weapons, which means that explanations for why so few states have actually proliferated should focus more on the supply side, as applied by Matthew Kroenig and Matthew Fuhrmann.

The findings here importantly suggest an additional reason why "proliferation begets proliferation," in the words of George Shultz (Shultz 1984: 18). If both parties to a crisis have nuclear weapons, the advantage is effectively cancelled out. When states develop nuclear weapons, doing so may encourage their rivals to also proliferate for fear of being exploited by the shifting bargaining positions. And once the rivals proliferate, the initial proliferator no longer has much bargaining advantage. On the one hand, this dynamic adds some restraint to initial proliferation within a rivalry relationship: states fear that their arsenal will encourage their rivals to pursue nuclear weapons, which will leave them no better off (Davis 1993; Cirincione 2007). On the other hand, once proliferation has occurred, all other states that are likely to experience coercive bargaining with the new nuclear state will also want nuclear weapons. The rate of proliferation has the potential to accelerate because the desire to possess the "equalizer" will increase as the number of nuclear powers slowly rises.

Our theoretical framework and empirical findings are complementary to Gartzke and Jo, who posit and find that nuclear states enjoy greater influence in the international realm. An interesting dynamic emerges when comparing the results to Rauchhaus, who finds that nuclear weapons in asymmetric dyads tend to increase the propensity for escalation. We have argued that nuclear weapons improve the bargaining leverage of the possessors and tested that proposition directly. It is important to note that the factors that shape conflict initiation and escalation are not necessarily the same factors that most shape the outcome of the conflict. Even so, one explanation for why a stronger bargaining position does not necessarily produce less escalation is that escalation is a function of decisions by both sides, and even though the opponent of a nuclear state is more willing to back down, the nuclear state should be more willing to raise its demands and push for a harder bargain in order to maximize the benefits from the nuclear weapons.

Nuclear weapons appear to need ever-greater shares of their bargains in order to be satisfied, which helps to explain both their proclivity to win and their proclivity toward aggressive coercive diplomacy. An important implication in light of these findings is thus that even though nuclear weapon states tend to fare better at the end of their crises, this does not necessarily mean that the weapons are a net benefit for peace and stability.

Notes

1 Replication data are available at http://jcr.sagepub.com/supplemental.
2 States that appear in the Hewitt (2003) data but not in the actor-level ICB data – when they are belligerents but do not actually perceive a crisis – are still included because their nuclear weapons still potentially shape their outcome from the dispute.
3 Another advantage of the ICB data is that they have multiple outcome measures coded that can be adapted easily for analysis of the dynamics under consideration here and, for this reason, have been used in recent quantitative studies of crisis outcomes (Gelpi and Griesdorf 2001; Chiozza and Goemans 2004; Lai 2004).
4 One might suspect that actors rarely express dissatisfaction with a crisis outcome because they face audience costs. This does not appear to be the case, as over a third of the crisis actors are coded as dissatisfied in the ICB data.
5 The high proportion of nuclear powers in international crises is partly explained by the opportunity for the superpowers to be involved in many different conflicts across the globe. The results control for superpower status to account for their disproportionate presence in international crises.
6 Issue type is not used solely as a measure of salience because it is, in part, picked up by the threat severity measure and there is tremendous variation of salience within each issue type.
7 The gravity variable itself is not sufficient because we believe that having 27 crisis dyads coded as having a threat of grave damage but without violence occurring allows for too many crises that might have had some potential for grave damage but that were really well contained.
8 The CINC index is the conventional measure of latent military capability in international conflict studies.
9 Also see Kroenig (this book: chapter 4) and Fuhrmann (this book: chapter 5).
10 By this operational definition, not all dyads have a targeted state if there are many dyads and some of the dyads consist of opponents that do not perceive each other as the key source of threat. That is, when actors are drawn into a conflict that is ongoing, there will sometimes be dyads in secondary conflicts in which neither state in the dyad perceive each other as the most serious threat, so those actors are not targets of aggression within that dyad.
11 A Schoenfeld test fails to reject the possibility of proportional hazards in the model. Weibull models produced similar results.
12 While rare, it is not impossible. When there are multiple issues, both actors could walk away feeling that they gained more than what they had under the status quo.
13 A linear combination confirms that states with nuclear weapons are significantly more likely to prevail against non-nuclear opponents when there is high salience.
14 The less restrictive measure of victory is used in these models, but similar results adhere when the other measure is used.

References

Arreguín-Toft, Ivan (2005) *How the Weak win Wars*, New York: Cambridge University Press.

Asal, Victor and Kyle Beardsley (2007) "Proliferation and international crisis behavior," *Journal of Peace Research* 44: 139–155.

Beardsley, Kyle and Victor Asal (2009) "Nuclear weapons as shields," *Conflict Management and Peace Science* 26: 235–255.

Beck, Nathaniel, Jonathan N. Katz and Richard Tucker (1998) "Taking time seriously: time-series–cross-section analysis with a binary dependent variable," *American Journal of Political Science* 42: 1260–1288.

Ben-Yehuda, Hemda (2001) "Territoriality, crisis and war in the Arab–Israel Conflict 1947–94," *Journal of Conflict Studies* 21: 78–108.

Betts, Richard K. (1987) *Nuclear Blackmail and Nuclear Balance*, Washington, DC: Brookings Institution.

Boehmke, Frederick J. (2005) "DURSEL: A program for duration models with sample selection (Stata version)," Version 2.0, Iowa City, IA: University of Iowa. Available at http://myweb.uiowa.edu/fboehmke/methods.

Boehmke, Frederick J., Daniel Morey and Megan Shannon (2006) "Selection bias and continuous-time duration models: consequences and a proposed solution," *American Journal of Political Science* 50: 192–207.

Brecher, Michael and Jonathan Wilkenfeld (2000) *A Study of Crisis*, Ann Arbor, MI: University of Michigan.

Carter, David and Curtis S. Signorino (2010) "Back to the future: modeling time dependence in binary data," *Political Analysis* 18: 271–292.

Chiozza, Giacomo and H.E. Goemans (2004) "International conflict and the tenure of leaders: is war still ex post inefficient?," *American Journal of Political Science* 48: 604–619.

Cirincione, Joseph (2007) *Bomb Scare: The History and Future of Nuclear Weapons*, New York: Columbia University Press.

Davis, Zachary (1993) "The realist nuclear regime," *Security Studies* 2: 79–99.

Desch, Michael C. (2002) "Democracy and victory: why regime type hardly matters," *International Security* 27: 5–47.

Dubin, Jeffrey A. and Douglas Rivers (1989) "Selection bias in linear regression, logit and probit models," *Sociological Methods and Research* 18: 360–390.

Fearon, James D. (1994) "Signaling versus the balance of power and interests: an empirical test of a crisis bargaining model," *Journal of Conflict Resolution* 38: 236–269.

Fuhrmann, Matthew (This Book) "Taking a walk on the supply side: the determinants of civilian nuclear cooperation."

Gaddis, John Lewis (1986) "The long peace: elements of stability in the postwar international system," *International Security* 10: 99–142.

Gartner, Scott Sigmund and Randolph M. Siverson (1996) "War expansion and war outcome," *Journal of Conflict Resolution* 40: 4–15.

Gartzke, Erik and Dong-Joon Jo (This Book) "Bargaining, nuclear proliferation, and interstate disputes."

Geller, Daniel S. (1990) "Nuclear weapons, deterrence, and crisis escalation," *Journal of Conflict Resolution* 34: 291–310.

Gelpi, Christopher F. and Michael Griesdorf (2001) "Winners or losers? Democracies in international crises, 1918–94," *American Political Science Review* 95: 633–647.

Hewitt, Joseph (2003) "Dyadic processes and international crises," *Journal of Conflict Resolution* 47: 669–692.

Horowitz, Michael (This Book) "The spread of nuclear weapons and international conflict: does experience matter?"

Huth, Paul (1988) "Extended deterrence and the outbreak of war," *American Political Science Review* 82: 423–443.

Huth, Paul (1990) "The extended deterrent value of nuclear weapons," *Journal of Conflict Resolution* 34: 270–290.

Huth, Paul and Bruce Russett (1988) "Deterrence failure and crisis escalation," *International Studies Quarterly* 32: 29–46.

Intriligator, Michael D. and Dagobert L. Brito (1981) Nuclear proliferation and the probability of nuclear war. *Public Choice* 37:247–260.

Intriligator, Michael D. and Dagobert L. Brito (1984) "Can arms races lead to the outbreak of war?," *Journal of Conflict Resolution* 28: 63–84.

Jervis, Robert (1989) *The Meaning of the Nuclear Revolution*, Ithaca, NY: Cornell.

Jo, Dong-Joon and Erik Gartzke (2007) "Determinants of nuclear weapons proliferation: a quantitative model," *Journal of Conflict Resolution* 51: 167–194.

King, Gary, Michael Tomz and Jason Wittenberg (2000) "Making the most of statistical analyses: improving interpretation and presentation," *American Journal of Political Science* 44: 347–361.

Kroenig, Matthew (This Book) "Importing the bomb: sensitive nuclear assistance and nuclear proliferation."

Lai, Brian (2004) "The effects of different types of military mobilization on the outcome of international crises," *Journal of Conflict Resolution* 48: 211–229.

Leeds, Brett Ashley, Jeffrey M. Ritter, Sara McLaughlin Mitchell and Andrew G. Long (2002) "Alliance treaty obligations and provisions, 1815–1944," *International Interactions* 28: 237–260.

Maoz, Zeev (1983) "Resolve, capabilities, and the outcomes of interstate disputes, 1816–1976," *Journal of Conflict Resolution* 27: 195–229.

Mueller, John (1988) "The essential irrelevance of nuclear weapons: stability in the postwar world," *International Security* 13: 55–79.

Powell, Robert (1987) "Crisis bargaining, escalation, and MAD," *American Political Science Review* 81: 717–735.

Powell, Robert (1988) "Nuclear brinkmanship with two-sided incomplete information," *American Political Science Review* 82: 155–178.

Powell, Robert (1990) *Nuclear Deterrence Theory: The Search for Credibility*, New York: Cambridge University Press.

Rauchhaus, Robert (This Book) "Evaluating the nuclear peace hypothesis: a quantitative approach."

Reed, William (2000) "A unified statistical model of conflict onset and escalation," *American Journal of Political Science* 44: 84–93.

Reiter, Dan and Allan C. Stam (2002) *Democracies at War*, Princeton, NJ: Princeton University Press.

Sagan, Scott (1997) "Why do states build nuclear weapons? Three models in search of a bomb," *International Security* 21: 54–86.

Sagan, Scott (2003) "More will be worse," in Scott Sagan and Kenneth Waltz (eds) *The Spread of Nuclear Weapons: A Debate Renewed*, New York: W.W. Norton & Company.

Schelling, Thomas C. (1966) *Arms and Influence*, New Haven, CT: Yale University Press.

Shultz, George (1984) "Preventing the proliferation of nuclear weapons," *Department of State Bulletin* 84: 17–21.

Signorino, Curtis S. and Ahmer Tarar (2006) "A unified theory and test of extended immediate deterrence," *American Journal of Political Science* 50: 586–605.

Singer, J. David (1987) "Reconstructing the Correlates of War Dataset on material capabilities of states, 1816–1985," *International Interactions* 14: 115–132.

Singer, J. David, Stuart Bremer and John Stuckey (1972) "Capability distribution, uncertainty, and major power war, 1820–1965," in Bruce Russett (ed.) *Peace, War, and Numbers*, Beverly Hills, CA: Sage, pp. 19–48.

Singh, Sonali and Christopher Way (2004) "The correlates of nuclear proliferation," *Journal of Conflict Resolution* 48: 859–885.

Snyder, Glenn H. and Paul Diesing (1977) *Conflict among Nations*, Princeton, NJ: Princeton University Press.

Stam, Allan C. (1996) *Win, Lose, or Draw: Domestic Politics and the Crucible of War*, Ann Arbor, MI: University of Michigan Press.

Tannenwald, Nina (1999) "The United States and normative basis of nuclear nonuse," *International Organization* 53: 433–468.

Tannenwald, Nina (2005) "Stigmatizing the bomb: origins of the nuclear taboo," *International Security* 29: 5–49.

Tomz, Michael, Jason Wittenberg and Gary King (2003) *CLARIFY: Software for Interpreting and Presenting Statistical Results*. Version 2.1, Stanford University, University of Wisconsin, and Harvard University, January 5. Available at http://gking.harvard.edu/.

Waltz, Kenneth N. (1990) "Nuclear myths and political realities," *American Political Science Review* 84: 731–745.

Waltz, Kenneth N. (2003) "More may be better," in Scott Sagan and Kenneth Waltz (eds) *The Spread of Nuclear Weapons: A Debate Renewed*, New York: W.W. Norton & Company.

Werner, Suzanne (1998) "Negotiating the terms of settlement: war aims and bargaining leverage," *Journal of Conflict Resolution* 42: 321–343.

Zagare, Frank C. and D. Marc Kilgour (2000) *Perfect Deterrence*, Cambridge: Cambridge University Press.

12 Risk analysis of nuclear deterrence

Martin E. Hellman[1]

Especially where human lives are at stake, good design practice demands large safety margins to account for unforeseen conditions producing stresses beyond those normally expected. Such "over design" saved the Golden Gate Bridge, along with the lives of the 300,000 people who thronged onto it in 1987 to celebrate its fiftieth anniversary. The weight of all those people presented a load that was several times the design load,[2] visibly flattening the bridge's arched roadway. Observing the roadway deform, bridge engineers feared that the span might collapse. However, engineering conservatism saved the day.

Similarly, current nuclear reactor designs require that the failure rate for a significant release of radioactivity be less than 10^{-6} per reactor per year. Estimating such small failure rates is difficult because they depend on events that have never occurred, and that we hope never will. Even so, order of magnitude estimates are possible using tools such as fault or event trees. In these approaches, the failure rates of small events (e.g., the failure of a cooling pump or a backup system) and conditional probabilities are combined to produce an overall failure rate for the much rarer catastrophic event that results when a critical subset of those partial failures occurs.

While significant resources have been expended estimating the failure rate of nuclear reactors, the author has been unable to find any similar studies for an even more dire event: the failure of nuclear deterrence. It is proposed that such studies be undertaken and, if the failure rate is found to be unacceptable, a follow-on effort be initiated to find ways to reduce the threat to an acceptable level.[3] This chapter, and the one that follows by Paul Nelson, are intended to help initiate this research agenda.

A failure of nuclear deterrence can be partial, as in the case of a nuclear terrorist incident, or complete, as in a full-scale nuclear war. Currently, the threat of nuclear terrorism looms much larger in the public's mind than the threat of full-scale nuclear war. A terrorist attack involving a nuclear weapon would be a catastrophe of immense proportions:

A 10-kiloton bomb detonated at Grand Central Station on a typical work day would likely kill some half a million people, and inflict over a trillion dollars in direct economic damage. America and its way of life would be changed forever.

(Bunn et al. 2003)

The likelihood of such an attack is significant. Former Secretary of Defense William Perry has estimated the chance of a nuclear terrorist incident within the next decade to be roughly 50 percent (Bunn 2007). David Albright, a former weapons inspector in Iraq, estimates those odds at less than 1 percent, but notes:

We would never accept a situation where the chance of a major nuclear accident like Chernobyl would be anywhere near 1 percent … A nuclear terrorism attack is a low-probability event, but we can't live in a world where it's anything but extremely low-probability.

(Hegland and Webb 2005)

In a survey of eighty-five national security experts, Senator Richard Lugar found a median estimate of 20 percent for the "probability of an attack involving a nuclear explosion occurring somewhere in the world in the next 10 years," with 79 percent of the respondents believing "it more likely to be carried out by terrorists" than by a government (Lugar 2005).

Because it provides a more complete picture of the risks we face, this chapter defines the failure rate in terms of a complete failure of deterrence, involving a full-scale nuclear war. Terrorism is one of the potential trigger mechanisms for a full-scale nuclear war, so the risk analyses proposed herein will require estimating the risk of nuclear terrorism as one component of the overall risk. If that risk, the overall risk, or both are found to be unacceptable, then the proposed remedies will be directed to reduce whichever risk(s) warrant attention. Similar remarks apply to a number of other threats (e.g., nuclear war between the US and China over Taiwan, or between India and Pakistan).

This chapter would be incomplete if it only dealt with the threat of nuclear terrorism and neglected the threat of full-scale nuclear war. If both risks are unacceptable, an effort to reduce only the terrorist component would leave humanity in great peril. In fact, society's almost total neglect of the threat of full-scale nuclear war makes studying that risk all the more important.

The cost of World War III

The danger associated with nuclear deterrence depends on both the cost of a failure and the failure rate.[4] This section explores the cost of a failure of nuclear deterrence, and the next section is concerned with the failure rate. While other definitions are possible, as noted earlier, this chapter defines a failure of deterrence to mean a full-scale exchange of all nuclear weapons available to the United States and Russia, an event that will be termed World War III.

Approximately 20 million people died as a result of WWI. World War II's fatalities were double or triple that number – chaos prevented a more precise determination. In both cases humanity recovered. Many people therefore implicitly believe that a third World War would be horrible but survivable, an extrapolation of the effects of the first two global wars. In that view, World War III, while horrible, is something that humanity will just have to face and from which it will then have to recover. In contrast, some of those most qualified to assess the situation hold a very different view.

In a 1961 speech to a joint session of the Philippine Congress, General Douglas MacArthur, stated:

> Global war has become a Frankenstein to destroy both sides.... If you lose, you are annihilated. If you win, you stand only to lose. No longer does it possess even the chance of the winner of a duel. It contains now only the germs of double suicide.

Former Secretary of Defense Robert McNamara expressed a similar view: "If deterrence fails and conflict develops, the present U.S. and NATO strategy carries with it a high risk that Western civilization will be destroyed (McNamara 1986)." More recently, George Shultz, William Perry, Henry Kissinger, and Sam Nunn[5] echoed those concerns when they quoted President Reagan's belief that nuclear weapons were "totally irrational, totally inhumane, good for nothing but killing, possibly destructive of life on earth and civilization" (Shultz *et al.* 2007).

Official studies, while couched in less emotional terms, still convey the enormous toll that World War III would exact:

> The resulting deaths would be far beyond any precedent. Executive branch calculations show a range of U.S. deaths from 35 to 77 percent (i.e., from 79 million to 160 million dead) ... a change in targeting could kill somewhere between 20 million and 30 million additional people on each side ... These calculations reflect only deaths during the first 30 days. Additional millions would be injured, and many would eventually die from lack of adequate medical care ... millions of people might starve or freeze during the following winter, but it is not possible to estimate how many ... further millions ... might eventually die of latent radiation effects.
>
> (OTA 1979)

This OTA report also noted the possibility of serious ecological damage (OTA 1979), a concern that assumed a new potentiality when the TTAPS Report (Turco *et al.* 1983) proposed that the ash and dust from so many nearly simultaneous nuclear explosions and their resultant firestorms could usher in a nuclear winter that might erase *Homo sapiens* from the face of the earth, much as many scientists now believe the K-T Extinction which wiped out the dinosaurs was caused by an impact winter caused by ash and dust from a large asteroid or comet striking Earth. The TTAPS report produced a heated debate, and there is still no scientific consensus on whether a nuclear winter would follow a full-scale nuclear war. Recent work (Robock et al. 2007; Toon et al. 2007) suggests that even a limited nuclear exchange or one between newer nuclear-weapons states, such as India and Pakistan, could have devastating long-lasting climatic consequences due to the large volumes of smoke that would be generated by fires in modern megacities.

While it is uncertain how destructive World War III would be, prudence dictates that we apply the same conservatism that saved the Golden Gate Bridge from collapsing on its fiftieth anniversary and assume that preventing World War III is a necessity, not an option.

A common line of reasoning holds that World War III would be so destructive that no rational individual would instigate such a devastating conflict; and, therefore, there is no basis for concern. However, similar logic prevailed prior to World War I, demonstrating that in times of crisis individuals do not behave entirely rationally. If civilization is destroyed in a nuclear holocaust, it is likely to start in a manner similar to World War I – with a sequence of events that spirals out of control.

Former Secretary of Defense Robert McNamara sums up what he learned from participating in three world crises – Berlin in 1961, Cuba in 1962, and the Mideast war of 1967 – each of which had the potential to go nuclear:

> In no one of the three incidents did either ... [the US or the Soviet Union] intend to act in a way that would lead to military conflict, but on each of the occasions lack of information, misinformation, and misjudgments led to confrontation. And in each of them, as the crisis evolved, tensions heightened, emotions rose, and the danger of irrational decisions increased.
>
> (McNamara 1986)

To counter society's apparent belief that the threat of full-scale nuclear war evaporated with the end of the Cold War, it should be noted that the only time the Russian "nuclear football" was opened was in January 1995, when Boris Yeltsin had to decide whether or not to launch his nation's missiles. This was the result of a meteorological rocket launched from Norway being mistaken by Russian air defense for an American submarine launched ballistic missile. Such an event would have been much more dangerous if it occurred during a time of Russo-American tension, such as the Georgian war of August 2008, or if Yeltsin's mental state had been impaired more than usual. Similarly, former CIA analyst Peter Vincent Pry recounts that, in October 1993, during the attempted Russian coup, he and half a dozen other intelligence officers at NORAD headquarters called their families and told them to leave Washington, DC out of fear the Russians might launch an attack (Pry 1999). In addition to a number of other post-Cold War events that had the potential to escalate to a Russian–American crisis, a successful nuclear terrorist attack would have similar possibilities.

Because the Cuban Missile Crisis was the closest the world has come to nuclear war, it is worthwhile studying its evolution. In 1961, over strenuous Soviet objections, America started deploying nuclear-armed Jupiter missiles in Turkey. From our perspective, installing these weapons made sense. They secured NATO's southern flank, helped cement relations with Turkey, and enhanced our nuclear deterrent. The Russians viewed these missiles very differently.

While other factors contributed to Khrushchev's 1962 deployment of similar missiles in Cuba, this disastrous decision started with a nuclear version of tit-for-tat as noted by Khrushchev's speech writer and advisor, Fyodor Burlatsky:

> Khrushchev and [Soviet Defense Minister] R. Malinovsky ... were strolling along the Black Sea coast. Malinovsky pointed out to sea and said that on the other shore in Turkey there was an American nuclear missile base. In a matter of six or seven minutes missiles launched from that base could devastate major centres in the Ukraine and southern Russia.... Khrushchev asked Malinovsky why the Soviet Union should not have the right to do the same as America. Why, for example, should it not deploy missiles in Cuba?
>
> (Burlatsky 1991)

Once the crisis started, it developed a life of its own. George Ball, a member of the White House ExComm,[6] stated that when a group of Kennedy's advisors met years later:

> Much to our own surprise, we reached the unanimous conclusion that, had we determined our course of action within the first forty-eight hours after the missiles were discovered, we would almost certainly have made the wrong decision, responding to the missiles in such a way as to require a forceful Soviet response and thus setting in train a series of reactions and counter-reactions with horrendous consequences.
>
> (Ury 1985)

Douglas Dillon, another member of Kennedy's ExComm, was less concerned and, at a 1987 conference commemorating the crisis' twenty-fifth anniversary stated:

My impression was that military operations looked like they were becoming increasingly necessary.... The pressure was getting too great.... Personally, I disliked the idea of an invasion [of Cuba] ... Nevertheless, the stakes were so high that we thought we might just have to go ahead. Not all of us had detailed information about what would have followed, but we didn't think there was any real risk of a nuclear exchange.

(Blight and Welch 1989)

In contrast to Dillon's belief that some other ExComm members had detailed information about what would have followed an invasion of Cuba, information that later became available showed that none of them had the least idea of what would likely have transpired. Unknown to Kennedy and his ExComm, the Russians had battlefield nuclear weapons in Cuba and came close to giving permission for their use against an American invasion, without further approval from Moscow (Chang and Kornbluh 1998; Blair 1993; Fursenko and Naftali 1997). Not knowing of these weapons, there was strong pressure within the ExComm and from Congress (Fursenko and Naftali 1997) to invade Cuba and remove Castro once and for all.

Another ominous aspect of the crisis was uncovered when key players from both sides met on the fortieth anniversary of the crisis. A Soviet submarine near the quarantine line had been subjected to signaling depth charges, commanding it to surface, which it eventually did. Not until forty years later did Americans learn that this submarine carried a nuclear torpedo and that the Soviet submarine captain, believing he was under attack, had given orders to arm it. Fortunately, the submarine brigade commander was on board, overruled the captain, and defused the threat of a nuclear attack on the American fleet (Blanton 2002).

The critical moment occurred when Soviet ships approached the American blockade. If neither side backed down, war seemed inevitable. Finally, Khrushchev stopped the Soviet ships just short of the blockade. Although Kennedy appeared to win that round of the Cold War, nuclear chicken may not always have a victor. It is a dangerous game, especially when, as in the Cuban Missile Crisis, winning depends on an opponent that has less concern for maintaining political power.[7]

After facing the possibility of World War III, a similar crisis seemed inconceivable post-1962. Unfortunately, at least two events that could have initiated a new scenario similar to the Cuban Missile Crisis have since occurred. In the 1980s, President Reagan was so disturbed by Cuba supplying weapons to a leftist insurgency in El Salvador that he threatened to reimpose a naval blockade of Cuba (LeoGrande 1981). Such an action would have violated one of our key concessions (lifting the blockade) in return for which the Russians removed their Cuban missiles. Had Reagan reimposed the blockade, the Russians might have threatened to redeploy missiles unless the blockade was immediately lifted. Such a reaction was made more likely by the fact that, at that time, Reagan was in the process of deploying Pershing MRBMs (so-called "Euromissiles") in Western Europe. While not as close to the Soviet border as the Turkish Jupiters, the only way the Soviets could match such weapons was with missiles in Cuba.

Currently, the US is in the process of deploying a missile defense in Russia's backyard despite strenuous Russian objections.[8] A possible Russian response would be to threaten deployment of a similar missile defense in Cuba, much as the US Jupiter missile deployment in Turkey was the stimulus for Khrushchev deploying their Cuban missiles (Burlatsky 1991).[9] While these Cuban missiles would be defensive in nature, many Americans would view the missiles as an intolerable security concern. Among other concerns, there would likely be fears that these were offensive weapons disguised as defensive ones. (The Russians have voiced a similar concern over our deployment.)

Another Cold War nuclear near miss was a 1983 NATO exercise code-named "Able Archer." Former CIA Director and current Secretary of Defense Robert M. Gates describes the danger in his memoirs:

> One of the potentially most dangerous episodes of the Cold War was prompted by a NATO command post exercise ... [This] exercise, to practice nuclear release procedures, came at the moment of maximum stress in the U.S.–Soviet relationship described above [the Euromissile deployment, Reagan's Strategic Defense Initiative, and the Soviets shooting down Korean Airlines flight 007]. But it also came against the backdrop of Andropov's seeming fixation on the possibility that the United States was planning a nuclear [first] strike against the Soviet Union.... Our sources claim to have seen documents that betrayed genuine nervousness that such a strike could occur at any time, for example, under cover of an apparently routine military exercise.... According to [KGB defector] Gordievsky, "the KGB concluded [during Able Archer] that American forces ... might even have begun the countdown to nuclear war." ...we in the CIA did not really grasp how alarmed the Soviet leaders might have been until ... our British colleagues issued an assessment in March 1984.
>
> (Gates 1996)

Nuclear proliferation and the specter of nuclear terrorism are creating dangerous, new possibilities for initiating major crises. If an American or Russian city were devastated by an act of nuclear terrorism, the public outcry for immediate, decisive – and possibly disastrous – action would be even stronger than the public outcry during the Kennedy administration when the Cuban missiles first became known to the American public. Fortunately, a likely byproduct of an effort to reduce the threat of full-scale nuclear war would be to augment efforts to reduce the threat of nuclear terrorism, an activity that currently is not proceeding rapidly enough.

The failure rate of nuclear deterrence

A full-scale nuclear war is not the only threat to humanity's continued existence. A large asteroid colliding with the Earth could destroy humanity in the same way it is believed the dinosaurs disappeared 65 million years ago. Such NEO (Near Earth Object) extinction events have a failure rate on the order of one in 100,000,000 per year (Chapman and Morrison 1994), corresponding to a time horizon of approximately 100 million years.

During one century that failure rate corresponds to one chance in a million of the complete destruction of the human species. While that is a small probability, the associated cost is so high – infinite from our perspective – that some might argue that a century is too long a delay before working to reduce the threat. Fortunately, significant threat reduction has recently occurred. Over the last twenty years, NASA's Spaceguard effort is believed to have found all such potentially hazardous large asteroids, and none is predicted to strike Earth within the next century. With a 100-year safety window in place, resolution of later potential impacts can be deferred for a few decades when our technology should be significantly enhanced. Comets also pose a threat and their more eccentric orbits make them harder to catalog, but their lower frequency of Earth impact makes the associated risk acceptable for a limited period of time.

Using similar reasoning, if the failure rate of nuclear deterrence were one in 1,000,000 per year, waiting a decade to reduce the threat might be acceptable, resulting in a one in 100,000 probability of a failure, although good engineering practice[10] might disagree. If the failure rate of deterrence is an order of magnitude higher, one in 100,000 per year, then the risk is increased proportionately and it is difficult to tolerate even a decade's delay in solving the problem.

Considering the next hypothetical failure rate of one in 10,000 per year, the probability of humanity destroying itself during a decade-long effort would be one in 1,000, which is much too large. If the failure rate is 0.1 percent per year,[11] the probability increases to approximately 1 percent over a decade and 10 percent over a century, and delay is clearly unacceptable. At that level of failure rate, a significant reduction would be required within a matter of years.

If the failure rate of nuclear deterrence is closer to 1 percent per year, then anything short of an all-out effort to change course might be considered criminally negligent. Each year of delays in reducing the risk brings with it a 1 percent chance of disaster, and a decade's delay entails roughly a 10 percent chance.[12]

Although the following estimate of the failure rate of nuclear deterrence is preliminary and additional research is warranted, it is hoped that readers will agree that the evidence presented makes it difficult to support an estimate of one in 1,000,000 per year or less, implying that even a decade's delay in starting to solve the problem is intolerable.

While much less accurate than the in-depth studies proposed herein, it is instructive to estimate the failure rate of deterrence due to just one failure mechanism, a Cuban Missile Type Crisis (CMTC). Because it neglects other trigger mechanisms such as a second Russo-Georgian war, command and control malfunctions and nuclear terrorism, this appendix underestimates the threat. This simplified analysis uses the time-invariant model described in footnote 4. It also assumes that the experience of the first fifty years of deterrence can be extended into the future, at least approximately.

The annualized probability of a CMTC resulting in World War III, denoted $\lambda_{CMTC}(t)$, is

$$\lambda_{CMTC} = \lambda_{IE}\, P_1\, P_2\, P_3$$

where λ_{IE} is the annualized probability of an initiating event that could lead to a CMTC, P_1 is the conditional probability that such an initiating event results in a CMTC, P_2 is the conditional probability that the CMTC leads to the use of a nuclear weapon, and P_3 is the conditional probability that the use of a nuclear weapon results in full-scale nuclear war.

As noted above, there have been at least three possible initiating events in the first fifty years of nuclear deterrence: the Turkish missiles in 1962, President Reagan's threat to re-impose a naval blockade of Cuba in the 1980s, and the current deployment of an American missile defense system in Eastern Europe. Taking the average rate of occurrence of these possible initiating events, three in fifty years, results in an estimate $\lambda_{IE} = 0.06$. A higher estimate would result if other crises were included as possible initiating events. Examples include the Berlin crisis of 1961, the Six Day War of 1967, and the Yom Kippur War of 1973, all of which involved at least implied nuclear threats. To temper the possibility of this chapter being interpreted as alarmist, it only considers the first three possible initiating events and therefore uses $\lambda_{IE} = 0.06$.

Because one of the three possible initiating events actually resulted in a CMTC, the empirical probability that a possible initiating event results in a CMTC is $P_1 = 1/3$. Because only the first initiating event led to a full-blown CMTC, it could be argued that society learned from its mistake and $1/3$ is too large an estimate today. But, the fact that the latter two possible initiating events occurred at all is evidence that society did not learn from 1962's near miss, or that it learned the wrong lesson (e.g., if you stand up to the Russians, they will always back down), or that the wrong safety measures were employed. Because these two factors tend to cancel each other and only rough estimates are possible, this chapter uses $P_1 = 1/3$ as reasonable.

P_2, the conditional probability that a CMTC leads to the use of a nuclear weapon, is difficult to estimate because, fortunately, that has never happened. Statements from the participants in the Cuban Missile Crisis[13] support a range of $(0.01, 0.5)$. Because invasion of Cuba was a strong possibility[14] and the participants stated their estimates before the Russian battlefield nuclear weapons were known in the West, this chapter replaces the 1 percent lower bound estimate with 10 percent, resulting in an estimated range of (0.1, 0.5) for P_2. If the actions of all parties with access to nuclear weapons (e.g., the Soviet submarine commander discussed above) are included, an even larger lower limit might be considered.

The last step is to estimate P_3, the conditional probability that the use of a nuclear weapon results in full-scale nuclear war. Again, it is difficult to estimate the probability of this event that has never happened. While Kennedy did not specify what he meant by the crisis ending in war, his evacuation order to the families of White House staff lends some support to the hypothesis that he meant full-scale nuclear war. McNamara's stated fear that he would not live out the week is also consistent with that interpretation. In that case, the upper bound of 0.5 for P_2 is really an upper bound for the product $P_2 P_3$. Again to avoid being interpreted as alarmist, this chapter uses an estimated range (0.1, 0.5) for P_3.

Since conditional probabilities were used, they can be multiplied, yielding an estimated range of (2E-4, 5E-3) for λ_{CMTC}, the failure rate of deterrence based on just this one failure mechanism. The upper limit 5E-3 is within a factor of two of the author's estimate that the failure rate of deterrence from all sources is on the order of 1 percent per year, and even the lower limit is well above the level that any engineering design review would find acceptable.

Because this estimate is based on a simplified, time-invariant model, it does not apply to the current point in time when relations between the US and Russia are better than they were, on average, during the last fifty years. However, that does not invalidate its conclusions. NATO expansion and disparate views on missile defense have strained Russian–American relations and new trigger mechanisms are coming into play – notably nuclear proliferation and terrorism – making it possible that the next fifty years could be even more dangerous than the last.

Furthermore, atypical times have a disproportionate effect on risk. A significant fraction of the total risk during the last fifty years occurred during the thirteen days of the Cuban Missile Crisis – a period that constituted just 0.07 percent of that time period. Because crises produce so much of the overall risk, it is important to look beyond today's relatively benign world and also consider the rare, disruptive times when events tend to unfold much less rationally and predictably.[15]

Next steps

One possible solution toward reducing the risk of a failure of nuclear deterrence would be for prestigious scientific and engineering bodies to undertake serious studies to estimate its failure rate. This would serve three important purposes. First, it would either correct or confirm the beliefs of nuclear optimists (Waltz 1981; Mueller 1989), who argue that fears of a nuclear catastrophe are overblown. Second, assuming the risk is found to warrant such action, the studies could help galvanize public support for change. That is critical because public support is a prerequisite for a change of this magnitude. Third, analyzing the failure rate of nuclear deterrence would identify the most probable failure mechanisms, thereby allowing ameliorative efforts to be focused where they would be most useful in reducing the risk.[16]

Estimating the failure rate of nuclear deterrence has similarities with estimating the failure rate of a nuclear reactor design that has not yet failed. In addition to estimating the failure rate, such a study also identifies the most likely event sequences that result in catastrophic failure. Such a failure is composed of a cascade of small failures, and reasonable estimates are often available for many of the variables (e.g., the failure rate of a cooling pump in a reactor). Because some probabilities are difficult to estimate, the resultant failure rate will be accurate at best to an order of magnitude. But, as shown in the previous section, even an order of magnitude estimate will almost surely suffice for determining whether corrective action is required.

It would be beneficial to have several independent studies both to cross-check one another and to reduce the likelihood that potential failure modes have been overlooked. Another benefit of multiple studies would be increased public awareness.

If the proposed studies show too high a risk, some individuals who grasp that reality will naturally want to jump to a new societal condition in which the nuclear threat is absent, for example by calling for rapid and complete nuclear disarmament, even though such discontinuities are unachievable. Nuclear disarmament is neither the first step nor the last in solving the problem. Because it is not the first, demanding it before earlier steps have laid an appropriate foundation is counterproductive. Most individuals will discount such demands as impossible – which they are in the current environment. Shultz, Perry, Kissinger, and Nunn, while calling for an eventual end to nuclear weapons, recognize this when they state:

> In some respects, the goal of a world free of nuclear weapons is like the top of a very tall mountain. From the vantage point of our troubled world today, we can't even see the top of the mountain, and it is tempting and easy to say we can't get there from here. But the risks from continuing to go down the mountain or standing pat are too real to ignore. We must chart a course to higher ground where the mountaintop becomes more visible.
>
> (Shultz *et al.* 2008)

Like a complex engineering project, formulating a solution to the nuclear threat requires breaking it down into a sequence of manageable steps, but with one major difference. The engineer who designed the Golden Gate Bridge knew it was necessary to construct strong piers at each end before hanging the cables that attached to the piers, and knew, with a high degree of certainty, the environment that the cables would find when they were attached. In contrast, the environment in which the solution to the nuclear threat evolves depends on highly unpredictable factors.

While the intermediate steps in the process must be formulated with due regard for the uncertain environment in which they will be carried out, it does help to try to picture the ultimate state in which survival of the human species is ensured. If the failure rate of nuclear deterrence is on the order of 1 percent per year and it must be reduced below one in 1,000,000 per year, then the world literally needs to become at least 10,000 times safer than it is today *and* not be allowed to revert to anything remotely resembling today's risk level. This last emphasized phrase is crucial because temporarily reducing the risk, without getting society to recognize the long-range goal, would produce a false sense of security that would dampen efforts to solve the problem long before that was appropriate.

Such a false sense of security allowed the inaction of recent years. During the 1980s, when the threat of nuclear war was in sharp focus, public concern helped produce progress that was unattainable in prior decades. But the resultant, friendlier relations between the superpowers reduced public support to the point that we are now facing a renewal of the pushing and prodding that is one of the primary trigger mechanisms for a global war. The Cold War thaw, while welcome, needed to be accompanied by an ongoing commitment even after the immediate threat was significantly reduced.

Making the world 10,000 times safer than at present may sound utopian and infeasible, and until recently it was. But, with approximately 20,000 nuclear weapons in existence today and the ability to build many times that number, the choice is between creating such a world and having no world at all. The international community is challenged to adapt to a sudden change in the environment and, fortunately, adaptability is one of humanity's defining characteristics. Through adaptations of clothing and shelter, humanity has extended its range from a small tropical region to the entire globe, and even walked on the Moon.

Social structures have also been adapted in ways initially thought to be impossible. Abolishing slavery, a laughable idea just 200 years ago, became the law of the land sixty years later. Women's suffrage, which was initially even more unrealistic,[17] also came to pass. Many of the arguments that individuals make today about the impossibility of moving beyond nuclear deterrence were also used as supposed proofs that those earlier changes could never occur. But occur they did.

While conservatism is demanded when designing systems where human lives are at stake, exuberant optimism is a hallmark of successful breakthroughs in the brainstorming phase, which is the position now with respect to ending reliance on nuclear deterrence. "Fulton's Folly" was the first step in supplanting sails with steam. The original proposals to span the Golden Gate were derided as impossible, but a few who were undeterred by conventional wisdom, optimistically persisted and ultimately succeeded. In 1961, when President Kennedy committed the US to putting a man on the Moon and returning him safely to Earth, society did not cry that this violated human nature and should not be considered. Rather, we devoted ourselves to overcoming seemingly insurmountable obstacles and again prevailed. In the same manner, the author hopes society will courageously rise to the unprecedented challenge posed by nuclear weapons, and succeed once more.

Notes

1 For helpful discussions, comments, and suggestions, I wish to thank Drs Duane Steffey and Rose Ray of Exponent, Inc., Prof. Nozer Singpurwalla of George Washington University, Profs Elisabeth Paté-Cornell and David Luenberger of Stanford University, Ms Loretta Rendall (formerly of Stanford), and Dr Richard Lawhern (LTC, USAF Retired).

2 At approximately 100 lb/ft², the density of a human being is about five times that of today's typical automobile traffic. A 2008 Ford Taurus has a density of 40 lb/ft². Inter-car spacing lowers that density by approximately a factor of two, to 20 lb ft², even in bumper-to-bumper traffic.

3 Classified studies may exist, but could not be used in this effort. Unclassified studies that were missed by this search may also exist and, if adequate, could be substituted for some of the proposed studies. However, experts on national defense, nuclear weapons, and risk analysis whom the author consulted as part of that search were unaware of any such studies.

4 This study uses failure rate, rather than the more usual Mean Time To Failure (MTTF). The latter quantity is a good indicator of risk in a time-invariant problem where the failure rate $\lambda(t)$ is a constant λ_0. In that case MTTF = $1/\lambda_0$. For example, it has been estimated that $\lambda_0 = 10^{-8}$ per year for an extinction event due to a large asteroid or comet hitting Earth, and the corresponding MTTF of 100 million years is an equally good indicator of the risk. But when $\lambda(t)$ is time-varying, the term MTTF is technically incorrect since it is no longer a meaningful average. The quantity that can be meaningfully averaged is $\lambda(t)$. In a time-varying problem, such as a failure of nuclear deterrence, a simplified but useful model averages $\lambda(t)$ over a time period and uses its average value λ_{AVG} in a time-invariant approximation to the actual process during that period. Unless otherwise noted, this chapter tacitly uses that time-invariant approximation.

5 Two Democrats and two Republicans, respectively Secretary of State under President Reagan, Secretary of Defense under President Clinton, Secretary of State under Presidents Nixon and Ford as well as National Security Advisor to President Nixon, and former Democratic Chairman of the Senate Armed Services Committee.

6 The Executive Committee of the National Security Council (ExComm) was the group Kennedy created to help him develop strategies to deal with the Cuban Missile Crisis.

7 Kennedy's victory was only apparent because Khrushchev got three key American concessions: lifting of the blockade, a pledge not to invade Cuba, and the removal of the Jupiter missiles in Turkey. Kennedy insisted that the

third concession be kept secret, giving the illusion of an American victory. The 1962 midterm elections occurred soon after the crisis ended and, with Kennedy seen as winning the standoff, the Democratic Party fared significantly better than previously anticipated. In contrast, Khrushchev fell from power two years later, partly due to Russia's humiliation in the Cuban Missile Crisis.

8 When this chapter was originally published in March 2008, elements of the system in Poland and the Czech Republic were of greatest concern to the Russians (Hellman 2008). Since then, a new administration in Washington has delayed those components of the system. While this helped defuse the tension, recent plans to base parts of the system in Romania and Bulgaria have rekindled Russian concerns.

9 Somewhat ominously, after the original version of this chapter was written but before it was published, Russian President Vladimir Putin likened the current American deployment to the Cuban Missile Crisis (Putin 2007). Although he disclaimed that such a crisis would occur in the friendlier climate that currently exists, those good relations are clearly fraying. After this chapter's original publication in March 2008, elements within the Russian military did in fact threaten to deploy nuclear-armed bombers to Cuba as a response (Finn 2008). Air Force Chief of Staff Norton Schwartz responded that such actions would cross "a red line" (Morgan 2008). Fortunately, the Russians later disclaimed the earlier threat, and a crisis was averted (Rodriguez 2008).

10 Engineers design modern nuclear reactors to have catastrophic failure rates less than once per million operating years, and such a failure is far less catastrophic than that of deterrence.

11 The remainder of this chapter provides preliminary evidence for such an estimate.

12 To put these numbers in human terms, a child born today in the United States has an expected lifetime of seventy-eight years. A 0.1 percent per year failure rate would imply roughly a 10 percent chance of that child not living out his or her natural life, and a 1 percent per year failure rate would give worse than even odds. These two rates correspond to expecting deterrence to work for 1,000 and 100 years.

13 Kennedy ordered families of White House staff to either leave Washington or be near a telephone (Burlatsky 1991), providing evidence for his estimate that the crisis could have ended in war as being between one-in-three and even (Blight and Welch 1989). During the height of the crisis, Robert McNamara thought he might not live out the week (McNamara 1986). At the other extreme, ExComm member McGeorge Bundy estimated 1 percent (Blanton 1997).

14 In addition to pressure for an invasion within ExComm, Kennedy was subjected to pressure from Congress (Fursenko and Naftali 1997).

15 Conversely, friendly Russian–American relations reduce the risk. For that reason, and as noted by Putin (2007), the current deployment of a missile defense system in Eastern Europe, by itself, is unlikely to precipitate a crisis. But, if relations continue to deteriorate, deployment without regard for Russia's fears carries significant danger.

16 For example, a preliminary analysis done by the author suggests that the state of relations between the US and Russia is a more important determinant of risk than the number of nuclear weapons. The period 1988–90, when both arsenals were near their peak, presented almost no risk, while short periods of high tension produced almost all of the risk. Improved relations also create more fertile ground for reducing the number of weapons.

17 The early abolitionists included women's suffrage in their platform, but removed it out of fear that it would prolong slavery by decades. In point of fact, the nineteenth Amendment did not pass until fifty-five years after the thirteenth.

Bibliography

Blair, Bruce G. (1993) *The Logic of Accidental Nuclear War*, Washington DC: The Brookings Institution.

Blanton, Thomas (1997) "Annals of blinksmanship," *The Wilson Quarterly*. Available at www.gwu.edu/~nsarchiv/nsa/cuba_mis_cri/annals.htm.

Blanton, Thomas (2002) Interview, "The Cuban Missile Crisis: 40 years later," *The Washington Post Online*, October 16. Available at http://discuss.washingtonpost.com/zforum/02/sp_world_blanton101602.htm.

Blight, James G. and David A. Welch (1989) *On the Brink: Americans and Soviets Reexamine the Cuban Missile Crisis*, New York: Hill and Wang.

Bunn, Matthew (2007) *Guardians at the Gates of Hell*, Doctoral Thesis in Technology, Management and Policy, MIT. Available at http://esd.mit.edu/people/dissertations/bunn_matthew.pdf.

Bunn, Matthew, Anthony Wier, and John P. Holdren (2003) *Controlling Nuclear Warheads and Materials: A Report Card and Action Plan*, Project on Managing the Atom, Belfer Center for Science and International Affairs, John F. Kennedy School of Government, Harvard University. Available at www.nti.org/e_research/cnwm/cnwm.pdf.

Burlatsky, Fedor (1991) *Khrushchev and the First Russian Spring*, New York: Charles Scribner's Sons.

Chang, Laurence and Peter Kornbluh (1998) Introduction to *The Cuban Missile Crisis, 1962: A National Security Archive Documents Reader*, 2nd edn, New York: The New Press.

Chapman, Clark and David Morrison (1994) "Impacts on the Earth by asteroids and comets: assessing the hazard," *Nature* 367: 33–40, 6.

Finn, Peter (2008) "Russian bombers could be deployed to Cuba," *Washington Post*, July 22, p. A10. Available at www.washingtonpost.com/wp-dyn/content/story/2008/07/22/ST2008072200062.html.

Fursenko, Aleksandr and Timothy Naftali (1997) *One Hell of a Gamble*, New York: W.W. Norton & Company.

Gates, Robert (1996) *From the Shadows: The Ultimate Insider's Story of Five Presidents and How They Won the Cold War*, New York: Simon & Schuster.

Hegland, Corine and Greg Webb (2005) "Terrorism: the threat," *National Journal*, April 15. Available at http://nationaljournal.com/about/njweekly/stories/2005/0415nj1.htm.

Hellman, Martin (2008) "Risk analysis of nuclear deterrenece," *The Bent of Tau Beta Pi* 99: 14–22.

LeoGrande, William (1981) "Getting Cuba," *The New York Times*, November 17, Section A, p. 31, column 2. Available at http://american.edu/faculty/leogrande/getting-cuba.htm.

Lugar, Richard (2005) *The Lugar Survey on Proliferation Threats and Responses*, Office of Senator Lugar, Washington, DC, June. Available at http://lugar.senate.gov/reports/NPSurvey.pdf.

McNamara, Robert (1986) *Blundering into Disaster*, New York: Pantheon Books.

Morgan, David (2008) "U.S. general warns against Russian bombers in Cuba," July 22, *Reuters* dispatch. Available at www.reuters.com/article/politicsNews/idUSN2229801920080722.

Mueller, John (1989) *Retreat from Doomsday: The Obsolescence of Major War*, New York: Basic Books.

Office of Technology Assessment (1979) "The effects of nuclear war," available from NTIS, order #PB-296946. Available at www.fas.org/nuke/intro/nuke/7906/.

Pry, Peter (1999) *War Scares*, Praeger, CT: Westport, p. x.

Putin, Vladimir (2007) "Press statement and answers to questions following the 20th Russia–European Union Summit, Marfa, Portugal," October 26. Available at www.kremlin.ru/eng/speeches/2007/10/26/1918_type82914type82915_149706.shtml.

Robock, A., L. Oman, G.L. Stenchikov, O.B. Toon, C. Bardeen, and R.P. Turco (2007) "Climatic consequences of regional nuclear conflicts," *Atmos. Chem. Phys.* 7, 2003–2012. The paper and a discussion are available at www.atmos-chem-phys.net/7/2003/2007/acp-7-2003-2007.pdf and www.cosis.net/members/journals/df/article.php?paper=acpd-6-11817.

Rodriguez, Alex (2008) "Are Russians deploying a hoax," *Chicago Tribune*, July 26.

Shultz, George, William Perry, Henry Kissinger, and Sam Nunn (2007) "A world free of nuclear weapons," *The Wall Street Journal*, January 4, p. A15. Available at http://media.hoover.org/documents/0817948429_3.pdf

Shultz, George, William Perry, Henry Kissinger, and Sam Nunn (2008) "Toward a nuclear-free world," *The Wall Street Journal*, January 15, p. A13. Available at www.hoover.org/pubaffairs/dailyreport/13796412.html.

Toon, O.B., R.P. Turco, A. Robock, C. Bardeen, L. Oman, and G.L. Stenchikov (2007) "Atmospheric effects and societal consequences of regional scale nuclear conflicts and acts of individual nuclear terrorism," *Atmos. Chem. Phys.* 7, 1973–2002. Available at www.atmos-chem-phys.net/7/1973/2007/acp-7-1973-2007.pdf.

Turco, R.P., A.B. Toon, T.P. Ackerman, J.B. Pollack, and C. Sagan (1983) "Nuclear winter: global atmospheric consequences of nuclear war," *Science* 222.

Ury, William (1985) *Beyond the Hotline: How We Can Prevent the Crisis that Might Bring on a Nuclear War*, Boston, MA: Houghton Mifflin Company.

Waltz, Kenneth (1981) "The spread of nuclear weapons: more may be better," *Adelphi Papers*, London: International Institute for Strategic Studies.

Zamoshkin, Yuri (1988) "Nuclear disarmament: ideal and reality," in Anatoly Gromyko and Martin Hellman (eds) *Breakthrough: Emerging New Thinking*, New York: Walker and Company, pp. 209–213. Available at http://www-ee.stanford.edu/%7Ehellman/Breakthrough/book/chapters/zamoshkin.html.

13 Nuclear disarmament

Can risk analysis inform the debate?

Paul Nelson

Introduction

Beginning roughly coincident with the April 5, 2009 speech of President Obama in Prague[1] there has been a widespread resurgence of interest in nuclear disarmament. While most publicly expressed opinions are favorable toward nuclear disarmament, there remains a minority of presumably knowledgeable individuals who have expressed strong reservations.[2] This note seeks to explore the possibility of adapting tools from the field of risk analysis to understand better the apparently strong divergence of opinions among experts who presumably have in common a desire for the best in the future of humankind.

As applied here[3] the fundamental idea of risk analysis is to choose, from among competing alternatives, on the basis of minimizing some disutility function (or "risk function") that depends upon the expected (adverse) consequences and probabilities of occurrence of various threats potentially associated to each of the alternatives. A disutility function is monotonically nondecreasing in either consequence or probability.

In the context of such disutility functions the term "risk" refers to the expected value, over all possible threats, of the consequences. In the simplest case of an alternative having a single threat, with specified values of probability and consequence, the associated risk is simply the product of the two. Disutility functions can be expressed as functions of risk and either of consequence or probability. A disutility function that depends only on risk often is termed "risk neutral," while one that is monotonically increasing or decreasing with consequence for fixed risk is termed respectively as "risk averse" or "risk seeking."[4]

Risk analysis is an instance of "science-based" methods[5] for deciding between various possible alternatives. In the realm of public policy this class of approach is not universally accepted, with rules based on moral intuition often being suggested as an alternative approach to decision making.[6]

The naïve application of risk analysis described above would require evaluations of probability and (expected) consequences of the various threats. A consensus on such evaluations is elusive. This is one oft-encountered objection to the use of risk analysis, and more generally to science-based methods. This especially is true for low-probability high-consequence threats such as nuclear explosions, because (fortunately) there is little empirical basis for assignment of value to either probability or consequence. Nonetheless, the viewpoint adopted in this note is that elements of such evaluations are implicitly inherent in any position on nuclear disarmament, and that risk analysis can make these elements more nearly explicit, thereby serving as a prism through which to view and better understand various widely divergent viewpoints of nuclear disarmament.

The application of risk analysis to nuclear disarmament requires a time-dependent (dynamic) model of the alternatives, rather than the "static" model portrayed above. The model employed in this note, as developed in more detail in the following Section 2, incorporates dynamic effects via specification of "threat profiles," which is to say time-dependent frequencies (probabilities per unit time) of occurrence of the various associated threats. Initially the expected value (over threats and time) of time-discounted consequence is taken as the associated disutility function. Eventually this approach is extended to accommodate the case that one of the threats is considered so dire as to have infinite consequence compared to the others.

In Section 3 we define two threat profiles corresponding respectively to maintenance of the status quo relative to nuclear weapons, and to disarmament at some specified future time, and carry out detailed calculations and comparison of the corresponding disutility functions, for the case of finite consequences. In Section 4 these results are extended to the case of an infinite consequence for nuclear threats. (Alternately, the consequences of conventional conflict are considered *de minimis* relative to those of nuclear events.) Section 5 is devoted to the corresponding developments for two different disutility functions: the "maximum risk rate" disutility function, and the "long-term risk rate" disutility function, both of which are related to arguments that have appeared in the literature.

In all of these cases the mathematical conditions that would imply nuclear disarmament is preferred to the status quo are found to have a degree of commonality. They involve first what we term as a "conventional nondeterrence" proposition, which is an algebraic reflection of the belief that nuclear weapons have little or no deterrent effect on conventional conflict. Second they involve some form of what is termed here as a "benign disarmament" proposition, which is a mathematical representation of the belief that the (two separate discounted expected) consequences in first achieving and second maintaining a global condition of nuclear disarmament are not sufficient to counter that associated with maintaining the nuclear-armed status quo.[7]

The conventional nondeterrence proposition of course occurs only in the cases where the consequences are taken as finite, but it has the same mathematical form in all cases where it does occur. By contrast some form of the benign disarmament proposition appears in all cases, but a total of four different (achievable) algebraic forms of that proposition occur: weak form, gamma form, lambda form and strong form. The weak form is implied by all of the others, and is therefore the easiest to believe. The strong form implies all of the others, and is therefore the most difficult to argue the validity of. (It in fact holds only under very restrictive circumstances.) The gamma and lambda forms are not comparable, except that they are identical if the discount rate is taken as the rate at which nuclear-weapons catastrophes occur.

In Section 6 an extension of these considerations to scenarios involving a continuum of consequences is briefly sketched. Section 7 is devoted to a brief summary, substantially in tabular form, of algebraic forms of the results described in the two preceding paragraphs. This table demonstrates that:

- The strongest case for the status quo arises from taking the disutility function either as discounted expected risk in the limit of arbitrarily large discount rate (always) or as the maximum risk-rate risk function (strong form of benign disarmament), according respectively as the consequences of conventional war are or are not considered commensurate to those of nuclear-weapons catastrophes.
- The strongest case for nuclear disarmament arises from the long-term risk rate disutility function (only the weak form of benign disarmament is required, regardless of whether the consequences of a nuclear-weapons catastrophe are taken as finite or infinite).

Thus conclusions favoring the status quo or disarmament correlate respectively with a bias toward the current generation, or a decision to give generations however far into the future the same weight as those now alive. The concluding Section 8 is an effort to put the results of this work into the broad context of the current discussion of nuclear disarmament.

The basic model

Consider two alternative types of threats (potential untoward events), indexed as $i = 1,2$. Suppose the occurrence of each is governed by a Markov model with (possibly time-dependent) transition rate $\lambda_i(t)$, and with instantaneous recovery.[8] Let C_i be the expected value of the consequences associated to threats of type i. Then the corresponding expected risk, discounted from present time $t = 0$, is

$$R(\lambda_1,\lambda_2) = \int_0^\infty e^{-\gamma t} \left[C_1\lambda_1(t) + C_2\lambda_2(t)\right] dt, \tag{1}$$

where γ is the discount rate.[9]

Given two different "rate profiles," say $(\lambda_1^{(a)}, \lambda_2^{(a)})$ and $(\lambda_1^{(d)}, \lambda_2^{(d)})$ one can in principle select the more desirable as that having the smaller value of the associated time-discounted expected risks,[10]

$$R_a = R\left(\lambda_1^{(a)}, \lambda_2^{(a)}\right) \text{ vs. } R_d = R\left(\lambda_1^{(d)}, \lambda_2^{(d)}\right).$$

This rather naïve depiction masks a number of well-known and widely discussed difficulties that affect any actual implementation of such an approach, such as obtaining an evaluation of consequences, and uncertainty in the frequencies. These matters are especially acute for the high-consequence low-probability threats that motivate the present work, but here we set them aside in order to focus on a different difficulty.

The difficulty of interest here arises when one of the threats, say the second, is assigned the value infinity,[11] $C_2 = \infty$. In such a case then the associated discounted expected risk is also infinite, if only the second component of the rate profile (i.e., λ_2) is not identically zero.[12] If neither $\lambda_2^{(a)}$ nor $\lambda_2^{(d)}$ is identically zero, then both of the corresponding discounted expected risks are infinite, and therefore provide no basis for discrimination between the two rate profiles.[13]

Even though the discounted expected risk provides no basis for discrimination, there is a rational basis. One can reasonably prefer the rate profile that has the largest expected time to "doomsday,"

$$T(\lambda_2) = \int_0^\infty t\lambda_2(t)e^{-\int_0^t \lambda_2(\tau)d\tau}\, dt. \tag{2}$$

In case $T(\lambda_2^{(a)}) = T(\lambda_2^{(d)})$, one could reasonably "break the tie" by choosing the rate profile having the discounted risk with smallest "finite part,"

$$R_1(\lambda_1) = C_1 \int_0^\infty e^{-\gamma t}\lambda_1(t)\, dt.$$

Other alternatives for an algorithm that chooses a preferred rate profile on the basis of the values of $T(\lambda_2)$ and $R_1(\lambda_1)$ also are possible.[14]

Use of nuclear weapons as a limited catastrophe

Under the status quo case of a nuclear-armed world assume the corresponding rate profile satisfies

$$\lambda_1(t) = \tilde{\lambda}_1^{(a)} \text{ and } \lambda_2(t) = \tilde{\lambda}_2^{(a)},$$

where $\lambda_1^{(a)}$ and $\lambda_2^{(a)}$ are nonnegative constants that represent respectively the corresponding status quo frequencies of occurrence of conventional war or a nuclear-weapon catastrophe of some type. The associated discounted risk of nuclear armament is

$$R^{(a)} = R\left(\lambda_1^{(a)}, \lambda_2^{(a)}\right) = \gamma^{-1}\left[C_1 \tilde{\lambda}_1^{(a)} + C_2 \tilde{\lambda}_2^{(a)}\right],$$

where the C_i, $i = 1, 2$, are the (finite) consequences of respectively a conventional war or a nuclear-weapon catastrophe.

We take the rate profiles corresponding to nuclear disarmament as

$$\lambda_1^{(d)}(t) = \begin{cases} \tilde{\lambda}_1^{(a)}, t < t_0, \\ \tilde{\lambda}_1^{(d)}, t > t_0, \end{cases}$$

and

$$\lambda_2^{(d)}(t) = \Lambda_0 \delta(t - t_0) + \begin{cases} \tilde{\lambda}_2^{(a)}, t < t_0, \\ \tilde{\lambda}_2^{(d)}, t > t_0. \end{cases}$$

Here t_0 is some "zero time" at which disarmament is assumed to occur instantaneously,[15] $\lambda_1^{(d)}$ and $\lambda_2^{(d)}$ are nonnegative constants that represent respectively the corresponding frequencies of occurrence of conventional war or a nuclear-weapon catastrophe during a state of worldwide nuclear disarmament, δ is the Dirac delta function, and Λ_0 is the expected number of nuclear-weapon catastrophes that occur "at"[16] the disarmament time t_0. The corresponding time-discounted expected risk of nuclear disarmament is

$$R^{(d)} = R\left(\lambda_1^{(d)}, \lambda_2^{(d)}\right) =$$
$$\gamma^{-1}\left\{\left[C_1 \tilde{\lambda}_1^{(d)} + C_2 \tilde{\lambda}_2^{(d)}\right]\left(1 - e^{-\gamma t_0}\right) + \left[C_1 \tilde{\lambda}_1^{(d)} + C_2 \tilde{\lambda}_2^{(d)}\right]e^{-\gamma t_0}\right\} + C_2 \Lambda_0 e^{-\gamma t_0}.$$

Risk analysis then dictates that disarmament is the preferred course of action if $R^{(a)} > R^{(d)}$, while retaining nuclear arms is indicated if the opposing inequality holds. A bit of algebra reveals that this is equivalent to rationally choosing disarmament or armament according respectively as

$$\gamma^{-1}\left[C_1 \tilde{\lambda}_1^{(a)} + C_2 \tilde{\lambda}_2^{(a)}\right] > \gamma^{-1}\left[C_1 \tilde{\lambda}_1^{(d)} + C_2 \tilde{\lambda}_2^{(d)}\right] + \Lambda_0 C_2 \qquad (3)$$

or the reverse inequality holds.

The various terms in (3) have simple interpretations. The term on the left is the discounted expected risk of the status quo, as calculated at the contemplated time of disarmament (t_0). The first term on the right has the same interpretation, except for maintenance of disarmament rather than the status quo. The last term on the right is the "instantaneous" risk of attaining disarmament, also as evaluated at the proposed time of disarmament.

This simple criterion seems to permit illustration of many of the arguments advanced in favor of nuclear disarmament, and many against. The most straightforward arguments in favor of nuclear disarmament seem more or less to involve two distinct propositions:

1   The *conventional nondeterrence* proposition[17] that the risk per unit time of conventional war is no less with nuclear arms than without, so that

$$C_1 \tilde{\lambda}_1^{(a)} \geq C_1 \tilde{\lambda}_1^{(d)}, \tag{4}$$

and (3) is assured if

$$\gamma^{-1} \tilde{\lambda}_2^{(a)} > \gamma^{-1} \tilde{\lambda}_2^{(d)} + \Lambda_0. \tag{5}$$

2   The *benign disarmament* proposition that the rate of nuclear-weapon catastrophes under nuclear disarmament and the expected number of nuclear-weapon catastrophes at disarmament are (or can be made) so small, relative to the rate of such catastrophes while some states legally possess nuclear weapons, that (5) certainly holds.

In the following (5) will be termed as the *gamma form* of benign disarmament, whenever necessary to distinguish it from other versions of a benign disarmament proposition, which have different algebraic representations, but similar interpretations.

Both of the immediately preceding propositions can be questioned, and have been. For example the idea has been offered (Brown 2007–2008) that nuclear disarmament will tend to increase the frequency of conventional wars (i.e., $\lambda_1^{(d)} > \lambda_1^{(a)}$), which negates (4). The question of the impact of nuclear arms on the frequency of conventional wars has been discussed empirically, seminally by Kugler (1984), who concluded as follows "... there is no evidence that nuclear weapons have added stability to the relation between the three nuclear giants. The terror created by nuclear devastation cannot, in sum, be directly linked to the preservation of peace."

This conclusion seems to support conventional nondeterrence, but more recent empirical work, as exemplified by many of the contributions to this volume, seem in some measure to challenge that conclusion; cf. especially Rauchhaus (this book), as summarized in Note 17. To exemplify this, note the following from the prefatory Chapter 1 to this volume, by Erik Gartzke, Matthew Kroenig and Robert Rauchhaus: "nuclear weapons on average and across a broad variety of indicators enhance the security and diplomatic influence of their possessors"; and, in their summary of the contribution by Michael Horowitz (Chapter 9) "nuclear weapons improve the strategic position of their possessor. The longer a state possesses nuclear weapons, the less likely it is to become involved in disputes." See also the first two of these authors, in their preface to the April 2009 issue of the *Journal of Conflict Resolution* that contained initial versions of many of these contributions, summarized as follows:

> The second set of articles considers the consequences of nuclear proliferation. Taken together, they find that nuclear weapons do not affect the frequency of conflict, but they do affect the timing, duration, severity, and outcome of conflict. These articles provide considerable support for the argument that nuclear weapons enhance the security and diplomatic power of their possessors. Nuclear weapon states are neither more nor less conflict prone, but their conflicts are shorter and less intense, and they tend to emerge victorious from them. Furthermore, the authors find that nuclear powers enjoy enhanced international bargaining power.

While these conclusions are not diametrically opposed to that of Kugler quoted above, they are substantially different in tone, and seem not supportive of the general concept of conventional nondeterrence. Taken together the two different conclusions suggest that while nuclear disarmament might not increase the frequency of conventional war, it might increase the consequences, and thus the associated (discounted expected) risk, which is really what is at issue in the proposition of conventional nondeterrence. The conclusions of Gartzke, Kroenig and Rauchhaus also perhaps indicate why it might be difficult for the current nuclear-armed states to forgo those weapons. Even though these empirical results might not be conclusive regarding validity of conventional nondeterrence, they arguably should be better known among those prone to qualitative discussion of such matters, if only to temper claims that might someday be subject to empirical validation.

If anything the benign disarmament proposition has been the subject of even greater critical scrutiny. It requires both that the expected number of nuclear-weapon catastrophes during nuclear disarmament be less than the discounted expected number occurring during an infinite period of nuclear armament,

$$\Lambda_0 < \gamma^{-1}\tilde{\lambda}_2^{(a)} \tag{6}$$

and that the rate at which nuclear-weapon catastrophes occur under nuclear disarmament be less than that at which they occur while nuclear armed,[18]

$$\tilde{\lambda}_2^{(d)} < \tilde{\lambda}_2^{(a)}. \tag{7}$$

Both of these inequalities can be questioned, and have been.

The inequality (6) is contrary to the classical theory of Kenneth Waltz (1981) to the (loose) effect that the more widely nuclear weapons are spread among and within states the more effectively they will deter nuclear warfare (i.e., the smaller $\lambda_2^{(a)}$ will be).[19] The recent tendency is to discount this theory,[20] and argue that (6) holds more now than in the past because terrorists are much more likely to use nuclear weapons than states, as the latter are more subject to deterrence by threat of counterattack.

Yet another reason the Waltzian theory often is minimized in the (usually tacit) context of (6) is the perceived large value of $\lambda_2^{(a)}$ associated with the possibility of an unintentional nuclear detonation. Any discussion of "accidental launches," as for many of the issues discussed here, tends to be contentious if for no other reason than lack of availability of empirical data, at least that are accessible to the public.[21] For example, Iklé (2009a) offers "the fact that nuclear weapons have not been used for sixty-four years" as reason for "hope." This could be taken as a suggestion that $\lambda_2^{(a)}$ is small, and thus as nonsupportive of benign disarmament. Blechman (2009) counters this with (among other things) the observation that "cases of near uses of nuclear weapons during the Cold War are well known."

If a perfect state of nuclear disarmament could be achieved, then one would have $0 = \lambda_2^{(d)} < \lambda_2^{(a)}$, so that the inequality (7) certainly would be attained. The concern associated with attaining that inequality is the difficulty of detecting and countering efforts to cheat on a disarmament regime. The associated difficulty lies in both the technical challenge of detecting small amounts of nuclear materials that might be either created by an entirely clandestine facility or diverted from a legitimate facility, and the enforcement challenge of having the international community formulate an effective response if such an effort were detected. This difficulty is exacerbated by the fact that any such effort at "breakout" would create precisely a situation (small number of nuclear weapons in the hands of a single state) under which the Waltzian theory already referenced above would predict maximum temptation to use employ nuclear weapons. These considerations have been reinforced by recent events, and mandate that one not naively assume $\lambda_2^{(d)} = 0$. Chyba (2008) notes that nuclear disarmament could have effects contrary to (7),[22] for example through tacitly encouraging states currently dependent upon US nuclear deterrence to develop their own deterrence.

Perkovich and Acton (2008) very forthrightly acknowledge the difficulties inherent in achieving each of (6) and (7), or more generally benign disarmament. Their objective is not to cast doubt on the ability to attain benign disarmament, but rather to focus upon the steps that might be taken in order to attain it. Somewhat interestingly, although they seem to acknowledge that of the two challenges indicated in the preceding paragraph the foremost is the enforcement challenge, the bulk of their discussion seems focused upon the perhaps more tractable – albeit far from easy – technical challenge of detecting illegal attempts to acquire nuclear weapons.

There is not, and cannot be, any significant empirical evidence regarding the benign disarmament proposition, because nuclear disarmament has never really been tried (as opposed to discussed). Thus it may be, as Blechman (2009) suggests, nonsensical to believe the 64 years of disuse of nuclear weapons while in a nuclear-armed regime provides evidence that the rate of nuclear-weapon catastrophes under such a regime is small. However, there is *no* empirical evidence the corresponding probabilities for achieving, or failure rates for remaining in, a nuclear-disarmed state (while nuclear weapons are known to be feasible) are smaller, because there is no prior experience of either.

In the limits $\gamma \to 0$ and $\gamma \to \infty$, the benign disarmament proposition becomes simply (7) or $\Lambda_0 < 0$ respectively. That is, in the case that one values future lives equally with current ones the benign disarmament proposition requires only the easy belief that nuclear-weapon catastrophes will be less frequent if nuclear arms are abolished than if they are not;[23] i.e., the consequences of "going to" (as opposed to "being at") a state of disarmament are negligible. For this reason we term (7) as the *weak form* of the benign disarmament proposition. On the other hand, in the alternative case that one values current certain lives sufficiently more highly than uncertain future lives (i.e., $\gamma \to \infty$), the benign disarmament proposition can *never* hold, because Λ_0 can never be negative. Thus a belief in benign disarmament seems to correlate with a higher value accorded to future generations.

If both the conventional nondeterrence and benign disarmament propositions are false, then nuclear disarmament is not indicated (i.e., the inequality (3) does not hold). It is conceivable that nuclear disarmament could be considered as indicated in the presence of only one of these propositions. Such an argument is most likely to be encountered in the context of an assertion, most likely tacit, that the potential consequences of a nuclear-weapon catastrophe are so much greater than those of a conventional war (i.e., $C_2 \gg C_1$) that the benign disarmament proposition alone is sufficient to assure desirability of nuclear disarmament, even without the conventional nondeterrence proposition.

We shall not consider this argument in detail, as in the following section we consider it in the even stronger form of this argument that is associated with the evaluation $C_2 = \infty$. Here we simply note there is some room to question the proposition that $C_2 \gg C_1$. Posner (2004: 71–72) estimates that about 150 million deaths could be directly occasioned by 1000 Hiroshima-sized bombs, as compared to the 40–50 million deaths in World War II. As horrific as either of these events certainly would be, the numbers are not indicative of an orders-of-magnitude difference between the consequences of conventional and nuclear warfare. This would be even more the case if the nuclear threat were expanded to include terrorist-caused events of even improvised nuclear explosives, because the probable lack of technological prowess among such parties will tend to make their nuclear devices less destructive.[24] Such considerations notwith-standing, no less a person than former Secretary of Defense William Perry (2007) has stated that "the greatest danger today is that a terror group will detonate a nuclear bomb in one of our cities." Hellman (2008; also Chapter 12 of this volume) appears to advocate a disaggregation of the various types of nuclear threats.

Nuclear weapons as a global catastrophe

The discussion of the preceding section contains elements of a rational trade-off study between risks of conventional war versus some type of threat of nuclear-weapon catastrophe, and between the zero-time risk of nuclear-weapon catastrophe as opposed to the long-term risk associated with indefinite retention of nuclear arsenals. But there seem to be voices in the discussion of nuclear disarmament that simply do not brook discussion of any possible merit attaching to retaining nuclear arsenals even one second longer.[25] Here we explore the possibility that this viewpoint of nuclear disarmament as a moral imperative that trumps all contrary indications can be understood in the context of expected risk theory by assigning the evaluation $C_2 = \infty$ to the consequence of a nuclear-weapon catastrophe, in the manner discussed above for the abstract two-threat model underlying (1).[26]

Before proceeding to this exploration it is appropriate to discuss whether there is a basis for the evaluation $C_2 = \infty$, on a scale such that this corresponds to a doomsday threat, as previously discussed. Such a discussion is particularly indicated by the preceding indication of estimates that even a nuclear exchange of 1000 Hiroshima-sized weapons would cause about 150 million deaths. While such an event certainly would be horrific – much more so than for any possible threat emanating directly from an act of "nuclear terrorism" – Posner (2004: 71) notes that is about 2.5 percent of the world's population, and thus is well short of being a dooms-day event.

On the other hand, the total number of nuclear weapons in nuclear arsenals across the world has been recently estimated (Borger 2009) at greater than 20,000. Further, some of those are thermonuclear weapons, and thus have destructive capacity far exceeding that employed so effectively at Hiroshima. Posner (2004: 74) indicates that it "is less certain ... the human race would survive ... an all-out war with hydrogen bombs," which he suggests "could produce consequences similar to that of a major aster-oid collision."[27] Further one can certainly envision even a nuclear incident that is relatively minor, on the scale being discussed here, as breaking the "nuclear taboo" that has been theorized,[28] and thereby unleashing an arms race that could lead to stockpiles of nuclear weapons in multiple sovereign states that dwarf those existing today. These possibilities certainly suggest it is not totally irrational to assign the value infinity to the consequences of even a minimally destructive nuclear-weapon catastrophe. Nonetheless there remains strong dissent to the danger, even the significance, of nuclear weapons, as exemplified by the recent work of John Mueller (2009).

Now consider nuclear-armed and nuclear-disarmed rate profiles exactly as above. For the status quo nuclear-armed case the expected time to first use is then

$$T^{(a)} = T(\lambda_2^{(a)}) = \int_0^\infty t\tilde{\lambda}_2^{(a)} \exp\left(-\tilde{\lambda}_2^{(a)}t\right) dt = \frac{1}{\tilde{\lambda}_2^{(a)}}.$$

Similarly

$$T^{(d)} = T(\lambda_2^{(d)}) = \int_0^{t_0} t\tilde{\lambda}_2^{(a)} e^{-\tilde{\lambda}_2^{(a)}t} dt + \Lambda_0 t_0 e^{-\tilde{\lambda}_2^{(a)}t_0} + \int_{t_0}^\infty t\tilde{\lambda}_2^{(d)}\left(1-\Lambda_0\right)e^{-\left(\tilde{\lambda}_2^{(a)}t_0 + \tilde{\lambda}_2^{(d)}(t-t_0)\right)} dt =$$

$$-t_0 e^{-\tilde{\lambda}_2^{(a)}t_0} + \frac{1}{\tilde{\lambda}_2^{(a)}}\left(1-e^{-\tilde{\lambda}_2^{(a)}t_0}\right) + \Lambda_0 t_0 e^{-\tilde{\lambda}_2^{(a)}t_0} + \left(t_0 + \frac{1}{\tilde{\lambda}_2^{(d)}}\right)e^{-\tilde{\lambda}_2^{(a)}t_0}.$$

is the expected time to nuclear-weapon catastrophe under the disarmament profile. Disarmament at time t_0 is therefore indicated if

$$t_0 + \frac{1}{\tilde{\lambda}_2^{(a)}} < \Lambda_0 t_0 + \left(1-\Lambda_0\right)\left(t_0 + \frac{1}{\tilde{\lambda}_2^{(d)}}\right). \tag{8}$$

The criterion (8) for nuclear disarmament (at time t_0) has a simple interpretation. The quantity on the left (right) is the expected time of first nuclear-weapon catastrophe, given that time t_0 is reached without nuclear-weapon catastrophe and that disarmament never occurs (respectively, occurs at time t_0). Further the apparent dependence on the specific time of disarmament is illusory. The various occurrences of t_0 cancel algebraically, and the criterion (8) simplifies into

$$\frac{1}{\tilde{\lambda}_2^{(a)}} < \frac{1-\Lambda_0}{\tilde{\lambda}_2^{(d)}}. \tag{9}$$

Thus if the three parameters in (9) were independent of time, then disarmament would either be desirable now or never. Of course this assumption of constancy with time does not comport with reality, because these parameters depend upon both technological capabilities and institutional relations between states within the international system, and both of these are highly dynamic.

The criterion (9) also has a ready interpretation. The left- and right-hand sides are the amounts by which the expected time of first nuclear-weapons catastrophe exceeds any given disarmament time t_0, under the respective rate profiles of a nuclear-armed world and nuclear disarmament, given that such a catastrophe does not occur prior to t_0. Comparing these obviously is equivalent to comparing the expected times of first use, because the probabilities that such a catastrophe occurs prior to t_0 are the same under the two profiles, and therefore so are the respective probabilities of nonoccurrence.

Qualitative arguments regarding the magnitude of the three parameters in (9) already have been extensively discussed above, and need not be repeated here. This inequality can be considered an alternative form of the (gamma form of the) benign disarmament proposition (5), and even a simpler version in that the ethically troubling discount rate does not appear. Note that if λ in (5) were replaced by $\lambda_2^{(d)}$, the result would be identical to (9); for that reason we term (9) as the *lambda form* of benign disarmament. This form implies the weak form (7).

Alternative risk functions

One could reasonably seek to minimize risk functions other than the discounted expected risk (1). One such example is the maximum risk-rate risk function

$$R_{\max}\left(\lambda_1,\lambda_2\right)=\max_{0\le t<\infty}\left\{C_1\lambda_1(t)+C_2\lambda_2(t)\right\}.$$

As applied to the status quo and disarmament profiles considered above, with finite consequences, this criterion always would select the status quo, provided only that C_2 and Λ_0 are positive. (Because under the disarmament profile the maximum risk rate is infinite, at the time of disarmament.) Thus under this criterion, and in this case, it is necessary to accept both $\Lambda_0 = 0$ and the weak form, (7), of benign disarmament, in order to conclude that it is not acceptable to maintain the status quo indefinitely. We term this combination as the *strong form* of the benign disarmament proposition, in note of the fact that it implies all forms previously encountered in this note.

On the other hand, if C_2 is infinite, and neither of the rates of occurrence of nuclear-weapon catastrophes are almost everywhere zero, then the maximum risk rate is infinite for both profiles, so fails to discriminate. In this case the philosophically kindred criterion would seem to be minimization of the maximum risk rate for nuclear catastrophe,

$$T_{\max}\left(\lambda_2\right)=\max_{0\le t<\infty}\lambda_2(t).$$

Again this maximum risk rate is infinite for the disarmament rate profile (provided Λ_0 is positive), but finite for the status quo. Similarly one therefore concludes that the status quo either is preferable or equivalent, unless the same strong form of the benign disarmament proposition holds.

Thus the maximum risk-rate risk function seems to favor maintaining indefinitely the status quo circumstances of nuclear armament. This criterion suggests that the societal objective should be to minimize the risk (from nuclear arms or the absence thereof) that any generation will ever face. In that respect it is similar to the "maximizing the worst possible outcome" theory of justice that has been proposed as a basis for equity or morality, in a variety of contexts (e.g., Rawls 1971). Becker (1982) has applied this "maximin principle"[29] to the type of intergenerational equity issues that necessarily underlie the issue of nuclear disarmament.

Yet another alternative objective that can be considered is that of minimizing the long-term risk rate,

$$R_\infty\left(\lambda_1,\lambda_2\right)=\lim_{t\to\infty}\left\{C_1\lambda_1(t)+C_2\lambda_2(t)\right\}, \tag{10}$$

with preference going to profiles that achieve a minimal asymptotic risk rate sooner rather than later. In the case of finite consequences this always leads to the choice of immediate disarmament, provided only that

$$C_1\lambda_1^{(a)}+C_2\lambda_2^{(a)}>C_1\lambda_1^{(d)}+C_2\lambda_2^{(d)}.$$

This is the earlier criterion (3), except that under the present long-term risk-rate risk function the risk at time of disarmament is completely discounted. It therefore leads to the same form (4) of the conventional non-deterrence proposition, but the weak form (7) of the benign disarmament proposition.

If the consequence of a nuclear-weapon catastrophe is taken as infinite, then both the status quo and disarmament profiles have infinite long-term disutilities. In this case the logical extension of this criterion seems to be to prefer that having the smaller value of the long-term risk rate,

$$T_\infty\left(\lambda_2\right)=\lim_{t\to\infty}\lambda_2(t).$$

If ties again are broken by a preference for profiles leading soonest to this asymptotic minimal rate, then immediate disarmament is the preferred course of action, provided only that the benign disarmament proposition holds in the weak form (7).

Thus the long-term risk-rate risk function (10) seems to favor immediate disarmament. The author is unaware of any prior work explicitly considering such risk functions. Yet they would seem to be a reasonable consequence of a world view to the effect that whatever problems the current generation created, it is up to that generation to solve, as opposed to indefinite postponement of the difficulties attendant thereunto. There seems decidedly to be more than a little of that world view within the current discussion of matters such as nuclear disarmament and climate change.

Neither of the two alternative risk functions considered in this section requires consideration of the ethically troublesome discount factor. Nonetheless the maximum risk-rate risk function allows current generations to defer indefinitely the difficult task of nuclear disarmament, while the long-term risk-rate risk function puts the entire burden of shouldering the risk of nuclear disarmament upon the current generation, which of course increases the attendant implicit risk to future generations. Thus not explicitly allowing for a discount factor seems only to camouflage the issue of intergenerational equity, not to eliminate it.

Multiple types of threats

Of course one never really has the luxury of considering only two types of threats. Here we briefly illustrate the extension of the preceding considerations to the opposing extreme of a continuum of types of threats, as summarized by their associated consequences and risk rates. The associated expected discounted risk is

$$R(\lambda) = \int_0^\infty \int_0^\infty e^{-\gamma t} C\lambda(C,t)dCdt, \tag{11}$$

where the consequence C takes on a continuum of values, and $\lambda(C,t)$ now is "risk-rate density," denominated as events per unit time and consequence "at" time t and consequence C.

In this setting infinite time-discounted risks can arise in a variety of ways. However the appropriate generalization of the matters discussed above seems to be consideration of a risk of the form

$$R(\lambda) = \int_0^\infty \int_0^\infty e^{-\gamma t} C\lambda(C,t)dCdt + \infty \int_0^\infty e^{-\gamma t}\lambda_\infty(t)dt, \tag{12}$$

where $\lambda_\infty(t)$ is the (time-varying) rate of occurrence of events of infinite consequence. If $\lambda_\infty(t)$ is nonnegative and not almost surely zero, then the generalized risk denominated by (12) is infinite, regardless of its "finite part" (11). Nonetheless one can in principle distinguish between rate profiles based on the expected time to first event of infinite consequence, which now will be exactly the same as (2), except with λ_2 replaced by λ_∞.

Traditionally such globally catastrophic threats are dealt with by attempting to ensure the rate of occurrence from some threat associated to human actions is associated with a rate no larger than believed associated with natural threats (e.g., collision with an asteroid). Few such efforts seem to have been undertaken in the context of threats associated to nuclear weapons, but Hellman (2008; Chapter 12 of this volume) is one notable exception.

Summary

See Table 13.I for a summary of the versions of the "conventional nondeterrence" and "benign disarmament" propositions that are relevant to the various risk functions and associated parametric values considered in the present work. Here the various versions of benign disarmament have been placed in the unifying form

$$\tilde{\lambda}_2^{(a)} > \tilde{\lambda}_2^{(d)} + w\Lambda_0,$$

where w is the corresponding weight ($0 \leq w \leq \infty$) associated to the risk of achieving (as opposed to maintaining) a disarmament regime.

Conclusion

Risk analysis seems unlikely to dissuade those who have an established position, in either direction, on the advisability of nuclear disarmament. Even if one accepts the premise that such "science-based" methods are applicable,[30] there is simply too little evidence regarding rates of occurrence, and too many possible rational choices of risk function, to permit persuasive arguments either way. Nonetheless the methodology as applied in this note reveals two key issues that seem to contain the essential underlying propositions: "conventional nondeterrence" and "benign disarmament." Other things being equal, a belief in the benign disarmament proposition comes more easily the more nearly one gives the welfare of distant future generations nearly the same weight as that for the current generation and its immediate descendants (for example, via a lower discount rate).

Whether we have yet reached the point that either of these propositions is firmly established – in any of their various forms presented here – is a debatable proposition, albeit that debate seems unlikely to be advanced by suggesting those on the opposing side are purveying "nonsense." On the other hand, the work of Perkovich and Acton (2008) appears to be a concession by two proponents of nuclear disarmament that the conditions to validate the benign disarmament proposition do not yet exist, along with a call for concrete steps intended to bring that day closer.[31] Perhaps that notable work should be matched by a serious effort by doubters of nuclear disarmament to delineate the circumstances that would adequately resolve those doubts.

Finally, one view of the present work is as an exploration of the extent to which allowance for infinite consequences permits deontological justifications for disarmament to be formally incorporated into consequentialist models having the international community as decision maker. While some success is achieved, it ultimately appears likely that a full consideration of deontological justifications for disarmament will require models in

Table 13.1 Versions of the conventional nondeterrence and benign disarmament propositions appropriate to various risk functions and associated parametric values

	finite C_i, $i = 1,2$		$C_2 = \infty$
	conventional nondeterrence	*benign disarmament*	*benign disarmament*
discounted expected risk, $0 < \gamma < \infty$ (γ = discount rate)	(4)	gamma form, $w = \gamma$	lambda form, $w = \lambda_2^{(a)}$
discounted expected risk, $\gamma \to \infty$	(4)	impossible form, $\lim_{w\to\infty} \lim_{\Lambda_0\to 0}$	lambda form, $w = \lambda_2^{(a)}$
discounted expected risk, $\gamma \to 0$	(4)	weak form, $w = 0$	lambda form, $w = \lambda_2^{(a)}$
maximum risk rate	(4)	strong form, $\lim_{w\to\infty} \lim_{\Lambda_0\to 0+}$	strong form, $\lim_{w\to\infty} \lim_{\Lambda_0\to 0+}$
long term	(4)	weak form, $w = 0$	weak form, $w = 0$

which individual sovereign states are the agents of decision, and therefore will require models with at least some of the elements of game theory.

One could contemplate extensions of the current work in directions other than the approach to multiple types of threats that is outlined in Section 6 above. One arguably important such extension might contemplate two levels of nuclear threat e.g., single terrorist events versus full-out state-to-state exchanges. Rationally such consideration would tend to reduce the risk associated with achieving or maintaining nuclear disarmament. On the other hand it does seem somewhat less than compelling to argue for nuclear disarmament on the basis that it would trade the risk of high-consequence nuclear exchanges, which currently seem perceived to have low probability, for a higher probability of more nuclear events having more limited consequences.

Acknowledgements

This material is based upon work supported by the Department of Energy, National Nuclear Security Administration under Grant DE-FG52–06NA27606, entitled "Support for the Nuclear Security Science and Policy Institute, Texas Engineering Experiment Station at Texas A&M University." Any opinions, findings, and conclusions or recommendations expressed in this publication are those of the author and do not necessarily reflect the views of the US Department of Energy, National Nuclear Security Administration. Thanks are due to Dr Kevin T. Nelson for introducing the author to the elements of deontological theories of ethics. Comments and suggestions by Professors Martin Hellman, Matthew Kroenig and Robert Rauchhaus were most helpful. Any errors or misinterpretations are of course the sole responsibility of the author.

Notes

1 The most relevant passage in this respect is: "…today, I state clearly and with conviction America's commitment to seek the peace and security of a world without nuclear weapons." But then a cautionary note immediately follows: "This goal will not be reached quickly – perhaps not in my lifetime. It will take patience and persistence. But now we, too, must ignore the voices who tell us that the world cannot change." See Obama (2009) for the entire text.

2 There have been many recent discussions of the pros and cons of nuclear disarmament. This note was much motivated by a recent article by Fred C. Iklé (2009a), and an ensuing exchange of views (Kampelman 2009; Blechman 2009; Iklé 2009b). Even the official US presentation to the 2010 Review Conference of the Treaty on the Non-Proliferation of Nuclear Weapons contains artfully constructed hedges in its commitments to nuclear disarmament; cf. Clinton (2010). Some examples of the cited hedging, with emphasis added:

> I represent a President and a country committed to a vision of a world without nuclear weapons and to taking the concrete steps necessary that will *help us* get there…. We also recognize our responsibility as a nuclear

weapons state to *move toward* disarmament.... Our commitment to the NPT begins with our efforts *to reduce* the role and number of nuclear weapons in our own arsenal.... President Obama has made clear *the United States will retain a nuclear deterrent for as long as nuclear weapons exist....*

3 Hellman (2008, 2009) also has applied risk analysis to nuclear disarmament, albeit in an apparently somewhat different form from that employed here. See Footnote 26 for discussion of fitting the approach of Hellman into the framework of this note.

4 The respective terms "consequence neutral," "consequence averse" and "probability averse" seem more descriptive.

5 For example, Byrd and Cothern (2000). See Short (1984) for a general critique of science-based methodologies.

6 This dialog can be viewed as a reflection of the dichotomy in the field of ethics between consequentialists, who desire to make decisions based on "the state of affairs they bring about" (Alexander and Moore 2007), and deontologists who prefer judgments otherwise based (e.g., "intent"). Deontological theories often include a preference for inaction ("omission bias," defined as "people are more willing to cause harmful outcomes through their omissions than through their acts"; cf. Baron 1993). See Parfit (1984, esp. Section 10) for objections to consequentialism; one objection often voiced is the difficulty of predicting the state of affairs that might be brought about by a particular action. Nye (1986) is a classical treatise on the ethics of nuclear arms. He principally justifies and employs consequential theories of ethics, but discusses deontological theories under the term "ethics of virtue."

7 The term "benign disarmament" is intended to provoke the thought that it is at least conceivable there are nuclear-related risks associated with either achieving or maintaining a state of universal nuclear disarmament. Difficulty in achieving disarmament without adverse consequences can be (for example) associated with a perceived greater temptation to use (or threaten to use) nuclear weapons when the total number of such weapons is small. Difficulty in maintenance could stem from either imperfection in detecting clandestine facilities, or the short "latency" of states that do not technically have a nuclear arsenal, but do maintain the ability to (re)construct one on short notice. A definitive judgment about the desirability of nuclear disarmament necessarily invokes some judgment about the magnitude of these risks, even if only through implicitly assuming they are negligible.

8 The model employed here has some similarity to that of Hellman (2008). Specifically both employ failure (transition) rates as fundamental parameters, and both envision the international community as the agent making decisions.

9 Jason Matheny (2007: esp. Section 5) argues that many of the traditional justifications for discounting are inapplicable to the "doomsday scenarios" (i.e., to the "benefits of delaying human extinction") that are integral to the present note. The use of discounting here is justified by the rather more technical and pragmatic desire to have some hope of finite time-integrated risks for the apparently reasonable case that the two components of the rate profile are positive constants and the time horizon is infinite. Other alternatives are to impose some arbitrary finite time horizon, or to require all rate-profile components to approach zero asymptotically sufficiently strongly so as to be (finitely) integrable. Among these alternatives the use of discounting seems the least arbitrary, although in practice the choice of a discount rate – which is unnecessary for present purposes – is quite troublesome. Richard Posner (2004: 17) seems to argue for the alternative of a finite time horizon that is somewhere between thousands and millions of years. See also Chapter 3 of

Posner (2004) for a more detailed discussion of some of the alternatives mentioned above, and extensive references to further discussion in the literature. See Gollier and Weitzmann (2009) for an argument, in the context of climate change, favoring use of a discount rate that varies with time in a particular manner.

10 Alternatives to the time-discounted expected risk as the functional to be minimized are briefly considered in Section 5.

11 As already mentioned in the Introduction, valuation of consequences always is a subjective (and therefore troublesome) aspect of risk analysis. When the value infinity is assigned a threat is, if anything, even more troublesome, as will be exemplified in the ensuing discussion of nuclear disarmament. The one class of threats that most indubitably deserves such assignment is the doomsday events that have as their physical consequence the extinction of the human species. See Matheny (2007: esp. p. 1342) for a very explicit argument (attributed to Derek Parfit) that there is a bigger qualitative difference between the doomsday of a nuclear war killing 100 percent of the world's existing population and a nuclear war killing 99 percent than there is between the latter ("merely"?) catastrophic event and peace. Consideration of events with infinite consequences is by no means unique to the present work. For example such matters have been explicitly considered by Manson (1999, 2002), under the term "catastrophe argument." He regards this argument as an extreme instance of the "precautionary principle" that has found its way into some legal arguments (especially relating to environmental matters, including concerns related to climate change; cf. Gollier 2001), and sees "a strong similarity between the Catastrophe Argument and one of the most famous arguments of philosophy: Pascal's Wager." See Bostrom and Ćirković (2008) for discussion by various authors on both specific possible doomsday scenarios (under the term "global catastrophic risks"), methodologies for response and a variety of related perspectives. Note also that at sufficiently large consequences the assumption of instantaneous recovery that underlies the present model necessarily becomes invalid. This is certainly the case for doomsday events. Recovery from events having infinite consequences must be considered as impossible, which is the most extreme form of recovery that is not instantaneous.

12 Technically, is not almost everywhere zero on $[0, \infty)$.

13 The subtlety associated with the mathematical indeterminacy arising when λ_2 is identically zero also will not be considered here.

14 The temptation to "tradeoff" between T and R_1 is especially strong if both $T(a)$ and $T(d)$ are large compared to a typical human lifespan, their difference is small compared to the uncertainty in either, and the larger of $R_1^{(a)}$, $R_1^{(d)}$ is associated with a (now time-dependent) consequence that is largest in the near-term. The current discussion of possible actions attendant to the threat of anthropogenic global warming seems such an example. Tonn (2009) suggests criteria for acceptability that might be modifiable into decision criteria, but seem to presuppose existence of some accepted time (year 1 billion) for human extinction.

15 No serious thinker about this matter expects nuclear disarmament to occur within a duration that is short on the scale of human lifetimes. Indeed some of the deeper thinkers among the advocates of nuclear disarmament (e.g., Perkovich and Acton 2008) suggest a great deal of preparatory work will be required to develop the necessary underlying international agreements, and the corollary technological means necessary to enforce those agreement. That is essentially because as the total number of nuclear weapons becomes smaller, the temptation a state faces to use its few remaining weapons to accomplish its purposes is perceived to become larger; therefore when the total number becomes

very small it is necessary to be able to detect small numbers of (illicitly held) weapons, and possibly even more critically to respond appropriately. The assumption here of an instantaneously occurring disarmament merely simplifies the final results, and therefore the subsequent discussion, while retaining (via the factor Λ_0) the key possibility that there may be a nonzero risk associated with the *step* of disarming, as opposed to the *state of being* disarmed.

16 More precisely, this term is intended to capture the various difficulties previously discussed in Notes 7 and 15.

17 This proposition is very close to being the negation of the *nuclear peace hypothesis* formulated by Rauchhaus (this book). The results of that reference suggest that in a state of nuclear disarmament conventional conflicts will be less frequent, hence $\lambda_1^{(a)} > \lambda_1^{(d)}$, especially if the nuclear-armed state is asymmetric. The results also suggest conflicts might tend to higher consequences under disarmament. The latter suggests that one should allow for different values of the consequences of conventional conflict, according as to whether the world is nuclear armed or not. This generalization is not carried forward notationally in the current work, but could be simply by inserting appropriate superscripts on occurrences of C_1 as indicated by those on the adjacent occurrence of λ_1.

18 One could reasonably assign different values to the consequences of a nuclear-weapons catastrophe under the status quo and under a disarmament regime, for example under the reasonable hypothesis that the expected consequence of a nuclear-weapons catastrophe during the status quo is larger than that under legal disarmament. That generalization will not be pursued here; but see Note 27.

19 The concern is that in the process of achieving disarmament it will be necessary to go through circumstances in which only a few states – perhaps only one – have nuclear weapons, which are precisely the circumstances in which the Waltz theory predicts the greatest likelihood of use.

20 For example Barnaby (2009: 10) brushes such considerations aside with a reference to "some misplaced faith in the continued value of nuclear deterrence." Somewhat similarly, if a bit more vehemently, Blechman (2009) suggests it is typical that "opponents of elimination: hyperventilate about the potential risks of a world without nuclear weapons, but shut your eyes to the rising risks of the real, proliferating world in which we live today." Nonetheless the theory of Waltz is supported by the circumstances underlying the only use of nuclear weapons, and some find additional support for it in "the serious consideration at high levels of the U.S government of preventive nuclear war" (Rosenberg 1983) during the early 1950s.

21 But Sagan (1993) is an excellent publicly available discussion of such matters. However it employs the methodology of case studies, so is largely anecdotal and qualitative. Approaches for quantifying such information are not readily apparent; however, see Hellman (2008) for an initial effort in that regard, as well as an appeal for a more substantive effort in that direction.

22 The fundamental point of Chyba's note is to call for a careful study of "what impact changes in the U.S. nuclear posture would have on nuclear weapons proliferation."

23 This assumption raises the question of exactly what it means to "abolish nuclear arms." Under some conceivable definitions of disarmament, some states could remain in a position to reconstitute a nuclear arsenal in a very short time. Perkovich and Acton (2008) correctly devote a great deal of attention to this "latency problem," particularly how to assure current non-weapons states that the weapon states have not retained a short latency, without enhancing the weapons-production capability of those non-weapons states. The seriousness of the latency problem is enhanced by the rather large number of non-weapons

states that currently are thought to have latencies in the order of months. Some seem to think the objective of the Iranian nuclear program is to enroll Iran in this club. See Juzaitis and McLaughlin (2008) for a more extensive discussion of the latency problem, and references to the extensive related literature.

24 Cf. Mueller 2009: esp. Chapter 15, for elaboration on these thoughts.

25 This reflects what Jervis (2009) has termed "a general stance that put(s) nuclear weapons into a uniquely dangerous and indeed immoral category. The preceding (Note 20) quotations from Blechman (2009) and Barnaby (2009) seem to suggest they are among the many informed by this viewpoint.

26 One reasonably could permit a different value for C_2 under the status quo and under disarmament, and assign the former a finite value and the latter an infinite value. Such an assignment of values would always dictate immediate disarmament as the only acceptable course of action (i.e., the only alternative having a finite value of the associated risk function). This seems very close to the viewpoint adopted by Hellman (2008, 2009).

27 One scenario widely discussed in the 1980s was that of "nuclear winter," under which an extensive nuclear exchange would cloud the atmosphere with "debris that would shut down photosynthesis, maybe for years" (Posner 2004: 72). See Turco *et al.* (1983) for a summary of a once widely noted study of this possibility. Robock and Toon (2010) have very recently reconsidered this concern, in the context of an India–Pakistan nuclear-weapons exchange.

28 Cf. Tannenwald (2007).

29 In the present context this would be a "minimax" principle, because disutility is considered rather than utility.

30 See Stirling and Scones (2009) for a summary of discussions regarding applicability of science-based risk assessment, in quite a different context from nuclear disarmament.

31 In the context of the simple two-alternative model that was the focus of this note, those steps would constitute changes to the probability of nuclear-weapon catastrophe during nuclear disarmament and to the rate of nuclear-weapon catastrophe during nuclear disarmament so as to move toward satisfying the gamma form (5) or the lambda form (9) of the benign disarmament proposition.

References

Alexander, L. and M. Moore (2007) "Deontological ethics," *Stanford Encyclopedia of Philosophy*, November 21. Available at http://plato.stanford.edu/entries/ethics-deontological/ (accessed December 29, 2009).

Barnaby, F. (2009) *The Nuclear Renaissance: Nuclear Weapons Proliferation and Terrorism*, London: Institute for Public Policy Research, March.

Baron, J. (1993) Morality and Rational Choice.

Becker, R.A. (1982) "Intergenerational equity: the capital-environment trade-off," *Journal of Environmental Economics and Management* 9: 165–185.

Blechman, B.M. (2009) *National Interest Online*, November 5. Available at www.nationalinterest.org/Article.aspx?id=22436#Kampelmanan (accessed November 8, 2009).

Borger, J. (2009) "Nuclear weapons: how many are there in 2009 and who has them?," *Guardian*. Available at www.guardian.co.uk/news/datablog/2009/sep/06/nuclear-weapons-world-us-north-korea-russia-iran (accessed May 18, 2010).

Bostrom, N. and M. Ćirković (2008) *Global Catastrophic Risks*, New York: Oxford University Press.

Brown, H. (2007–2008) "New nuclear realities," *Washington Quarterly*, winter.

Byrd, D.M. and C.R. Cothern (2000) *Introduction to Risk Analysis: A Systematic Approach to Science-based Decision Making*, Rockville, MD: Government Institutes.

Chyba, C.F. (2008) "Time for a systematic analysis: U.S. nuclear weapons and nuclear proliferation," *Arms Control Today*, December. Available at www.armscontrol.org/act/2008_12/Chyba (accessed December 30, 2009).

Clinton, H.R. (2010) *Statement by Secretary of State Hillary Rodham Clinton to the 2010 Review Conference of the Treaty on the Non-Proliferation of Nuclear Weapons*. Available at www.un.org/en/conf/npt/2010/statements/pdf/usa_en.pdf (accessed May 16, 2010).

Gollier, C. (2001) "Should we beware of the precautionary principle?," *Economic Policy* 16: 301–328.

Gollier, C. and M.L. Weitzmann (2009) "How should the distant future be discounted when discount rates are uncertain?," Preprint, November 7. Available at http://idei.fr/doc/by/gollier/discounting_long_term.pdf (accessed November 30, 2009).

Hellman, M.E. (2008) "Risk analysis of nuclear deterrence," *The Bent of Tau Beta Pi*, spring, pp. 14–22.

Hellman, M.E. (2009) "Soaring, cryptography and nuclear weapons," *Defusing the Nuclear Threat*. Available at http://nuclearrisk.org/soaring_article.php (accessed May 22, 2010).

Iklé, F.C. (2009a) "Nuclear abolition, a reverie," *National Interest*, September/October, 103: 4–7.

Iklé, F.C. (2009b) *National Interest Online*, November 5. Available at www.nationalinterest.org/Article.aspx?id=22436#Kampelmanan (accessed November 8, 2009).

Jervis, R. (2009) "Or: how I learned to stop worrying," *National Interest*, November/December, 104: 73–85. (Review of Mueller 2009).

Juzaitis, R.J. and J.E. McLaughlin (2008) "Challenges of verification and compliance within a state of universal latency," in G.P. Shultz, S.P. Andreasen, S.D. Drell and J.E. Goodby (eds) *Reykjavik Revisited: Steps toward a World Free of Nuclear Weapons*, Stanford, CA: Hoover Institution Press, pp. 159–203.

Kampelman, M.M. (2009) *National Interest Online*, November 5. Available at www.nationalinterest.org/Article.aspx?id=22436#Kampelmanan (accessed November 8, 2009).

Kugler, J. (1984) "Terror without deterrence: reassessing the role of nuclear weapons," *Journal of Conflict Resolution* 28: 470–506.

Manson, N.A. (1999) "The precautionary principle, the catastrophe argument and Pascal's wager," *Ends and Means*, 4. Available at www.abdn.ac.uk/philosophy/endsandmeans/vol. 4no1/index.shtml (accessed November 30, 2009).

Manson, N.A. (2002) "Formulating the precautionary principle," *Environmental Ethics* 24: 263–274.

Matheny, J.G. (2007) "Reducing the risk of human extinction," *Risk Analysis* 27: 1335–1344.

Mueller, J. (2009) *Atomic Obsession: Nuclear Alarmism from Hiroshima to Al-Qaeda*, New York: Oxford University Press.

Nye, J.S. (1986) *Nuclear Ethics*, New York: The Free Press (Macmillan).

Obama, B. (2009) *President Obama's Visit to Prague, April 4–5, 2009*. Available at http://prague.usembassy.gov/obama.html (accessed May 15, 2010).

Parfit, D. (1984) *Reasons and Persons*, New York: Oxford University Press.

Perkovich, G. and J.M. Acton (2008) *Abolishing Nuclear Weapons*, New York: Routledge.

Perry, W.J. (2007) "Testimony before the House Armed Services Committee, Strategic Forces Subcommittee," July 18. Available at www.nuclearsecurityproject. org/atf/cf/%7B1FCE2821-C31C-4560-BEC1-BB4BB58B54D9%7D/PERRY_TES-TIMONY071807.PDF (accessed November 11, 2009).

Posner, R.A. (2004) *Catastrophe: Risk and Response*, Oxford: Oxford University Press.

Rauchhaus, R. (This Book) "Evaluating the nuclear peace hypothesis: a quantitative approach."

Rawls, J. (1971) *A Theory of Justice*, Cambridge, MA: Harvard University Press.

Robock, A. and O.B. Toon (2010) "Local nuclear war, global suffering," *Scientific American* 302: 74–81.

Rosenberg, D.A. (1983) "The origins of overkill: nuclear weapons and American strategy, 1945–1960," *International Security* 7: 3–71.

Sagan, S. (1993) *The Limits of Safety: Organizations, Accidents, and Nuclear Weapons*, Princeton, NJ: University Press.

Short, J.F. (1984) "The social fabric at risk: toward the social transformation of risk analysis," *American Sociological Review* 49: 711–725.

Stirling, A.C. and I. Scones (2009) "From risk assessment to knowledge mapping: science, precaution, and participation in disease ecology," *Ecology and Society* 14: 14. Available at www.ecologyandsociety.org/vol. 14/iss2/art14/ (accessed December 5, 2009).

Tannenwald, N. (2007) *The Nuclear Taboo: The United States and the Non-use of Nuclear Weapons since 1945*, Cambridge: Cambridge University Press.

Turco, R.P. *et al.* (1983) "Nuclear winter: global consequences of multiple nuclear explosions," *Science* 222: 1283–1292.

Waltz, K.N. (1981) "The spread of nuclear weapons: more may be better," *Adelphi Paper no. 171*, London: International Institute for Strategic Studies.

14 The perils of predicting proliferation

Alexander H. Montgomery and Scott D. Sagan

The systematic study of the causes and consequences of the spread of nuclear weapons is at an early stage of development. The essays in this special volume signal a renaissance of interest in quantitative empirical studies of nuclear proliferation, an approach that was mostly dormant after early attempts at predicting proliferation in the 1980s (Kegley 1980; Meyer 1984). A new generation of political scientists, however, has recently taken up the charge of assessing the causes and consequences of the spread of nuclear weapons (Singh and Way 2004; Asal and Beardsley 2007; Jo and Gartzke 2007; Fuhrmann 2008). The authors in this book continue that important effort by creating new datasets to widen the scope of inquiry, using new and innovative methodologies, and testing a variety of theories to explain how and why states acquire nuclear weapons and to predict the effects of the spread of nuclear weapons on the likelihood and outcome of military conflicts.

This chapter reviews and critiques this second wave of quantitative literature on nuclear weapons proliferation. These new studies provide an important counterpart to the mainstream proliferation literature, which generally focused on in-depth individual case studies or small-n cross-case variation rather than attempting to test hypotheses in a systematic way across all states over long periods of time. The various chapters in this book demonstrate the advances made since early attempts at quantifying the causes and effects of proliferation, significantly improving our understanding of these phenomena. This new research on the causes of proliferation usefully focuses on the attempts that states have made to regulate proliferation (Brown; Erickson and Way; Benson and Wen), the causes of nuclear assistance from other countries (Kroenig) and estimates the effects of that assistance on nuclear weapons acquisition (Fuhrmann). They demonstrate convincingly that the NPT regime has been influenced by the degree of delegation of responsibilities given to the International Atomic Energy Agency by member states and that the NPT membership has been encouraged by conventional arms transfers to countries who sign the treaty. The new work has usefully identified how the NPT regime can create incentives for potential proliferators to make their nuclear programs ambiguous; has shown that general nuclear technology assistance is affected by patterns of enmity and alliance; and has demonstrated that receiving sensitive nuclear assistance (help with uranium enrichment, plutonium reprocessing, or nuclear weapon design) significantly increases the chances of acquiring nuclear weapons.

The chapters in this book also offer innovative insights into the nuclear optimism/pessimism debate (Sagan and Waltz 2003): does the proliferation of nuclear weapons make states more cautious and reduce the likelihood of war, or does it lead to nuclear-armed states seeking additional gains, experiencing accidents, and risking catastrophe? The findings are mixed. States that have nuclear weapons are more likely to initiate Militarized Interstate Disputes (MIDs), and this tendency increases with experience (Horowitz; Gartzke and Jo). However, one chapter argues that the increase in MID initiation is due to endogeneity (Gartzke and Jo), while another demonstrates that as states become more experienced with nuclear weapons, they become less likely to reciprocate military challenges or have their challenges reciprocated (Horowitz). The first two findings bolster the pessimism argument, while the latter two support the nuclear optimists' position. Theoretical extensions of the optimism/pessimism debate to nuclear disarmament seem to come down more heavily on the pessimists' position; two risk analyses chapters conclude that the risk of nuclear war is much higher than what should be considered acceptable by several orders of magnitude (Hellman), and that if future generations are considered, the benefits of disarmament due to a decreased likelihood of nuclear war outweigh the benefits of decreased conventional conflict (Nelson).

These chapters also offer insights into the effects of nuclear weapons on the outcomes of crises and conflicts. Here the authors find that dyads where only one state has nuclear weapons are more likely to experience all levels of force in MIDs, with the nuclear state winning more often and achieving a settlement more quickly in ICB (International Crisis Behavior) crises. Dyads where both have nuclear weapons are much less likely to experience the maximum level of force (War) in a MID, but are no more or less likely to win or to experience a shorter conflict in an ICB crisis (Asal and Beardsley; Rauchhaus). Thus, nuclear states seem to have incentives to be belligerent against both nuclear and non-nuclear states (which helps the pessimists' case), refraining from escalating to war only against other nuclear states (which helps the optimists' case).

The authors in this volume also usefully raise new and intriguing questions about nuclear proliferation that will need to be addressed in subsequent research. To what degree is public support for nuclear weapons necessary for a state to acquire a bomb or expand the size of its arsenal (Wirtz)? How should we evaluate the risks of nuclear war that exist despite deterrent effects from the maintenance of existing nuclear arsenals compared to the risks of nuclear use that could remain in a world without nuclear weapons, given that the former nuclear states might cheat or could rearm quickly in a crisis (Hellman and Nelson)? Are "side-payments" really necessary to get states to join the NPT, and other nuclear non-proliferation efforts, and if so, what are the broader unintended security consequences of giving governments side-payments such as civilian nuclear power technology or conventional armaments (Kroenig; Fuhrmann; Erickson and Way; also see Fuhrmann 2009).

These new studies of nuclear proliferation, however, despite using the most up-to-date datasets and techniques available, do not solve five serious problems that have also plagued earlier quantitative studies of nuclear proliferation. First, it is inherently difficult to have accurate coding of the dependent variables regarding whether states are exploring, pursuing, or have acquired nuclear weapons: some governments' civilian nuclear power programs reflect internal ambivalence about whether the state should pursue a bomb option, and the intense secrecy surrounding weapons programs has meant that earlier published datasets left out many cases of covert programs or the creation of "hedging" options, a problem likely to remain persistent for the foreseeable future. While the chapters in this book use a common dataset for nuclear weapons possession, increasing the comparability of results across this set of chapters, their use of a common dataset decreases the robustness of their findings because, as we will demonstrate, other reasonable codings on when states initiated or completed nuclear weapons programs produce very different results. Second, the coding rules used for existing independent variables in nuclear proliferation analyses are also problematic. Too often quantitative researchers measure what is easily measured rather than find ways of accurately capturing the concepts that our theories suggest should be important. Regarding the causes of proliferation, for example, important factors that have been discussed in historical case studies of proliferation such as leaders' psychology, bureaucratic power and military autonomy, and the desire for prestige are often excluded altogether or measured poorly in statistical studies. The problem also exists for the quantitative literature on the consequences of proliferation, in which the relevant independent variable is assumed to be a state's first nuclear weapon, despite a long-standing debate in the historical literature about whether states are deterred by virtual nuclear weapons, a single bomb, a small arsenal, or a second-strike nuclear capability. Instead of developing new datasets to test for the effects of such factors, the literature too often conveniently uses proxy variables based on pre-existing datasets, making the studies particularly vulnerable to the "looking for the key under the lamppost" charge, as we will demonstrate below. Third, methodologies and datasets need to be tightly coupled to the empirical questions under investigation. Including a broader set of states in a dataset without proper controls allows states that cannot have any influence on processes or outcomes to skew results, as we will also demonstrate. Fourth, some quantitative proliferation pieces have findings that are trivial, providing us with insights that we already knew or at least believed to be true. While it is always valuable to provide tests of commonly held views to see if they are indeed logically consistent or empirically accurate, many of the new studies have failed to produce counter-intuitive insights, which would add more significantly to our understanding of proliferation. Fifth, and finally, statistical findings can ignore or gloss over individual data points that are crucially important for policymaking and wider scholarly debates. We note in this chapter, for example, that the 1999 Kargil war between India and Pakistan – the only undisputed case of a war between nuclear-armed states – is simply ignored by these studies, as it does not appear as a separate dispute in the MID database, and is not listed as a war in the COW or ICB databases.[1]

It is valuable in this light to compare the study of nuclear proliferation to the study of the "democratic peace" in international relations. In both of these research areas, the scholarship has slowly expanded from qualitative theoretical and historical inquiry to include more game-theoretic approaches and systematic quantitative testing of hypotheses. The development path of research in the democratic peace has progressed significantly in the past two decades in ways that are instructive. This literature began with deductions based on political theory and limited historical evidence that suggested that democratic states rarely, if ever, go to war against each other (Kant 1917 [1795]; Doyle 1986). Vigorous debates about the democratic peace theory emerged in political science starting in the 1980s, and a progressive research program of many scholars using multiple methods eventually produced a significant, though by no means complete, degree of consensus about how and why democracies differ from non-democracies in their foreign policy and international security behavior (Lake 1992; Maoz and Russett 1993; Fearon 1994; Mansfield and Snyder 1995; Elman 1997; Schultz 1998; Russett and Oneal 2001; Reiter and Stam 2002; Gartzke 2007). Our understanding of the effect of democracy on the likelihood and conduct of war has been significantly enhanced by both rich historical and rigorous quantitative scholarship on the democratic peace. We hope that this book and our critique can lead scholars to emulate the democratic peace literature, produce more multi-method research, and contribute further to improved understanding of the causes and consequences of nuclear proliferation.

In the first section, we review the earlier historical case-study and quantitative research on nuclear proliferation and compare its findings with the more recent quantitative literature on proliferation. Here we note improvements as well as lingering problems with the coding, methodology, and empirical findings. Having established the context for the remainder of the essay, we proceed by discussing the accomplishments and remaining problems in the essays in this book. Here we analyze all four topics discussed in the volume: (1) the supply and regulation of nuclear technologies; (2) the effects of the spread of nuclear weapons on the likelihood of conflict; (3) the effects of nuclear weapons on the consequences of crises and conflict; and (4) risk assessments of nuclear disarmament. We conclude with a discussion of the implications for future research and policy debates about how to deal with nuclear proliferation.

Previous studies of proliferation

Different studies of the causes of nuclear proliferation divide incentives and actors in different ways. In a widely cited analysis of nuclear non-proliferation, Scott Sagan compares three models: security, domestic politics, and norms. The first focuses on military security motivations; the second emphasizes domestic political or bureaucratic coalitions that form to support or oppose nuclear weapons; and the third focuses on norms and prestige considerations that encourage acquisition of nuclear weapons (Sagan 1996/97; 1999). He finds strongest support for the security model, though he argues that domestic interests and prestige concerns are "sufficient, but not necessary" conditions for proliferation in a limited number of cases. Scholarly debate continued about how to weigh these different motivations for proliferation, with some realists arguing for the singular importance of security motivations (Mearsheimer 1990; Frankel 1993) and other scholars focusing on the constraints stemming from domestic economic interests or normative opposition against nuclear weapons (Solingen 1994; Katzenstein 1996; Solingen 1998, 2007). Suzette Grillot, Alexander Montgomery, and others have, in contrast, argued that role conceptions and identity play a major role in producing interests in starting and ending nuclear weapons programs (Chafetz *et al.* 1996; Grillot and Long 2000; Montgomery 2005). Additional studies include cognitive and psychological factors that may contribute to decisions to acquire the bomb (Ogilvie-White 1996: 51–53; Hymans 2006).

Much of this historical case-study work, however, examined only cases in which governments had developed nuclear arsenals. In order to overcome the limits of research that "selects on the dependent variable," scholars have also focused on specific cases in which governments chose to get rid of nuclear weapons or forgo the option before they had acquired an arsenal. T.V. Paul, for example, discusses the effects of power and norms, and finds that states' security positions are primarily responsible for their willingness to accept nuclear disarmament (Paul 2000). Some valuable case-study-focused accounts include all of these factors without seeking to analytically separate them into individual accounts (Reiss 1988; Reiss and Litwak 1994; Reiss 1995; Levite 2002/2003; Campbell *et al.* 2004).

The first wave of quantitative studies sought to rectify the weaknesses of limited case studies. Charles Kegley's original quantitative study attempted to measure twenty different national and systemic measures for proliferation in a scattershot fashion, finding significant variation in three categories: threat perception, achievement of international status, and domestic satisfaction. His study is unique among quantitative studies in that it attempts to measure directly a state's social role-conception in the international system rather than using a proxy for overall status (Kegley 1980). Stephen Meyer divided incentives into three categories: political power–prestige, military–security, and domestic politics, then measured these using fifteen indicators. He found that fear of a well-armed rival, pariah status, and desires for regional preeminence were the most important proliferation incentives, but that alliances with a nuclear power, membership in the NPT, and fear of pre-emptive strikes helped to dissuade states (Meyer 1984: 44–74).

In the second, more recent, wave of proliferation studies, Sonali Singh and Christopher Way divide incentives between internal (regime type and liberalization-related incentives) and external (security threats and guarantees) determinants, while Dong-Joon Jo and Erik Gartzke divide their incentives along Sagan's three models (Singh and Way 2004: 862–865; Jo and Gartzke 2007: 168–171). Singh and Way find strong support for both enduring rivalries and militarized disputes on the external side, and limited support for economic openness and liberalization as domestic political factors. Jo and Gartzke find considerable support for status-driven motives and somewhat less support for domestic political and international security motives, with an especially interesting finding that rivalry with a nuclear weapons state is negatively correlated with a government's proliferation decisions.

These studies also include supply-side factors that may limit proliferation, a subject that is given less attention in the qualitative literature. Meyer developed a set of fourteen factors that contribute towards a domestic capability, divided into factors that influence mining and processing of nuclear materials, construction and operation of nuclear facilities, and weapons fabrication; a subset of his indicators were extended through 1992 by Jo and Gartzke. Singh and Way also analyze technological determinants using more general indicators, which are coded into three variables: GDP, a general industrial threshold, and specific industrial capabilities (Meyer 1984: Appendix B; Singh and Way 2004: 867–869; Jo and Gartzke 2006: 5–7). All three models find consistently strong support for supply-side factors as major determinants of proliferation.

The meaning of proliferation

An important insight from these studies and their descendants is that more gradations exist regarding the status of a state than simply being nuclear or non-nuclear. The contribution of the quantitative proliferation literature here is important, but because quantitative studies of nuclear proliferation by Meyer, Singh and Way, and Jo and Gartzke have adopted different methods of coding nuclear activity, they are difficult to compare. Meyer simply coded whether a state had made a "decision" to seek nuclear weapons or not, and did not examine whether states succeeded or not. Jo and Gartzke operationalized this variable as a measure of whether the "highest decision maker in a given state authorized [or ended] a nuclear weapons program" for official programs or the year in which "nuclear activities increase noticeably" for clandestine programs. They also added acquisition data for the dates on which "each state was ready to quickly assemble nuclear components into nuclear weapons." Singh and Way measure nuclear status along a continuum with four "degrees of nuclear-ness": no interest, exploration, pursuit, and assembly. The first degree is simply no interest in nuclear weapons. The second degree is exploration, which is "demonstrated by political authorization to explore the option or by linking research to defense agencies that would oversee any potential weapons development." To qualify as pursuing nuclear weapons, states must take steps such as "a political decision by cabinet-level officials, move-ment toward weaponization, or development of single-use, dedicated tech-nology." Finally, both Jo and Gartzke and Singh and Way code states as having fully acquired weapons if they either test or possess a "functional nuclear weapon" (Meyer 1984: Appendix A; Singh and Way 2004: 866–867; Jo and Gartzke 2006: 1–2). The codings from Meyer, Singh and Way, and Jo and Gartzke are compared in Table 14.1.

The key idea that nuclear proliferation should not be viewed as a single end-state is valuable. Proliferation is a process by which countries move closer to or away from different thresholds toward developing the bomb. Countries will not necessarily stay solidly in one state of "nuclear latency" or another, as internal and external conditions that fuel or suppress pro-liferation may change over time. Governments do not actually need to "decide" to "go nuclear" until the moment that they test a nuclear device; even then, the decision to develop a deliverable weapon or declare nuclear weapons status can be independent of a nuclear test. The case of India is instructive; the 1974 test device was declared a "Peaceful Nuclear Explo-sive" and India did not claim nuclear weapons state status, nor did they weaponize for a number of years. In 1998, the New Delhi government made two decisions: the first was to test; the second was to declare their status as a nuclear weapons state.

The ambiguity of nuclear proliferation – and consequently, the pitfalls of selecting one coding system or another – becomes apparent when com-paring different coding systems for exploration, pursuit, and acquisition of nuclear weapons. Even the dates of the programs for the initial five nuclear states (N5) are debatable; Meyer has China starting in 1957, while Jo and Gartzke start in 1956 and Singh and Way have China jumping directly to pursuit without actually exploring nuclear weapons first in 1955. After the N5, the data quickly becomes quite murky. Dates for Israeli acquisition range from 1966 to 1972 (with Meyer not even coding Israel as deciding to seek nuclear weapons until 1968). The new datasets diverge significantly from each other regarding nuclear weapons programs: Libya,

Switzerland, Australia, Algeria, and Taiwan's second attempt to develop nuclear weapons in the 1980s do not appear in Jo and Gartzke; Iran's suspected first attempt in the 1970s is excluded from Singh and Way, as are Germany and Japan's World War II programs. Moreover, neither of these datasets include the now well-known cases of attempted nuclear weapons acquisition as Germany (Müller 2003) and Italy (Nuti 1993) in 1958 or Egypt's exploration of proliferation options in the 1960s (Rublee 2006, 2009).[2]

Complete agreement between Jo and Gartzke/Singh and Way should not be expected, given their different definitions of nuclear programs and different coding rules. Moreover, variation in coding rules and datasets can be good in social science research, if the coding rules and decisions are matched up with the appropriate theories and if the similarity in results demonstrate the robustness of the findings. That is not the case in these studies, unfortunately, as we will demonstrate. Part of the problem is the ambiguity of the coding rules, as both sets of authors include deliberately broad language in order to capture more ambiguous cases: Jo and Gartzke code a program for states other than the N5 when nuclear activities "increase noticeably," by which they explicitly include such potentially benign activities as purchasing a nuclear reactor or constructing a uranium mill; Singh and Way, meanwhile, allow for coding of ambiguous cases of pursuit simply on "movement towards weaponization." Yet under Jo and Gartzke's broader definition any number of states – including Japan and Germany – could be coded as having a nuclear program.

Meanwhile, strictly applying Singh and Way's definition of exploration yields a number of additional suspect cases not in their dataset, including Norway and Japan. The governments of both of these countries at one point commissioned studies examining the costs and benefits of acquiring nuclear weapons, and both resoundingly concluded that the costs exceeded the benefits. These cases would better be defined as examples of good governance and thorough policy review, rather than covert exploration of nuclear weapons acquisition (Forland 1997; Levite 2002/2003; Campbell and Sunohara 2004; Mackby and Slocombe 2004).

As can be seen in Table 14.1, Meyer's dataset, coded to end in 1980, missed many programs – including Pakistan, Brazil, Iraq, Iran, Argentina, Sweden, Yugoslavia, Taiwan, and Romania – primarily due to lack of data at the time. While we presumably have somewhat more confidence in some of these estimates now, new information could change these historical or current proliferation datasets at any point. For example, how should we code Syria, in light of the evidence that a covert nuclear facility was destroyed in 2007 (Albright and Brannan 2008)? Even if we had reliable and complete information on states' nuclear programs, however, the ambiguity about states' programs is not confined to our perceptions and estimates; it is inherent in the phenomenon itself. States do not necessarily make decisions "to go nuclear"; often, the meanings of the programs are

Table 14.1 Nuclear status coding schemes

	Meyer (1942–1980)	Jo and Gartzke (1941–2002)		Singh and Way (1945–2000)		
	Decide	Programs	Possession	Explore	Pursue	Acquire
Acquisition						
USA	1942–	1942–	1945–	*	*	1945–
Russia	1942–	1943–	1949–	*	1945–	1949–
United Kingdom	1947–	1941–	1952–	1945–	1947–	1952–
France	1956–	1954–	1960–	1946–	1954–	1960–
China	1957–	1956–	1964–	1955–	1955–	1964–
Israel	1968–	1955–	1966–	1949–	1958–	1972–
India(1)	1964–1966	1964–1965		1954–	1964–	1974–1974
India(2)	1972–	1972–	1988–	1975–	1980–	1988–
South Africa	1975–	1971–1990	1979–1991	1969–	1974–	1979–1993
Pakistan		1972–	1987–	1972–	1972–	1990–
Pursuit						
Korea, South	1972–1975	1971–1975		1959–	1970–1978	
Libya				1970–	1970–	
Brazil		1978–1990		1953–	1978–1990	
Korea, North		1982–		1965–	1980–	
Iraq		1973–2002		1976–	1982–	
Iran(1)		1974–1978				
Iran(2)		1984–		1984–	1985–	
Argentina		1976–1990		1968–	1978–1990	

Exploration		
Germany	1941–1945	1946–1969
Japan	1943–1945	1954–1969
Switzerland		1954–1965
Sweden	1946–1969	1974–1988
Yugoslavia(1)	1953–1963	1956–1973
Yugoslavia(2)	1982–1987	1967–1977
Australia		1987–1988
Taiwan(1)	1967–1976	1983–
Taiwan(2)		1985–1993
Algeria		
Romania	1981–1989	

Notes

*Before initial observation in dataset.

constructed by multiple actors within each state as the program progresses. The sociology of nuclear proliferation argues that these programs are better understood by examining the broader political and historical discourses of which nuclear science is a part (Flank 1993–1994; MacKenzie and Spinardi 1995; Abraham 1998); proliferation is a contingent historical phenomenon, not the inevitable result of the workings of the pressures of the international system.

India is often offered as an example of what appears externally as ambiguity, which internally might be better characterized as ambivalence. Itty Abraham (2006) argues that India developed a nuclear program as part of a grand modernization scheme with the ultimate end of legitimating its role as an independent, autonomous, self-sufficient postcolonial nation. To this end, India remained "ambivalent" about its nuclear program. It adopted the seemingly contradictory stances of leading the global charge for a robust non-proliferation regime and championing the advances of its nuclear program, to the exclusion of all mentions of the foreign aid it received in its development. "Ambivalence," writes Abraham, "is a permanent feature of the nuclear condition ... a recognition of the inability to wholly control nuclear events." (Abraham 2006: 56) As nuclear programs evolve, bureaucracies are established and independent political interests become entrenched. Beyond organizational pressures, however, ambivalence is a result of the awareness that the potential uses for and demands of nuclear science can change over time. The *role* that the program plays as an expression of state identity, too, can change as the relationship between the state and larger normative–ideational structures changes. Along the road to nuclear weapons, there are many potential paths; the meaning of specific nuclear technology programs is therefore contingent, not set. Consequently, it is not simply that scholars or the CIA must develop estimates of ambiguous "intent" on the part of potential proliferators; the process of proliferation itself may often be better understood as "ambivalence" inside the governments involved.

Comparing methods and results

In addition to the difficulties of defining proliferation, there are also methodological problems with the second wave of quantitative proliferation studies that create further questions about the comparability and validity of their conclusions. Both Singh and Way and Jo and Gartzke have multiple stages of proliferation, but they deal with them in very different ways, and adopt very different options for analysis. Contained in their methods are implicit assumptions that make little substantive sense. In Singh and Way's analysis, even states that have no nuclear program are included in their models of nuclear acquisition. Yet states cannot acquire weapons without first pursuing them,[3] and it seems unlikely that states will not pursue nuclear weapons without first exploring the option first, even if only for a short period of time. Jo and Gartzke effectively count each and every year a state has nuclear weapons as a separate decision to go nuclear, thereby placing excessive weight on states that went nuclear very early. We explore the results of changing these assumptions below. We use these two datasets to demonstrate our first three critiques of the literature: the problems with existing codings of nuclear programs; the lack of proper proxies for important variables; and the need for tighter correspondence between methodologies and empirical questions.

Due to their finely grained coding, Singh and Way look at four different potential transitions. Singh and Way have possible transitions from no nuclear weapons program to exploration (0 to 1) or pursuit (0 to 2), from exploration to pursuit (1 to 2), and from pursuit to acquisition (2 to 3). States that cancel their nuclear programs revert back to 0, with the exception of India, which moves from acquisition (3) in 1974 to exploration (1) in 1975. Due to left-censoring, the USA never enters any analysis, the USSR only enters into the analysis for acquiring nuclear weapons, the UK enters only for moving to pursuit, and Japan and Germany's World War II programs never show up. Libya, Pakistan, and China move directly from no nuclear weapons program to pursuit, skipping exploration. The coding that excludes these programs is potentially problematic, since it removes five of the twenty-six possible cases due to left-censoring and three more from the analysis of exploration moving to pursuit.

Singh and Way try two different tacks for analysis: first, a hazard analysis of their three different levels, then a multinomial logit. A hazard model for each level (1,2,3) with the pool restricted to states at the previous level of development (0,1,2) is the most empirically relevant way to analyze this data, since it models each level as a prerequisite for the next. We drop all states not already in the first stage (exploring a program) from an analysis of the second stage (pursuit of nuclear weapons) while adding a year of exploration for Libya, Pakistan, and China before they began pursuing; this drops the number of data points from 5578 to 250.[4] We further correct for time by setting the first year of exploration as the first year of being at risk for pursuing nuclear weapons;[5] Once these changes are made, the only variables that remain significant are related to *gross domestic product* (*GDPpc* and *GDPpc squared* jointly), *dispute involvement*, and the *percentage of democracies*. Dropping all states that were not already pursuing from the analysis of nuclear acquisition takes the number of data points from 5,784 to 210, making all variables except *industrial threshold* statistically insignificant; the data is so sparse that the algorithm does not even converge correctly.[6] Moving to a more empirically relevant methodology thus undercuts a number of the results. Finally, Singh and Way omit entirely measures of status or any effects that the non-proliferation regime might have; while there are good methodological reasons for not simply putting in measures of NPT membership or systemic acceptance (see below), eliminating them entirely from the analysis is problematic.

Jo and Gartzke, by contrast, only have two stages: nuclear weapons programs and nuclear weapons possession. Unlike Singh and Way, they disregard relatively poorly documented suspected programs such as those in Algeria that did not progress very far. While this choice is consistent with their coding rules, they nevertheless do exclude a number of empirically relevant confirmed nuclear weapons programs such as Libya, Australia, Taiwan's second attempt, and Switzerland. Moreover, their regressions end much earlier (1992) than those of Singh and Way (2000).[7]

Their methodology also differs from Singh and Way. They perform a probit analysis on the complete dataset to determine the effects of the independent variables on starting a nuclear program. However, unlike Singh and Way, states do not exit the risk pool for starting a nuclear program once they begin; they remain in the pool the entire time. Consequently, the results are biased towards programs that exist for a longer period of time. The United States, for example, is coded as having a nuclear program for fifty-two years, while North Korea only contributes eleven towards the algorithm.

If Jo and Gartzke's analysis is corrected to eliminate this bias from the risk pool, several very important substantive results change. In addition, if one adds additional known cases of states that started nuclear weapons programs, and later abandoned them, apparently important findings are reversed. In Table 14.2, we report the first differences that result for variables that were significant in any of the three models. We replicate their model for states starting nuclear programs in Model 1, then run the same model while only counting the first year of nuclear acquisition rather than every year in Model 2. In Model 3 we add the following five states to the dataset of countries with nuclear programs: Australia 1956–72 (Walsh 1997), Germany and Italy 1957–8 (Nuti 1993; Müller 2003), Egypt 1960–7 (Rublee 2006), and Libya 1970–2003 (Bowen 2006). Then in Model 4, we substitute the Singh and Way dates for exploration for the Jo and Gartzke dates.[8] The lack of robustness in the findings is apparent. *Latent production capability* drops across all three variations, but remains statistically significant. *Economic capacity* flips sign and becomes significant in both Models 2 and 4. *Diffusion* becomes negative and insignificant in Models 2–4. We suspect that this is due to improper variable specification; instead of diffusion being based on direct connections to potential suppliers (as some of the chapters in this book address), here it is simply based on time. *Nuclear threat* flips sign and becomes insignificant in Models 2–4. Although it is not significant, the estimated effect is quite strong in Model 3, increasing the likelihood of starting a nuclear program by 165 percent. In Models 3 and 4, the effects of being a *Major power* drop, and being a *Regional power* is no longer significant in Model 4. However, we believe that this is in part due to mismeasurement; rather than a measure of prestige, the measures of status here are based on material power.

Table 14.2 Percentage change in the corrected likelihood of a nuclear program (Jo and Gartzke methods, bold = *p* < .10)

Variable (change)	Model 1: Replication (%)	Model 2: Onset (%)	Model 3: Extra States Onset (%)	Model 4: Singh and Way Onset (%)
Latent production capability	**142.1**	**110.7**	**57.0**	**83.4**
Economic capacity	0.7	**−7.2**	−3.7	**−10.8**
Diffusion	**61.8**	−5.5	−6.5	−3.4
Conventional threat	**246.2**	**298.1**	**149.0**	**197.4**
Nuclear threat	**−81.0**	19.2	165.8	86.5
NPT membership	**−81.1**	−60.3	−56.4	59.7
NPT system	23.2	45.9	12.7	**−36.1**
Major power	**1,125.8**	**1847.5**	**844.8**	**847.3**
Regional power	**794.9**	**378.2**	**300.4**	108.4
n	4,697	4,273	4,224	4,118

Jo and Gartzke usefully grapple with the notions of norms as potential constraints on proliferation. They find that *NPT membership* (whether a state has ratified the treaty) "decreases the likelihood of having nuclear weapons programs," not a surprising finding, although in our models, it becomes insignificant. But Jo and Gartzke also find that their *NPT system* variable (the proportion of NPT joiners to the total number of states in the world) does not produce a statistically significant effect on nuclear proliferation and conclude that this "indicates that the NPT has not curbed proliferation incentives since the 1970s" (Jo and Gartzke 2007: 179). This last finding, however, is neither robust to alternative measures, nor is it likely to represent a causal relationship. In Model 2 of our tests, the *NPT system* variable is positive and significant, then becomes negative and significant in Model 4. The NPT system effect measured in this manner, however, may just reflect the generally increasing trend for more states joining the treaty regime through 1992.[9] Moreover, the Jo and Gartzke NPT membership coding fails to distinguish between states that join the NPT in order to cement a non-proliferation bargain with regional rivals (where we would expect to see an effect), cheater states that join the NPT with existing nuclear weapons programs such as Taiwan, North Korea, and Libya, and states that join as a part of joining the world order and have no intent of ever developing a civilian nuclear infrastructure, much less nuclear weapons, such as Bhutan, Papua New Guinea, and Fiji. Indeed, even the Holy See, hardly a candidate for nuclear power or a nuclear weapons concern, is a member of the NPT. Given these complex and diverse sets of motives for joining the treaty, we should not conclude that NPT status and norms are unimportant in curbing nuclear proliferation, but rather that they have not been properly tested yet.

Finally, the sparsity of the data for nuclear acquisition is particularly troubling. For example, although the official *n* is 250 and 210 for *pursue* and *acquire* respectively in Singh and Way, in effect there are only twenty-one unique subjects with fifteen failures for moving from *explore* to *pursue* and only fifteen subjects and nine failures for moving from *pursue* to *acquire*. At these levels, perhaps something like Qualitative Comparative Analysis, which uses fuzzy logic to explore complex interactions between different variables in datasets with a low number of observations, might be more appropriate (Ragin 2000) than traditional statistical analysis.

Progress in prediction

The authors in this volume further this initial work by focusing on the supply and regulation of nuclear technologies through the NPT regime (Brown; Erickson and Way; Benson and Wen; Wirtz; Kroenig; Fuhrmann) and the effects of the spread of nuclear weapons on the propensity of states to get into conflicts (Gartzke and Jo; Rauchhaus; Asal and Beardsley; and Horowitz) as well as how nuclear weapons affect the dynamics and net outcomes of such conflicts (Asal and Beardsley; Horowitz) and the future risks of proliferation and disarmament (Hellman; Nelson).

Methodologically, these studies have much to recommend them. They increasingly take into account strategic interaction and endogeneity in various ways, through testing to see if selection into crises affects their conduct and outcomes (Asal and Beardsley; Horowitz), and by using instrumental variables for proliferation (Gartzke and Jo). They carefully include sophisticated notions of the effects of time through splines (Gartzke and Jo; Horowitz), Taylor-series approximations (Asal and Beardsley), autoregression (Fuhrmann; Rauchhaus; Brown; Erickson and Way), dummies for particular periods (Fuhrmann; Erickson and Way) or hazard models (Kroenig; Asal and Beardsley). These are valuable methodological innovations. At the same time, these authors replicate some of the weaknesses of earlier quantitative work on proliferation. We discuss how our first four critiques apply to each of the individual chapters below, then turn to the curious case of Kargil to elaborate on the fifth critique about the importance of analyzing outliers.

Proliferation determinants

Brown tackles an important question about international law and organization: Why do sovereign states delegate authority to deal with their security problems to an international organization, in this case the International Atomic Energy Agency (IAEA)? Brown develops three plausible hypotheses derived from realist, liberal institutionalist and constuctivist theories: the degree of delegation reflects the interests of the most powerful state in the system, functional needs for safeguarding nuclear facilities, or the strength of global non-proliferation norms. Brown has usefully created a newly coded dataset, including three measures of his dependent variable (the level of nuclear delegation given to the IAEA): indicators related to the independent authority of the IAEA (e.g., can the agency order special investigations or deny members benefits if it suspects violations of agreements?), the amount of resources provided to the IAEA, and a sum of all delegation indicators. Brown also comes up with two innovative measures of the functional need for the IAEA: the number of nuclear weapons states and the "Minutes to Midnight" as reported by the Bulletin of Atomic Scientists.

Brown's study, however, is weakened by the use of independent variables that do not fit tightly to the underlying concepts in his theories. His measure of the strength of the NPT norms, the NPT accession share, is driven, as we have just discussed, by many causes, including states that covet nuclear weapons programs seeking to avoid scrutiny by joining the treaty, and microstates that were persuaded by the United States to join the treaty prior to the 1995 NPT extension vote, and is unlikely to reflect on its own the strength of the norms surrounding the NPT regime

(Graham 2002). A better measure might be the number of states that have accepted the IAEA's Additional Protocol for stronger safeguard inspections or the number of states that have supported efforts to create an international fuel bank for low-enriched uranium for reactors. Similarly, neither the number of nuclear weapons states nor the number of Minutes to Midnight is a good reflection of the functional need for IAEA inspectors and hence its "resource delegation" as measured by its budget. Indeed, since confirmed NPT member nuclear weapons states (NWS) require no major IAEA safeguard inspections and the non-NPT member NWS do not let inspectors into their facilities, every additional NWS likely decreases the need for more IAEA inspections. The lack of strong results Brown finds for functional variable may be due to these faulty measures and we suspect that two better measures of the functional institutional variable would be either: (1) the number of states with nuclear power reactors or the number of nuclear facilities worldwide that are covered by IAEA safeguard agreements; or (2) the rise and end of specific nonproliferation crises in which the IAEA is given significant responsibilities (the South African disarmament effort, the Iraqi nuclear inspections, and the DPRK crisis in the 1990s). Moreover, information on both the nuclear power measures and the budgetary estimates for the special IAEA crisis inspection and monitoring regimes are available, making it particularly puzzling that Brown looked under the NWS and "Minutes to Midnight" lampposts to find evidence to test functionalist theories. Finally, we are not convinced that Brown's sophisticated study has taught us much that we did not already know: it is not surprising to learn that "the results indicate that the IAEA changes over time for complicated reasons" (p. 21) or that "power, purpose, and beliefs are all important to a complete explanation of why the IAEA is asked to intervene in international nuclear nonproliferation efforts" (p. 14).

Erickson and Way's chapter is an excellent and novel investigation of the influence of NPT status on major conventional arms transfers. In doing so, they seek to discover whether countries gain other "side-payment" benefits from NPT status other than the explicit bargains inherent in the treaty. They convincingly demonstrate that countries that accede to the NPT import significantly more arms than do countries outside the treaty, although this effect is much stronger with the US than with Russia, and is nonexistent with respect to the United Kingdom. Their analysis is pioneering, for although we know that side-payments are often given in international negotiations, this is the first attempt to measure it with respect to the NPT. The study, moreover, raises several intriguing questions for future research. Are the higher level post-ratification arms sales due to suppliers selling arms more cheaply and freely as a side-payment, or are they caused by domestic demand in the recipient due to the cancellation of nascent nuclear weapons programs? If the latter, is the bump really a "benefit" of NPT membership to the recipients, or is it a cost to them? Moreover, are these arms transfers best seen as a payment to increase security of a country overall, or are they perhaps side-payments to domestic constituencies such as the military in exchange for their support of NPT ratification? Finally, it would be valuable to link the Erickson and Way research findings to the other authors' foci on the consequences of nuclear proliferation and non-proliferation: how do these conventional arms transfers impact the likelihood of conflict, the consequences of conflict and the risks and benefits of future nuclear disarmament?

Kroenig is the only author who directly extends upon the proliferation determinants' literature, adding a potentially significant cause of proliferation acquisition: sensitive nuclear assistance. Kroenig's coding of whether states received sensitive assistance or not (and from whom) is a significant improvement over past efforts to determine the supply-side factors influencing proliferation. Kroenig fixes both of the major methodological problems present in previous pieces, counting each nuclear weapons acquisition only once, and includes a censored model with only states that are already pursuing a program. It is worth noting that in the censored model, similar to the results above, very few of the independent variables are significant. In this light, it is particularly important to note that sensitive nuclear assistance is still highly significant; commendably, Kroenig tests his model against both earlier datasets as well as the consensus dataset for this book for robustness, although he does not report the full results.

What Kroenig does not highlight is also important: in robustness checks, he finds that one particular type of civilian nuclear assistance (a state's first reactor) and NPT membership decrease the probability that a state will acquire nuclear weapons. The notion that the spread of civilian technology will inevitably lead to more proliferation has received a lot of attention, primarily due to a few important cases such as India, Iran, and North Korea. Furthermore, Fuhrmann argues that defining civilian cooperation more broadly as nuclear cooperation agreements (NCAs) does increase the probability of exploration, pursuit, and acquisition. Kroenig offers an important counterpoint here in the form of evidence that both the NPT and some civilian technologies do decrease the likelihood of weapons proliferation, providing some evidence that the bargain of the NPT is holding, although our caveats regarding NPT membership apply here as well.

Kroenig's main findings are useful, but are hardly counter-intuitive. He concludes that "states that have the ability to acquire nuclear weapons, either through international assistance or domestic capability, are more likely to do so." (p. 62). It is valuable to know that important sensitive assistance has been for new proliferants' programs, but it is not surprising, to give the most extreme example, that states that received bomb designs from other states were more likely to develop a bomb than states that did not receive such designs.

While Kroenig focuses primarily on the effects of sensitive assistance, Fuhrmann adds to our knowledge about who gives what kind of nuclear assistance to whom, finding that states make agreements with allies and with other states that share the same enemies. Fuhrmann, uniquely among these chapters, breaks down his analysis into several time periods, commendably allowing for greater scrutiny of his results and giving a more accurate picture of the evolution over time of assistance. Fuhrmann's finding that membership in the NPT actually decreases the probability that a state will receive civilian nuclear cooperation agreements (NCAs) is an interesting and potentially troubling finding, given that this evidence seems to run counter to one of the major incentives for states to join the NPT.

This result, however, while statistically sound, appears to be substantively misleading: it is likely to be an artifact of the widespread growth and legitimacy of the NPT, since virtually all states, including many who have no reason to sign such nuclear cooperation agreements, have signed the treaty. Fuhrmann's NPT result is strictly applicable to the period 1992–2000; this outcome, then, likely comes from comparing the small number of states outside the treaty, who generally are interested in nuclear technologies of all kinds but did not wish to submit to the demands of the NPT, with the vast majority of states (84 percent in 1992) within the NPT, many of whom have no interest in nuclear technology of any kind. In short, another interpretation of Fuhrmann's finding is that NPT member states that do not wish to acquire nuclear technologies are less likely to get nuclear cooperation agreements than states who wanted nuclear technology before they signed the NPT, or the small number of states (India, Pakistan, and Israel) that have remained outside the treaty. This is not a surprising finding. Fuhrmann also finds that "countries exploring nuclear weapons are 107 percent more likely to receive nuclear aid for peaceful purposes" than are countries not exploring a nuclear weapons option (p. 100). This too appears to be a startling finding (albeit one that decreases over time as well). Yet again it seems to be caused by comparing states that are exploring nuclear weapons programs (all of which have civilian programs as well), with states that have never even explored a nuclear weapons program, a large number of which never had nuclear power programs and therefore never received nuclear technology assistance at all.

Wirtz's chapter in this volume is an outlier in two ways. First, it is the only chapter utilizing comparative historical case-study methodology in a volume emphasizing new quantitative research on proliferation. Second, Wirtz focuses neither on the decision to acquire nuclear weapons nor on the consequences of proliferation, but rather on how domestic political support, or lack thereof, for a state's nuclear program influences the maintenance or growth of existing nuclear arsenals. His case studies of a set of US nuclear doctrine and deployment decisions from 1950 through 2010 are designed to test his claim that "nuclear weapons have to enjoy broad-based societal and institutional support or governments and the organizations within them will turn their attention to more pressing issues or more politically and bureaucratically popular programs" (p. 138).

Wirtz's chapter does illustrate one important strength of comparative case-study methodology: the author can "process trace" whether the independent variable in question actually can be seen to be influencing the dependent variable in question (George and Bennett 2005). Wirtz thus provides direct and compelling evidence of leaders expressing concerns about public support for nuclear programs and shows how it influences decisions. At the same time, however, his chapter illustrates two common weaknesses in comparative case-study approach. First, one cannot tell from this research design whether the finding is generalizable. In Wirtz's case, we suspect not, for there is no theoretical reason to think that autocratic governments need to have "broad-based societal" support for their nuclear policies to maintain or improve nuclear arsenals. Wirtz would need to add a quantitative analysis of all cases, or at least have some carefully chosen case studies from autocratic nuclear weapons states, to make credible claims that his insights apply to other states than the US. Second, the important assumptions made by case-study authors are often more opaque and underspecified than is the norm in statistical studies in which clear definitions of variables are needed for coding decisions. In Wirtz's chapter, for example, he claims that criticism of the George W. Bush administration's 2001 Nuclear Posture Review was "immediate, overwhelming and shallow," (p. 149), but he never defines such terms in a way that would enable to the reader to know whether Wirtz is correct about this historical case, much less being able to compare the timing, the effectiveness, and the analytic depth of criticism of the 2001 Review to earlier or later administrations' Nuclear Posture Reviews.

Benson and Wen develop a two-person bargaining model between potential proliferators and counter-proliferators to examine the possible dynamics between the two. We applaud their use of game theory to address proliferation issues and their use of historical case studies to trace whether the factors they think are causing the results are actually doing so. Such mixed-methods research is rare in this field and can lead to innovative insights. In this case, we think that Benson and Wen creatively identify what they call the "nuclear security dilemma": the possibility that one state seeks nuclear weapons because it fears a conventional attack by another, but that threat of conventional attack is due entirely to the fear that the first state is acquiring nuclear weapons. This kind of security dilemma may be more common than we know and this chapter could therefore lead to useful future theoretical and empirical research on this phenomenon and mutual security guarantees that might ameliorate the problem.

Although game-theoretic models are a very different approach from statistical studies, Benson and Wen's work nevertheless shares one of the shortcomings of the other quantitative literature: the treatment of "nuclear ambiguity." In Benson and Wen's model, potential proliferators have a strategic choice, a "mixed strategy" equilibrium between arming and not arming, which they label as the nuclear ambiguity decision. Yet as Abraham reminds us, what appears to be ambiguity regarding a nuclear weapons program may actually be ambivalence rather than a strategic choice. If that is the case, what Benson and Wen model as bargaining between two unitary actors may well be a simpler form of a two-level game, with actors within the potential proliferator having very different conceptions of their state's interests and appropriate strategies.

Proliferation consequences

The second major theme of this volume is the consequences of nuclear proliferation. The previously existing scholarly debate on this subject is both theoretically rich and vigorous, but deeply unresolved, in part because it revolves around making predictions about a highly uncertain future. The nuclear optimists (Mearsheimer 1990; Waltz 1990; Mearsheimer 1993; Karl 1996; Sagan and Waltz 2003: Chapter 1, 3–4), following realist theory, envision a "perpetual nuclear peace," maintaining that states and statesmen behave with extreme rationality and will be therefore be deterred from using nuclear weapons in crises or wars against other nuclear states. They argue that overcoming preventive war incentives, developing second-strike capabilities, and developing command and control systems is easy. Nuclear pessimists (Feaver 1992; Miller 1993; Sagan 1993, 1994; Feaver *et al.* 1997; Sagan and Waltz 2003: Chapters 2–3, 5; Sagan 2004) use organization theory and maintain that nuclear weapons are not controlled by states, but rather by normal fragile humans in imperfect organizations. Their exploration of nuclear history has uncovered much evidence suggesting that there were close calls to nuclear war during the Cold War, and they predict therefore that new proliferators, especially those with poor command and control systems, will be particularly dangerous nuclear weapons states.

There have been surprisingly few statistical studies, however, designed to determine how common nuclear "near accidents" are or to learn how the acquisition of nuclear weapons influences a state's propensity to engage in conventional or sub-conventional war. The exceptions focus on the success rate of extended deterrence and on the effects of nuclear weapons in regional settings. Paul Huth, for example, finds that nuclear weapons increase the likelihood of successful deterrence of attacks on one's allies (Huth 1988, 1990). S. Paul Kapur combines case-study research and statistical methods in his study of the effects of nuclear weapons in South Asia and finds that nuclear weapons have led to an increase in the likelihood of MIDs between India and Pakistan (Kapur 2007). But we lack broader studies of the consequences of nuclear proliferation on different states' war and crisis behavior.

The remaining chapters in this book help fill that gap and make significant contributions. They turn the dependent variable in the causes of proliferation studies – a state's nuclear weapons acquisition – into the independent variable to assess the consequences of proliferation. Unfortunately, although these chapters use the same dates for when individual states acquired their first nuclear weapon, increasing comparability, it is unclear what is the theoretically appropriate threshold in a state's nuclear weapons capabilities for nuclear weapons to have an effect on its own or its rivals' calculations and behavior. Even if the correct date of a state's first nuclear weapon could be definitively determined (which is not the case today for many new proliferators), should we expect to see deterrent or compellent effects when a state is close to getting a weapon, when it has one weapon, after it has acquired a small arsenal, or only once it has a secure second-strike capability? An opaque proliferating state without a useable nuclear weapon yet might still act more belligerently to encourage other governments to back down in crises; similarly different adversaries to suspected proliferators may react quite differently to challenges if they have different intelligence estimates of the opponent's nuclear capabilities.

Take the secret Israeli nuclear program, for example: some scholars date Israel's nuclear weapons capability from a covert "decisive test" performed in November 1966, while others claim a crude weapon was first assembled in or just on the eve of the 1967 war; yet the US thought that Israel did not have nuclear weapons as late as 1969 (Cohen 2000: 112–114; Richelson 2006: 236–273; Montgomery and Mount 2010: 13–16). When should one expect, therefore, that the USSR or Arab states would be influenced by a possible Israeli nuclear weapon? Similar difficulties apply to other states. India tested its "Peaceful Nuclear Explosive" in 1974, which apparently was not easily deliverable, according to some accounts; weaponization was not completed until 1988; and this capability was not definitively demonstrated until the May 1998 nuclear tests. Dates for Pakistan's capabilities range from 1987 to 1990, although again the May 1998 test date could also apply. North Korea is even more enigmatic; the amount of plutonium that the North Koreans possessed after reprocessing a limited number of fuel rods by 1992 may not have been enough for even a first weapon; further reprocessing in 2003 definitely gave North Korea a sufficient amount for a few weapons, but this capability was not demonstrated definitively until October 2006. The ambiguity of the status of the arsenal of South Africa in the 1970s and 1980s (Albright 1994: 43) and the inherited Soviet weapons in Belarus, Kazakhstan, and Ukraine in the 1990s are further cases in point. Even using a first test date is ambiguous; how should the suspected Israeli or South African test in 1979 or the October 2006 North Korean test (which many analysts believe was a failure) be coded?

A second common methodological problem in the consequences of proliferation literature has been how to deal with selection effects and endogeneity. If nuclear states are found to win more disputes than non-nuclear states, is that because they are more powerful, or because they cautiously enter only into disputes that they are likely to win? If states that acquire nuclear weapons engage in more conflicts than non-nuclear states, are they really more conflict-prone because they have nuclear weapons or do they have nuclear weapons because they are conflict-prone? The authors contributing to this book make important progress in dealing with the selection effects and endogeneity problems. But they are less success-ful in dealing with the difficulties of matching the coding independent variables to the theory being tested. Some of their findings are also, as was the case with the causes of proliferation chapters, quite obvious and unlikely to overturn conventional wisdom.

Gartzke and Jo's essay is a significant and creative contribution, assess-ing the effects of the possession of nuclear weapons on militarized dispute (MID) onset and escalation. They find two contradictory effects: while actual nuclear weapons possession is found to increase the likelihood of initiating a dispute, when substituting an instrument (effectively, the prob-ability of nuclear weapons possession) instead to correct for possible endo-geneity, they find no effect.[10] Gartzke and Jo suggest that "nuclear weapons have no net effect on dispute propensity" because some nuclear states become more aggressive and others more cautious and these effects wash each other out. Moreover, they suggest that when facing a nuclear-armed state, non-nuclear target states acquiesce before a dispute reaches the dispute stage, but nuclear states escalate their demands such that new dis-putes still occur. Again, the net effect of nuclear weapons acquisition on dispute propensity will be minimal. This is an intriguing finding and their explanation is one plausible potential cause of the results. We suggest two others. Possession of nuclear weapons should deter disputes with non-nuclear states, but may not if: (1) a nuclear taboo exists and both actors believe the dispute is below the threshold of plausible nuclear use (Paul 1995; Tannenwald 2007); or (2) the non-nuclear initiator wishes to dem-onstrate that they will not be deterred by nuclear weapons, as Stalin did at the beginning of the Cold War (Holloway 1996).

Gartzke and Jo have an additional intriguing finding – that "states with nuclear weapons are more likely to receive diplomatic missions from other states than states without nuclear weapons." They interpret this result as evidence of an increased diplomatic influence that nuclear weapons may bring to a state. This interpretation, however, is problematic for two reasons. First, while having a higher number of connections to other states may result in increased prestige or influence, whether this is the case depends heavily on whom you are connected to and whether the connection is a positive one or seen as a necessary evil (Hafner-Burton and Montgomery 2006; Hafner-Burton *et al.* 2009). Second, Gartzke and Jo conflate the legal status of official diplomatic recognition with the political influence – arguing that "nations with demands need to be recognized before those demands can be satisfied" – despite the fact that negotiations commonly exist between states that do not have formal diplomatic recognition of each other. In short, diplomatic recognition, political influence and international esteem are three very different things and it is difficult to avoid the impression that this measure of "diplomatic influence" was chosen because it was readily available in the COW dataset. Gartzke and Jo usefully focus our attention on the connection between nuclear weapons and diplomatic influence, but they have not, contrary to their claims, demonstrated that "proliferators appear to prosper by becoming more influential diplomatically."

Asal and Beardsley's chapter "Winning with the bomb" nicely follows on their early work on the effect of nuclear weapons on crisis outcomes, using the ICB dataset (Asal and Beardsley 2007). The earlier work demonstrated that as the number of nuclear powers increases, the violence level of a crisis decreases. Asal and Beardsley's new chapter demonstrates that states that have nuclear weapons have a bargaining advantage as well; the probability of victory (defined as either outright victory or satisfaction with a compromise settlement) in a crisis increases by 14 percent when a nuclear state faces a non-nuclear opponent in any crisis, and by 30 percent in "high salience" crises. Moreover, Asal and Beardsley find that, controlling for other factors, the crises that nuclear weapons states have with non-nuclear weapons states are significantly shorter on average than are crises between two non-nuclear weapons states. They conclude that "nuclear weapons provide more than prestige, they provide leverage. They are useful in coercive diplomacy and this must be central to any explanation of why states acquire them."

Upon further examination, however, the evidence for this conclusion is less impressive than Asal and Beardsley acknowledge. Is a 14 percent increase in the probability of winning an international crisis sufficiently high for statesmen to justify an investment that costs millions of dollars and runs the risk of preventive war and potential opprobrium from the international community? The higher "victory" percentage in high-salience asymmetrical nuclear weapon cases is more impressive, but more than half of those victories are actually compromise settlements.[11] Moreover, the Asal and Beardsley salience measurement, while a commendable attempt to measure the relevance of nuclear weapons to a crisis, is likely to be endogenous to the conflict itself, since the presence of these weapons affects both the level of violence and the stakes involved. Their salience definition, including both actual military violence and threats of grave damage, strangely excludes cases in which no violence occurred or when only regional threats existed even if nuclear weapons were highly relevant. Their coding thus leaves out many of the Cold War and post-Cold War crises in which nuclear weapons use was contemplated or in which threats to attack suspected nuclear weapons production facilities were made, including the 1954 Dien Bien Phu crisis, the 1961 Berlin crisis, the 1969 Usurri River crisis, the 1987 Brass Tacks crisis, and the 1993–4 crisis over the North Korean nuclear program, and the 1999 Kargil crisis (see below).

Finally, Asal and Beardsley include a robustness check to ensure that the results are not a function of nuclear states selecting themselves into crises, which implies that nuclear states are actually more likely to start crises in the first place. This offers empirical evidence that nuclear states are more likely to enter into crises – even with other nuclear states. Yet it is not clear that this finding is robust across different codings of nuclear status; indeed, an earlier iteration of the same work with a much broader dataset of nuclear weapons states demonstrated that nuclear states were *less* likely to enter into crises.[12] A logical extension of this work would be to study how the outcomes of asymmetrical crises influence the likelihood of further nuclear proliferation; if nuclear states win asymmetric fights, how often do the losers then start nuclear programs?

Rauchhaus's essay – "Evaluating the nuclear peace hypothesis" – tests a long-standing proposition in studies of nuclear deterrence theory and proliferation: the stability–instability paradox. This paradox holds that while symmetrical possession of nuclear weapons may prevent all-out war between two states, it may also increase the likelihood of low-level military conflicts, because one or both of these states might believe that the other government would fear escalation and accept defeat rather than move to higher levels of violence. The logic of the stability–instability paradox led analysts during the Cold War to worry that the USSR might be tempted to use military force against US allies after Moscow had acquired nuclear weapons or a position of nuclear parity. If both governments in a nuclear dyad believed that the other would back down rather than escalate further in a conflict, however, this could lead to a dangerous game of chicken with unpredictable consequences.

The value of Rauchhaus's essay is not in its statistical finding that "when two states have nuclear weapons, the negative coefficient indicates that they are less likely to go to war with one another." We knew that already and that result was perfectly predictable given his historical data. Indeed, as he notes, "the dataset does not include any instances of two nuclear states engaging in war with one another. Thus, there is a perfect correlation between the absence of war and dyads where both states possess nuclear weapons." The value of the essay is its sophisticated statistical test of whether two nuclear-armed states are more likely to use threats and military force at lower levels of violence against each other once both have nuclear weapons. This chapter provides substantial proof of this proposition: MIDs, the use of force in MIDs, and fatal MIDs are all more likely to occur in symmetrical dyads of nuclear states. Moreover, Rauchhaus carefully controls for potential selection effects and provides a robustness check of his findings by using an alternative coding of the nuclear weapons acquisition date variable. However, the methodology used here (looking at undirected dyads) does not give as precise a measurement of crisis behavior as directed dyads would, since we cannot tell which state in an asymmetrical dyad started the crisis.

Horowitz, unlike most of the literature on proliferation, takes into account the possibility that states may change their behavior over time due to learning, and carefully assesses who initiates and reciprocates each dispute. His valuable chapter finds that "new" nuclear states are slightly more likely to have their disputes reciprocated (and are much more likely to reciprocate others' initial moves) than non-nuclear states, but that over time, this diminishes to the point where experienced nuclear states are less than half as likely as non-nuclear states to have their disputes reciprocated. "Mature" nuclear states are also slightly less likely to reciprocate others' disputes than are non-nuclear states.

Horowitz robustly tests different codings for nuclear acquisition, finding that including nuclear inheritors (Belarus, Kazakhstan, and the Ukraine) does not affect the results. Vicarious learning, a particularly difficult-to-measure but potentially important concept, is partially addressed in a robustness test. Presumably new nuclear states enter a world in which all states have learned something about nuclear disputes, so that their learning curve might be less steep. Future research could attempt to model vicarious learning as a diffusion process that occurs proportional to the strength of network ties between states; e.g., the United Kingdom is likely to learn lessons from the United States, but not from the Soviet Union; Iran might learn more effectively from Pakistani experience with nuclear weapons than from the Israeli or US experience.

These are valuable chapters presenting intriguing findings. Further research will be needed, however, to assess whether the causal mechanisms suggested in these studies are actually driving the results. More statistical work will also be needed, as noted above, to provide more robust confidence in the statistical findings. Future work, however, must be more careful than past research in taking into account disconfirming evidence as noted below.

This book also includes two risk analyses that attempt to estimate the probability of nuclear catastrophes; Hellman attempts to estimate the likelihood of a catastrophe given the future likelihood of a Cuban Missile Crisis-level event and the chance that such an event will lead to a nuclear exchange. Nelson takes a broader view, comparing the presumed increased risk of conventional war in a world without nuclear weapons with the risk of nuclear war today.

Both Hellman and Nelson usefully highlight that the risks of war impact both current and future generations, and we find their insights about discount rates to be novel and intriguing. And certainly, Nelson is correct to note that divergent views about the wisdom of nuclear disarmament are due, in part, to different estimates of both the likelihood of nuclear war and the likelihood of major conventional war in a world without nuclear weapons. However, it is not clear that we learn anything significantly new from using the tools of risk analysis to study the probability of nuclear war. Hellman concludes that the risk of nuclear war is much higher than what might be termed an acceptable risk. While this is an important reminder and a warning not to let such dangers be ignored, it is neither clear that formal risk analysis was needed to do so nor that it will be persuasive; Nelson admits as much, in that "Risk analysis seems unlikely to dissuade those who have an established position, in either direction, on the advisability of nuclear disarmament." (p. 285).

Most importantly, Hellman does not look at the flipside of disarmament; the belief among some analysts that nuclear disarmament might result in a net increase in the likelihood of nuclear weapons use due to the risks of rapid rearmament and what Thomas Schelling has called "the instability of small numbers" (Schelling 1962; Glaser 1998; Sagan 2009b; Schelling 2009). Nelson does include this chance, but argues that "...the benign disarmament proposition requires only the easy belief that nuclear-weapon catastrophes will be less frequent if nuclear arms are abolished than if they are not" (p. 279). Clearly, however, there are many nuclear weapons experts who do not share this "easy" assumption.

It is especially puzzling that Hellman does not compare the risks of nuclear use today and in a disarmed world since he focuses so much attention on American leaders' estimates of nuclear war during the Cuban Missile Crisis. After all, John F. Kennedy decided to accept the risks of nuclear escalation during the crisis precisely because he believed that the longer-term risks of nuclear war would be even higher if he permitted the Soviet Union to deploy nuclear-armed missiles in Cuba after having promised that they would not do so.

Finally, formal risk analyses such as these should try to leverage statistical studies in order to try to estimate their inputs. The studies in this book provide good starting points for making estimates of the increased likelihood of conflict, escalation, and full-blown war given the possession of nuclear weapons that could serve to make future risk analyses more concrete.

The curious case of Kargil

Statistical studies are a useful, indeed essential, method of testing social science theories about how the world works and the chapters in this book have clearly helped generated new insights about the sources of nuclear proliferation and its consequences. The use of quantitative research methods, however, too often leads scholars to ignore important disconfirming evidence or to treat it as "measurement error." Such disconfirming evidence should instead lead to questioning about the accuracy of the initial test of a theory or research about why there may be exceptions to the rule. Consider, for example, the curious case of Kargil.

The Kargil war of 1999 is curious in two ways: first, because it offers apparently damning evidence against both the democratic peace theory and the nuclear peace theory; second, because quantitative scholars on both subjects have largely ignored the implications of the Kargil war. The war occurred in the spring of 1999, when Indian armed forces discovered that Pakistani northern infantry soldiers, disguised as *Mujahideen* guerilla fighters, had crossed the Line of Control in Indian-held Kashmir and had taken up fortified positions in the mountains above the town of Kargil. India and Pakistan were clearly nuclear weapons states after their 1998 nuclear tests. The 1999 conflict should be coded as an interstate war, since the most reliable estimates of the fatalities in Kargil, from the Kargil Review Committee (2000), set the number of Indian dead at 474 (2000: 23) and the "lowest estimate of regular Pakistani Army casualties is 700 killed," (2000: 98) for a conservative minimum of 1,174. This is well above the 1,000 battle deaths for war criteria used in the COW and other data-sets. Kargil is an exception to the democratic peace theory as well because India and Pakistan score a +9 and +7 respectively in the Polity IV dataset for 1999 (Marshall and Jaggers 2003). Still, all the chapters in this book have ignored this fact and its implications for the robustness of the tests about the consequences of proliferation. A leading work in the democratic peace literature does at least address the Kargil war: Russett and Oneal recognize Kargil as an apparent exception to the theory, but incorrectly suggest that it may not count as a war because many of the deaths were "Islamic guerrillas, not regular Pakistani troops" (Russett and Oneal 2001: 48).

It would be better to analyze apparent exceptions to the rule to develop alternative theories and hypotheses for future research. In the case of Kargil, the Pakistani decision to send troops into Indian-held Kashmir was apparently taken by military leaders, with minimal involvement of the democratically elected prime minister (Bennett-Jones 2002: 102–103; Sagan 2009a). This leads to a testable hypothesis that military-run governments or civilian governments with inadequate operational control over the military may behave differently regarding nuclear weapons and war initiation. The fact that the Pakistani military also opposed the withdrawal from Kashmir and the cease-fire settlement in 1999 also suggests that such governments may behave differently regarding nuclear weapons and escalation in crises and conflicts (Sagan and Waltz 2003: 97; Musharraf 2006: 96). Future qualitative and quantitative research will be needed to test these hypotheses.

Implications

This revival of the quantitative study of proliferation is a welcome advance-ment in nuclear proliferation studies. Some of the questions and debates in this subfield can only be fully tested when using statistical methods. Others will require mixed methods, combining historical case studies, deductive reasoning, and quantitative research. The authors in this volume have made significant progress in our understanding of the causes of nuclear proliferation, the propensity of states to initiate disputes, the outcomes of those disputes, and incentives for nuclear disarmament. As with much good research, they provoke as many questions as they answer. Here we have noted some of the puzzling and potentially contradictory results, offered some tentative explanations, and proposed an agenda for further research.

The findings of the chapters on the causes of proliferation usefully focus attention on the technology assistance to potential proliferators. The next wave of research will need to disaggregate the kinds of assistance much more than Fuhrmann and Kroenig do in their chapters. While it is not surprising that designs for nuclear weapons make proliferation more likely, it would be helpful to know, for example, whether uranium enrichment or plutonium reprocessing were more commonly abused by covert proliferators, including states that started weapons programs and did not complete them. It would also be helpful to differentiate between NCAs signed and those that were actually implemented, to avoid giving inappropriate weight to cases, like the German NCAs with Brazil, which were not in the end honored and thus could not contribute to nuclear weapons programs or acquisition (Squassoni and Fite 2005). Disaggregation of different types of NCAs would also be useful; nuclear assistance with medical devices and light-water power reactors are unlikely to aid nuclear weapons programs, while other types of civilian assistance are much more contentious. The relationship between the NPT, covert nuclear weapons programs, and civilian nuclear assistance also needs to be examined more thoroughly before jumping to negative conclusions about the treaty. Further historical and statistical study is required to unravel some of these puzzles. Why have different states joined the treaty and how has the treaty influenced their subsequent behavior (Sasikumar and Way 2010)? How do different technologies affect proliferation? How much does sensitive assistance decrease the time to acquisition of nuclear weapons? With the potential for a dramatic increase in the use of nuclear power expected in the future, these questions have an immediate policy relevance (Miller and Sagan 2009, 2010).

The chapters on the consequences of proliferation also point to the need for further research. One important research agenda would focus more on initiation of conflicts to learn if possession of nuclear weapons makes states more likely to initiate or be the target of disputes. In their raw results, all the chapters on proliferation consequences suggest that possessors are more likely to be in crises, although only two have specific results for initiation (Gartzke and Jo; and Horowitz). Gartzke and Jo posit that increased initiation is not due to nuclear possession itself, but Horowitz's results also suggest possessors become more likely to initiate disputes with experience. This is a very bleak conclusion for nuclear optimists: while nuclear weapons states may have their challenges reciprocated less often over time, they may issue more challenges. Future research could usefully focus on whether all states fit into that pattern, since some types of regimes or leaders are more likely than others to be aggressive if they get nuclear weapons. While Asal and Beardsley, and Horowitz have taken important first steps in understanding the net effect of nuclear weapons on conflict and bargaining outcomes, additional research is clearly also required here. If initiation is actually not affected (or increased) by nuclear weapons, this should have an effect on the bargains that these states get with or without crises or threats of force. Future work in this important area of research could focus less on the overall trends and more on the outliers: for example, are there certain states or certain kinds of regimes that do not become more prudent over time after getting nuclear weapons? Finally, a useful follow-on study regarding the stability–instability paradox would be to combine Rauchhaus' statistical methods and histor-ical case studies to examine directly the dynamics of escalation from the threat to the use of force and from uses of force to fatal MIDs to deter-mine whether the fear of escalation by one side or both determined the governments' behavior or whether other factors were more important. That research could provide insights into how confident we should be about the likelihood that the "nuclear peace" will continue to exist in the future if more states acquire nuclear weapons.

The exclusion of important theories of proliferation (or their inclusion with inadequate measures) also tempers some of the conclusions reached here, and requires additional research. Scholars have grappled for a long time with the notions of prestige, norms, social roles, and psychology as motivations for the causes of proliferation. Yet since Kegley, none of the quantitative pieces on the causes of proliferation have successfully incor-porated these theories into their analysis. This affects both chapters on the likelihood of proliferation and its consequences, as the reasons for prolif-eration could potentially have significant effects on how nuclear weapons are used once they are acquired. Difficult-to-measure concepts such as civil–military relations and bureaucratic power and autonomy have also rarely been incorporated into quantitative analyses (with the notable exception of Sechser 2004), or when incorporated have been measured using existing measures of regime type, which were developed for other purposes. Yet civilian control of the military and central government control over nuclear scientists could have important effects on both the likelihood of proliferation and its consequences.

Finally, the results that quantitative studies produce do not necessarily make for sound policy advice; what may be true across an entire popula-tion does not necessarily make good sense for dealing with individual cases. The finding that civilian nuclear assistance may often lead to prolif-eration, for example, should not lead scholars to oppose the Clinton and Bush administrations' agreements to give light-water-moderated nuclear power reactors to North Korea, for that policy option is conditional on North Korea dismantling its more proliferation-prone graphite-moderated reactor and returning its weapons-grade plutonium stockpile to the IAEA. The observation that nuclear-armed dyads are less likely to go to war against each other similarly should not necessarily lead to the prescription that more nuclear states would be better, since the possible destruction of a full-scale war between nuclear powers could outweigh the benefits of decreased likelihood of conventional conflict.

The curious case of Kargil underlines this final lesson for both the democratic peace and the nuclear peace: rare does not mean never. This is less damaging for the democratic peace; as long as democracy decreases war, there is still a net benefit that results from an increase in the number of democratic states. But if nuclear weapons do not eliminate the possibility of nuclear war entirely, their proliferation could lead to a disastrous outcome over time. While nuclear optimists may therefore take some comfort in the results of some of these chapters, nuclear pessimists will remind us that unless the probability of nuclear war is zero, the potential consequences of nuclear proliferation may still outweigh the benefits.

Notes

1 MID 3.10 does include Kargil as a dispute that had a maximum hostility level of war, but has it as the end point of a dispute starting in 1993; see Kapur 2007: 19. COW 3.0 only has wars through 1997, while ICB 8.0 lists Kargil as "serious clashes," not "full-out war."

2 See Müller and Schmidt 2010 for a list of additional possible states with "nuclear activities."

3 The cases of Belarus, Kazakhstan, and Ukraine are excluded from both datasets, since the temporary location of nuclear weapons on their soil resulted from the breakup of the Soviet Union rather than from a domestic program.

4 Singh and Way footnote this variant in their analysis (2004: 875, fn. 32); we believe that this is the more empirically relevant question.

5 This corrects for entry and exit times of the risk pool. In Singh and Way's analysis, a state is at risk of moving to the third stage (pursuing) nuclear weapons from its first date of entry into the system. In this corrected analysis, states enter the risk pool for pursuit of nuclear weapons only in their first year of exploring nuclear weapons.

6 We omit a full analysis here due to space constraints; STATA datasets and do-files for replication are available on the *JCR* website.

7 Like the Singh and Way left-censoring, the right-censoring of this data at 1992 is potentially important, but beyond the scope of this analysis.

8 We replicate their Table 1, Model 1 (Jo and Gartzke 2007: 178). We used Clarify 2.1 (King *et al.* 2000; Tomz *et al.* 2003) to analyze these differences; all variables were set to their medians for the baseline except *Latent production capability*, which was set to 5, and increased to their 75th percentile value except for dummy variables and variables whose 75th percentile is still zero (i.e., *Conventional threat*), which were set to 1.

9 The NPT system variable is correlated 0.9131 with the year; the fraction of states in the system increases rapidly from 0.47 in 1970 to 0.84 in 1992.

10 While we critique Jo and Gartzke's 2007 paper for including multiple observations for nuclear possession, in the Gartzke and Jo paper, this model makes

more sense in this context, since it is attempting to produce an instrument that correlates with the presence of nuclear weapons, not just with the initial acquisition. Nonetheless, we find the instrument to be potentially problematic since probit and logit functional forms can lead to misspecification (see Angrist and Krueger 2001: 80), and important variables such as status are excluded from the instrument.

11 Similarly, in high-salience crises with symmetrical nuclear dyads, they record a 21 percent increase in victory compared to a dyad with two non-nuclear weapon states; however, this is entirely due to an increase in compromise settlements, as absolute victory actually decreases.

12 The APSA 2007 (Beardsley and Asal 2007) version of the paper had a negative coefficient on Nuclear A and a small positive coefficient on Nuclear B. This dataset had earlier dates for India (1974), Pakistan (1987), and North Korea (1992), and included Ukraine, Kazakhstan, and Belarus from 1991 until 1996, 1995, and 1996 respectively.

References

Abraham, Itty (1998) *The Making of the Indian Atomic Bomb: Science, Secrecy and the Postcolonial State*, London, UK: Zed Books.

Abraham, Itty (2006) "The Ambivalence of Nuclear Histories," *Osiris* 21: 49–65.

Albright, David (1994) "South Africa and the Affordable Bomb," *Bulletin of the Atomic Scientists* 50: 37–47.

Albright, David and Paul Brannan (2008) *The Al Kibar Reactor: Extraordinary Camouflage, Troubling Implications*, Institute for Science and International Security.

Angrist, Joshua D. and Alan B. Krueger (2001) "Instrumental Variables and the Search for Identification: From Supply and Demand to Natural Experiments," *Journal of Economic Perspectives* 15: 69–85.

Asal, Victor and Kyle Beardsley (2007) "Proliferation and International Crisis Behavior," *Journal of Peace Research* 44: 139–155.

Beardsley, Kyle and Victor Asal (2007) "Winning with the Bomb," Paper read at 103rd Annual Meeting of the American Political Science Association, August 30–September 2, at Chicago, IL.

Bennett-Jones, Owen (2002) *Pakistan: Eye of the Storm*, New Haven, CT: Yale University Press.

Bowen, Wyn Q. (2006) "Libya and Nuclear Proliferation: Stepping Back from the Brink," *Adelphi Papers*, International Institute for Strategic Studies.

Campbell, Kurt M. and Tsuyoshi Sunohara (2004) "Japan: Thinking the Unthinkable," in K.M. Campbell, R.J. Einhorn and M. Reiss (eds) *The Nuclear Tipping Point: Why States Reconsider Their Nuclear Choices*, Washington, DC: Brookings Institution Press.

Campbell, Kurt M., Robert J. Einhorn, and Mitchell Reiss (eds) (2004) *The Nuclear Tipping Point: Why States Reconsider Their Nuclear Choices*, Washington, DC: Brookings Institution Press.

Chafetz, Glenn, Hillel Abramson, and Suzette Grillot (1996) "Role Theory and Foreign Policy: Belarussian and Ukranian Compliance with the Nuclear Nonproliferation Regime," *Political Psychology* 17: 727–757.

Cohen, Avner (2000) "Nuclear Arms in Crisis under Secrecy: Israel and the Lessons of the 1967 and 1973 Wars," in P.R. Lavoy, S.D. Sagan, and J.J. Wirtz (eds) *Planning the Unthinkable*, Ithaca, NY: Cornell University Press.

Doyle, Michael W. (1986) "Liberalism and World Politics," *American Political Science Review* 80: 1151–1169.

Elman, Miriam Fendius (1997) *Paths to Peace: Is Democracy the Answer?*, Cambridge, MA: MIT Press.

Fearon, James D. (1994) "Domestic Political Audiences and the Escalation of International Disputes," *American Political Science Review* 88: 577–592.

Feaver, Peter D. (1992) "Command and Control in Emerging Nuclear Nations," *International Security* 17: 160–187.

Feaver, Peter D., Scott D. Sagan, and David J. Karl (1997) "Proliferation Pessimism and Emerging Nuclear Powers," *International Security* 22: 185–207.

Flank, Steven (1993–1994) "Exploding the Black Box: The Historical Sociology of Nuclear Proliferation," *Security Studies* 3: 259–294.

Forland, Astrid (1997) "Norway's Nuclear Odyssey: From Optimistic Proponent to Nonproliferator," *Nonproliferation Review* 4: 1–16.

Frankel, Benjamin (1993) "The Brooding Shadow: Systemic Incentives and Nuclear Weapons Proliferation," in Z.S. Davis and B. Frankel (eds) *The Proliferation Puzzle: Why Nuclear Weapons Spread and What Results*, Portland, OR: Frank Cass.

Fuhrmann, Matthew (2008) "Exporting Mass Destruction? The Determinants of Dual-Use Trade," *Journal of Peace Research* 45: 633–652.

Fuhrmann, Matthew (2009) "Spreading Temptation: Proliferation and Peaceful Nuclear Cooperation Agreements," *International Security* 34: 7–41.

Gartzke, Erik (2007) "The Capitalist Peace," *American Journal of Political Science* 51: 166–191.

George, Alexander L. and Andrew Bennett (2005) *Case Studies and Theory Development in the Social Sciences*, Cambridge, MA: MIT Press.

Glaser, Charles (1998) "The Flawed Case for Nuclear Disarmament," *Survival: Global Politics and Strategy* 40: 112.

Graham, Thomas (2002) *Disarmament Sketches: Three Decades of Arms Control and International Law*, Institute for Global and Regional Security Studies, Seattle: University of Washington Press.

Grillot, Suzette R. and William J. Long (2000) "Ideas, Beliefs, and Nuclear Policies: The Cases of South Africa and Ukraine," *Nonproliferation Review* 7: 24–40.

Hafner-Burton, Emilie M. and Alexander H. Montgomery (2006) "Power Positions: International Organizations, Social Networks, and Conflict," *Journal of Conflict Resolution* 50: 3–27.

Hafner-Burton, Emilie M., Miles Kahler, and Alexander H. Montgomery (2009) "Network Analysis for International Relations," *International Organization* 63(3): 559–592.

Holloway, David (1996) *Stalin and the Bomb*, London: Yale University Press.

Huth, Paul K. (1988) "Extended Deterrence and the Outbreak of War," *American Political Science Review* 82: 423–443.

Huth, Paul K. (1990) "The Extended Deterrent Value of Nuclear Weapons," *Journal of Conflict Resolution* 34: 270–290.

Hymans, Jacques E.C. (2006) *The Psychology of Nuclear Proliferation: Identity, Emotions, and Foreign Policy*, Cambridge, UK: Cambridge University Press.

Jo, Dong-Joon and Erik Gartzke (2006) Codebook and Data Notes for "Determinants of Nuclear Weapons Proliferation: A Quantitative Model". Available at www.columbia.edu/~eg589/datasets.htm.

Jo, Dong-Joon and Erik Gartzke (2007) "Determinants of Nuclear Weapons Proliferation: A Quantitative Model," *Journal of Conflict Resolution* 51: 167–194.

Kant, Immanuel 1917 [1795] *Perpetual Peace: A Philosophical Essay*, M.C. Smith (ed.), London, UK: G. Allen and Unwin.

Kapur, S. Paul (2007) *Dangerous Deterrent: Nuclear Weapons Proliferation and Conflict in South Asia*, Stanford, CA: Stanford University Press.

Kargil Review Committee (2000) *From Surprise to Reckoning: The Kargil Review Committee Report*, New Delhi: Sage Publications.

Karl, David J. (1996) "Proliferation Pessimism and Emerging Nuclear Powers," *International Security* 21: 87–119.

Katzenstein, Peter J. (1996) *Cultural Norms and National Security: Police and Military in Postwar Japan, Cornell Studies in Political Economy*, Ithaca, NY: Cornell University Press.

Kegley, Charles W. (1980) "International and Domestic Correlates of Nuclear Proliferation: A Comparative Analysis," *Korea and World Affairs* 4: 5–37.

King, Gary, Michael Tomz, and Jason Wittenberg (2000) "Making the Most of Statistical Analyses: Improving Interpretation and Presentation," *American Journal of Political Science* 44: 347–361.

Lake, David A. (1992) "Powerful Pacifists: Democratic States and War," *American Political Science Review* 86: 24–37.

Levite, Ariel E. (2002/2003) "Never Say Never Again: Nuclear Reversal Revisited," *International Security* 27: 59–88.

Mackby, Jenifer and Walter Slocombe (2004) "Germany: The Model Case, a Historical Imperative," in K.M. Campbell, R.J. Einhorn, and M. Reiss (eds) *The Nuclear Tipping Point: Why States Reconsider Their Nuclear Choices*, Washington, DC: Brookings Institution Press.

MacKenzie, Donald and Graham Spinardi (1995) "Tacit Knowledge, Weapons Design, and the Uninvention of Nuclear Weapons," *American Journal of Sociology* 101: 44–99.

Mansfield, Edward D. and Jack Snyder (1995) "Democratization and the Danger of War," *International Security* 20: 5–38.

Maoz, Zeev and Bruce Russett (1993) "Normative and Structural Causes of Democratic Peace, 1946–1986," *American Political Science Review* 87: 624–638.

Marshall, Monty G. and Keith Jaggers (2003) "Polity IV Project: Political Regime Characteristics and Transitions, 1800–2002: Integrated Network for Societal Conflict Research." Available at www.cidcm.umd.edu/inscr/polity/.

Mearsheimer, John J. (1990) "Back to the Future: Instability in Europe after the Cold War," *International Security* 15: 5–56.

Mearsheimer, John J. (1993) "The Case for a Ukrainian Nuclear Deterrent," *Foreign Affairs* 72: 50–66.

Meyer, Stephen M. (1984) *The Dynamics of Nuclear Proliferation*, Chicago, IL: University of Chicago Press.

Miller, Steven E. (1993) "The Case against a Ukrainian Nuclear Deterrent," *Foreign Affairs* 72: 67–80.

Miller, Steven E. and Scott D. Sagan (2009) "The Global Nuclear Future Volume 1," *Daedalus* 138: 4.

Miller, Steven E. and Scott D. Sagan (2010) "The Global Nuclear Future Volume 2," *Daedalus* 139: 1.

Montgomery, Alexander H. (2005) "Ringing in Proliferation: How to Dismantle an Atomic Bomb Network," *International Security* 30: 153–187.

Montgomery, Alexander H. and Adam J. Mount (2010) "Misunderestimation: Explaining US Failures to Predict Nuclear Weapons Programs," Paper read at Intelligence and Nuclear Proliferation Conference, June, London, UK.

Müller, Harald (2003) "German National Identity and WMD – Proliferation," *The Nonproliferation Review* 10: 1–20.

Müller, Harald and Andreas Schmidt (2010) "The Little Known Story of De-Proliferation: Why States Give up Nuclear Weapons Activities," in W.C. Potter and G. Mukhatzhanova (eds) *Forecasting Nuclear Proliferation in the 21st Century: Volume 1, the Role of Theory*, Stanford, CA: Stanford University Press.

Musharraf, Pervez (2006) *In the Line of Fire: A Memoir*, New York, NY: Free Press.

Nuti, Leopoldo (1993) "'Me Too, Please': Italy and the Politics of Nuclear Weapons, 1945–1975," *Diplomacy and Statecraft* 4: 114–148.

Ogilvie-White, Tanya (1996) "Is There a Theory of Nuclear Proliferation? An Analysis of the Contemporary Debate," *Nonproliferation Review* 4: 43–60.

Paul, T.V. (1995) "Nuclear Taboo and War Initiation in Regional Conflicts," *Journal of Conflict Resolution* 39: 696–717.

Paul, T.V. (2000) *Power Versus Prudence: Why Nations Forgo Nuclear Weapons, Foreign Policy, Security and Strategic Studies*, Montreal, Quebec: McGill-Queen's University Press.

Ragin, Charles C. (2000) *Fuzzy-Set Social Science*, Chicago, IL: University Of Chicago Press.

Reiss, Mitchell (1988) *Without the Bomb: The Politics of Nuclear Nonproliferation*, New York, NY: Columbia University Press.

Reiss, Mitchell (1995) *Bridled Ambition: Why Countries Constrain Their Nuclear Capabilities, Woodrow Wilson Center Special Studies*, Washington, DC: Woodrow Wilson Center Press.

Reiss, Mitchell and Robert S. Litwak (eds) (1994) *Nuclear Proliferation after the Cold War, Woodrow Wilson Center Special Studies*, Washington, DC: Woodrow Wilson Center Press.

Reiter, Dan and Allan C. Stam (2002) *Democracies at War*, Princeton, NJ: Princeton University Press.

Richelson, Jeffrey (2006) *Spying on the Bomb: American Nuclear Intelligence, from Nazi Germany to Iran and North Korea*, 1st edn, New York, NY: Norton.

Rublee, Maria Rost (2006) "Egypt's Nuclear Weapons Program: Lessons Learned," *The Nonproliferation Review* 13: 555–567.

Rublee, Maria Rost (2009) *Nonproliferation Norms: Why States Choose Nuclear Restraint*, Athens: University of Georgia Press.

Russett, Bruce M. and John R. Oneal (2001) *Triangulating Peace: Democracy, Interdependence, and International Organizations*, New York, NY: Norton.

Sagan, Scott D. (1993) *The Limits of Safety: Organizations, Accidents, and Nuclear Weapons*, Princeton, NJ: Princeton University Press.

Sagan, Scott D. (1994) "The Perils of Proliferation: Organization Theory, Deterrence Theory, and the Spread of Nuclear Weapons," *International Security* 18: 66–107.

Sagan, Scott D. (1996/97) "Why Do States Build Nuclear Weapons? Three Models in Search of a Bomb," *International Security* 21: 54–86.

Sagan, Scott D. (1999) "Rethinking the Causes of Nuclear Proliferation: Three Models in Search of a Bomb," in V.A. Utgoff (ed.) *The Coming Crisis: Nuclear Proliferation, U.S. Interests, and World Order*, Cambridge, MA: MIT Press.

Sagan, Scott D. (2004) "The Problem of Redundancy Problem: Why More Nuclear Security Forces May Produce Less Nuclear Security," *Risk Analysis* 24: 935–946.

Sagan, Scott D. (ed.) (2009a) *Inside Nuclear South Asia*, Stanford, CA: Stanford University Press.

Sagan, Scott D. (2009b) "Shared Responsibilities for Nuclear Disarmament," *Daedalus* 138: 157–168.

Sagan, Scott D. and Kenneth N. Waltz (2003) *The Spread of Nuclear Weapons: A Debate Renewed*, 2nd edn, New York, NY: W.W. Norton.

Sasikumar, Karthika and Christopher R. Way (2010) "Paper Tiger or Barrier to Proliferation? What Accessions Reveal about NPT Effectiveness," Paper read at CISAC Social Science Research Seminar, April 15, at Stanford, CA.

Schelling, Thomas C. (1962) "The Role of Deterrence in Total Disarmament," *Foreign Affairs* 40: 392–406.

Schelling, Thomas C. (2009) "A World without Nuclear Weapons?," *Daedalus* 138: 124–129.

Schultz, Kenneth A. (1998) "Domestic Opposition and Signaling in International Crises," *American Political Science Review* 92: 829–844.

Sechser, Todd S. (2004) "Are Soldiers Less War-Prone than Statesmen?," *Journal of Conflict Resolution* 48: 746–774.

Singh, Sonali and Christopher R. Way (2004) "The Correlates of Nuclear Proliferation: A Quantitative Test," *Journal of Conflict Resolution* 48: 859–885.

Solingen, Etel (1994) "The Political Economy of Nuclear Restraint," *International Security* 19: 126–169.

Solingen, Etel (1998) "Regional Orders at Century's Dawn: Global and Domestic Influences on Grand Strategy," *Princeton Studies in International History and Politics*, Princeton, NJ: Princeton University Press.

Solingen, Etel (2007) "Nuclear Logics: Contrasting Paths in East Asia and the Middle East," *Princeton Studies in International History and Politics*, Princeton, NJ: Princeton University Press.

Squassoni, Sharon A. and David Fite (2005) "Brazil as Litmus Test: Resende and Restrictions on Uranium Enrichment," *Arms Control Today*, October.

Tannenwald, Nina (2007) *The Nuclear Taboo: The United States and the Non-Use of Nuclear Weapons since 1945*, Cambridge, UK: Cambridge University Press.

Tomz, Michael, Jason Wittenberg, and Gary King (2003) *Clarify: Software for Interpreting and Presenting Statistical Results* Ver. 2.1. Available at www.stanford. edu/~tomz/software/clarify.pdf.

Walsh, Jim (1997) "Surprise Down Under: The Secret History of Australia's Nuclear Ambitions," *Nonproliferation Review* 5: 1–20.

Waltz, Kenneth N. (1990) "Nuclear Myths and Political Realities," *American Political Science Review* 84: 731–745.

Index

Page numbers in *italics* denote tables, those in **bold** denote figures.

For Product Safety Concerns and Information please contact our EU
representative GPSR@taylorandfrancis.com
Taylor & Francis Verlag GmbH, Kaufingerstraße 24, 80331 München, Germany